MW00579948

Mel Bay Presents
Everything You Wanted to Know About
Clawhammer Banjo

by Ken Perlman

A Complete Tutor
for the Intermediate
and Advanced Player:
A Clawhammer
Encyclopedia for
Players of All Levels

Includes Over 120
Tunes and Almost 200
Musical Examples in
Clear Tablature.

Based on nearly two decades of
"Melodic Clawhammer" columns
in *Banjo Newsletter*.

Cover Photo by David Bagnall

Music type-setting & book design
by John Roberts

1 2 3 4 5 6 7 8 9 0

© 2004 BY MEL BAY PUBLICATIONS, INC., PACIFIC, MO 63069.
ALL RIGHTS RESERVED. INTERNATIONAL COPYRIGHT SECURED. B.M.I. MADE AND PRINTED IN U.S.A.
No part of this publication may be reproduced in whole or in part, or stored in a retrieval system, or transmitted in any form
or by any means, electronic, mechanical, photocopy, recording, or otherwise, without written permission of the publisher.

Visit us on the Web at www.melbay.com — E-mail us at email@melbay.com

ACKNOWLEDGMENTS

I would like to extend my heartfelt thanks to:

♦ The Nitchie family: Hub, Nancy, Don, and Spencer for keeping Banjo Newsletter going and extending their blessing for me to compile and publish this book.

♦ John Burke, John Cohen, Stu Jamieson, Tom Paley, Art Rosenbaum, Mike and Pete Seeger, Tommy Thompson and to all the other great players and teachers whose recordings and books got the 5-string banjo and clawhammer revivals going.

♦ Linda Abrams for help in proof-reading the banjo tablatures.

♦ Ed Britt for suggestions and corrections for the "History and Observations" chapter.

♦ Jim Bollman and Ed Britt for help in assembling the Discography.

♦ The many pickers and friends who contributed tunes and ideas to this column:

Linda Abrams, Andy Alexis, Mac Benford, Clarke Beuhling, Bruce Boyer, Gene Brown, Jim Crumpley, George Davies, Bart Dewolf, Scott Didlake, Dwight Diller, Bob Douglas, Ernie Fasse, Ray Gavens, Robb Goldstein, Taylor Grover, Darrell Hensley, Al Janssen, Ken Jennings, Judy Jones, Elias Kaufman, Beth Kirkland, Ike LaJoie, Deborah Lempke, Steve Loring, Barry Luft, Rob Mairs, Abe & Malka Mandel, Jack Marcovitch, Reed Martin, Tim McCarthy, Rick McCracken, Joe McGuire, Doyle McKey, Michael Miles, Steve Miller, Ken Miner, Bob Momich, Wendy Morrison, Marc Nerenberg, Tom Paley, Roy Patchell, Larry Peterson, Bob Pliskin, Fred Pribac Roger Rankin, Gil Ricard, Clark Robbins, John Rossbach, Mike Rovine, Mike Seeger, Anthony Shostak, Marjorie Skora, Bob Solosko, Dave Stacey, Joel Stafford, Barry Sullivan, Tony Sullivan, Ed Sweeney, Peter Taney, Ed Topolnicki, Larry Unger, Harry Van Lunenberg, Bart Veerman, Joe Weidlich, Christian Wig, Frank Wilson, Bill Wisdom, John Wright.

Ken Perlman

Ken Perlman with fiddler Alan Jabbour, May '02
(Photo by Susanne Even)

TABLE OF CONTENTS

Chapter 5: Tunings and Keys

Chapter 6: Learning, Arranging and Backup

Chapter 7: The Instrument

Chapter 8: Clawhammer Miscellany

**Chapter 9: History and Observations on the Banjo
        and Old Time Music**

Chapter 10: More Great Tunes

Appendices:

ABOUT THE AUTHOR

Ken Perlman is one of today's best-known clawhammer banjo players. He is considered a pioneer of the melodic style, which has greatly expanded the range and flexibility of clawhammer, and he is known in particular for his skillful adaptations to banjo of reels, jigs, hornpipes and other Celtic tunes. As *Bluegrass Unlimited* notes, "He has stretched the boundaries of what can be done on the clawhammer banjo. His techniques open up a new world to the clawhammer banjoist."

Ken's solo recordings include *Northern Banjo* (Copper Creek), *Island Boy* (Wizmak), *Devil in the Kitchen* (Marimac), *Live in the U.K.* (Halshaw), and *Clawhammer Banjo and Fingerstyle Guitar Solos* (Folkways). His other banjo instruction books include *Clawhammer Style Banjo* (Centerstream), *Melodic Clawhammer Banjo* (Music Sales) and *Basic Clawhammer Banjo* (Mel Bay). He has recorded a video companion to *Clawhammer Style Banjo*, and he has also recorded several other audio and video banjo-instruction series for Mel Bay and Homespun.

His "Melodic Clawhammer" column has run in *Banjo Newsletter* for almost two decades.

Ken has been active internationally since the mid-1970s as a prominent teacher of clawhammer banjo. He has taught at such prestigious teaching festivals as the American Festival of Fiddle Tunes, the Celtic College (Ontario, Canada), the Harrietville Folk Festival (Victoria, Australia), the Living Tradition Summer School (Ayrshire, Scotland), the Northern Lights Festival (Northern Ireland), the Puget Sound Guitar Workshop, the Rocky Mountain Fiddle Camp, the Reading Banjo Festival (England), the Tennessee Banjo Institute and the Woods Music Camp (Ontario). He has also served as music-director or co-director for several banjo-teaching festivals, including the American Banjo Camp, the Bath Banjo Festival, Banjo Camp North, the Maryland Banjo Academy, and the Suwanee Banjo Camp.

Also a well-known guitarist, Ken's specialty is adapting traditional Celtic and Southern fiddle tunes to fingerpicking. His guitar books include *Fingerstyle Guitar*, *Advanced Fingerstyle Guitar* and *Fingerpicking Fiddle Tunes* (all published by Centerstream Music). He has also recorded a guitar-instruction video for Centerstream. Ken is guitar columnist for *Sing Out!* magazine, and he has written on guitar instruction for *Acoustic Guitar*, *Acoustic Musician* and several other periodicals.

Ken has produced several works devoted to old-time fiddling on Prince Edward Island in eastern Canada.. Among them are the tune-book, *The Fiddle Music of Prince Edward Island* (Mel Bay), and a two-CD anthology entitled *The Prince Edward Island Style of Fiddling* (Rounder Records).

He lives and works in the Boston area.

Ken (at left) poses with banjo class by a canal in Heerde, Holland, June '95.
To Ken's left is workshop organizer Wim Vande Weg.

INDEX OF TUNES[1] AND CD PLAYLIST

---

[1] Tunes marked with an asterisk were transcribed by Ken Perlman from field recordings of traditional Prince Edward Island fiddlers; standard notation for them appears in his *Fiddle Music of Prince Edward Island* (Mel Bay).

FOREWORD
from the Publishers of BANJO NEWSLETTER

Ken Perlman has written a monthly column in *Banjo Newsletter* since 1982. Ken's own style has been characterized as "melodic clawhammer," and his writing on the subject has helped pickers understand his approach to music, and the work involved in both collecting and playing it tastefully. It has meant a great deal to our readers that Ken has not only shared tips about his individual playing style, but he has also focused on general issues that concern the typical clawhammer banjoist. There aren't too many players of traditional music who are willing *and* able to share and explain their music, and this has made Ken's column all the more valuable and appreciated in the banjo world.

While keeping up a busy travel, writing and performance schedule, Ken has somehow been able to put much time and more effort in researching various types of traditional acoustic folk music, most notably on Prince Edward Island in eastern Canada. It had not occurred to me until Ken's friend and P.E.I. banjoist Rik Barron explained to me that many of the musicians there had never shared their music or allowed their playing to be taped until Ken Perlman came along. And of course, Ken often let his readers know what he was up to on P.E.I., and as he tracked down tunes and old-time fiddlers his monthly columns sometimes read like a mystery story.

Over the last few years, *Banjo Newsletter* has sponsored a number of weekend festivals devoted to all aspects of banjo teaching, the best known of which we call the Maryland Banjo Academy. Since we started planning the very first of these in 1997, Ken has devoted considerable time and energy to helping us with M.B.A. organization. He has also taken on the job of coordinating the "old-time" banjo faculty and setting up class schedules. Certainly without the help of Ken and a few others there wouldn't even be an M.B.A!

My sons Don and Spencer, who are now co-editors of *BNL*, and I all thank Ken Perlman for being the team banjo player that he is!

Nancy Nitchie
co-founder of *Banjo Newsletter*

INTRODUCTION

"This is the first of a series that will appear in BNL. Clawhammer pickers of a 'melodic' persuasion are invited to send in tunes and/or essays on technical aspects of playing. These will be used as the basis for future articles."

With the above words nearly two decades ago, my *Melodic Clawhammer* column was launched in *Banjo Newsletter,* the monthly periodical generally considered to be the voice of the American 5-string banjo community. I had managed to convince BNL's founder and editor Hub Nitchie that what his magazine really needed was a column devoted to adventuresome and experimental approaches to clawhammer. In essence, Hub was offering me a mandate to act as spokesman for an entire "faction" of clawhammer banjo players, and in the years since I have taken this role quite seriously and tried to the best of my ability to carry it through.

The *Melodic Clawhammer* column began running on a bimonthly basis in the winter of 1983; two years later it switched to a more-or-less monthly basis and has continued in that format ever since. Each time a column was due, Hub — and after his passing, his sons Don and Spencer — let me write about whatever aspect of clawhammer technique, history or lore most interested me at the time. Nearly two decades and over 150 columns later, I realized that I had covered a pretty wide variety of topics in the field! Clearly it was time to put this body of work together in a more permanent and easily accessible form, and this volume is the result!

Melodic vs. "Traditional" Clawhammer

To the best of my knowledge, the first association of the words "melodic" and "clawhammer" was the *Melodic Clawhammer* LP, an anthology released by the Kicking Mule Record Co. back in 1977. The term "melodic" was already in use in bluegrass circles to distinguish the modern improvisational style of Bill Keith and others from conventional Scruggs-picking. The word "clawhammer" had at that time only recently supplanted "frailing" as the term-of-choice for describing the method of banjo *down-picking* that formed my column's core subject matter.

Some of the history of clawhammer is described in detail later in this volume, but by the 1970s a definite split had developed among active clawhammer banjo players. Although it's hard to even describe the nature of the split without in some way taking sides, two "camps" grew up, which ultimately became known respectively as *traditional* clawhammer and *melodic* clawhammer.

Those players in sympathy with the traditional camp generally took the position that they were keeping faith with the style of clawhammer that was played throughout the south in the heyday of old-time music. Because clawhammer style banjo "traditionally" had a specific — and somewhat limited — role in the string-band ensemble, they felt that this was the only legitimate role that the style could assume.

The melodic camp had a different notion. As I put it in my '97 BNL interview, our aim was "to create a style of clawhammer that was essentially a full-fledged solo instrumental style. In other words, it would give the banjoist the ability to play a large range of musical genres with speed, accuracy, power, and (within the limitations of the instrument) a wide range of expression."

This controversy has continued unabated ever since; in some ways it has hardened, as more and more members of the traditional camp look to a specific set of musical role models from a single community of players from the region surrounding Galax, Virginia and Mt. Airy, North Carolina.

The irony is that much of what is called "traditional" clawhammer today is no more a creation of the past — and no less a reflection of the present — than is the melodic style. First of all, the melodic style has its own substantial historical precedent: to wit, the *minstrel style* of the mid-19th century (see cols. 9.3-5). Second, there simply never was a widespread, consistent method of Southern old-time banjo playing that had a specific role in a consistently constituted ensemble. If nothing else, clawhammer was only one of a constellation of styles, and each community (if not each separate player) practiced a different variant or hybrid of two-finger, three-finger and down-picking styles. What's more, ensembles tended to be ad hoc, without any specific rules about how banjo players were expected to conduct themselves. Even more telling, the brand of Galax/Mt. Airy old-time music so widely emulated today is itself a relatively modern development: it is quite different from the music played in that area by the previous generation of players, and it was in all likelihood influenced rhythmically to at least some extent by bluegrass and western swing.

About This Book

I put quite a bit of thought into deciding on the best way to organize these columns in book form. It would have been easiest to just present them chronologically, but I decided that this work would be most valuable to the banjoist if I organized them thematically. Along these lines, the first two chapters are devoted to technique, while other chapters have such organizing principles as playing fiddle tunes or other kinds of musical genres, banjo-tunings, arranging and backup, the instrument, "miscellany" and history/observations. Within each chapter, I've tried to arrange the columns so that when read in order they create a coherent vision. On the other hand, you can approach the book anecdotally, and dip in and out as the spirit moves you.

Putting together this book involved quite a bit of editing. I cut repetitious and dated material, straightened out inconsistencies, revised where my knowledge of a topic had grown since its original presentation, and updated where hindsight or changing technology suggested a different approach or set of conclusions.

As for the tunes, the biggest job was just getting them all into a single tablature-format (at least half a dozen different tab-formats have been employed by BNL over the last two decades). In addition, "typos" in the tabs were painstakingly corrected, and many arrangements were updated or otherwise revised.

As a result of this process, there are about 120 highly readable tablatures in this volume, all representing tunes that are both fun to play and interesting to listen to. They range from Southern hoedowns to Scottish reels and marches, from Irish jigs and polkas to New England hornpipes and waltzes, from Cape Breton strathspeys to Prince Edward Island set tunes. In addition, you'll also find tunes from Québec, Ontario, Shetland, Sweden, France and Hungary, plus ventures into genres as diverse as ragtime, bluegrass and klezmer.

Although all the tunes in this volume were originally published along with one of my *Melodic Clawhammer* columns, I've taken considerable liberties in terms of their presentation. To begin with, in many cases I didn't feel the need to maintain the same association of tune and column that originally appeared in BNL. Instead, I elected to treat the entire repertoire as a "pool" from which I could select the very best available example to illustrate a particular set of ideas.

Since quite a number of columns actually required no tune for illustration, I created a separate chapter that just features more than two dozen great tunes.

It probably makes sense to describe how *Everything You Wanted to Know About Clawhammer* fits in with my other banjo instruction books. First, although this is a valuable book for beginners to own as a resource, it should be stressed that both the instruction and the level of the tunes begin at the *intermediate* level. Beginners are encouraged to start with another of my books, namely *Clawhammer Style Banjo*.

Some of the material in the two instructional chapters necessarily parallels some areas I've dealt with in previous books, but the wide-ranging nature of topics in the other chapters is pretty much unique to this volume. In addition to banjo technique, the reader will find considerable discussion of how to approach a variety of fiddle-tune types and musical genres, tips on learning, arranging and backup, and suggestions on instrument care, accessories and tuning. Last but far from least, there's also quite a bit of background — not only on banjo and clawhammer history — but also on the histories of both "old-time" and Celtic musics.

The Tablature System Explained

Banjo tablature has become fairly standardized but I'll briefly go over the elements of the system used here. There's no need to dwell here on explanations of techniques: these are dealt with in chapters 1 and 2.

The Staff. 5-string banjo "tab" is written on a 5-line staff, with each line corresponding to a string: the top line signifies "string 1" (the thinnest long string), the bottom line signifies string 5 (the short drone string), and so on. Numbers on the lines indicate frets: "0" means an open (unstopped) string, "1" means first fret, "5" means fifth fret, and so on.

Time Signatures: Time signatures are the same as in standard music notation: 2/2 or cut time (¢), 3/4, 4/4, 6/8 etc.

Time Value: Time value is shown via a system that more or less parallels the one used for standard notation, as shown in Example i-1. Illustrated from left to right are a pair of eighth notes (i-1a), a single eighth note (i-1b), a quarter note (i-1c), and a dotted quarter note (i-1d). Values of a half note or larger are shown by surrounding a tab-entry with a box. Shown here are a half note (i-1e), a dotted half note (i-1f) and a whole note (i-1g). Following these are illustrated a grace note (i-1h), a double grace note (i-1i) and four sixteenth notes (i-1j).

Example i-1

(a) (b) (c) (d) (e) (f) (g) (h) (i) (j)

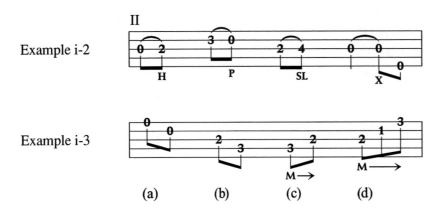

Example i-2

Example i-3

(a)   (b)   (c)   (d)

Directions for the Left or Fretting Hand: Indications for the left hand include Hammer-ons (H), Pull-offs (P), Slides (SL) and Skip-Strokes (X). All these techniques are explained in various columns (see chapter 1). Observe that I use a *slur* sign (arc) to indicate Hs, Ps and SLs: some computer-based tab programs nowadays use a dash for this purpose.

Roman numerals above the staff indicate left-hand fingering *position* (see col. 1.6).

Directions for the Right or Plucking Hand for tunes in 4/4 and cut-time (2/2):

♦ For all entries a quarter note or longer, use the picking finger (M), *unless otherwise indicated.*
♦ For all pairs of eighth notes, use M on the first note and the thumb (T) on the second note, *unless otherwise indicated* (Example i-3a and b).
♦ All 5th-string notes are played by T.
♦ An M followed by an **arrow** indicates an *arpeggio stroke* (i-3c and d; see col. 2-9).

Right Hand directions for 3/4 time are discussed in col. 3.5-6. Right Hand directions for 6/8 time are discussed in col. 3.7-8.

Basic Banjo Tunings

Directions follow for the few most common 5-string banjo tunings.

G tuning (**gDGBD**) is obtained as follows:

♦ Tune string 3 to G below middle C
♦ Tune open string 2 to fret 4, string 3
♦ Tune open string 1 to fret 3, string 2
♦ Tune open string 5 to fret 5, string 1
♦ Tune fret 5, string 4 to open string 3.

Standard C tuning (**gCGBD**): start with G tuning, then tune string 4 down so that fret 7 matches open string 3.

Mountain minor tuning (**gDGCD**): start with open G tuning, then tune open string 2 up to fret 5, string 3.

For Double C tuning (**gCGCD**): start with G tuning, then:

♦ Tune open string 2 up to fret 5, string 3
♦ Tune string 4 down so that fret 7 matches open string 3.

Capo-2 means, "place your capo at the 2nd fret. In this case you would also tune your 5th string up the equivalent of two frets, or place it in a 5th string capoing device at the second 5th-string fret (equivalent to the seventh long-string fret).

Tuning for Musical Examples:

Unless otherwise indicated, all musical examples are in open G-tuning.

Fingering for Chord Diagrams:

In this book, fingering for chord diagrams appears at the base of the vertical line that corresponds to a fretted string.

CHAPTER 1: FUNDAMENTALS

Ken Perlman playing banjo in proper clawhammer position
(Photo by David Bagnall)

1.1 The Right Hand's the Key

(Jan. '94)[1]

Contrary to popular belief, the key to effective melodic clawhammer playing is in the right or plucking hand, not the left or fretting hand. In other words, you can be as fancy or elaborate as you want on the fingerboard, but unless your right hand is solid, responsive and adaptable, your efforts will in all likelihood be for nought.

The basic right hand stroke of clawhammer is unique to the banjo and its African ancestors (for more on the banjo's African roots, see cols. 9.1-2). Generally, it involves plucking *down* on the strings with alternating strokes performed by the *back* of the index or middle fingernail (referred to in this book as *M* or the *M-finger*), and the thumb (*T*). The three most basic strokes: *brush-thumbing,* the *single-string brush*, and *drop-thumbing* are explained in col. 1.2.

Here's a bunch of tips on what to cultivate and avoid in your efforts to come up with an effective right hand attack:

◆ *Keep a compact hand.* All fingers should form a loose "fist" with the picking finger protruding slightly. Your fingers should be touching each other but not pressing into each other.

◆ *Keep a slightly elevated wrist.* The right hand wrist should be very slightly arched. Avoid both a high arch, and a collapsed wrist.

◆ *Brace your forearm* on the rim or armrest and avoid resting any part of your hand or forearm on the banjo head.. Observe that simple contact of the M-finger or T with the head in the course of the stroke is often unavoidable and presents no real problem.

◆ *Let gravity do the work.* Don't throw your M-finger at the strings. Once you start the plucking motion, relax and let gravity carry your hand down.

◆ *Get both wrist and forearm into the act.* Direct the stroke with the wrist, but make sure you allow your forearm to travel along with it. In other words, allow the forearm to roll a bit along the rim or arm rest as the wrist directs the stroke. This transfers the power of your arm via the wrist to your down-stroke.

◆ *Avoid flicking at the strings.* Don't flick out at the strings with your picking finger. Keep your finger rigid as you strike down on the string with your hand and wrist.

---

[1] Each column's original date of publication in *Banjo Newsletter* is listed beside the title.

♦ *Avoid "giving way."* Make sure your M-finger has enough resistance to produce a good strong tone.

♦ *Use "rest strokes."* Rest briefly on the next string "down" at the conclusion of your "M-stroke." For example, rest on string 1 after striking string 2; rest on string 2 after striking string 3, etc.

♦ *Avoid the "polite teacup" stroke.* Don't allow your pinky to stick out during the stroke.

♦ *Avoid the "pistol pointer."* Don't allow your index finger to stick out during the stroke.

1.2 Drop and Double Thumbing

(June '94)

Back in the early days of my banjo experience, the players I knew spoke of "double-thumbing" as a skill reserved only for virtuosos. If someone managed to throw in a drop thumb here or there in his or her playing, it made quite a sensation. Moreover, it was generally considered that drop-thumbing was a skill far removed from ordinary brush-thumbing, and that vastly different mechanics were involved.

I'm not exactly sure how my own method of drop and double-thumbing developed. I read descriptions in a couple of books and watched a couple of local players do it. At first, my efforts could be described as "backwards fingerpicking" (this came naturally, since I was a fingerpicking guitarist first). Gradually my hand usage became more compact and efficient. When I moved to New York City in the mid-70s, I watched some

players who had been influenced by Kyle Creed and Fred Cockerham play. From them I picked up a few mechanical changes that allowed me to develop more power and projection in my stroke (see col. 1.4).

It was only after I started teaching banjo that I began to analyze the actual mechanics of the technique. And it was probably several more years before the inter-connectedness of all clawhammer picking techniques became clear.

Example 1-1 not only shows the progression from brush-thumbing to drop thumbing, but it also serves as template for an excellent exercise to help you develop good drop-thumbing habits.

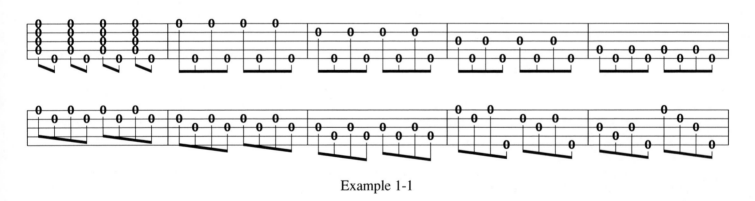

Example 1-1

Measure 1 shows basic *brush-thumbing* (that is, a full four-string brush followed by a fifth-string note). Remember to keep the picking finger relatively still as your wrist guides it across the banjo's four long strings from fourth to first. As the hand nears the bottom of its stroke, the thumb is more or less "dragged" into the fifth string. It hangs there a moment, then plucks the string. Both brush- and thumb- strokes have the same time value: half a beat each.

Moving to measure 2, there's a maneuver I call the *single-string brush*. In other words, the player uses the brush-thumb motion, but hits only a single string with the picking finger. The trick here is to space your thumb (relative to your hand) so that

it is brought precisely into contact with the fifth string as the picking finger crosses the first string. Without this precise thumb-spacing, your single-string brushes (and subsequently, your drop-thumbs) will never achieve that tight, highly rhythmic sound that clawhammer players strive for.

Observe that achieving this spacing between thumb and plucking hand on a habitual basis requires what is known as *muscle memory*.

Measure 3 shows single-string brushes on the second string. Two factors come into play here. First, (as was the case for single-string "brushes" on the first string) the hand must be spaced so that the thumb is brought into contact with the fifth string as your picking finger crosses the second string. Second, your picking finger must perform a *rest stroke*. In other words, it rests briefly on the first string at the conclusion of your downstroke. This gives you more control, and makes the plucked note project much better .

Measures 4 and 5 show single-string brushes on strings 3 and 4. In both cases, space your hand so that the thumb is brought into contact with the fifth string as your picking finger crosses a long string. Remember also to rest after your stroke on the string beneath (rest on string 2 after playing string 3, rest on string 3 after playing on string 4).

By the time you've mastered the fourth-string "single-string brush," you are ready to begin drop-thumbing. The fourth and fifth strings are adjacent, so the spacing achieved by your thumb and picking finger is identical to that required for drop thumbing.

Moving on to measure 6, maintain your "spacing" from measure 5 and drop your *wrist* down until your picking finger and thumb are in position to play strings one and two. Make sure

that you bring your thumb into contact with the second string as the picking finger crosses the first string. Remember to use the same brush-like motion described above.

Measures 7 and 8 show drop-thumbing beginning on strings two and three. Again the thumb is spaced so it lands precisely on its string as the picking finger crosses its string. And the picking finger rests on the string underneath its path, just as for single-string brushes, For example, when you begin a drop-thumb on string 2, bring the thumb into contact with string 3, and rest (at the conclusion of the down-stroke) on string 1.

Measures 9 and 10 show what is sometimes called *double-thumbing*, which is an alternation of drop-thumbing and single string brushes.

Try some pretty straight drop and double thumbing in the following arrangement of a tune called *Puncheon Camps* by Kentucky banjoist Clyde Davenport.[2] Observe that Part B, meas. 4 is only half the length of the tune's other measures: to integrate that measure in the piece, "count" Part B, measures 3-5 as follows: 1-2-3-4-/1-2-/1-2-3-4-.

Puncheon Camps

Banjo Arrangement: Clyde Davenport

Tuning: gCGCD (capo–2) or aDADE

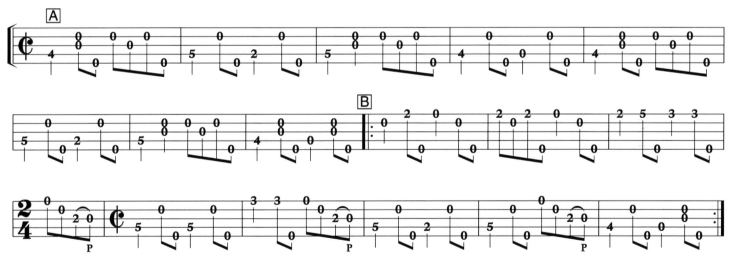

Setting © 1996 by Clyde Davenport, Tablature © 1996 by Ken Perlman

1.3 Drop Thumbing and the Left Hand

(July '94)

When you drop-thumb a pair of strings, there are five left hand (L.H.) possibilities, each of which is illustrated in Example 1-2. We'll look at each in turn (observe that in this book, the term *M-string* means "the string to be played by the picking finger, or M," while the *T-string* means "the string to be played by the thumb, or T").

♦ Both M- and T-strings are open (Ex. 1-2a).

♦ Both M- and T-strings are part of a *chord form* (C, D7, F, etc.), barre, or partial barre (Ex. 1-2b assumes you are fretting a C-chord).

♦ The M-string is fretted and the T-string is open (Ex. 1-2c).

♦ Both M- and T-strings are fretted (Ex. 1-2d).

♦ The M-string is open and the T-string is fretted (Ex. 1-2e).

---

[2] This arrangement was initially published along with an interview I conducted with Mr. Davenport, published in the Oct. 1996 issue of *Banjo Newsletter*.

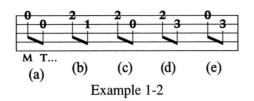

Example 1-2

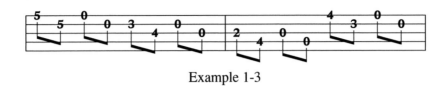

Example 1-3

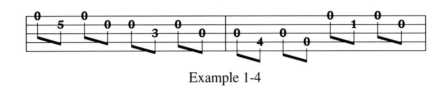

Example 1-4

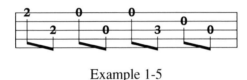

Example 1-5

For the first three situations mentioned above, no special L.H. adaptations are required. If both strings are open or part of a chord, barre or partial barre, just feel free to drop or double thumb with impunity. The same is true when the M-string is fretted and the T-string is open.

Complications arise for the last two situations. When *both* M- and T- strings are fretted (but not part of a chord form or barre) it is very important from the point of view of getting a smooth sound to *stop both strings at the same time*. In other words, when you pluck the M-string, you should stop *both* M- and T-strings together. Looking at Example 1-3, as you pluck string 1 with M, stop fret 5, string 1 *and* fret 5, string 2 simultaneously. Then pluck string 2 with T half a beat later. At the start of the next measure, as you pluck string 3 with M, stop fret 2, string 3 *and* fret 4, string 4 simultaneously. Then pluck string 4 with T half a beat later.

My observation has been that most pickers naturally stop both strings simultaneously for an all-fretted drop thumb on the first two strings. As the pair of notes moves down towards the third and fourth strings, however, many pickers need to train themselves to accomplish this.

The last situation (open M-string, fretted T-string) is perhaps the most problematic. To get a smooth sound, it is very important that the T-string be fretted *when the M-string is plucked*. This means that the T-string is fretted a half beat *before* it is actually played. Another way to think of it is that you *anticipate* the fretting of the T-string by half a beat.

Remembering to anticipate the fretting of the T-string seems to drive some of my students crazy, particularly since they would probably not perceive much difference in sound until they have achieved a certain level of playing fluidly and speed. I guarantee, however, that using this particular L.H. modification increases speed and smoothness markedly.

Looking at Example 1-4, stop fret 5, *string 2* with the L.H. *at the same time you pluck open string 1* with M. Then pluck string 2 with T half a beat later. In the next instance, stop fret 2, *string 3* with the L.H. *at the same time you pluck open string 2* with M. Then pluck string 3 with T half a beat later.

These rules for doubly-fretted drop-thumbs, and open-M, fretted-T drop-thumbs apply even for situations where the drop-thumb strings are *not* adjacent. Example 1-5 shows two non-adjacent string drop-thumbs. In the first example (doubly fretted), stop fret 2, string 1 and fret 2 string 3 simultaneously. In the second example, (open-M, fretted-T), stop fret 3, string 3 when you pluck open string 1.

The following setting for the Southern tune *Jay Bird* provides a good illustration for both doubly fretted and open-M, fretted-T drop-thumbs (observe that the purpose of the Roman numerals above the staff is explained in col. 1.6). After that, try some more open-M, fretted-T drop thumbs in *Sid Baglole's Tune,* which I collected from fiddler Sid Baglole of Freetown, Prince Edward Island. The tune had no title, so I went ahead and named it for its source.

14

Jay Bird

Banjo Arrangement: Ken Perlman

Tuning: gCGCD (capo–2)

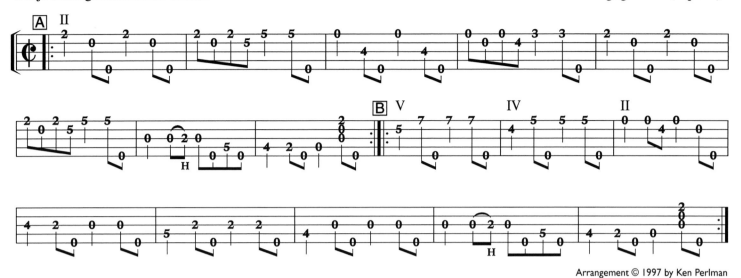

Arrangement © 1997 by Ken Perlman

Sid Baglole's Tune

Banjo Arrangement: Ken Perlman

Tuning: gDGBD

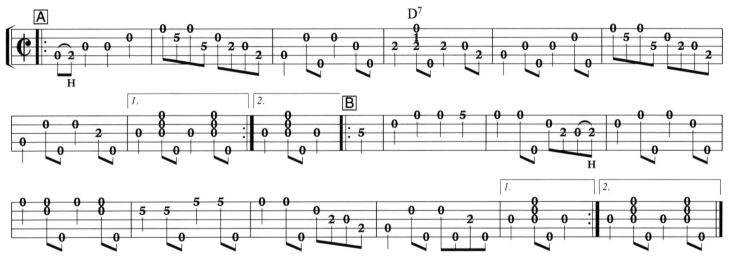

Arrangement © 1993 by Ken Perlman

1.4 The Rationale for Drop-Thumbing

(Sept. '98)

Back when I was getting started playing "melodic" style, I remember my first temptation was to use lots of hammer-ons and pull-offs for melody, and to only make use of drop-thumbs in relatively obvious situations. Since I came from a guitar background, and Hs and Ps required pretty much the same technical approach on both instruments (they are actually easier on banjo, because the strings are generally lighter), this seemed the obvious choice, especially since my drop thumbing — to put it charitably — was still in the developmental stage.

It was not until I had moved to New York City and began hanging out with other frailers like Henry Sapoznik and Ray Alden — and playing in string bands and in large sessions — that I fully understood the wisdom of using as much drop thumbing as possible. The major advantages of drop thumbing were essentially twofold. First, you had a lot more control over the shape of the melody when you got notes via drop thumbing. Second, drop thumbed notes simply *cut* better — you could hear all your drop thumbed notes clearly ringing out through the din

15

of a jam session or string band, whereas notes that came via Hs and Ps tended to get lost in the shuffle.

To play melodies made up primarily of drop thumbs, however, I simply had to improve my technique. Specifically, I had to come up with a way of playing that was extremely smooth and had a capacity for high sound volume. I solved the volume problem by adopting some elements from the style of Ray Alden, who in turn had developed his right-hand technique by watching Round Peak players like Kyle Creed and Fred Cockerham. Essentially, what I got from him was bringing the support of the forearm into every stroke.

The secret to smoothness, as I have preached in all my books and videos for the last twenty years, is to a great extent due to thumb "placement." On every downstroke, the thumb is brought firmly into contact with a drone or long string. It then sits there until it's time for it to play. The thumb's force in striking a string is then derived directly from the energy provided by the force given to the original downstroke.

Above all, there should be no essential difference in stroke, hand or arm motion between the single-string brush (that is, stroke on long string/thumb on fifth) on the one hand, and drop-thumbing (stroke on long string/thumb on lower long string) on the other.

In recent years, it has come to my attention that many practitioners of the most popular contemporary styles of "traditional" clawhammer have severely limited the role of drop-thumbing in their playing, on the theory that drop thumbing somehow interferes with the ability to exactly match the rhythm of a fiddler. Only *stroke-drone* (that is, single-string brush)

maneuvers — this viewpoint continues — are sufficiently strong and controllable for this task.

Personally, I don't buy it. Since the drop-thumb maneuver can be done with *exactly* the same motion as the stroke-drone, a player should be able to continue his exact match of fiddle-rhythm through all his drop-thumbing. Plus, he or she now has the added advantage of being able to precisely match *more* of the melody (matching as much of the fiddler's melody as possible *without* allowing the rhythm to falter is, after all, the way that born-to-the tradition old-time banjo pickers actually saw their role).

As someone who's been teaching workshops and observing players around the country, I feel the real problem is that most pickers don't work on their right hand technique enough. Many pickers simply need better technique in order to explore drop thumbing to its full potential. Even small hitches in the stroke can — over the course of a single tune, let alone a whole evening of playing — throw things off considerably.

A number of pointers that will help you improve your drop-thumbing are discussed in col. 1.1.

Appearing here is a tune from West Virginia called *Ducks on the Pond*. I picked up this version a few years ago from fiddler Doug Van Gundy of Marlinton, West Virginia. Note in the arrangement how judicious use of drop thumbing allows for matching the fiddle on just about a note-for-note basis.

If you don't yet know how to perform off- (or alternate-) string pull-offs, see column 1.8.

Ducks on the Pond

Banjo Arrangement: Ken Perlman

Tuning: gDGCD (capo–2)

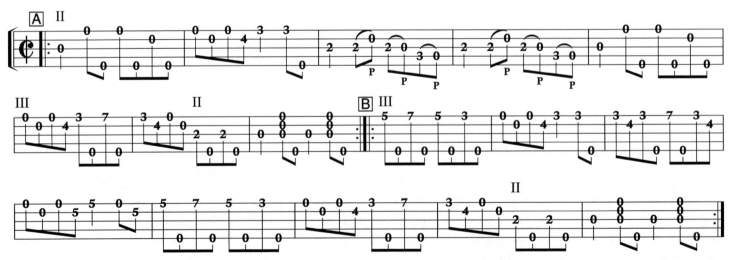

Arrangement © 1998 by Ken Perlman

Lately I've been coming around to the idea that banjoists should probably start each day's practice session with about five to ten minutes worth of exercises. For the player who is learning the craft, this is a period when he or she can work on technique without the distractions created by needing to be musical. For the advanced player, exercises can provide a nice warm-up that prepares the hands to take on the various movements that are characteristic to the style.

Warming up before playing is particularly important to players over the age of 30. One's muscles and tendons naturally get a bit less flexible beginning at around this stage of life, and jumping into rapid picking or intricate left-hand maneuvers without preamble can lead to undue stress or even injury.

Pickers who tour a lot would also benefit from a daily exercise regimen. If a banjoist is performing every day, there's a real temptation to skip concentrated practice. And without such practice, one's technique tends to drift ever so slightly off-kilter with each passing day. Daily hand exercises provide an excellent opportunity to focus totally on the process of playing, allowing the performer to center his or her technique and keep entropy at bay.

An ideal set of exercises focuses on several commonly used skills. Plus, each skill should be broken down in such a way that most of its commonly employed aspects are touched on. In the exercises that accompany this column, I'll do that for the right or plucking hand (note that additional right-hand warm-up exercises appear in col. 2.10; exercises for the left or fretting hand are dealt with in col. 2.20).

At any rate, here's my suggestion for an effective daily right-hand regimen that pretty much covers all the bases.

Exercises A1–7

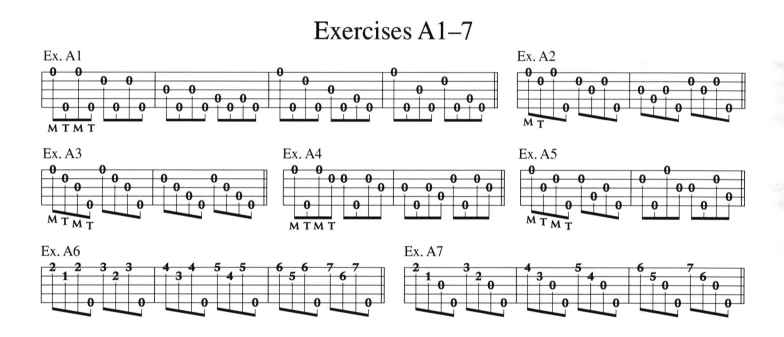

Start off in Exercise A1 with some plain old single-string brushes (long-string/drone alternations), going through all combinations of strings. In Exercises A2 and A4 we move on to the most basic form of double-thumbing: an alternation of a single-string brush and a drop-thumb, in which the long string played is the same. In A2, the drop-thumb is first in each pattern; in A4, the single-string brush is first.

Exercises A3 and A5 allow you to practice more advanced forms of double-thumbing. In A3 the single-string brush is on a different long string from the drop-thumb; in A5 the thumb drops a couple of strings behind the M-finger, *and* the single string brush is on a different long string from the drop thumb.

All of these exercises are quite short, and one can quickly grow bored playing exactly the same open strings over and over.

To increase interest, I've borrowed an idea from classical guitar pedagogy. Specifically, play a given pattern while fretting a single left-hand fingering "shape," then move that shape one fret up the neck and repeat the same right-hand pattern. Continue moving the shape up the neck, repeating the right hand pattern at each fret level. Maximum interest is obtained when at least one of the strings in the fingering shape is open, because moving that shape up the neck produces interesting combinations of harmonies and dissonances.

Exercises A6 and A7 demonstrate this process. In A6, the right hand plays the very first pattern from Exercise A2 (namely, strings 1-2-1-5) over and over again. At the beginning of the exercise, play the pattern over a C-chord. Then, move the C-chord up a fret and repeat the pattern. Next, move the chord up another fret, repeat the pattern, and so on.

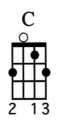

Example 1-6

In Exercise A7, the right hand plays the first pattern from Exercise 3 (strings 1-2-3-5) over and over again. Again, start by fretting a C-chord, then move the fingering pattern up one a fret for each repetition of the exercise.

Named for a famous clipper ship, *Flying Cloud Cotillion* should give your right hand a good work out. Note that the ending of the B-part leads back to the A-part, and is not meant to sound "final." Again, see columns 1.7 and 1.8 for coaching on all sorts of hammer-ons and pull-offs.

Flying Cloud Cotillion

Banjo Arrangement: Ken Perlman

Tuning: gDGBD

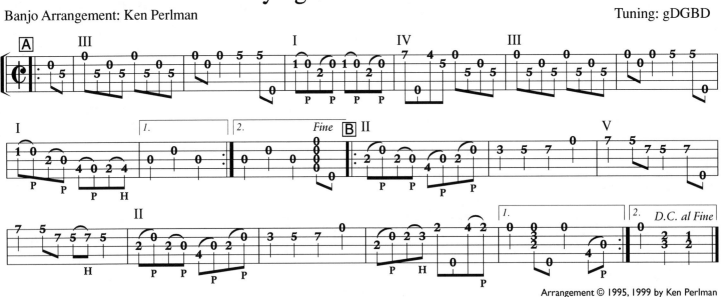

Arrangement © 1995, 1999 by Ken Perlman

1.6 Left Hand Fingering Tips

(May '94)

Here are a number of common sense directives that should assist you in your journeys around the fingerboard. Remember that in the following discussion, the first finger refers to the fretting-hand index finger, the second finger refers to the middle finger, the third finger refers to the ring finger and the fourth finger refers to the pinky (this is different from the piano system where the thumb is counted as the first finger, to the initial confusion of the many fretted-instrument students who have taken piano lessons in their youth).

Most simple fingering situations are covered by two directives I call the *vertical rule* and the *horizontal rule*. The vertical rule, which refers to movement up and down the frets, states that in general *one finger is assigned to duty on a given fret*. In other words, if you're playing near the nut, the first finger covers all notes on the first fret of any string, the second finger covers all notes on the second fret of any string, the third finger covers all notes on the third fret of any string and (if you use it) the fourth finger covers the fourth fret of any string. The horizontal rule 1.7

covers situations when more than one string is stopped (pressed down) at the same fret. In this case, *the lower number finger plays the higher number string*. So for an ordinary C chord in G-tuning where fret 2 is stopped on both strings 1 and 4, the (lower numbered) second finger plays the (higher numbered) fourth string, and the (higher numbered) third finger plays the (lower numbered) first string. If you need to refer to a diagram of the chord, see Example 1-6 above.

Again, both these rules are merely common sense directives derived from the general shape and mechanics of the human hand. Most students will in fact hit upon them when left entirely to their own devices. There are exceptions, however. I taught a guitar class once that was attended by a student whose sense of finger mechanics had led him to learn all common chords with a reverse-horizontal rule (to get the idea try reversing the positions of the second and third fingers in the above-mentioned C chord). To accomplish this, he had to hold his left elbow virtually over his navel. So much for innate musical instincts!

The vertical rule is easily adapted to up the neck playing via the concept of *positions*. We have seen how for basic playing, the first finger plays the first fret, and so on. This is called playing in *first position*. Let's say, however, (and this situation comes up all the time in double C tuning) that you have a tune with no notes at all on the first fret. Instead, all of its notes are distributed between frets 2 and 5. What you do here is an extension of the vertical rule: you just assign each finger to duty on a given fret. Specifically, the first finger now handles all notes on fret 2 (regardless of the string), the second finger now handles all notes on fret 3, the third finger handles all notes on fret 4, and the fourth finger handles all notes on fret 5. Simultaneous or consecutive notes that fall on the same fret of different strings can then be dealt with via the the horizontal rule.

What has just been described is referred to as playing in *second position*. Obviously, there's no need to stop at just one other playing position. We can, in fact, set a position up for each reachable fret on the neck. In *third position* then, the first finger covers all notes on the third fret, regardless of string. The second finger then covers the fourth fret, the third finger covers the fifth fret, and so on. In *fifth position,* the first finger covers the fifth fret, the second covers the sixth, and so on. In seventh position, the first finger covers the seventh fret; in tenth position, the first finger covers the tenth fret; in fifteenth position, the first finger covers the fifteenth fret. Well, you get the idea!

Another way of expressing this is that in *position playing* we essentially set up fingering "territories" at various locations around the neck. We think of moving from territory to territory, instead of from fret to fret. Within each territory, finger movement is identical to the basic banjo fingering moves of first position (namely the simple fret-assignments of the vertical rule).

The concept of position playing is particularly useful when you have a tune in which the way the notes fall requires you to move frequently around the neck. Instead of just flying wildly about with your fingers trying to get all the notes in their proper time-slots, you can design a fingering plan that allows you to move calmly from *position to position*. In other words, lets say a tune starts off with a cluster of notes near the nut. These can be handled in first position. Farther along in that tune the notes move up the neck and there's a cluster that can be handled between the seventh and ninth frets. Play these out of seventh position. Then there's a bunch of notes that fall between the fifth and seventh frets. Play these out of fifth position.

Years ago, I adopted the method of using Roman numerals in tablature to show fingering positions (I for first position, V for fifth position, XII for twelfth position and so on). The idea was that there were already so many "Arabic" numbers on a page of tab that inserting still more of them to indicate fingering was just not practical. Using Roman numerals has run me into trouble only once. When I did the tab book for my *Live in the UK* recording, the British publisher refused to allow me to use Roman numerals on the grounds that the British public was no longer educated in their use. Instead, I had to use 5p for fifth position, 10p for fifth position, etc. (The problem there of course, was that the term 5p would just make the British public think of five pence — but who's counting?)

The trick to devising fingering plans is to know when to switch positions. One good time to shift is the split second *following* the playing of any open string (including the fifth). If you shift just before, or simultaneously with the playing of the open string, the listener can hear a break in the flow of notes. If you wait to shift until *just after* the open note, no such break is perceptible.

Alternatively, a good time to shift is just before the upbeat of a measure, or just prior to the start of any new *phrase* or *motive* (see columns 3.15-16). At these junctures, there is a natural pause in the music, and a rapid shift around the neck goes unnoticed by the listener.

I can't stress too much the importance of mental flexibility in devising workable fingering plans. If your approach is working, and you can easily finger all the notes in tune up to speed, don't "fix" it! If you find that you are running into trouble mastering the fingering of a tune, however, try revising your plan. Sometimes the same sequence of notes is easier to obtain in a different fingering position. Sometimes notes along the borders of a phrase need to be shifted from one position to another. In fact, one really neat trick is to make the next passage of a tune easier to play by going so far as to switch fingers on an already stopped fret!

Speaking of flexibility, it is crucial to bear in mind that a positional approach is not always the best method of handling fingering. Sometimes when there is a very short-lived shift — or a series of short-lived shifts, it is best to just go ahead and perform them without trying to figure out what "position" they might belong to. In the tabs that follow, this is usually dealt with by avoiding a positional indicator for passages of this sort, thereby leaving it up to the player to sort out from the context his or her own fingering.

Here's an old Scottish Dance tune called *Lass o' Gowrie* (known in Irish traditional-music circles as *Lakes of Sligo*). Try to be conscious of the vertical and horizontal rules. And be sure to follow the position notations in the B part. If you are unfamiliar with dotted quarter notes, see column 1.10.

Lass o' Gowrie

Banjo Arrangement: Ken Perlman

Tuning: gCGCD (capo–2)

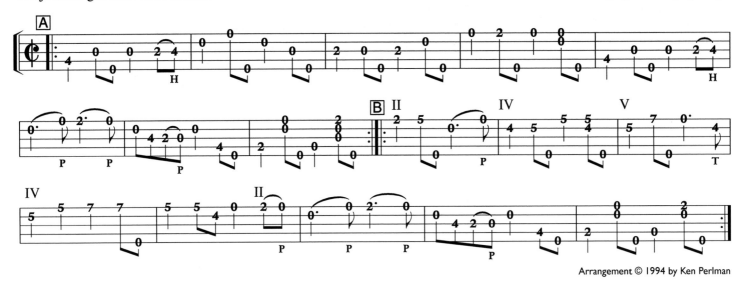

Arrangement © 1994 by Ken Perlman

1.7 Minding Your P's and H's

(Mar.' 94)

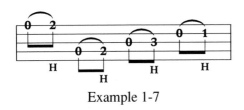

Example 1-7

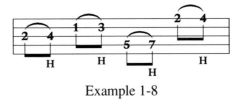

Example 1-8

Pull-offs and Hammer-ons are probably more important to the clawhammer player than to most other fretted instrument players. Sometimes they're the only way we can get certain combinations of notes, and the strategic use of "hammers" and "pulls" helps give our style its own distinctive sound.

Let's look at Hammer-ons first. In a hammer-on (H), a finger of the fretting hand is brought down sharply on a sounding string to produce another note. We'll start with the simplest case — hammering from an open string to a fretted note on that string. In the first entry of Example 1-7, pluck the first string with the right hand to produce one note (the open first string) then sharply strike the fingerboard with a left hand finger to produce a second note (string 1, fret 2).

Now for some tips. Many inexperienced players straighten their finger as they raise it up in preparation for starting the hammer. The trick, however, is to *keep the finger arched* (that is, with all joints bent) as you raise it up. Then as you begin your hammer you can concentrate the full force of your finger muscles into a rapid descent to the fingerboard. You don't have to lift your finger very high off the board, but you need to come sharply and cleanly onto it, so that the string is literally "hammered" into the board. Picture actually trying to drive a nail into the fingerboard with the tip of your finger.

My experience as a teacher prompts me to add — for the benefit of the literal minded — that this directive is only a

metaphor, and that you don't need to go overboard on the aforementioned nail-driving.

When performing *fretted hammer-ons* (that is, hammering from one fretted note to another on the same string) the same basic principles apply. Make sure, however, that you hold on to the struck-note fret so that it continues to sound (in fact, it should continue to sound until the hammering finger reaches the fretboard). Then, make sure to stretch your finger out towards the destination fret *before* you actually start the finger's descent. In Example 1-8, strike fret 2, string 3, and hold the fret down with your first finger. Then (before the sound begins to die) s-t-r-e-t-c-h your third finger out towards the fourth fret. Finally (maintaining your finger-arch all the while) hammer forcefully down on the fourth fret with a sharp, quick motion.

Most intermediate and advanced students that I encounter seem to have a pretty good handle on hammer-ons. Pull-offs on the other hand seem to be much more problematic, and it is a rare clawhammer student who doesn't need at least some correction. In a pull-off (P), strike a fretted string, then produce another note by in effect plucking that string *with the fretting finger*. In the first instance of Example 1-9, strike string 1 (*stopped* at the second fret by a finger of the fretting hand). Then, *without allowing the sound to die,* pluck that string by catching it with that same finger tip and drawing the tip ever so slightly *in* towards the palm of the hand. To do a proper pull-off, you once again must maintain the finger arch (that is, keep all joints bent) throughout the maneuver.

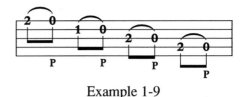

Example 1-9

Example 1-10

Example 1-11

Some things to avoid while pulling off:

♦ Merely raising your finger off the string. You get no sound this way!

♦ Keeping the finger still and twisting your hand to produce the pull-off. I've seen lots of people do this one! This puts your hand way out of position.

♦ Pulling-off with an outward trajectory (creating the pull-off sound by pushing your finger in the direction of the fifth string). I know that at least one very famous bluegrass player recommended this method in his book, but this really isn't very effective and puts great stress on your fretting hand over time.

When pulling off over "inner" strings (second through fourth entries in Example 1-9), special care must be taken to avoid string collisions. In other words (looking at the second instance), when pulling off at fret 1, string 2, it is all too easy to collide with the open first string, thereby making an unwanted noise. To do this maneuver cleanly, you must either pull just over the top of string 1 (be careful not to pull too far over, or you won't get a strong sound out of the P), or pull down so that the

pulling finger actually rests for a moment in the space between strings 2 and 1.

Fretted pull-offs (pulling from a higher to a lower fret note on the same string) require anticipation. To get an effective sound your must place two fingers on the board, then pull from the higher fret to the lower one. In the first instance of Example 1-10, stop both fret 3 and fret 2 on string 1 *when you strike fret 3*. Then, keeping fret 2 firmly pressed down — and using the technique described above — pull off fret 3.

When a triplet is made up of two fretted pull-offs, start with three left hand fingers down on the board. In the first entry of Example 1-11, start with the first, second and fourth fingers on the first string at frets 2, 3 and 5 respectively. Then — holding frets 2 and 3 firmly down — pull off from fret 5 to fret 3. Then — still holding on to fret 2 — pull off from fret 3 to fret 2. Think of it as putting three fingers down at once, then peeling them off one at a time.

I learned *Tina's Schottische* from fiddler Alvin Bernard of Long River, Prince Edward Island. This arrangement should give you a good opportunity to practice your H's and P's.

Tina's Schottische

Banjo Arrangement: Ken Perlman

Tuning: gCGCD (capo–2)

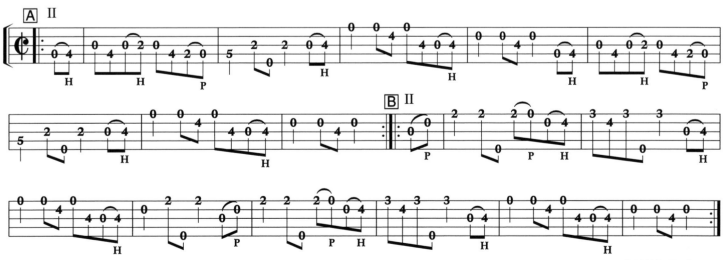

Arrangement © 1998 by Ken Perlman

21

One group of related techniques that seems to apply more to banjos than to most other stringed instruments is off-string hammer-ons and pull-offs. In an off-string (or alternate-string) hammer-on, the player strikes one string, then hammers on to *another* string at any reachable fret. In an off-string (or alternate-string) pull-off, he or she strikes one string, then pulls off *another* string. These techniques are important to the clawhammer picker for two reasons. First, those who wish to avoid drop thumbing find alternate-string H's and P's an acceptable alternative in certain cases. Second, even those clawhammer players who drop thumb fluidly must face a certain limitation in the technique. Specifically, the mechanics of drop thumbing make it much easier to play a pair of notes in which the second note is *lower* than a pair of notes in which the second note is

higher. Alternate-string H's and P's sometimes offer an acceptable solution to this problem.

Let's look at off-string H's first. In the simplest case strike an open string, then, half a beat later, strike with full force of the finger on the desired fret of its *lower* neighbor. So, in the first instance shown in Example 1-12, strike string 3 but hammer on to fret 3, *string 4*. In the second instance you strike string 2 but hammer on to fret 2, *string 3*. In the third instance, you strike string 1, but hammer on to fret 5, *string 2*. When you try these maneuvers, you'll hear that the off-string hammer-on can substitute for drop thumbing *but* it produces a much weaker note. On the other hand, sometimes off-string H's are neat to use for effect — especially when you strike the third string and hammer on to the fourth.

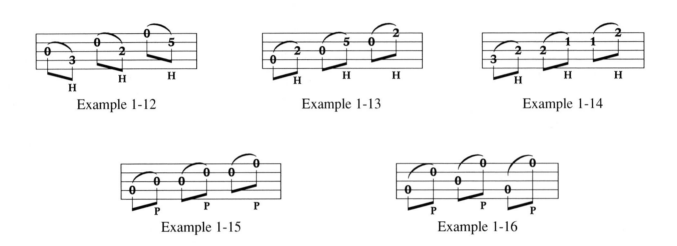

Example 1-12   Example 1-13   Example 1-14

Example 1-15   Example 1-16

You can also hit one string and hammer on to a *higher* string. In Example 1-13, strike string 4, then hammer on to fret 2, *string 3*. Alternatively strike a *fretted* string, then reach across and hammer to a higher string. In Example 1-14, strike fret 3, string 4 then reach across and hammer on to fret 2, *string 3*.

The time to use this last technique is when the second note of an eighth note pair is substantially higher than the first note. You'll notice as you try these examples, however, that the notes produced are fairly weak relative to the sounds of the original struck notes. Because these notes are so weak, I'd advise against using upward off-string H's unless there is no other way to get a particular sequence of notes. And although at one point in my career I used upward off-string H's fairly extensively, I have tended in recent years to use instead another technique known as the *arpeggio* (see col. 2.9).

Now on to off-string pull-offs. In the simplest case, strike one string, then pull-off its open higher neighbor. (Off-string pull-offs on lower neighbors are theoretically possible, but I've never encountered a situation that called for them). So

(Example 1-15), strike open string 4 but pull off open string 3 (for best results, have a finger waiting on the third string *when you strike the fourth string*). Similarly, you can strike string 3 but pull off string 2, or strike open string 2 and pull off string 1. You can also skip strings in an alternate string pull-off. So in Example 1-16, strike string 4 and pull off string 2, or strike string 3 and pull off string 1. You can even strike string 4 and pull off string 1.

You can also perform off-string pull-offs where the struck note is fretted. For best results, fret both the struck note *and the string to be pulled off* at the same time. You can place your pulling-finger at any convenient location on the string that is to be pulled off. For example (Example 1-17) strike fret 3, string 4 — and place a finger somewhere on string 3 (the first or second finger at the second fret will do) — at the same time. Then after half a beat, use the finger waiting on string 3 to pull off that string. Similarly, you can strike fret three, string three (simultaneously placing a finger somewhere on string 2) then pull off string two, and so on.

Example 1-17

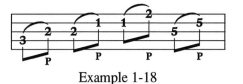

Example 1-18

The off-string pull-off is often an effective method for obtaining eighth note pairs where the second note is higher than the first. Although I have replaced it to some degree by the arpeggio, I still use it quite a bit. Plus it is also a great technique to use for effect when the spirit moves you.

One last case remains, namely an off-string pull off where *both* strings are fretted. Let's look at Example 1-18. In the first instance, strike fret 3, string 4, then pull off to fret 2, *string 3*. To break that down, you must stop *at the same time*, the struck string (i.e. fret 3, string 4), the note to be sounded by the pull off (fret 2, string 3), and *some point on string 3 higher than fret 2*. Half a beat later, pull off from the higher location on string 3, thereby sounding fret 2. This technique yields a somewhat

stronger note than an off-string hammer to an upper neighbor string. Some excellent players — one who immediately comes to mind is Mac Benford — use it to good effect.

Observe that the most effective method for accomplishing the last maneuver of 1-18, is through use of a barre. In other words, place, at the same time, the barre at the fifth fret plus a finger on string 2 above the barre. Then pluck string 3 and — half a beat later — pull off a finger from string 2, thereby producing a pulled note at fret 5, string 2.

The Shetland reel *Spoodis Skeery* offers some good practice in off-string pull-offs.

Spoodis Skeery

Banjo Arrangement: Ken Perlman   Tuning: gDGBD

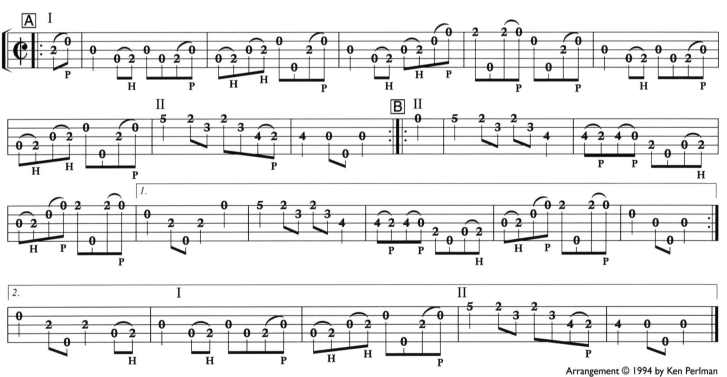

Arrangement © 1994 by Ken Perlman

1.9 Slides on Fretted Banjos   (Aug. '94)

One of the great joys of playing on a fretless banjo is the freedom to effortlessly slide around the neck. You can start your slide at any point on any string, continue it as far up or down as you want, and take (within reasonable limits) just about as long as you wish to get there.

Sliding on fretted banjos is far more problematic. There are now frets in the way for your fingers to stumble over. More

important, those same frets can become obstacles that break up your nice sliding sound into discrete units, each one half step long. What to do?

While a fretted banjo will never give you as good a sliding response as a fretless, there are a number of methods to counter-act the nastier effects of frets on your slides. Let's start by making two kinds of distinctions. First we need to separate

23

slides which are to be treated as full fledged notes, and slides which are to be regarded as grace notes. Second, we need to distinguish between slides that are one fret in length, and those that are longer than a single fret.

Slides that are full-fledged notes start off with a *stopped*

(pressed down) sounding string. The stopped string is held down for its full value (quarter note, eighth note, etc.), then the stopping finger glides with full pressure up or down the neck to a destination fret. The actual time that this *SL-note* sounds is made up two parts: (1) the sound of the sliding motion and (2) the sound of the note sounding at its destination fret.

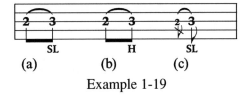

(a)   (b)   (c)

Example 1-19

Example 1-20

Let's look at example 1-19a, where you slide from fret 2, string 3 to fret 3, string 3. Here, fret 2 is plucked and allowed to sound for half a beat. Then the stopping finger quickly glides with full pressure up the neck to fret 3, and lingers on fret 3 until its full time value has elapsed. The over-all effect of a slide of this kind is similar to that of a hammer-on (Example 1-19b).

In an ornamental or quick-slide, there is no initial stopped note with a definite time value. Instead, the player stops a string and begins to slide at virtually the same time. In other words, the listener does not hear the initial note — he or she only hears a sliding sound and the note at the destination fret. So in Example 1-19c, the player stops fret 2, string 3 and begins a sliding motion all at the same time. He or she then completes the slide to fret 3 quickly, and permits fret 3 to sound for the remainder of its full notated value. Observe that the initial attack is written as a *grace note*, which has no specific allotted time-value (see col. 2.24).

On a fretless banjo, it's certainly possible to perform slides that fall *in between* the full-fledged and ornamental categories. You can also do this on a fretted banjo, but it requires more control. I won't deal with this aspect of slides here. I would definitely say the best way to approach this kind of slide, however, is to learn the two extremes discussed above, and then modify them according to what you hear banjoists do live or on recordings.

So far, the slides we've discussed were all one fret in length.

Playing longer slides on a fretted banjo requires additional adjustment. Let's look at the first slide in Example 1-20, from fret 2 to fret 4, string 3. If you slide two frets up with full pressure, the presence of a fretwire between the 3rd and 4th frets will cause the sliding sound to break up into two distinct notes. If you slide two frets up with only a small amount of pressure, your slide will be virtually inaudible. The trick to doing an effective multi-fret slide on a fretted banjo is as follows. Once you leave the initial fret, glide with full pressure only up to the next fretwire in your path (in this case, the one between frets 3 and 4). As you pass over that fretwire, you relax pressure slightly, thereby preventing the production of a discreet extra note. Then as you pass the final fretwire in the path of your slide (in this case, that same one), you resume full pressure on your slide.

Similarly, if you wish to perform a slide from fret 2 to fret 5 on string 3 (second entry in example 1-20), start your slide with full pressure, relax that pressure as you pass over the first fretwire in your path (between the 3rd and 4th frets), and resume full pressure as you pass over the last fretwire in your path (between the 4th and 5th frets). Example 1-21 is a schematic diagram that depicts the path your finger needs to take during a multi-fret slide.

You should also be aware that slides of all kinds can be performed in a "reverse" or downward direction, as shown in Example 1-22.

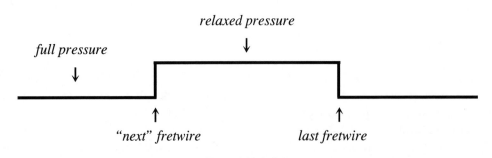

Example 1-21

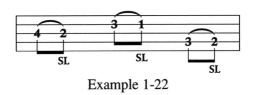

Example 1-22

Waitin' for The Federals, also known as *Seneca Square Dance*, offers some practice in slides. Observe that the symbol "X" indicates a skip-maneuver, which is explained in columns 1-12 and 1-13. Use up-the-neck fingering form #1 from col. 2.16 (Example 2-48) for Part B, meas. 5.

Waitin' for the Federals

Banjo Arrangement: Ken Perlman

Tuning: gDGBD

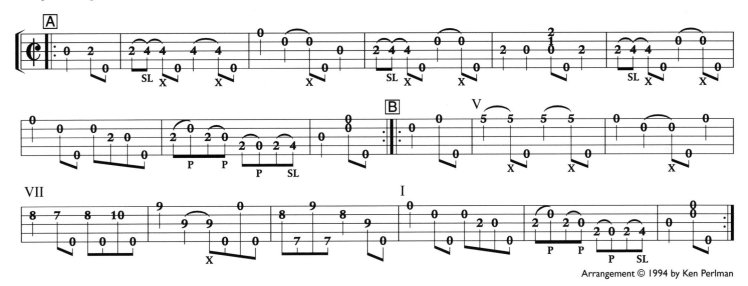

Arrangement © 1994 by Ken Perlman

1.10 Dotted Quarter Notes

(Sept. '94)

For some reason, playing dotted quarter notes in 4/4 or cut time (2/2) seems to give many of my students fits (in 2/4 time the analog would be playing dotted eighth notes). Even long after they have theoretically mastered how to handle this kind of note, its presence in a piece seems as likely to throw them as a huge jump around the neck, or a passage with especially difficult fingering.

In terms of music writing, a dot placed alongside a note increases that note's value by 50%. So (assuming 4/4 time) if a half note is allotted two beats, then a dotted half note gets three beats. Similarly, if a quarter note gets one beat, a dotted quarter gets one and a half beats. In most 4/4 or cut (2/2) time fiddle tunes, the dotted quarter note usually is followed by a single eighth note (½ beat). The dotted quarter and single eighth notes together yield a total of two beats, as shown in Example 1-23.

Count: 1 - 2 &   3 - 4 &

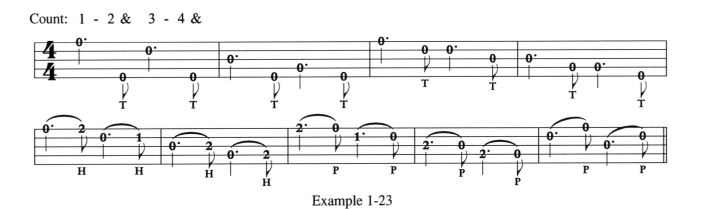

Example 1-23

25

My theory is that the dotted quarter is especially troublesome because it breaks the "stream" of notes that those of us who play a lot of fiddle tunes get so used to. Almost all notes played in a typical reel or hoedown are ordinary quarter notes or eighth notes. Each beat then is either entirely occupied by a single note (that is, a quarter note), or by a pair of evenly spaced notes (that is, two eighth notes). Dotted quarter notes, on the other hand, being *one and a half beats* long, are a decided departure from this pattern.

Let's look at the series of dotted quarter and single eighth notes in Ex. 1-23. Notice that the production of each single eighth note is linked to the dotted quarter that precedes it — either through some action of the thumb, or through some action of the fretting hand. In either case, the notes should be counted as follows: 1- 2&, 3- 4&. In other words, count the initial beat after you strike a dotted quarter as an indivisible unit, *then subdivide the second beat*. The single eighth note then comes in *exactly* half way through the second beat.

In the first four measures, the single eighth note is obtained with the thumb — either by hitting the fifth string or via drop-thumbing. Here the two notes (that is, dotted quarter *plus* single eighth) should be treated like an extended single-string brush or drop-thumb. In other words, when you play the M-string (the string played by the M or I finger), bring your thumb firmly into contact with the T-string (the string to be played by the thumb). The thumb then *waits* on the T-string for the full value of the dotted quarter (1½ beats) before actually playing the T-string. So in measure 1, strike the open first string at the start of count 1, simultaneously bringing T into contact with the fifth string. Then, 1½ beats later, strike the fifth string with T. At the start of measure 3, strike the open first string at the start of count 1, and simultaneously bring T into contact with string 2. Then, 1½ beats later, use T to strike string 2.

In the next four measures, the single eighth notes are obtained via hammer-ons and same-string pull-offs. In the case of a hammer-on, the left hand finger hovers for 1½ beats over a string before slamming down onto it. In the case of a pull-off, the left hand finger starts out firmly in contact with a sounding string. It then waits exactly 1½ beats before pulling that string off.

In the last measure, the single eighth notes are obtained via off-string pull-offs. When the M-string is plucked, a left hand finger is placed on a silent string. It then waits exactly 1½ beats before "plucking" that string.

Dotted quarter notes appear in a variety of contexts — old-time Southern tunes, Irish polkas and Scottish set tunes, ragtime pieces, and on and on. If you take the time to master the technique in the early stages of your playing you'll never have to worry about it later on.

This arrangement of the old time favorite *Sally's in the Garden Siftin' Sand* (sometimes known as *Hogeye*, or *Hogeyed Man*) contains quite a number of dotted-quarter/single eighth pairs. Incidentally, there's a whole slew of tunes named *Sally Gardens* or *Sally in the Garden* (there's another one in chapter 10, for example). Recently it has come to my attention that the Gaelic word for "willow" renders phonetically in English as *"sally."* Therefore the Scottish song and reel each known as *Sally Gardens* are actually referring to "willow gardens." This title then must have got transformed in the States (where "Sally" is a woman's name) to "Sally in the Garden."

Note that the two measure "bridge" at the conclusion of the B part repetition serves either as a conduit back to the beginning of the A part, or as a tag ending for the piece as a whole.

Sally's in the Garden Siftin' Sand

Banjo Arrangement: Ken Perlman

Tuning: gDGBD (capo–2)

Arrangement © 1994 by Ken Perlman

It is rarely possible to think one melody note at a time in clawhammer. Most often the clawhammerist must think in terms of pairs of notes. In other words, he or she must play one melody note while simultaneously preparing for the production of a second note. I like to refer to all the clawhammer techniques where such preparation is necessary as *anticipation techniques*.

The most basic anticipation techniques in clawhammer are the single-string brush and the drop thumb. In the single-string brush (refer back to column 1.2), the thumb (T) is brought into contact with the fifth string when the picking finger (M) plays a long string. In other words, T is resting on the fifth string in *anticipation* of playing that string. It is important to note that this principle applies no matter how much time elapses between M and T (see column 1.10).

For drop-thumbs (refer again to column 1.2), T is brought into contact with one long string (the T-string) when M plucks another long string (the M-string). In other words, T is set in *anticipation* some time before the T-string is actually played. This amount of time can be a half beat, a beat and a half, a third of a beat, or any other time interval.

A common fretting-hand anticipation technique is the alternate string pull-off (column 1.8, Example 1-15). A fretting-hand finger is placed on the string to be pulled off (the P-string) when the M-string is plucked. The finger then waits on the P-string until the time comes along for it to sound. When the M-string in an alternate-string P is fretted (column 1.8, Example 1-17), both the M-string and the P-string are stopped (pressed down) when the M-string is plucked. A finger then waits on the P-string until it is time for the pulled note to appear.

Richmond Cotillion

Banjo Arrangement: Ken Perlman   Tuning: gCGCD (capo–2)

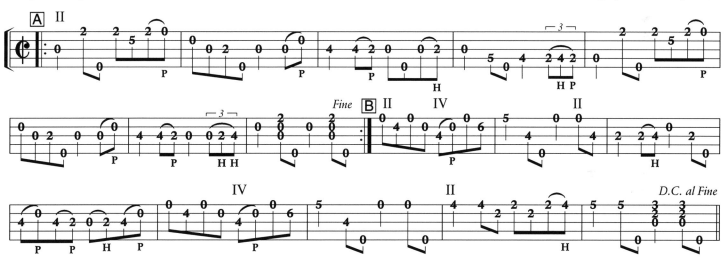

Arrangement © 1994 by Ken Perlman

The plot thickens further when situations arise where both plucking and fretting hands must anticipate simultaneously. I call these situations *compound anticipation techniques* (and you wondered why banjo players look like they're concentrating hard!). A very common example of a compound anticipation technique is a drop-thumb where both notes are fretted (Column 1.3, Example 1-3). I have already discussed how the plucking hand must anticipate by bringing T into contact with the T-string when the M-string is plucked. Now, however, the fretting hand must also anticipate by stopping the T-string at the same time it stops the M-string. T then waits on the T-string until it is time for it to be plucked.

A similar situation arises where the M-string is open but the T-string is fretted (column 1.3, Example 1-4). Here a finger of the fretting hand stops the anticipated T-string when the open M-string is played. T then waits on the T-string until it is time for it to sound.

There's quite a number of *anticipation* techniques to be found to *Richmond Cotillion*. Doubly fretted drop thumbs appear in A-part measures 1 and 5, and B-part meas. 7. Open-M, fretted-T drop thumbs are in B part meas. 1, 2, and 5. Off-string P's appear in A part meas. 6 and B part meas. 1, 4, and 5. Note the *triplets* in Part A, meas. 4 and 7; they are explained in columns 2.6 through 2.8. Observe also that the ending of the B-part leads back to the A-part, and is not meant to sound "final."

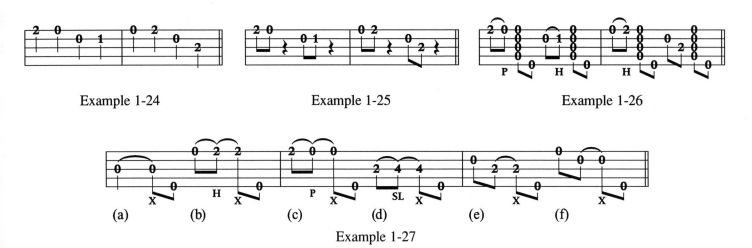

Example 1-24   Example 1-25   Example 1-26

(a)   (b)   (c)   (d)   (e)   (f)

Example 1-27

Strictly speaking, syncopation means placing an unexpected accent in a piece. Since strong accents are expected at the beginning of each measure, putting accents elsewhere in a measure is considered a form of syncopation.

Melody in its simplest form is often written in straight or *rectilinear* manner where most notes occur *on* the beat. Example 1-24 shows Part A, measures 6 and 7 of *Buffalo Gals* set in this manner.

If we move notes around in a tune relative to the beat, this is called *pushing* or *dragging* the beat. If we then accent those pushed or dragged notes, we get syncopation. In example 1-25, the second note of each pair has been *pushed* forward. In effect, a pair of quarter notes becomes a pair of eighth notes. The space that had been occupied by the second quarter note becomes a rest.

In clawhammer, we generally play pairs of eighth notes with hammer-ons, pull-offs, slides, or drop thumbs. Instead of playing rests, we tend to fill in with brush-thumbs. Bearing this in mind, lets try the same passage filled in with brush-thumbs, as shown in Example 1-26.

To create accents or syncopations, many clawhammer players use *skip strokes* instead of full brush-thumbs. In a skip stroke, the player begins an ordinary brush-thumb motion, but *intentionally misses the strings* on the way down. The thumb is dragged into the fifth string as in a normal brush, however. It waits there half a beat, then plucks the string with a pop.

Because the skip stroke calls for missing the strings entirely, the note that precedes the skip is followed by a brief silence. This silence calls attention to the preceding note. This in turn causes the listener to perceive this preceding note as stressed or *accented*.

Let's try the simplest skip, where the skip plus thumb-stroke follows a quarter note (Example 1-27a). Here, play your quarter note, let it ring for half a beat, and begin your brush

Buffalo Gals
"Straight" version

Banjo Arrangement: Ken Perlman   Tuning: gDGBD

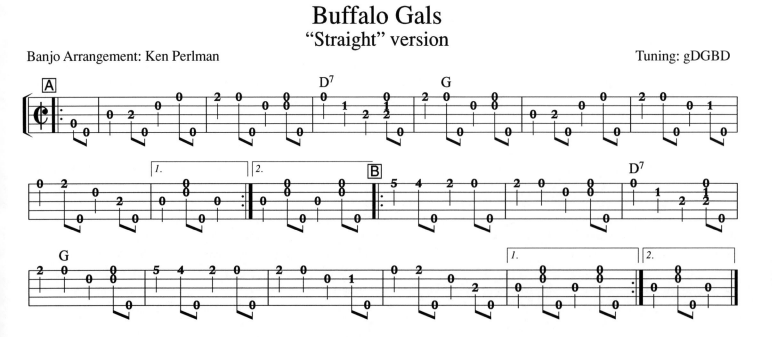

Syncopated

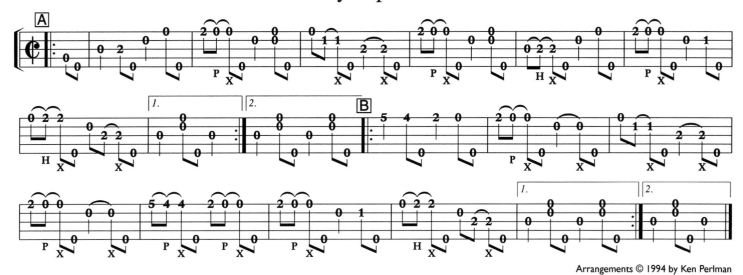

Arrangements © 1994 by Ken Perlman

thumb. *Miss* the strings on the way down, but drag the thumb (T) into the 5th string. Then, half a beat later, pluck the 5th string with T. Observe that a skip is shown in tablature by tying over the preceding note, then placing an "X" under the skip.

Instead of a quarter note, you can substitute a hammer-on (Example 1-27b), a pull-off (1-27c), a slide (1-27d) or a drop-thumb (1-27e and f). In each case, play the initial eighth note pair in the normal manner, then begin your brush thumb. Miss the

strings on the way down, but drag T into the fifth string. Then half a beat later, pluck the 5th string with T.

Buffalo Gals is presented here in two versions. The first version shows a "straight" approach to the melody. The second version shows how skips can be used for the purpose of syncopation. After trying both, you'll surely agree that the skip technique adds considerable interest to the arrangement.

1.13 The Skip-Stroke Revisited

(Jan. '98)

When I was reviewing Reed Martin's new recording *Old Time Banjo* for a recent column, I was struck how superbly Reed was able to create intricate syncopations by using a relatively simple banjo technique which I call the "skip stroke," explained in col. 1.12 (see Reed's arrangement of *Last Chance,* which appears along with col. 5.2).

Once you know what to listen for, you will hear skip-strokes in the playing of just about every accomplished clawhammer picker. The reason is that as you pick up speed, there is a tendency to brush the strings more and more lightly. Above a certain tempo, there is even a natural tendency to miss the strings altogether during brush-strokes. In the hands of an accomplished player, this natural tendency can be exploited to produce some interesting rhythmic effects.

Despite the fact that just about every player eventually hits on this technique spontaneously, for some reason students seem

to have a hard time mastering the skip-stroke when it is presented in a "pedagogical" framework. It seems hard for them to accept the notion that they should intentionally miss strings, and there is a tendency to let the hand merely rest limply after the plucked note instead of actually going through a brush motion. This leads to relatively weak-sounding thumb-notes where there should be very strong ones.

For those who would like to master the kind of syncopation that players like Reed Martin frequently use, I have the following words of advice: "Learn the skip stroke technique properly, and accept the fact that no strings are struck on the way down!"

There are a couple of interesting variants of this technique, both of which arise when the skip is preceded by a fifth-string note. In the first (Example 1-28a), a single-string brush is followed directly by a conventional skip (the fifth string itself is shown as being "tied over," but the skip is performed as usual

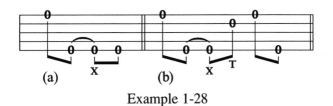

Example 1-28

by going through the motions of a "missed" brush). Alternatively, two skips can be performed in succession. This technique produces a figure — often heard in Southern banjo playing — where two strong fifth-string notes are played in a row without any intervening long-string notes (there's an example of this in the tune *Yew Pine Mountains*, which appears along with col. 2.2)

In the second technique (shown in 1-28b) — which Reed uses quite often in his playing — the skip is followed by a dropped-thumb instead of by a fifth string note. This is a bit tricky to accomplish, but yields an interesting rhythmic effect. The way I'd break it down, start to play a conventional drop-thumb, but intentionally miss the string on the down-stroke (again, it is the fifth string itself that is written as "tied over," but the skip is performed normally by going through the motions of a "missed" brush). At the conclusion of the "skip" motion, drag your thumb into the projected thumb-string (that is, string 2). Then, at the appropriate time, you'll be able to use the thumb to strike the second string with a nice "pop."

Try some of these techniques in an arrangement of the old minstrel tune *Old Jim River*, which I learned a couple of summers ago from banjoist/folksinger Jeff Warner when both of us were sojourning in England.

Old Jim River

Banjo Arrangement: Ken Perlman

Tuning: gCGBD

Arrangement © 1998 by Ken Perlman

Ken in lower Manhattan with his New York band, The Metropolitan Opry, c.1980.
L-R: Ken, Marty Laster, Will Osborne, Peter Langston. (Photo by Wren D'Antonio).

CHAPTER 2: ADVANCED AND EXPERIMENTAL TECHNIQUES

2.1 Role of the Fifth String

(Jan. '83)

In "traditional" clawhammer style, the fifth string is used primarily as a *drone* (that is, a continually sounding tone that serves as background for a melody). Example 2-1 shows a series of notes, along with a separate staff that shows that same series of notes accompanied by fifth-string drone notes.

Occasionally in "traditional" style — and frequently in melodic style — the fifth string is used for melody, as in the run of notes in Example 2-2. In this case the thumb hits the fifth string with a somewhat different attack than for drone notes. Since the fifth string should sound more like the long strings when used melodically, you should be shooting here for less "pop" and more pure tone.

There's another interesting thing you can do with the fifth string when you are playing a tune with a lot of notes obtained via hammer-ons, pull-offs or slides, and there really doesn't seem to be much room for drone notes. If you leave out drone notes entirely — particularly when you are playing with a band — you tend to lose a lot of drive and to also lose some of the five string banjo's unique character. On the other hand, if you go for drone notes and leave out melody notes, you're confining yourself to the restrictions of "traditional" style.

One good solution here is to play drone notes *simultaneously* with your hammers, pull-offs and slides. This is best achieved by timing each left hand maneuver to coincide with the striking of each drone note by the thumb. Practice some of these in Example 2-3.

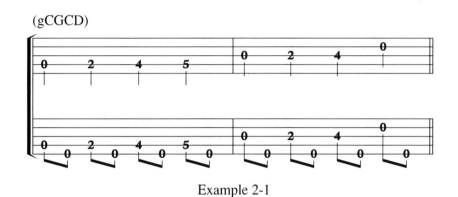

Example 2-1

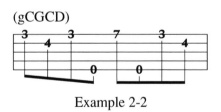

Example 2-2

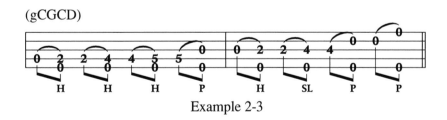

Example 2-3

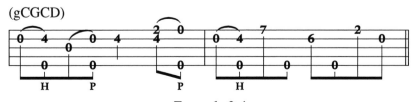

Example 2-4

31

I learned *Levantine's Barrel* from fiddler Sterling Baker of Montague, Prince Edward Island. My arrangement contains quite a few instances of fifth-string melody notes, specifically in meas. 2, 4 and 6 of both parts. In case you'd like to try playing some drone notes simultaneous with your H's and P's, I've illustrated in Example 2-4 how this might go for the first two measures. Observe that the tune opens with a *triplet*: triplets are explained in cols. 2.6-8 (this one is of the "MPP" variety).

Levantine's Barrel

Banjo Arrangement: Ken Perlman

Tuning: gCGCD (capo–2)

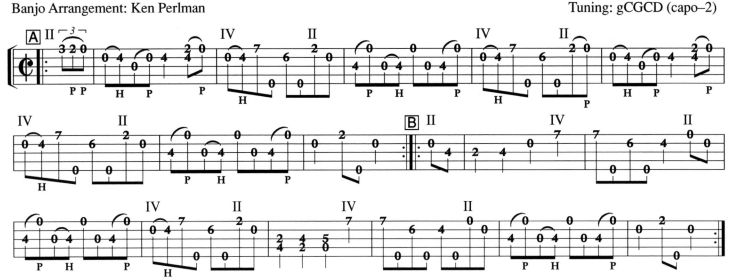

Arrangement © 1998 by Ken Perlman

2.2 Adding Drone Notes to Melodic Tabs

(Dec. '89)

In a recent column, I remarked that in performance it was quite routine to ad-lib drone notes when playing "melodic" arrangements. It occurs to me that it might also be fruitful for many readers if I discussed just how this is done. So here goes!

There are basically three ways to add drone notes to a melodic tab, each of which will be discussed in turn, then Rolls illustrated in Example 2-5. The top staff (2-5a) shows the melody for the first two measures of *Nine Points Of Roguery*, an Irish reel which I recorded on *Clawhammer Banjo & Fingerstyle Guitar Solos*. The staffs labeled 2-5b-d show various methods for adding drones, and the bottom staff (2-5e) shows a suggested composite method for adding drones.

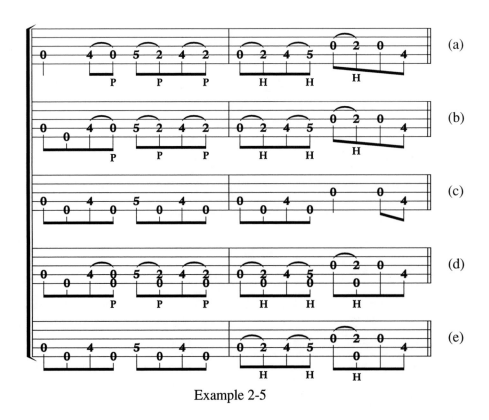

Example 2-5

32

First and simplest, any quarter note in a 4/4 or 2/2 melody can — with the addition of a drone note — be converted into the two eighth notes that make up a single-string brush. An example here is shown at the beginning of 2-5b, where an open fourth string quarter note from the melody was changed into two eighth notes (open fourth string plus open fifth).

Second, you can simplify the melody by *substituting* drone notes for melody eighth notes falling between the beats. So, if you look at 2-5c, all the H and P notes have been replaced by drone notes, yielding a series of single-string brushes. This is a nice way of dealing with fiddle accompaniment. In other words, the banjo offers support for the melody without stepping on the fiddler's toes.

Third (as described in column 2.1), you can actually play drone notes at the same time as your H-, P- or SL-notes, which makes the semi-educated listener think you have four hands. This is shown in 2-5d. Here, perform your ordinary single-string brush (that is, M-note plus drone note) with the right hand, but get your left hand to perform an H, P or SL that exactly coincides with the playing of the T-note. At first, this will feel very much like simultaneously patting your head and rubbing your stomach, but once you get it down it's really easy-as-pie (well, almost!).

In practice you'll probably want to combine all the methods, a suggestion for which is shown in 2-5e. For practice, try adapting these approaches to the rest of this tune (it's printed in its entirety in chapter 10), then try to similarly modify other melodic tabs. After all, just because you're a melodic player doesn't mean you must play melody all the time. It just means you're *capable* of playing the melody — or carrying the lead — for any tune at any time!

Yew Pine Mountains is a West Virginia tune arranged for banjo by Dwight Diller, who routinely keeps his fifth string going simultaneously with his H's, P's and SL's. Observe that there are two 2/4 measures (that is, they are "half" the normal length: one in the second ending of the A-part, and one at the end of the B-part). There is also an instance of consecutive 5th string notes in the A-part, 2nd ending (performed by playing two skip-strokes in succession: see col. 1.13). The piece is in gGDGD tuning, which is obtained as follows:

♦ Tune string 3 down to match open string 4.
♦ Tune string 2 down to match the new pitch of fret 5, string 3.
♦ Tune string 4 down so that its 7th fret matches the new pitch of open string 3.

Yew Pine Mountains

Banjo Arrangement: Dwight Diller

Tuning: gGDGD

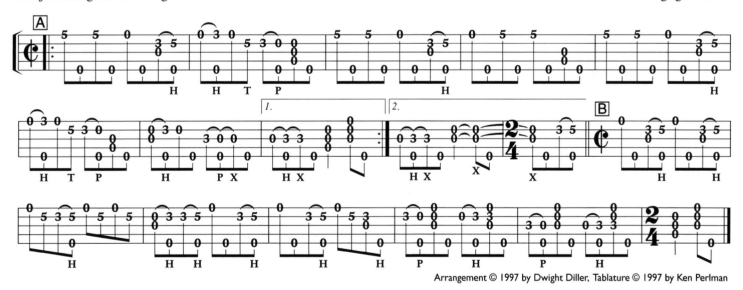

Arrangement © 1997 by Dwight Diller, Tablature © 1997 by Ken Perlman

2.3 Brushes and Drones in Clawhammer

(Nov. '89)

This column was prompted by two recent letters — one from a reader in Oregon lamenting the absence of brush strokes in the tabs recently published along with this column, and the other from a reader in Maine pointing to a dearth of drone notes in those same tabs.

I'll deal with the second issue first: as the reader puts it, "Why play the 5-string if you ignore the fifth string?"

Why indeed! And in fact I use the fifth string in my own playing all the time — especially when accompanying fiddlers or vocalists, or when jamming in sessions (see chapter 6). In fact, any clawhammer player worth his salt should be able to set up a nice rolling rhythm involving both fifth and long strings, and keep up that rhythm all day long.

Every full-fledged clawhammer player knows this, and most can do it just fine. I therefore never felt the need to deal much with the drone in a column devoted to experimental approaches to the instrument. Moreover, just because the tab indicates few drones doesn't mean that one shouldn't ad lib additional drones during performance (see columns 2.1-2). It should more or less be *understood* that drones are to be added, the way that Irish fiddlers know that certain ornaments are to be added to the relatively bare-bones notation of fiddle tunes that appears in tune-books.

I think that in general written music — whether in tab or standard notation — should not be regarded as a "final authority." Tabs should be seen as points of departure for a players' efforts rather than as ends in themselves.

Moving on to next issue, the reader from Oregon makes the point that because my tabs do not feature frequent full brushes, the style I present is not truly representative of clawhammer. I'll respond by pointing out that full brushes were considered a major focus of the style for only a relatively short period of its development — namely the first generation of the "revival"

(roughly 1945-70: see cols. 9-13 thru 9-15). The earliest clawhammer instruction books written c. 1850, for example, rarely indicate full brush strokes beyond the elementary level. What's more, in the version of "traditional" clawhammer most often encountered after 1970, players tend to avoid using full brushes except for effect. Instead of the full brush, they tend to focus on the technique referred to in these pages as the "single-string brush" (that is, M-note plus drone: see column 1.2).

The most important reason for using the single-string brush rather than the full brush is that the banjo is an extremely resonant instrument. When you pluck one string, you can generally hear all its neighbors sounding softly. Therefore, when you play a bumm-titty rhythm (quarter note plus two eighths) with the first eighth note on a long string and the second on the fifth (Example 2-6), the entire instrument is resonating nearly as much as if you had performed a full brush. Under these conditions, as one approaches fiddle tune speed full brushes are simply "overkill": they are just too harsh and cumbersome to be of much use. The single-string brush, on the other hand, becomes the "elegant" method of brushing the banjo.

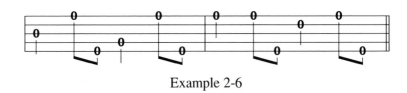

Example 2-6

2.4 Improvisation and "Breaks"   (May '87)

Playing variations on a melody is a particularly interesting way of handling a banjo solo. A *variation* has the same basic harmony and overall feel as the original melody, but differs from it sufficiently to be musically distinct. A bluegrass banjo *break* that significantly embellishes the basic melody, for example, is actually a variation on that melody.

As the last statement implies, one very effective variation technique involves taking a very simple melody and making it more complex. One straight-forward method for accomplishing this is called *Baroque improvisation*.

"Baroque improvisation" may sound like a $20 expression, but the idea behind it is quite simple. Starting with the basic melody line, the musician surrounds each note with adjacent notes drawn from the scale in use. The term Baroque is used here because the process is associated with the compositional style of the Baroque Period of Music (c. 1600-1750).

Example 2-7 shows the notes for the key G-mixolydian (G-A-B-C-D-E-F-G). To the left of the full octave are the lowest G-mixolydian notes on the banjo (F-E-D). To the right of the full octave are some higher G-mixolydian notes (A-B-C-D).

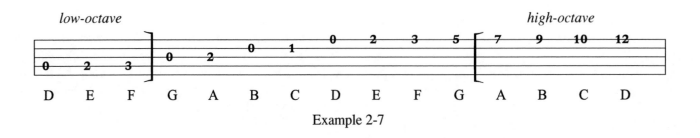

Example 2-7

Baroque improvisation can be approached via a series of formulas. For example, we can employ the following prescription:

♦ Take a melody note
♦ Follow it by the scale note below it
♦ Return to the original note
♦ Play the scale note above it
♦ Repeat the process, beginning two notes above the original melody note

Looking at the first two measures of Example 2-8, a Baroque improvisation using the above formula has been applied to an ascending full-octave G-mixolydian scale. Starting with the melody note (open G), we follow it with the lower scale note (F: fret 3, string 4); return to G; pass through the next melody note (A: fret 2, string 3). Next, starting at open B, we play the next lower scale note (A), return to B, move through the next melody note C (fret 1, string 2) to the note open D, and so on.

The next four measures of 2-8 apply the following formula to a descending G-mixolydian scale (G-F-E-D-C-B-A-G):

♦ Take a melody note
♦ Follow it by two successively lower scale notes
♦ Return to the original melody note
♦ Move on to the next melody note and repeat the process.

Following this formula, I've started my improvisation at high A (fret 7, string 1), which is one note above the octave scale. Starting with A, I play G below it (open 5th string) and F (fret 6, string 2), followed by A again. Moving on, I play G (fret 5, string 1), follow it with F and E (fret 5 string 2), return to G, and so on.

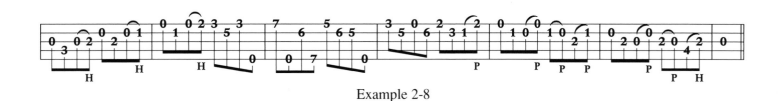

Example 2-8

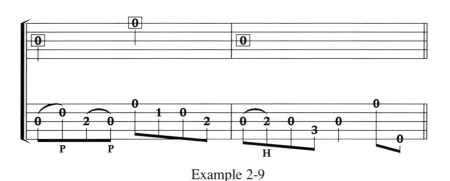

Example 2-9

Another aspect of Baroque Improvisation involves *arpeggiation* (moving directly from note-to-note within a chord). In other words, you can move from chord note to chord note, returning to the original note via a series of scale notes. In the top staff of Example 2-9, there's a very sparse melody line harmonized by a G chord (the G chord is made up of the pitches G, B and D). We can create a Baroque improvisation (bottom staff) by going from melody note G (open 3rd string), to fellow chord-note B (open second string), then returning to the G-note via scale step A (fret 2; string 3). Then we can skip up directly to melody note (and fellow chord note) D, and return to the next Clawhammer melody note G via the intervening scale notes C (fret 1, string 2), B (open string 2) and A.

Finally, I filled in the last long note with a "marching in place" kind of improvisation which employs this formula: Take a note, follow it with the next higher scale note, return to the original, play the next lower scale note, then return to the original.

Try some of these ideas in this arrangement for the well-known tune *Old Joe Clark*. The top staff shows the basic melody while the bottom staff displays the variation.

Old Joe Clark "Break"

Banjo Arrangement: Ken Perlman

Tuning: gDGBD (capo–2 optional)

Arrangement © 1987 by Ken Perlman

2.5 Playing Octave Up Variations

(Dec. '84)

Taking the basic melody of a tune up an octave makes an exciting and impressive break. This is true even for quite simple tunes whose octave-up versions are not particularly demanding technically. Three reasons for this immediately come to mind. First, the banjo really sings out at these upper registers — not only is projection much greater, but the timbre (tone-quality) of the instrument takes on a rich, complex character, akin to that of high notes on a French horn. Second, audiences are not accustomed to hearing banjos — particularly open-back banjos — played way up-the-neck, and just about anything you do up there will seem fresh and original. Third, merely the sight of a banjoist's fretting hand obtaining a full melody line way up-the-neck tends to impress.

Be aware that in the following discussion I will refer to the *actual* pitches on banjo, and *not* to how those pitches are written (pitches on the banjo are by convention written an octave higher than their actual sound).

Finding your octave-up melody notes is not particularly hard. As you probably know, the 12th fret on each string is exactly an octave above the open string (most banjos in fact draw attention to the 12th or octave fret of the long strings with a special decorative marker).

So, if the pitch of open string 4 in G-tuning (gDGBD) is D below middle C, the pitch of fret 12, string 4 is D above middle C. Similarly, if the pitch of open string 2 in double C tuning is middle C, the pitch of fret 12, string 2 is C above middle C, and so on.

Above the 12th fret on any string, all the pitches found near the nut repeat themselves at an octave-higher level. The open fourth string in G-tuning, for example, is D below middle C. Fret 1, string 4 is therefore D♯ or E♭ below middle C, fret 2, string 4 is E below middle C, fret 3, string 4 is F below middle C, and so on. Since we know that fret 12, string 4 is the octave fret with a pitch of D above middle C, we instantly know that fret 13, string 4 corresponds to fret 1, string 4, and has a pitch of D♯ or E♭ above middle C. Similarly, fret 14, string 4 corresponds to fret 2, string 4 and has a pitch of E above middle C, fret 15, string 4 corresponds to fret 3, string 4 and has a pitch of F above middle C, and so on.

In fact, to find an octave-higher note on any string, just add 12 to the original fret number. If your original melody note is at fret 2 on any string, for example, the note an octave up is found at fret 14 (2 + 12 = 14). If your original melody note is at fret 5 on any string, your octave-up note is at fret 17 (5 + 12 = 17).

Example 2-10 shows a fingering diagram for some basic octave-up natural-note locations in G tuning. Example 2-11 shows a fingering diagram for some basic octave-up natural-note locations in double C tuning (gCGCD). For both these

tunings, be aware that pitches on the fifth string are identical to pitches on the first string at all upper fret levels.

Here's a trick I like to use to create instant octave-up breaks. I barre across strings one through three at the 12th fret with my first finger, and keep that barre firmly in place throughout the duration of the break. This approach has several advantages. First, my barring finger serves as a line of demarcation — immediately indicating where the octave-fret is. I can then imagine that the 12th fret is the nut and know instantly where to

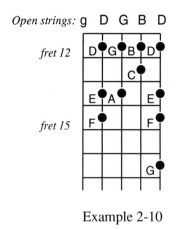

Example 2-10

Example 2-11

Old Joe Clark (Octave Up)

Banjo Arrangement: Ken Perlman

Tuning: gDGBD (capo–2 optional)

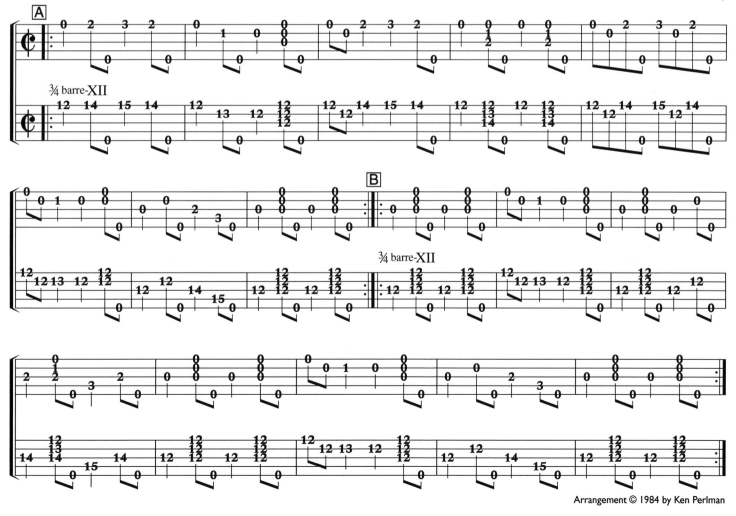

Arrangement © 1984 by Ken Perlman

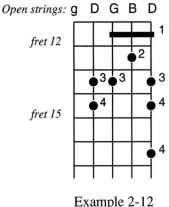

Example 2-12

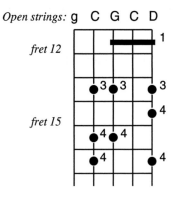

Example 2-13

find octave-up versions of all the other pitches I need. Second, keeping pressure on a three-string barre allows the high notes on these top three strings to vibrate together somewhat, preventing your arrangement from sounding unpleasantly staccato. Third, barring no more than three strings allows the still open fourth string to also vibrate sympathetically, providing nice low overtones and preventing your arrangement from sounding too shrill.

Example 2-12 suggests fingering for various natural notes

when using a three-string barre (I call it a ¾ barre in the tab) across the 12th or octave fret for G tuning. Example 2-13 offers the same information for double C tuning.

For practice, here are two old-time standards — *Old Joe Clark* and *Angeline the Baker* — each arranged in both conventional "open-position" form (top staffs) and octave-up form (bottom staffs). The up-the-neck version of each tune is to be played while holding down a ¾ barre at the twelfth fret throughout.

Angeline the Baker (Octave Up)

Banjo Arrangement: Ken Perlman

Tuning: gCGCD (capo–2 optional)

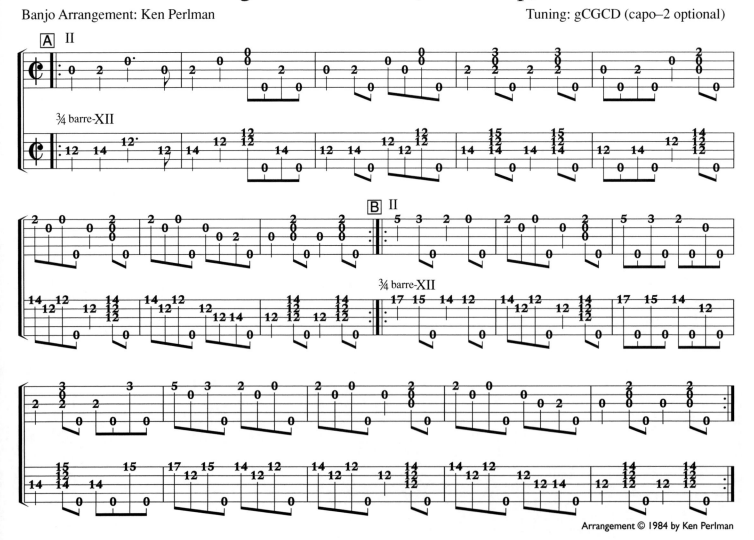

Arrangement © 1984 by Ken Perlman

38

2.6 Using Triplets to Ornament a Simple Melody

 (Nov. '82)

Say that you have a pretty but simple melody and need a way to make repetitions interesting. One method is to decorate or *ornament* certain notes in the melody. If done wisely, ornamentation leaves the character of the melody intact, but adds considerable texture and complexity to the overall performance.

Although several kinds of ornamentation are employed by clawhammer players, this discussion will be confined to the use of triplets (for other kinds of ornamentation, see col. 2-24). A triplet is a group of three notes played in the time ordinarily occupied by one quarter note. As shown in Example 2-14, a

measure of triplets in 4/4 time is counted as 1-&-a, 2-&-a, 3-&-a, 4-&-a.

The first note of each triplet in clawhammer is usual played by the middle or index fingernail, while the second and third notes of each triplet are generally obtained by some combination of hammer-ons and pull-offs. Example 2-15 shows how quarter notes (or eighth note pairs in which the second note is a fifth string drone) can be turned into M-H-P triplets — the most frequently used clawhammer ornament. Observe how M strikes the original melody note, an H is performed to the next note of the scale, and a P is performed from the hammered note back to the original note.

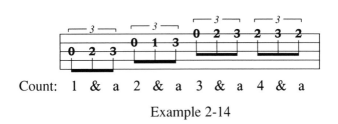

Count: 1 & a 2 & a 3 & a 4 & a

Example 2-14

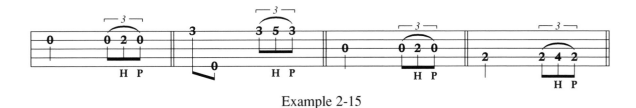

Example 2-15

The next issue to be dealt with is which notes to ornament. While there are no hard and fast rules, there are some criteria to bear in mind. Three such criteria are concepts I call *economy, variety* and *balance*. By economy, I mean that you should generally be sparing in your use of ornaments. It's more effective to ornament a few strategically placed notes than to change every quarter note in sight into a triplet.

By variety I mean that when certain melodic phrases or rhythmic patterns are repeated in a tune, you will probably want to ornament each phrase or pattern somewhat differently.

Balance refers to what beat in a given measure is ornamented, relative to those beats ornamented in other measures.

Let's look at the accompanying tune *Sean Ryan's Polka*, which comes from County Kerry in southwestern Ireland. The top staff is the basic melody (drone notes included) while the lower staff is ornamented with MHP triplets. Play through the A Part and you'll note that the most distinctive phrase is stated in measure 1, repeated in measure 3 and again in measure 5. Measures 2, 4 and 6 are very similar to each other in both melody and rhythm. Measures 7 and 8 form one of the many cliche endings that occur again and again in fiddle tunes.

Because measures 1, 3 and 5 are so distinctive and because the phrase contained in them is musically dense ("chock full of notes"), I've decided in the interests of economy to let them pass unornamented. Measure 2 on the other hand, which is simple and repetitive is a good candidate for ornamentation. For variety's sake, I've ornamented the second open string-3 note, which falls on the second "full" beat of the measure (note that the tune is in 2/2, not 4/4 time so each beat is a half measure long). To balance this triplet, I've also ornamented the fret 2, string 4 note which falls on the second beat of measure 4. Then, for variety, I've ornamented the first open-string 3 note of measure 6. Also in the interest of variety, I chose to ornament the open-string 1 note in measure 7.

Now play through the B Part, and note how its structure is considerably different from that of the A Part. There is a relatively distinctive phrase that covers measures 1 & 2 and is repeated in measures 5 & 6. Measures 3 and 4 form a phrase whose function is to echo measures 1 and 2, while measures 7 and 8 repeat the cliche ending of the A Part. Since the B Part's structure is much "looser" than that of the A Part (that is, it has much longer phrases), there are many acceptable ways to ornament it.

I've aimed here for maximum variety. In measure 1, I ornamented the first quarter note, in measure 2 the second quarter note, in measure 3 the third quarter note; I left measure 4 unornamented because it was already musically dense. Measures 5 & 6 repeat measures 1 & 2, so I ornamented different quarter notes: specifically the second note in measure 5 and the first in measure 6. Measures 7 represents the second time around for a cliche ending [yawn!]), so I ornamented two quarter notes.

Now remember that the method I've presented here is merely a representation of what might go on subconsciously in a player's mind. I don't mean to imply that you should actually write a tune out and systematically decide where the ornaments should go. I never do this myself. Economy, variety and balance are merely factors to be weighed, rather than ends in themselves. As always, the ultimate standard for musical decisions is how what you are playing sounds to your own ear.

Sean Ryan's Polka

Banjo Arrangement: Ken Perlman

Tuning: gCGCD (capo–2)

Arrangement © 1982 by Ken Perlman

2.7 Multiple Hammer-Ons and Pull-Offs

(June '90)

Playing a single hammer-on (H) or pull-off (P) from a single M-finger stroke is one of the most common clawhammer maneuvers. Playing more than one hammer or pull from that same M-stroke (Example 2-16) can be tricky to accomplish. To make matters worse, quite often it is difficult to get some multiple H- and P-notes to project sufficiently to be heard above the din of a string band or jam session. This of course tempts the sensible player to just leave them out altogether, thereby often detracting from the overall character of the tune being played. Is there anything to be done to improve this situation?

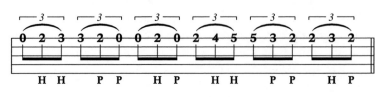

Example 2-16

The problem can actually be attacked from several angles. First, you can work to improve your left-hand technique. Practice multi-hammers on open strings (Example 2-17a) and fretted strings (Example 2-17b). Practice multi-pulls on open strings (Example 2-18a) and fretted strings (Example 2-18b). Practice hammer-pull combinations on open strings (Example 2-19a) and fretted strings (Example 2-19b). Each example shows Hs and Ps on the first string only, but you can also practice them — using the same frets — on all the other long strings. As for fingering, use the first finger on fret 2; the second finger on fret 3; the third finger on fret 4 and the fourth finger on fret 5.

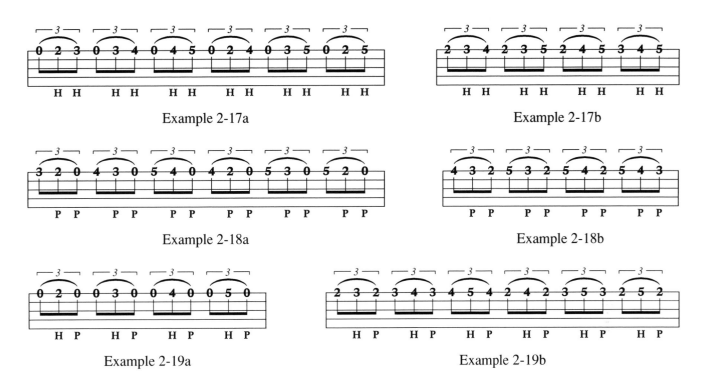

Example 2-17a

Example 2-17b

Example 2-18a

Example 2-18b

Example 2-19a

Example 2-19b

Once you have given these maneuvers a try, here are some tips to improve clarity and projection. For hammer-ons, make sure your arched finger drives the string sharply into the finger board, literally like a hammer driving a nail into wood. To get a little extra "pop" into your sound, you can actually wind up a bit before you hammer. In other words, keeping your finger arched, retract the hammering finger slightly relative to the other fingers of your hand prior to striking it down.

If you are going to perform two H's in succession from the same M-stroke (as in Examples 2-17a and b), the procedure is as follows: at the conclusion of the first H, balance firmly on the hammering finger while you stretch out your second hammering finger towards the "target" fret (that is, the fret targeted for the second hammer-on). Don't release pressure on the first hammering finger until just after the second hammering finger strikes down.

The High Reel

Banjo Arrangement: Ken Perlman

Tuning: gDGBD (capo–2)

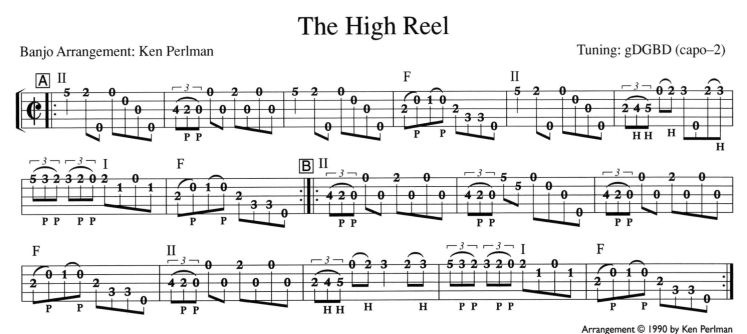

Arrangement © 1990 by Ken Perlman

41

For multiple pull-offs, start with all fingers down on the fingerboard, then peel them off one by one. In the first entry of Example 2-18a, press down the first and second fingers at the same time, then hold the first firmly while pulling off with the second. Then (1/3 of a beat later) pull-off with the first finger to the open string. In the first entry of Example 2-18b, press down the first, second, and third fingers at the same time. Hold down the first and second while pulling off the third, then hold down the first while pulling off the second.

One problem with multiple hammers and pulls on banjo is that the instrument doesn't have a lot of sustain. In other words, the sound created by the original plucked string can die away so quickly that there isn't much left to support the extra H's and

P's. In this situation, the sympathetic vibrations of neighboring strings (i.e., the sounds created by unstruck strings vibrating slightly from energy generated by struck strings) is sometimes sufficiently loud to interfere with the clear perception of these H- and P-notes. For this reason it is often effective to dampen out one or more neighboring strings with the right-hand thumb while performing multiple H's and P's on a given string. For example, you might let your thumb rest on the second string while doing a series of multi-hammer or multi-pull triplets on the first string, and so on.

The High Reel comes from the Irish repertoire. Multi-pull triplets appear in Part A (ms. 2 & 7) and in Part B (ms. 1, 2, 3, 5 & 7). Multi-hammer triplets appear in Part A & B (meas 6).

2.8 All Kinds of Triplets

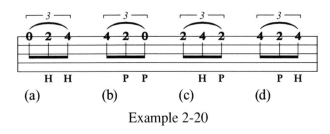

H H   P P   H P   P H

(a)   (b)   (c)   (d)

Example 2-20

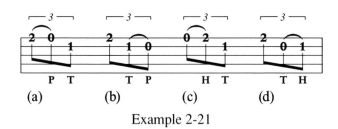

P T   T P   H T   T H

(a)   (b)   (c)   (d)

Example 2-21

Although in clawhammer it is most natural to play notes in pairs, there are numerous ways to obtain effective triplets. In this column I'll discuss some of the more common ways that triplets can be performed in clawhammer (see col. 2.6 for a definition of triplets and a method for *counting* them).

For the sake of convenience, I'll name each kind of triplet for the maneuvers used to produce it. In this discussion the symbol *M* indicates a downstroke of the picking finger, *T* means thumb, *H* means hammer-on, *P* means pull-off, and *A* means arpeggio (rolled note: see column 2.9).

Most of the common methods for making triplets in clawhammer involve an initial strike by the M-finger followed by some combination of *left-hand plucking* maneuvers (that is, hammering-on or pulling-off). Example 2-20 shows some common triplets of this ilk. Whenever applicable I'll suggest a tune or two in this book where each kind of triplet is illustrated. Observe that some of the techniques described below are also used for playing three-note-groupings in jigs (see cols. 3.7-10)

◆ *The MHH triplet* (Ex. 2-20a). This is accomplished by performing two successive hammer-ons on the same sounding string. Start by striking the open string with M. After ⅓ of a beat, do your first hammer-on to fret 2. Keep the note sounding for ⅓ of a beat, then perform a second H to fret 4. Featured in: *Richmond Cotillion, The High Reel.*

◆ *The MPP triplet* (Ex. 2-20b). This is accomplished by performing two successive pull-offs on the same sounding string. Start by striking fret 4, string 1 with M. After ⅓ of a beat, do your first pull-off to fret 2. Keep the note sounding for ⅓ of

a beat, then perform a second P to the open string. Featured in: *Levantine's Barrel, The High Reel.*

◆ *The MHP triplet* (Ex. 2-20c). This is obtained with an H followed by a P. Start by striking fret 2, string 1 with M. After ⅓ of a beat, do an H onto fret 4. Keep the note sounding for ⅓ of a beat, then perform a P back to fret 2. Make sure you keep fret 2 pressed down firmly throughout. Featured in: *Sean Ryan's Polka, MacNab's Hornpipe, Cooley's Reel.*

◆ *The MPH triplet* (Ex. 2-20d). This is obtained with a P followed by an H. Start by striking fret 4, string 1 with M. After ⅓ of a beat, pull off to fret 2. Keep the note sounding for ⅓ of a beat, then perform an H back to fret 4. Make sure you keep fret 2 pressed down firmly throughout. Featured in: *Nine Points of Roguery.*

Example 2-21 shows pull-offs obtained by a combining an H or P with a drop thumb pair.

◆ *The MPT triplet* (Ex.2-21a). Obtain this by inserting a P within a drop-thumb pair. Start by striking fret 2, string 1 with M (and bring T into contact with the second string). After ⅓ of a beat, pull off the open string. After another ⅓ of a beat, strike fret 1, string 2 with T. Featured in: *The Laird of Drumblaire.*

◆ *The MTP triplet* (Ex.2-21 b). Obtain this triplet by following a drop-thumb pair with a P originating from the T-note. Start by striking fret 2, string 1 with M (and bring T into contact with the second string). After ⅓ of a beat, strike fret 1, string 2 with T. After another ⅓ of a beat, do a P from fret 1, string 2 to the open string.

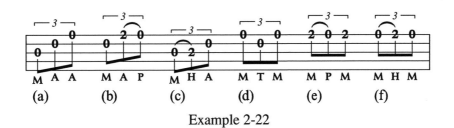

Example 2-22

♦ *The MHT triplet* (Ex. 2-21c). Obtain this triplet by inserting an H within a drop-thumb pair. Start by striking open string 1 with M (and bring T into contact with the second string). After ⅓ of a beat, do your H onto fret 2, string 1. After another ⅓ of a beat, strike fret 1, string 2 with T.

♦ *The MTH triplet* (Ex. 2-21d). Obtain this triplet by following a drop-thumb pair with an H off the T-note. Start by striking fret 2, string 1 with M. After ⅓ of a beat, strike open string 2 with T. After another ⅓ of a beat, do an H to fret 1, string 2.

Example 2-22 shows triplets that include *arpeggios* (explained in col. 2.9), or extra M-strokes:

♦ *The MAA triplet* (Ex. 2-22a). In this one, the second and third triplet notes are obtained via arpeggio. Start by striking string 3. After ⅓ of a beat, continue the M-stroke onto string 2. After another ⅓ of a beat, continue the M-stroke through string 1. Featured in: *Dinah*.

♦ *The MAP triplet* (Ex. 2-22b). Obtain this triplet by combining an arpeggio and pull-off. Start by striking open string 2 with M. After ⅓ of a beat, continue your arpeggio and strike fret 2, string 1. After another ⅓ of a beat, do a P to open string 1.

♦ *The MHA triplet* (Ex. 2-22c). Obtain this triplet by combining an arpeggio and hammer-on. Start by striking open string 3 with M, and leave it resting on string 2. After ⅓ of a beat, do an H on fret 2, string 3. After another ⅓ of a beat, continue your arpeggio and strike open string 2.

♦ *MTM, MPM, MHM triplets* (Ex. 2-22d-f). Obtained by adding an additional M stroke to a drop-thumb, pull-off or hammer-on, respectively. These techniques are most often employed in playing jigs and other 6/8 or 9/8 time tunes, but they will occasionally show up in 3/4, 4/4 or cut-time pieces: especially when the tempos are on the slow side. Featured in: *The Mariner, The Leard o' Drumblaire, Niel Gow's Lament*.

Try some MHP and MPP triplets in the accompanying tune *Harvest Home Hornpipe*. One unusual "wrinkle": the second triplet in meas. 4 of both parts (representing the "MHP" variety) features an *off-string* H. To make this work, perform the H to fret 4, string 3 with the third finger, and bring the first finger behind it to fret 2 in *anticipation* of the forthcoming pull-off. Then (after ⅓ of a beat) perform your P. If you're not quite sure how to approach playing hornpipes, see col. 3.2.

Harvest Home Hornpipe

Banjo Arrangement: Ken Perlman

Tuning: gCGCD (capo–2)

Arrangement © 2001 by Ken Perlman

43

To play an ordinary note on strings 2, 3, or 4 with the picking finger (M), the player strikes a string and comes to rest momentarily on the next higher string. After that moment of contact, the hand relaxes and M more or less removes itself from the contacted string. So, if M strikes string 2, it rests briefly on string 1; if M strikes string 3, it rests for a bit on string 2, and so on.

In an Arpeggio (arp) or roll-stroke, M strikes, say, string 2 but rests *heavily* on string 1. When it is time to pluck string 1, M plucks that string *without* a new wrist stroke. In other words, you get two notes off the same wrist movement. Observe that I notate the arp with an "M" plus an arrow that shows how far the stroke extends (Example 2-23). As you might expect, arps can cover more than two strings (Example 2-24). Just bear in mind that you must rest heavily on each succeeding string and then pluck that string with power deriving from the original wrist stroke. In the first arp of Ex. 2-24, for example, strike string 3 and rest heavily on 2; strike string 2 without a fresh wrist stroke and rest heavily on string 1; then strike string 1 without a fresh wrist stroke.

I have long felt the need for a technique like the arp because of an important limitation inherent to drop-thumbing. The problem is as follows: each time you drop-thumb a rapid pair of notes, the thumb (T) comes into play on a lower string than M. If the second note of the pair is higher than the first, you often cannot obtain that second note by drop-thumbing.

In my first few years of playing I learned to use numerous *compensation techniques* designed to overcome this limitation — such as the alternate string pull-off and the alternate string hammer-on (see column 1.8) — but these tended to have problems and limitations of their own. In addition, there seemed to be a need for simplification in melodic clawhammer: sometimes there were so many different techniques involved in playing a piece that it was hard to keep track of them all.

One peculiarity of arp-less clawhammer is that it often takes an entirely different fingering (or maneuver) to play the same pair of notes in a different order. Example 2-25 shows several pairs of notes — each played both in upward and downward order — on strings 1 & 2. Observe that every pair of notes is best obtained differently when the direction of play is reversed.

When using the arpeggio technique, on the other hand, you can at least use the same left-hand fingering for most pairs of notes, regardless of their direction of play. In other words, you can always use the arpeggio for upward motion and drop thumbing for downward motion (Example 2-26).

I first hit on the idea of using arps in the mid-70s, but it was quite a while before I actually used the technique in a finished version of a tune. In most circumstances I found that I could not perform an arp with enough speed and fluidity to avoid throwing my right hand completely off stride.

Eventually, I began finding some limited circumstances where arps could be used, such as the *Turkey In The Straw* lick (Example 2-27). I kept playing away, and after lots of practice using the technique for exotic fare like ragtime and ersatz bluegrass (see columns 2.17-18 and 4.4), my wrist loosened up sufficiently for me to use arps effectively in ordinary fiddle tunes.

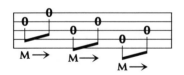

Example 2-23

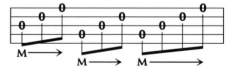

Example 2-24

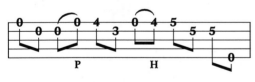

Example 2-25

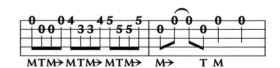

Example 2-26

Example 2-27

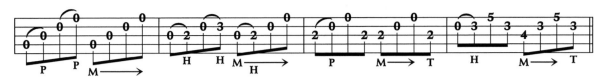

Example 2-28

By extending an arp across three or even fours strings, you get a nice run of ascending melody notes with a lot more simplicity than is offered by any other method I've encountered. Example 2-28 shows a series of four-note licks. In each measure, the lick is first obtained conventionally, then by means of an arp.

Observe that a hammer-on, pull-off, slide or drop thumb can be integrated into an arp. In the second measure, for example, M rests heavily on string 2, while you hammer onto string 3. M then continues its arp stroke onto string 1. In the last meas., M carries across three strings, dragging T into position on the second string. At the appropriate moment, T then plucks the second string as in a conventional drop-thumb.

Banjo purists can take heart here, since the arp technique is even older than "traditional" clawhammer. In fact, it shows up prominently in mid-19th Century minstrel-era "stroke style" banjo tutors (see cols. 9.3-4).

Try some arps in *Mackilmoyle,* a tune frequently heard in the New England contra dance scene and often associated with the playing of fiddler Don Messer, who was a major figure on the Canadian airwaves from the late 1930s through the early 70s. Observe that Part B, meas. 3 calls for some 5th-string fretting: this is discussed in cols. 2.16-18.

Mackilmoyle

Banjo Arrangement: Ken Perlman

Tuning: gCGCD (capo–2)

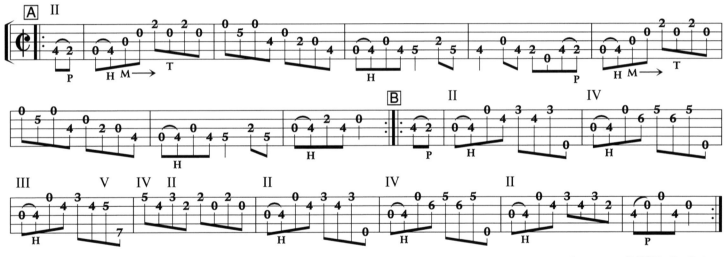

Arrangement © 1986 by Ken Perlman

2.10 Arpeggio Exercises (Excerpt from "Right-Hand Exercises") (June '98)

Once you learn to use arpeggios in your playing, you can also incorporate the following exercises into the daily routine suggested in column 1.5. In Exercise B1, you can practices a four-note group consisting of a 3-string arpeggio plus a drone note; in Exercise B2 it's a 3-string arpeggio plus a drop-thumb.

In Exercise B3, the right hand plays the first pattern from Exercise B2 throughout. The left hand *stops* (presses down) the fingering shape shown in Example 2-29a at the fifth fret, then moves it up one fret for each repetition. In Exercise B4, the right hand plays a variant of the second pattern from Exercise B2 2.11

throughout. The left hand stops the fingering shape shown in Example 2-29b at the fifth fret, then moves it up one fret for each repetition.

Example 2-29a

Example 2-29b

45

Exercises B1–4

Ex. B1

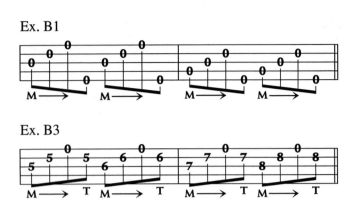

Ex. B2

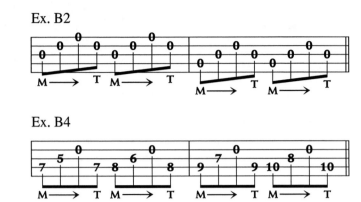

Ex. B3

Ex. B4

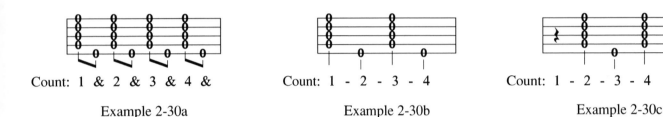

(Dec. '00)

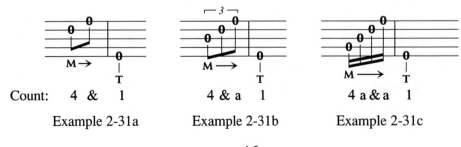

Count: 1 & 2 & 3 & 4 &

Example 2-30a

Count: 1 - 2 - 3 - 4

Example 2-30b

Count: 1 - 2 - 3 - 4 - 1

Example 2-30c

The roll in clawhammer is a truly exciting technique that dramatically punctuates passages of a tune. To perform a roll the plucking hand drags slowly and continuously across all four strings, thereby creating what amounts to a controlled brush. Just as an ordinary brush is usually followed by a thumb-stroke on the fifth string, the clawhammer roll also culminates in a precisely timed 5th string thumb stroke.

There are probably as many ways of playing rolls in clawhammer as there are accomplished clawhammer players. In this column I'll teach you my method, but you should be aware that others exist.

My own starting point is the simple brush-thumb stroke. In a brush, the back of the M finger is drawn across all four strings, thereby dragging the thumb (T) into the fifth string. T then hangs there a moment before it plucks the 5th string, generally with a loud pop. In most cases, the brush and thumb strokes are each half a beat long, as shown in example 2-30a.

You can also perform brush-thumbs slowly, with each

"half" of the maneuver played as quarter notes, as shown in example 2-30b. Observe that each brush and each thumb stroke gets a full "number count," and further observe that the odd-number counts are all brush strokes and the even number counts are all "thumbs."

In Example 2-30c, each brush and thumb stroke still gets a full "number count," but I've moved them off "phase," so that the thumbs are odd counts and the brush strokes are even counts. To bring this into sharp relief, I've started out the example with a rest. Then you brush on count 2, thumb on count 3, brush on count 4, thumb on count 1, etc.

The above position of brush vs. thumb in the measure is exactly the same as in a clawhammer roll. In other words, the roll always begins on an even numbered beat while the thumb strikes the 5th string on the downbeat or other odd-numbered beat. Think of the brushing part as "winding up" to a climax, with the climax being the striking of the 5th string by T on an important beat of the measure.

Count: 4 &   1

Example 2-31a

4 & a   1

Example 2-31b

4 a & a   1

Example 2-31c

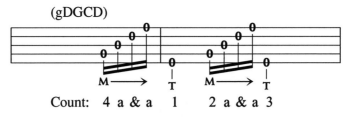

(gDGCD)

Count: 4 a & a   1   2 a & a 3

Example 2-32

Once you have the time-relationship established, the next step is breaking the brush up into separate notes. The obvious place to start is the "Galax lick" (Example 2-31a) which involves a two-string arpeggio, followed by a fifth string note on the following downbeat or other important beat. To perform a Galax lick, strike string 2 with M as you bring T into contact with the 5th string. Following the plucking of string 2, rest heavily with your picking fingernail on string 1, and — without a fresh wrist stroke — continue drawing M downward and pluck the first string. Finally, pluck the 5th string with T as in a normal brush. Note in the example how the arpeggio part of the lick falls on the upbeat count of the measure, while the 5th string stroke falls on the downbeat count (for an arrangement in these pages that uses a Galax lick, see *Arkansas Traveler,* in col. 2.12)

The next step is playing an arpeggio-triplet lead-in, shown in example 2-31b. The process is as follows: strike string 3 with M as you bring T into contact with the 5th string. Following the plucking of string 3, rest heavily with your picking fingernail on the string 2, and — without a fresh wrist stroke — continue drawing M downward and pluck string 2. Then rest heavily with your picking fingernail on string 1, and — without a fresh wrist stroke — continue drawing M downward and pluck string 1. Finally, pluck the 5th string with T as in a normal brush.

The timing of this maneuver is that of a triplet on the upbeat count of the measure, leading into a 5th string quarter note on the downbeat count of the measure (for an illustration of a tune using this technique see *Dinah,* in chapter 10).

The final step is playing a *full roll* covering all four long strings (example 2-31c). The process is as follows: strike string 4 with M as you bring T into contact with the 5th string. Following the plucking of string 4, rest heavily with your picking fingernail on string 3, and — without a fresh wrist stroke — continue drawing M downward and pluck string 3. Then rest heavily with your picking fingernail on string 2, and — without a fresh wrist stroke — continue drawing M downward and pluck string 2. Continuing the maneuver, rest heavily with your picking fingernail on string 1, and — without a fresh wrist stroke — continue drawing M downward and pluck string 1. Finally, pluck the 5th string with T as in a normal brush.

The timing of the maneuver is four sixteenth notes on the upbeat count of the measure, leading into a 5th string quarter note on the downbeat count of the measure.

Probably the most famous clawhammer rolls of all time were those performed by Clarence "Tom" Ashley in his recording of *The Cuckoo Bird.* Ashley blends roll after roll with regular clawhammer picking in such a way that the effect is like a rippling stream.

You can emulate Ashley's constant stream of rolls by using the style of roll-playing shown in Example 2-32, with your banjo tuned to mountain minor tuning, or gDGCD (for the entire tab, see my *Clawhammer Style Banjo* book). Start by practicing slowly, counting to yourself (4-a-&-a 1-, 2-a-&a 3-, and so on). When you eventually speed things up, it should sound just like the recording.

Long after I had perfected my own rolls-technique, I saw a film of Ashley playing *The Cuckoo.* It turns out that instead of using the controlled brush/arpeggio I've taught here, he used a technique similar to the one flamenco guitarists employ to perform continuous strumming. In other words, Ashley curls up all four fingers of the right hand and — on the upbeat — beginning with the pinky, he "unfurls" them backwards across all four long strings one finger-nail at a time (the back of the pinky-fingernail strikes the strings first, then the ring, the middle the finally the index). The 5th string is then popped by the thumb on the downbeat.

Does this point to a heretofore unheralded Spanish influence in old time music? Probably not, but it's certainly food for thought.

At any rate, you might want to also experiment with Ashley's manner of playing rolls and see what works best for you.

To illustrate this technique, I've selected the by now classic old-time tune, *Over the Waterfall,* which Alan Jabbour collected from West Virginia fiddler Henry Reed back in the mid-1960s.

Over the Waterfall

Banjo Arrangement: Ken Perlman

Tuning: gCGCD (capo–2)

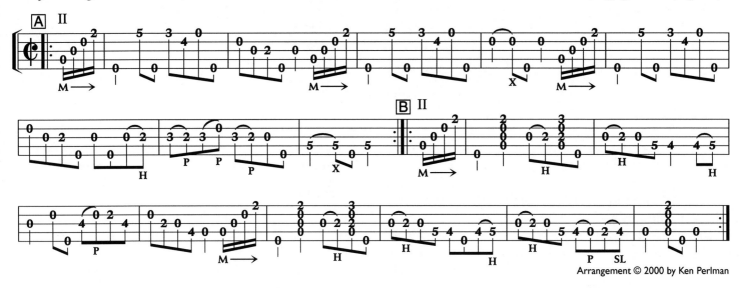

Arrangement © 2000 by Ken Perlman

2.12 Off-the-Beat Hammer-Ons & Pull-Offs (and M-T "Reversal") (Jan. '87)

Off-the-beat hammer-ons and pull-offs are used quite frequently by fingerpicking guitarists and bluegrass banjo players. Most clawhammer pickers have not really latched on to these techniques as yet, but they are highly effective in certain situations. I find myself using them more and more in my playing.

Conventional H's and P's start on the beat. In other words, the player strikes a long string with the picking finger (M) at the beginning of a beat (Example 2-33). In the case of a hammer-on, the hammering finger strikes the fingerboard at a point halfway between the original beat and the next beat. A similar principle applies to conventional pull-offs.

In off-beat hammer-ons and pull-offs, the procedure is reversed. M strikes a string at a point halfway between two beats

(that is, on an "&-count"), while the sounding of the H- or P-note coincides with the start of the *following* beat.

Example 2-34 shows off-the-beat hammer-ons. In the first instance, M strikes the open first string at a point exactly halfway between beats 1 and 2 (the first "&" count of the measure). The hammering finger then strikes the fingerboard at the start of beat 2. In the next instance, M strikes fret 1, string 2 on the second "&" count of the measure. The H is then made to sound at the start of beat 3.

Example 2-35 shows off-the-beat pull-offs. In the first instance, M strikes fret 2, string 1 halfway between beats 1 and 2. The pulling finger is then drawn away from the string at the start of beat 2. In the next example, M strikes fret 3, string 2 halfway between beats 2 and 3. The pull-off to fret 1, string 2 is performed at the start of beat 3.

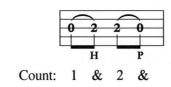

Count: 1   &   2   &

Example 2-33

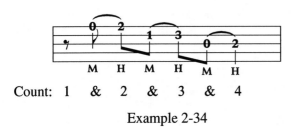

Count: 1   &   2   &   3   &   4

Example 2-34

1   &   2   &   3   &   4

Example 2-35

48

Conventional clawhammer practice, where M always seems to fall on the beat, tends to more or less discourage experimenting with such "off-center" subtleties as off-the-beat H's and P's. When every M-note is played with a hearty wrist-stroke, and is inexorably followed by either a drop-thumb, hammer-on, pull-off or slide, it offers an incomparable feeling of security. To consider the possibility that M-notes can also be played between the beats can therefore easily feel unsettling.

Be that as it may, let's go over a couple of instances of off-the-beat P's in the accompanying version of *Arkansas Traveler*. In Part A, measure 1, start out with an arpeggio (continuous M-stroke) from string 2 to string 1. The ensuing P is performed off the second arpeggio note and falls at the start of the second beat of the measure. Notice that following the P, the thumb sneaks in and performs a drop-thumb on string 2.

Part B begins with a Galax lick (or half roll), and the first note of Part B, measure 1, is the open fifth-string. M is then used between beats on the first "&-count" of the measure, and a P immediately follows that *ends* on count 2.

Observe that arrangements featuring off-beat H's and P's tend to also call for a technique I call *M-T reversal*. Since various H's and P's are played out of their "normal" slots, this sometimes also makes it desirable to use M or T in relatively unusual ways. Consequently, some M-notes occasionally show up in "slots" customarily occupied by T-notes, and vice versa. An example in *Arkansas Traveler* is Part B, meas. 1, where M is used between the beats (generally a T location) to start an off-beat P. See *Chicken Polka* in col. 2.14 for several additional examples of reversal, along with several examples of off-beat H's.

Arkansas Traveler

Banjo Arrangement: Ken Perlman

Tuning: gCGCD (capo–2)

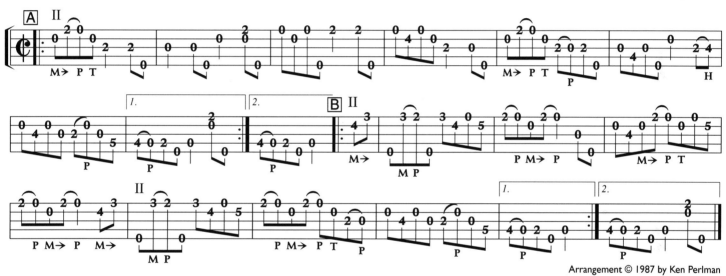

Arrangement © 1987 by Ken Perlman

2.13 "Keith" Picking vs. Alternating M and T strokes on the Same String

(Oct. '87)

Example 2-36

One maneuver which is quite basic to flatpickers but troublesome to both clawhammer and bluegrass banjo players is playing notes quickly up and down the same string. For the flatpicker, the series of notes in Example 2-36 (an ascending and descending major scale), is easy-as-pie. He or she play's the first note of each eighth note pair as down stroke (symbol: ⊓), and the second note of each eighth note pair as an upstroke (symbol: ∨).

Bluegrass banjo pickers have worked out two main approaches to playing series of scale-like notes. One employs thumb-strokes for downstrokes and index finger strokes for upstrokes. In the second method, known as *Keith-picking*, the scale is obtained by alternating open strings with up the neck fretted strings, as is illustrated later in Example 2-38.

Modern day clawhammer players have never completely come to terms with series of scale-like notes. The most common method of handling a scale involves playing the first note of each eighth note pair with M and the second note of each pair with either an H or P, as shown in Example 2-37. The main difficulty with this approach is that the resulting hammered or pulled notes are never quite as loud as the original plucked notes. Consequently, these H and P notes tend to get lost in a band or noisy gig situation. Another problem derives from the fact that H's and P's necessarily yield legato (i.e., "smooth") transitions between notes. There are occasions where, for one reason or another, a player wants a choppier or more abrupt transition between notes.

Keith-picking concepts can also be applied to clawhammer, as shown in Example 2-38. Observe that on both ascending and descending scales I've generally combined open M-notes with up-the-neck drop-thumbs. This provides a solution to our lem, but scale patterns don't always fall as neatly as the one in this example.

There are also numerous "hybrid" methods in clawhammer for playing ascending and descending scales, involving combinations of a variety of techniques. These can work quite well, but often require extensive planning. One elaborate alternative is suggested in Example 2-39, which combines arpeggios, drop-thumbs, pull offs and off-string pull-offs.

There is another, ultimately less cumbersome alternative for clawhammer that can be used at least in certain situations. Akin both to flatpicking and same-string bluegrass picking, this technique involves using M strokes in lieu of downstrokes and T-strokes in lieu of upstrokes, as shown in Example 2-40.

The major problem with M and T stroke alternation on the same string is getting the M-finger out of the way quickly

Example 2-37

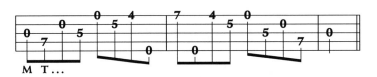

Example 2-38

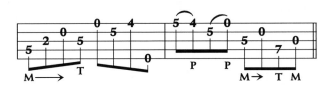

Example 2-39

Example 2-40

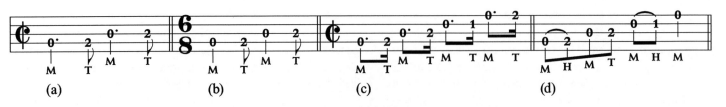

Example 2-41

50

enough so that a T-stroke can be performed smoothly and at the desired instant. This is extremely difficult to do convincingly at reel or hoedown speed. There are other situations, however, where same-string M-T alternation may be just what the doctor ordered. Some of these are illustrated in Example 2-41, and explained below:

♦ *Dotted quarter-single eighth note combinations* (Example 2-41a). One-and-a-half beats should be enough time to get the M finger out of the way, even during the fastest reel or hoedown.

♦ *Quarter-eighth note combinations in 6/8, 9/8 or 12/8 times* (Example 2-41b). Jigs move at about the same tempo as do reels, but have fewer notes per beat (a "beat" in 6/8 time is in effect three eighth notes long). You therefore have more time between notes in general and sufficient time in this situation to get the M finger out of the way.

♦ *Dotted eighth-sixteenth note combinations in hornpipes* (Example 2-41c). Hornpipes have the same number of notes per beat as do reels but move at a much slower tempo. Since the notes typically played by M are significantly longer those typically played by T (dotted eighth notes vs. sixteenth notes, respectively), you should have enough time to get the M-finger out of the way if you work at it. This is most effective in passages that are supposed to be somewhat choppy.

♦ *Strategically placed eighth notes in reels*, such as those occurring at the beginning of a "phrase" (Example 2-41d). If you listen carefully to a tune played by an expert fiddler you will notice that there are certain points where the last note of a group of eighth notes is joined via bowing to the following series of notes. Here, using a quick T-stroke allows you to mimic the sound of the fiddler's bowing.

I collected *The Mariner* from well-known fiddler Angus Grant of the Fort William, Scotland area. I originally tried playing this tune using mostly H's and P's but the resulting sound was unsatisfactory. Using some same-string M-T's on the other hand worked just fine (playing hornpipes in clawhammer style is explained in column 3.2).

One unusual feature: The first note of the MTM triplet in Part A, meas. 1, 2, 5 and 6 is also the last note of a three-string *arpeggio* (see cols. 2.8 and 2.9). At the conclusion of the triplet, T is used on a long-string quarter note.

Once you have gotten a handle on *The Mariner*, try your hand at *Chicken Polka*. This is an up-tempo tune in which same-string M-T alternation works fairly well to create a certain "effect" (namely, evoking the clucking of barnyard fowl). The tune also features several instances of off-beat H's and "M-T reversal" (col. 2.11), where M-notes and T-notes appear in unusual roles. One example of reversal is found in Part A, where M is used as the upbeat of measure 6 and T is used on the downbeat of measure 7.

The Mariner

Banjo Arrangement: Ken Perlman

Tuning: gCGCD (capo–2)

Arrangement © 1987 by Ken Perlman

Chicken Polka

Banjo Arrangement: Peter Taney

Tuning: gCGCD (capo–2)

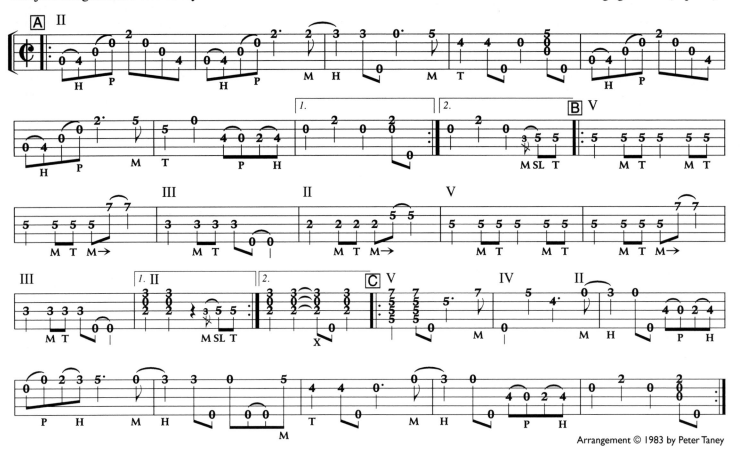

Arrangement © 1983 by Peter Taney

2.14 The Joys of Fifth String Fretting

(Aug.'86)

The primary role of the fifth-string in clawhammer is providing an open drone. Quarter notes in the melody are enhanced by the addition of the open fifth-string note — giving the banjo its characteristic twang. Occasionally, an open fifth-string note can be used as part of the melody (see column 2.1). Using a fretted fifth-string was not, until fairly recently, part of the clawhammer player's bag-of-tricks.

The reasons for this go back to the banjo's early days. Instruments of the minstrel era were fretless, the location of the fifth-string nut (sometimes called the *pip* by banjo makers) was not standardized, and the fifth string itself was set quite high off the fingerboard. For fifth-string fretting to be practical, the whole instrument would have had to be redesigned.

A lot of this re-designing took place in the 1870s, when frets were added, the pip was set permanently at or near the fifth fret, and overall string height was lowered. These new-style banjos were designed — not for minstrel or *stroke-style* playing — but for classical (three-finger) banjo playing.

Although it was used from time to time as an "effect," fifth string fretting was never adopted as a standard practice by classical banjoists. What's more, when the practice of clawhammer moved out of the cities and into rural areas of the South, the art of fifth-string fretting also failed to develop.

It was Bill Keith and other practitioners of the *melodic* style of bluegrass banjo playing who first explored the possibilities of fifth-string fretting in any detail. We melodic clawhammer pickers, I confess, got a lot of our ideas for using the fifth-string in this manner by observing them.

I had previously used a fretted fifth-string on a number of occasions, but I didn't fully understand how to use it until the early 80s when I started hanging out at the Thursday night bluegrass jam sessions held at Arturo's Pizza on Houston Street in New York City. Melodic bluegrasser Marty Cutler was banjo picker-in-residence and I watched with great interest as he set up fingering forms that yielded particular runs when played in a given sequence. I reasoned that the concept must be applicable to clawhammer, and eventually came up with several sequences of fingering forms that I now use continually in my playing. Example 2-42 shows one such sequence for G-tuning (for chord diagrams showing fingering see cols. 2.16-17). Be sure to fret all notes in each group of four simultaneously.

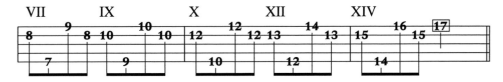

Example 2-42

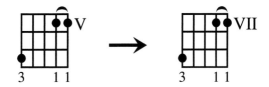

Example 2-43

If you are seriously interested in exploring fifth-string fretting, you may need to alter the height or location of the pip. If the pip is too high off the fingerboard, the fifth-string will always fret sharp. If the pip is set back too far behind the fifth fretwire, the fifth-string will always fret flat. There are two ideal locations for the pip: just behind, and very slightly higher than, the fifth fretwire, or *along-side* the fifth fret wire (in this last case some of the wire must be removed to make way for it).

Accompanying this column is a well-known Scottish dance tune called *The Duke of Perth*. The arrangement uses a few strategically placed fretted-fifth string notes to drive the B-part along. Part B, meas.1-3 and 5-6 are best played via a *half barre* (press strings 1 and 2 down with the underside of the first finger) at the fifth and seventh frets, as shown in example 2-43. Once your half-barre is firmly in place, you can reach across with your third or fourth finger to obtain fretted-fifth string notes at frets 7 and 9, respectively.

The Duke of Perth

Banjo Arrangement: Ken Perlman

Tuning: gDGBD

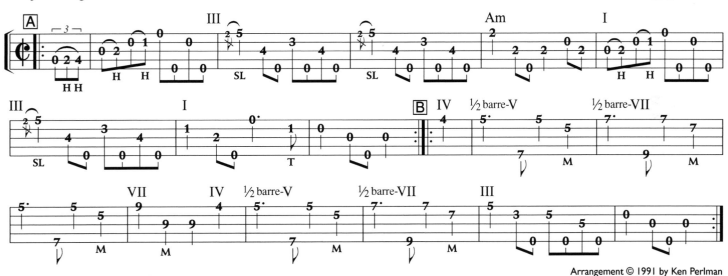

Arrangement © 1991 by Ken Perlman

2.15 Fretting the Fifth String: The Rationale

(May '96)

Those of you who have followed my career are probably aware that I am a firm believer in the virtues of fifth-string fretting — both in melodic passages and when the banjo is playing a backup role. Using the fifth string in this way greatly increases the number of powerful combinations of notes that can be played *without* sacrificing a strong rhythmic attack. It also makes life in general much, much easier on the left hand.

I am quite aware that most clawhammer players do not fret the fifth string. In fact, there are many clawhammerists who do

not believe it is *proper* to fret the fifth string. This belief is so strong that some of my students have reported being lectured on the subject by disgruntled banjo-conservatives at jam sessions.

I think it is pretty clear that restrictions of this kind are part of the baggage of the *art-music* or classical world, not of the folk world. The essence of playing a "folk" instrument is that anything goes *as long as it works*. If you want to create a tune where the fiddler plays on the wrong side of the bridge, or bangs on the face of the instrument with the end of his frog — so be it, if it's fun to listen to. If you want to create a banjo tune where mule sounds are imitated by scraping your picks on the wrong side of the bridge, or where exciting rhythms are created by pounding on the banjo-head like a drum, more power to you! If you want to create a guitar arrangement and fret an otherwise un-reachable bass note with your nose (I've actually seen this done by New York City guitarist Erik Frandsen), why not!

As noted in column 2.14, the first major use of fifth-string fretting was in the realm of melodic bluegrass playing. Fifth string fretting offers the same benefits for clawhammer as it does for bluegrass. For example, it allows the high-parts of key-of-G fiddle tunes like *Blackberry Blossom* to be played strongly and cleanly. Without a fretted fifth string, the opening phrase of the tune relies on weak sounding hammer-ons and pull-offs (Examples 2-44a-b). You can catch the rhythm of the main beats, but you can't capture the intricate sub-phrasing that makes the tune come alive. Using fifth string fretting, the tune just sings out (Example 2-44c; see the *Melodic Clawhammer Banjo* book for the complete tab).

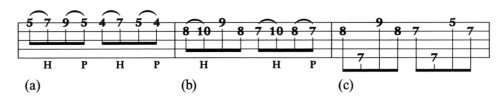

Example 2-44

In a backup role, there are certain occasions where you might want to fret the fifth string in order to make it compatible with the prevailing harmony. This allows you to continue a powerful double-thumbed accompaniment while cruising through the modes or the circle of fifths. Let's say you want to accompany a modal E-minor tune (with primary chords Em and D) out of G-tuning. Unfortunately, using an open fifth-string drone (that is, a G-note) sounds fairly weak against an Em chord, while using the same open fifth string for a drone against a D-chord just sounds plain-bad. If you use the Em and D forms shown in Example 2-45 which call for fifth-string fretting, on the other hand, the sound is infinitely better (Observe that Roman numerals in the chord diagrams indicate that diagram's top fret; for example VII means the diagram begins at the seventh fret).

Similarly, should a fiddler switch keys on you without giving you an opportunity to switch tunings, fifth-string fretting allows you to keep up a strong rhythm without becoming a harmonic pariah. Example 2-46 shows some common "out-of-key" chords in G tuning involving fifth string fretting.

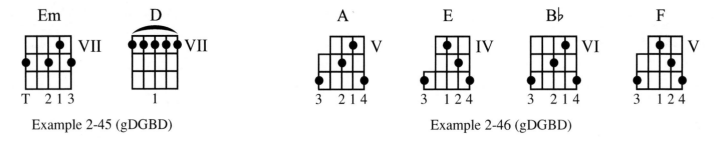

Example 2-45 (gDGBD)   Example 2-46 (gDGBD)

Loons on the Pond

By Ken Perlman   Tuning: gDGBD

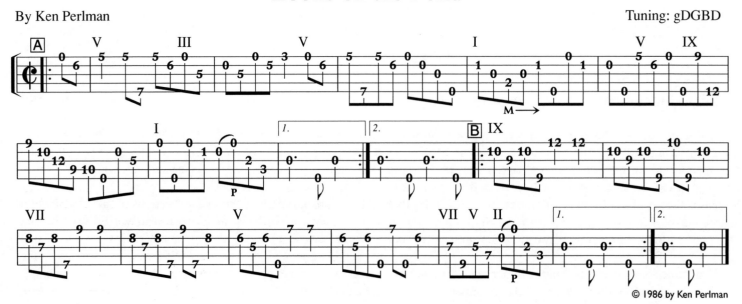

© 1986 by Ken Perlman

54

There's really no reason why fifth string fretting should not be universally adopted in clawhammer. It's a bona fide folk-technique that makes certain things work that otherwise would be problematic. Try it some time; you'll probably come back for more!

I wrote *Loons On The Pond* one summer when I was vacationing in Maine: the title is an obvious homage to the well known old-time tune *Ducks on the Pond*. There's a lot of up-the-neck work and I use a lot of fifth-string fretting in the arrangement (when I've played it with fiddlers, they have generally liked to take the B part down an octave). Observe that Part A, meas. 3 uses melodic fingering form #4, Part B, meas. 2 uses form #2, and Part B meas. 3-4 uses form #1 (see cols. 2.16-17).

2.16 Playing Up the Neck De-Mystified

Playing up the neck seems to intimidate a lot of clawhammer pickers. I've already discussed one non-intimidating means of getting yourself up the neck: using the twelfth-fret barre (column 2.5). In this column, I'll suggest two additional ways to approach up-the-neck playing, so you can face the prospect with a bit more equanimity.

The first new method involves what are known as *movable chords*. In a movable chord all strings on the banjo (or three strings in a row if you can trust yourself not to hit the remaining open string) are fretted. Then you can move these chord forms up the neck. Each time you move a movable chord up a fret it goes up one half step in pitch. Another name for movable chords is *position chords*.

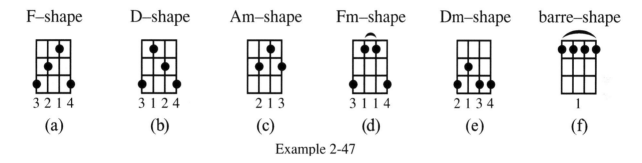

Example 2-47

Let's look at the F chord in G tuning (2-47a). If we raise this form to the second fret (symbol: F-II), it becomes F♯ or G♭. Raised to the third fret (F-III), it becomes an alternative way of playing a G chord. Similarly it becomes A at the fifth fret, C at the eighth fret, F again at the 13th fret, and so on.

Another common movable chord is D (2-47b), which starts at the second fret. If we lower D one fret it becomes D♭ or C♯. If we raise D one fret (D-III) it becomes E♭ or D♯. Raising D two frets to the fourth fret makes it E; raising D to the fifth fret makes it F; to the seventh fret yields yet another way to play G. And of course, raising D to the 14th fret gives us the D chord again, up an octave.

There are also three movable minor chords you should know: Am (2-47c), Fm (2-47d), and Dm (2-47e) Movable Am becomes Bm at the third fret (symbol: Am-III), Dm at the sixth fret, Em at the eighth, octave Am at the 13th.

Movable Fm becomes Gm (Fm-III) at the third fret, an alternative way of playing Am at the fifth fret, an alternative Bm at the seventh, etc. Movable Dm becomes Em at the fourth fret (Dm-IV), etc.

Finally, the full-barre itself (Example 2-47f) is actually another kind of movable major chord. It yields the chord A at the second fret, C at the fifth, D at the seventh and G at the twelfth.

Two exercises should help you grasp some of the possibilities for movable chords. First, try the following series, where you play the same chord in several locations around the neck:

♦ G-chord Exercise: play open banjo, F-III, D-VII, Barre XII, D-VII, F-III, open banjo.

♦ C-chord Exercise: play C, barre-V, F-VIII, D-XII, F-VIII, barre V, C.

♦ D-chord Exercise: play D, barre-VII, F-X, D-XIV, F-X, barre VII, D

♦ Am-chord Exercise: play Am, Fm-V, Dm-IX, Am-XIII, Dm-IX, Fm-V, Am.

♦ Em-chord Exercise: play Em, Dm-IV, Am-VII, Em-XII, Am-VII, Dm-IV, Em.

Next, try a *Chord-Scale Exercise* like the one at the top of the next page. By playing the indicated chords in succession, you get a harmonized major scale (this process is sometimes referred to as *chord melody*). You'll get the idea when you try it. Each chord form and fret are indicated first, followed in parenthesis by the actual pitch of the chord.

55

G-Major Scale:

F-III(G), Fm-V(Am), D-VII(G), F-VIII(C), F-X(D), Fm-XII(Em), D-XIV(Octave D), F-XV(Octave G), D-XIV (Octave D), Fm-XII (Em), F-X (D), F-VIII (C), D-VII (G), Fm-V (Am), F-III (G).

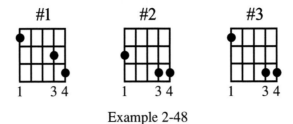

Example 2-48

The second up-the-neck method is what I call *melodic fingering forms*. These fingering forms can be memorized like chord forms, but — instead of sounding a particular harmony — they yield specific runs of notes. These forms are used quite frequently in melodic bluegrass banjo, and they are equally useful for clawhammer.

I'll suggest three fingering forms which I'll call #1, #2 and #3. These are shown in Example 2-48. If the indication is say, "1-VII", this means that fingering form #1 is to be played at the seventh fret (that is, the first finger in the pattern is at the seventh

fret, and the other fingers are distributed accordingly).

This being said, Example 2-49 shows a *Melodic Fingering Form Exercise* for G-tuning. For each fingering form, play the strings in the following order: string 2, string 5, string 1, string 2; in terms of the right hand, merely alternate your M and T strokes.

For more G-tuning forms, see col. 2.17; for forms in mountain minor and double C tunings, see col. 2.23.

Two Pathways

By Barry Luft

Tuning: gDGBD

© 1992 by Barry Luft

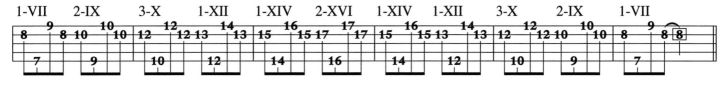

Example 2-49

Two tunes accompany this column. The first — *Two Pathways,* an original banjo tune by Barry Luft of Calgary, Alberta — is an excellent illustration for using up-the-neck chord forms. The second tune is *Shenandoah Falls,* presented as basic version and break. The up the neck break, which appears on my *Live in the UK* recording, uses quite a number of melodic fingering forms. Observe that the basic version of *Shenandoah* employs arpeggio-strokes to create ragtime-like syncopations. If you have problems with this lick, try consulting cols. 2.17-18 before proceeding.

Shenandoah Falls

Banjo Arrangement: Ken Perlman

Tuning: gDGBD (capo–2)

Break

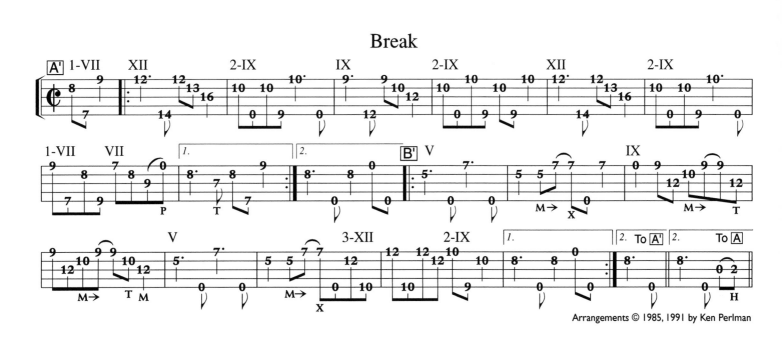

Arrangements © 1985, 1991 by Ken Perlman

57

There has never been, to my knowledge, a tradition of playing ragtime clawhammer. Clawhammer had all but disappeared from urban areas by the time that ragtime came along (about 1900), and the version of clawhammer that persisted in isolated pockets of the South was in general not sufficiently developed to be adapted to the demands of extended syncopated phrases. There is no reason, however, why clawhammer cannot be applied to ragtime. All that is needed are some minor modifications of existing right hand techniques, and some new ways of thinking about the left hand. I won't be able to discuss the entire subject in one column, but I will get you started playing some ragtime phrases.

One modified right hand technique you'll need is what I call the *indirect* thumb-crossover, which is discussed at length in my book, *Clawhammer Style Banjo*. The indirect crossover is a variant of the thumb-over technique I first presented in the *Melodic Clawhammer Banjo* book. In a thumb-over (that is, a *direct* thumb-crossover), the thumb (T) crosses over the position of the middle or index finger (M) to immediately play a note on a higher long string (Example 2-50a). In an indirect crossover, the hand has plenty of time to rotate to a position where T can easily cross over the position of M. Two very common situations where the indirect crossover is valuable are dotted

quarter/single-eighth-note combinations (Example 2-50b), and syncopated phrases containing tied notes (Example 2-50c and d). For practice, try both phrases in Example 2-50c & d, following closely the notated order of M's and T's.

Observe that both c and d can be played without crossing T over M, but the *phrasing* of the lick would not be nearly as effective for ragtime. The count here is 1-&-2-&-_-&-4- (where the note played on the second &-count is held through count 3). This second "&-count" note is then accented, yielding the characteristic *syncopation* pattern of ragtime (for more on syncopation, see cols. 1.12-13 and 2.18).

The indirect thumb-crossover can also be adapted to melodic fingering forms. As noted in col. 2.16, each pattern outlines a run of notes formed from a combination of up-the-neck long string notes and fretted fifth string notes. Diagrams for a new series of melodic fingering forms — called #'s 4, 5, and 6 — are shown in Example 2-51. A series of melody runs using those forms appears in Example 2-52, while Example 2-53 shows ragtime runs that use the forms. Observe that the indication "4-VII" means that fingering form #4 is to be played at the seventh fret.

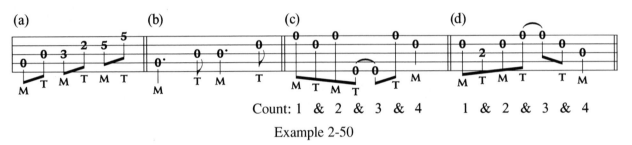

Example 2-50

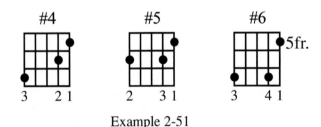

Example 2-51

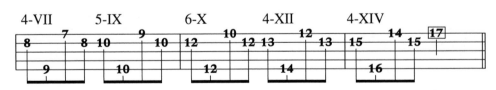

Example 2-52

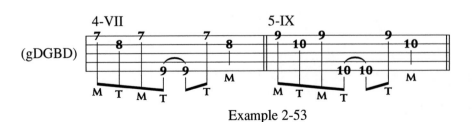

Example 2-53

The accompanying tune *Leavin' Home*, is presented in three staffs. The top staff is an arrangement of the basic melody. The middle staff is a break that includes some ragtime phrases, while the bottom staff is a more complex ragtime style break that makes use of melodic fingering forms.

Leavin' Home

Banjo Arrangement: Ken Perlman

Tuning: gDGBD

Arrangement © 1983 by Ken Perlman

59

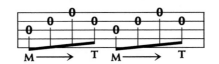

Example 2-54

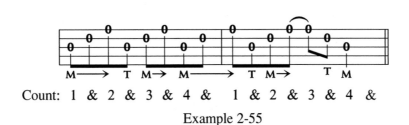

Count: 1 & 2 & 3 & 4 & 1 & 2 & 3 & 4 &

Example 2-55

The picking pattern where a two-, three-, or four-string arpeggio leads to a drop-thumb note (Example 2-54) is essentially the clawhammer version of *crosspicking*. Crosspicking is a flatpicker's technique for getting syncopated runs of notes. The flatpicker hits, say, string 3 on the guitar with a downstroke of his plectrum and rests on string 2. He then downstrokes string 2 and rests on string 1. He continues with a downstroke on string 1, and completes the lick with an upstroke on string 2. The analogy to a three-string M-arpeggio followed by a T-stroke is obvious.

Clawhammer crosspicking then, is a combination of two and three string arpeggios with strategically placed drop-thumbs. When arranged as in Example 2-55, the technique produces the exact phrasing of a complex characteristic ragtime lick.

This two measure long right-hand lick is interpreted as follows:

♦ Meas. 1, counts "1&2&": Perform a three-string arpeggio followed by a drop thumb. The drop thumb pivots M into position for the next segment.

♦ Meas. 1, counts "3&": Perform a two string arpeggio.

♦ Meas. 1, counts "4&" thru Meas. 2, counts "1&": Initiate a three string arpeggio (the last note of this arpeggio is the downbeat of the second measure), followed by a thumb stroke. Again, this drop thumb pivots M into position for the next segment.

♦ Meas. 2, counts "2&3": Perform a two string arpeggio, but let the last note carry an extra half beat, during which you bring the thumb into position for its next move.

♦ Meas. 2, counts "&4&": Strike string 2 with T, then use M for the concluding quarter note on string 3.

On the facing page is an arrangement for the first half of Scott Joplin's famous *Maple Leaf Rag*. Remember that Roman numerals indicate fingering positions (column 1.6). Note the frequent use throughout the piece of movable chords and up the neck fingering patterns (col. 2.16).

2.19 Being at Home Below the Range

One of the major challenges in arranging fiddle tunes for banjo occurs when the range of the tune moves below the fiddle's third or D string onto its fourth string. In other words, because the lowest note on the banjo is usually tuned to either C or D, special problems occur for the banjoist whenever a fiddle tune goes below these to include any of the following notes: B, B♭, A, A♭ or G. Naturally, when the banjo fourth string is tuned to D, the note low-C also becomes a problem.

Strictly speaking, a banjoist can match most low-range fiddle tunes note-for-note because the actual sound of a banjo's strings is an octave lower than their notation. Therefore, the third string (which is written as G above middle C) actually sounds as G *below* middle C. It is therefore exactly equivalent in pitch to the fourth or lowest string on the fiddle.

We banjo players, however, like to play fiddle tunes using as many open strings as possible, and with a minimum of up-the-neck maneuvering. We also want to make maximum use of the banjo's unique tone quality. Therefore we usually like to play fiddle tunes where the *notated* level of our banjo notes is equivalent to the fiddle's notes. In other words, we like to play our tunes an octave below the fiddle, where our open third or G-string is equivalent to the G that fiddlers play with the third

Maple Leaf Rag

Banjo Arrangement: Ken Perlman

Tuning: gDGBD

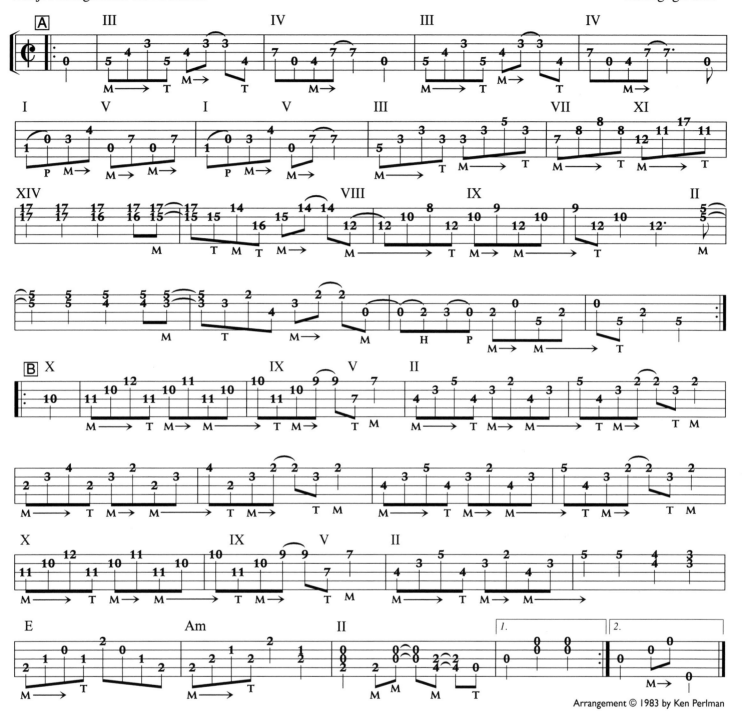

Arrangement © 1983 by Ken Perlman

finger on their own D or third string. Our low D is then in effect equivalent to the fiddle's open third or D string. Unfortunately, if the tune then goes lower than this, we banjoists must get inventive or be out of luck as far as that tune is concerned.

There are several options open to us when the fiddle moves into its low range; each of which I'll discuss in turn:

♦ Leave notes out entirely.

♦ Substitute equivalent or compatible higher notes for a few "too-low" notes.

♦ Move the entire tune up an octave so that the banjo matches the actual pitch of the fiddle, instead of playing the tune an octave lower than the fiddle.

♦ Move one part of the tune up an octave, leaving the second part in normal banjo range.

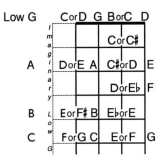

probExample 2-56

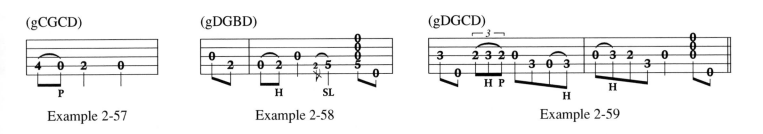

(gCGCD)   (gDGBD)   (gDGCD)

Example 2-57   Example 2-58   Example 2-59

In the first case, a tune might go below regular banjo range once or twice just in passing. In other words, the too-low notes are not really important to the general flow of the tune and there are just a couple of them at most. These notes should simply be left out. Let's say we have a key of C tune which includes a common ending: E-C-D-B-C. If this figure was to be played on the banjo's fourth string in double-C tuning (gCGCD), the B note would fall below banjo range. (It would show up on fret 4 of an imaginary low G string: see Example 2-56). One way of handling this situation quite effectively on banjo is to just leave the B out entirely, and play the figure E-C-D-C, as shown in Example 2-57.

In the second instance, only one small phrase (usually at the end of a part) goes below banjo range. To make the entire part banjo-friendly, you can take just that single phrase up an octave, or make up a new series of notes playable on the banjo that fills up the same amount of space and serves about the same function within the tune. For example, the tune *Georgia Railroad* ends with the figure E-D-B-A-G, where the notes B, A and G are below banjo range (see the imaginary super-low G-string above). When I arranged this tune for banjo (see my *Melodic Clawhammer Banjo* book), I substituted an equivalent phrase that fell within banjo range. This phrase is shown in Example 2-58. Similarly, the B Part in Growling Old Man and Cackling Old Woman goes down (not counting the capo that turns G modal tuning to A modal) to the lowest note on the imaginary super-low G-string. When arranging this tune, I recomposed the ending of the part so that it would hover around the banjo's third string, as shown in Example 2-59 (see *Basic Clawhammer Banjo* for the complete tab).

When substantial portions of a tune go below banjo range, or you judge that recomposition trivializes a tune, you really

have to take the tune up an octave if you want to play it. Needless to say, this is often a very challenging exercise, especially if the tune moves up any distance on the high end. One tune where I did this fairly early on was *Whiskey Before Breakfast* which (not counting the capo that turns double C tuning into D tuning) begins on the open imaginary string (that is on G below middle C). For my arrangement, which appears in *Melodic Clawhammer Banjo*, the A part (which is all quite low-range on the fiddle) fits very nicely on banjo in octave-up position. The B part, however, moves to normal high range on fiddle, and requires numerous fingering pyrotechnics to realize on banjo in octave-up position.

This same B part, on the other hand, is in a convenient range for playing on banjo if you *don't* take it up an octave. So this leads us to an interesting compromise. If you play the low part of the tune up an octave, and the high part of the tune at its normal pitch, you can often create a very playable arrangement. The downside of this approach is that you thereby change the pitch relationship between the two parts, and this sometimes can take away some of the tune's tension or excitement. Only you can judge if your arrangement works on this level. At any rate, my *Whiskey Before Breakfast* arrangement offers both options, reserving the octave-up B Part for use as a fancy break.

Following is a Scottish reel called *Miss Lyall* (sometimes spelled Lyle) which is also played by Irish musicians under the title *Paddy Ryan's Dream*. The A Part has been taken up an octave, while the second part is played in normal banjo range (I did have to alter the second ending of the B Part so that it would lead to the octave-up A Part, instead of down to the original A Part). An example in this book where an entire tune was moved up an octave is *Niel Gow's Lament for His Second Wife*.

62

Miss Lyall

Banjo Arrangement: Ken Perlman

Tuning: gDGCD (capo–2)

Arrangement © 1991 by Ken Perlman

2.20 Warm Up Exercises for the Left Hand

(Aug. '98)

A while ago I did a column on right hand warm-up exercises. It's time now to look at warm up exercises for the left hand. The idea here is that we want to attain as much strength and agility as possible in the shortest amount of time.

Hammer-on and pull-off exercises (Exercises C-1 through C-8) are ideal for this purpose. Note that the numbers in the tab for these exercises refer to *fingers* (1 = first finger, 2 = second finger etc.) not frets. This is so the exercises can be done at any fret level. To get maximum benefit assign a fret to each finger,

so that if the first finger plays fret 1, the second finger plays fret 2, the third finger plays fret 3, and the fourth finger plays fret 4. Similarly, if you are up the neck a bit and the first finger plays fret 3, then the second finger plays fret 4, the third finger plays fret 5, etc.

These exercises are presented in order of difficulty. If using them for a warmup, therefore, you are well-advised to play them in order.

Left Hand Exercises C1–10

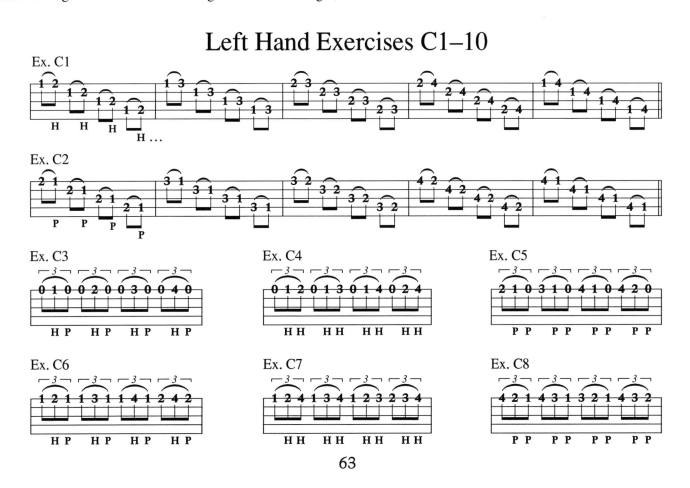

Ex. C9 (Go up and back)

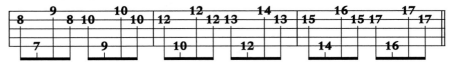

Ex. C10 (Go up and back)

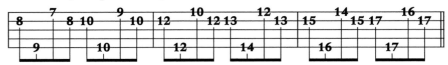

Exercise C-1 explores H's, going through several fingering combinations, while Exercise C-2 explores P's, going through several fingering combinations. Exercises C-3 through C-8 are made up of triplets (see cols. 2.6-8). For maximum benefit, make sure each triplet note is strong and even.

For C-3 through C-8, only maneuvers for the first string are shown. In each case, perform these same maneuvers on *all long strings* before going on to the next exercise. Following is a description of each of these exercises:

♦ Exercise C-3: H-P combinations on open strings.
♦ Exercise C-4: double H's on open strings
♦ Exercise C-5: double P's on open strings
♦ Exercise C-6: H-P combinations on fretted strings
♦ Exercise C-7: double H's on fretted strings
♦ Exercise C-8: double P's on fretted strings

Exercises C-9 and C-10 involve making one's way through two series of up the neck "melodic-fingering forms." C-9 uses the forms diagramed in column 2.16, while C-10 uses forms diagramed in column 2.17. Be sure to play each exercise in both ascending *and* descending directions.

2.21 The Change of Direction Technique: Alternating Arpeggio-Strokes & Drop-Thumbs (Nov. '87)

In conventional clawhammer style, it has always been a problem to play the kind of maneuvers shown in the first measure of Example 2-60, where a pair of adjacent-string eighth notes played in a downward direction must be quickly followed by the same pair played in an upward direction. Of course, the reverse sequence of string pairs is equally problematical (second measure).

Now, if all the strings are open, or if just the upward-moving pair of eighth notes is played open, it is quite effective to rely upon alternate string pull-offs (Example 2-61). The same maneuver can also be effectively used if only the second note of the

upwardly moving pair is an open string, as shown in Example 2-62.

The real difficulty in clawhammer arises when the top note of the upwardly moving pair of notes is fretted. Some players have tried to solve this by using doubly-fretted alternate-string pull-offs, but this can produce fairly weak notes (see column 1.8). Other solutions involve actual re-settings of the notes so they can be attained by conventional techniques like drop-thumbs, hammer-ons, or fifth string fretting. Example 2-63 shows two such troublesome melodic figures and a few methods to obtain the notes for each.

Example 2-60

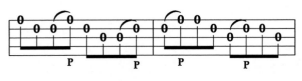

Example 2-61

Example 2-62

64

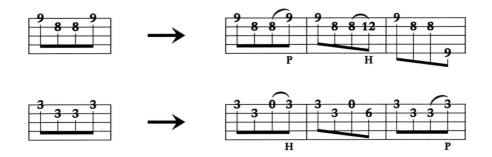

Example 2-63

The problem with all these approaches is that you are always busy re-thinking how to play what are actually simple melodic figures. It stands to reason that clawhammerists need to be able to easily reverse direction on a pair of strings without resorting to extraordinary means.

To deal with this situation, I have recently been experimenting with quick alterations between arpeggios and drop-thumbs, a method I call the *change of direction* technique. The advantage here is twofold. First, the upwardly directed notes are just as strong as the drop-thumbed notes; Second and most impor

tantly, you don't have to continually re-think fingering for every situation.

Exercise D should help you master a rapid drop-thumb/arpeggio alternation on the same string pair. Try the change of direction technique first on open strings, then continue to play it while you take a simple fretting form up the neck.

I've arranged the accompanying Tennessee tune *Merriweather* with a few change-of-direction maneuvers. Observe that Part A, meas. 4 uses fingering form #6 (see col. 2-17).

Exercise D

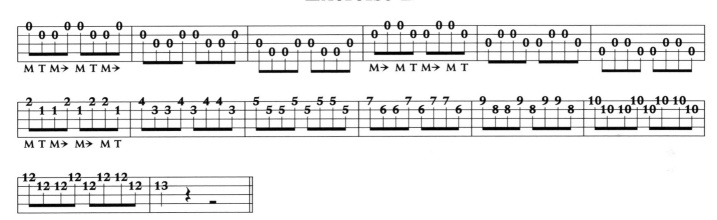

Merriweather

Banjo Arrangement: Ken Perlman

Tuning: gDGBD

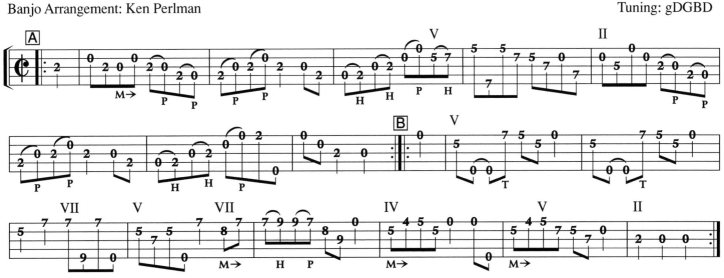

Arrangement © 1987 by Ken Perlman

65

Generally speaking, you won't see too many full sixteenth note groups (Example 2-64) in 4/4 or 2/2 time fiddle tunes unless the tune is moving at a fairly slow tempo. So, while you'll find sixteenth note groups occasionally in hornpipes and frequently in strathspeys (see below) — or in for-listening-only tunes like slow airs and laments — you won't encounter too many sixteenth note groups in up-tempo genres like reels, hoedowns or jigs. (I should mention that sometimes reels and hoedowns are written in 2/4 time, in which case sixteenth notes are standard and *thirty-second notes* are the ones you won't see too often).

Handling sixteenth notes at slow speed is more a question of mental adjustment than physical prowess. First, you need to learn to divide a 4/4 time beat into four parts. This is accomplished with the counting method shown in Example 2-64, where an extra syllable (-a-) Is added to the customary count for triplets (1 & a, 2 & a). The result: 1-a-&-a-, 2-a-&-a, and so on.

This still leaves the problem of how to play sixteenth notes. At the slow tempos that we are considering here, no new techniques are required. We just need to take some basic techniques that are used in the playing of eighth notes and triplets and redirect them.

Most eighth notes in 4/4 or 2/2 time are obtained via a few basic methods: M-stroke plus hammer-on (M-H); M plus pull-off (M-P), M plus slide (M-SL); M plus thumb (M-T) or arpeggio (M-A).There are also several ways to obtain triplets (see column 2.8).

You can make sixteenth notes by combining the techniques for creating two pairs of eighth notes, or by adding one note to the various techniques used for making triplets. For example combine M-T with M-H, M-P or M-A — or combine M-T with M-T — to make four sixteenth notes (Example 2-65). Alternatively, you can add an extra pull-off to an M-P-P triplet — or put in a T-note after M in a M-H-H triplet — and so on, as shown in Example 2-66.

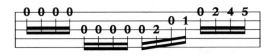

Count: 1 a & a   2 a & a   3 a & a   4 a & a

Example 2-64

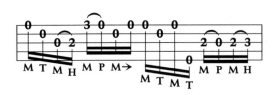

Example 2-65

Example 2-66

It does become necessary upon occasion to play sixteenth notes in faster fiddle tunes, in which case the same principles we've just discussed for arranging and counting them also apply. Generally, these sixteenth-note episodes are relatively brief, and the notes themselves are generally obtained via techniques that lend themselves to high-speed performance, such as H's and P's (one specialized use of sixteenth notes in fast tunes is the *birl*: see col. 2.25). Some up-tempo tunes in this book where you'll find sixteenth note groups include *The Black Hoe* and *Nine Points of Roguery*.

Try some sixteenth note groupings in *The Marquis Of Huntley*, which is an example of a kind of Scottish dance tune known as a *strathspey* (pronounced strath-SPEY). Since the beats are moving fairly slowly (the tempo here is about ♩ = 110) there's plenty of time to play all the sixteenth note groups with

the conventional techniques discussed above. The group in Part A, measure 2, for example, is obtained by a combination of a drop-thumb and a pull-off (M-T-M-P). while the group that appears in both parts A and B, meas. 8 and is obtained via two separate pull-off maneuvers (M-P-M-P). Alternatively, the group in part B meas. 2 and 4 is obtained by combining a single-string brush and a drop-thumb (M-T-M-T).

Observe that both the *snap-rhythm* (a two note grouping written as a sixteenth note followed by an eighth note) and the correct style for playing strathspeys are explained in column 3-11. Along these lines, it should be noted that in authentic performance of strathspeys, sixteenth note groupings such as the ones in this tune are often *not* played straight. Sometimes in fact they are played as two quick successive *snaps*, or as combinations of snaps and *dotted pairs* (see column 3.2). As is usual in such cases, you have to listen quite a bit to a style of music before you can perform it successfully.

66

The Marquis of Huntley

Banjo Arrangement: Ken Perlman

Tuning: gDGCD

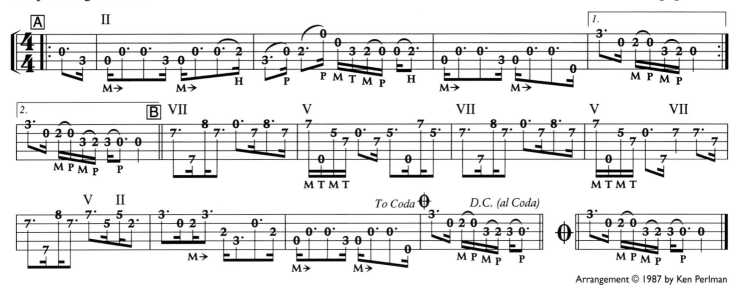

Arrangement © 1987 by Ken Perlman

2.23 The Tremolo

(May '85)

Every musical instrument family has a unique set of limitations that accomplished players must strive consistently to overcome. On wind instruments, for example, players must learn to create the illusion of note-articulation, when in fact there is a continuity of sound between notes. On fretted instruments we have the opposite problem, and we are constantly trying to create the illusion of legato (smoothness) and sustain, when in fact all the notes we play are *staccato*; (i.e., choppy) and short-lived.

We notice this property of fretted instruments most when a tune has a lot of long notes — such as notes in 4/4 time that have a duration of two beats or more. Let's say we have to play some long high-D notes in open-G tuning, perhaps two half notes and one whole note. (Example 2-67). If we merely play these melody notes unadorned, the sound of each note dies out quickly, and our rendition contains some unpleasant-sounding dead spaces. So, very early in our playing careers, we learn to fill in long notes with one or more "bumm-titty" strums (Example 2-68a). As we become more advanced, we learn to fill in with single string brushes and double-thumbing (Example 2-68b) or with "filler licks" (Example 2-68c).

Players of mandolin, tenor banjo and other flatpicked instruments have an additional weapon in their anti-dead-space arsenal known as the *tremolo*, which is indicated in standard music and tablature by placing a double-cross-bar on a note stem (or under a stemless note), as shown in Example 2-69. In a flatpicked tremolo, the player rapidly alternates downstrokes (⊓) and-upstrokes (∨) on the same string. These rapidly alternating strokes are continued for the entire duration of a long note, creating the illusion of sustain.

Although the exact number of strokes in a tremolo varies with the tempo of a given tune (the slower the tempo, the more

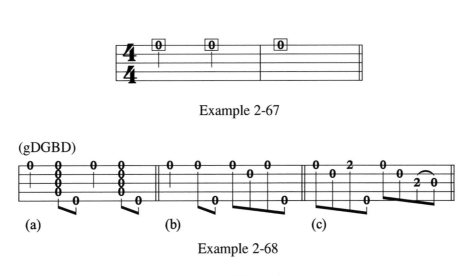

Example 2-67

Example 2-68

67

up-and-down strokes are required and vice versa) we can get a good start by notating a tremolo as a series of sixteenth notes. We can then get an approximate picture of how a given long note translates to a given number of up-and-down tremolo strokes. By this formula, a half note on the open first string would be replaced by a tremolo consisting of eight sixteenth notes at that same pitch (Example 2-70).

There is not really a true up-stroke in clawhammer, but I often wondered if there was perhaps some way in which the sound of a tremolo could at least be approximated. After much experimentation I managed to come up with a tremolo sound that is effective for certain notes.

No same-string tremolos are possible without an up-stroke, so I turned my attention to situations where I could get the same pitch on two different strings; for example at the open first string

and fret 3, string 2 in open G tuning. I could then play one string with my middle finger and one string with my thumb. By rapidly alternating M and T strokes, I could at least approximate the sound of a flatpicked tremolo (Example 2-71).

There were two major problems with this approach. First, there are no equivalent notes to some pitches (for example, low D, E and F in open G tuning), and sometimes holding down two same-pitch frets at the same time involves too great a stretch (for example, the A at fret 2, string 3 and the one at fret 7, string 4 in open G tuning). Second, when two equivalent notes are on strings of different thickness, they are often sufficiently different in timbre (tone quality) to spoil the tremolo effect.

Only when I tried alternating first string and fifth string notes on the same pitch did I get a sound approximating a true tremolo. In fact, I feel that the sound here is so successful it deserves to be in the repertoire of all clawhammer pickers.

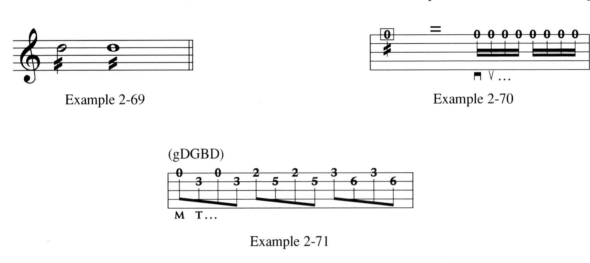

Example 2-69

Example 2-70

(gDGBD)

Example 2-71

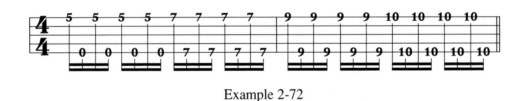

Example 2-72

The clawhammer tremolo works for any pitch that is equivalent to, or higher than the pitch to which the fifth string is tuned. In G, double C (gCGCD) and sawmill (gDGCD) tunings, for example, the fifth string is tuned to high G and the first string is tuned to D. The pitch *high G* is also found at fret 5, string 1, so a tremolo can be obtained by alternating M-strokes on fret 5, string 1 with T-strokes on the open fifth string. Example 2-72 gives appropriate tremolos for long notes on several pitches.

Let me re-state that I am not suggesting that each half note be replaced by exactly eight tremolo strokes. The number that is best for a given tune varies with tempo and overall feel. Note also that it will probably take you sometime to limber up your hand sufficiently to make this clawhammer tremolo sound like the real thing. If you listen to recordings of your favorite mandolin player (father-of-bluegrass Bill Monroe is of course always a safe bet in this regard), this should help you better understand the sound you want.

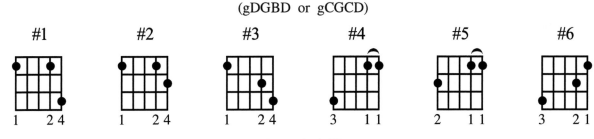

(gDGBD or gCGCD)

#1 #2 #3 #4 #5 #6

Example 2-73

Try another of my original tunes which, since it struck me as being sinisterly Slavic in feel, I call *Rasputin's Last Ride*. The long notes in Part B (marked with the double cross bar) are ideal for tremolo treatment. Observe that the piece uses quite a number of up the neck fingering forms, diagrammed in Example 2-73. These forms yield runs of notes in the same way as those suggested for open G tuning in cols. 2.16-17, but they have been adapted for mountain minor and double C tunings. Again, the notation "6-V" means, "fingering form #6 is played in fifth position."

Rasputin's Last Ride

By Ken Perlman

Tuning: gDGCD

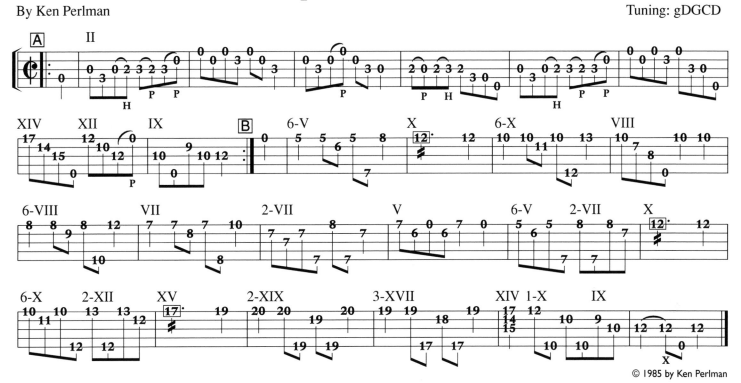

© 1985 by Ken Perlman

2.24 Grace Notes

(Jan. '01)

In column 2.6, I discussed using triplets for ornamentation. This column focuses on two other ornamenting techniques, namely grace notes and double grace notes. Grace and double grace notes are very quick notes that have no official time value of their own. Instead, they borrow a tiny amount of time from the note they are being used to decorate.

Single grace notes are generally performed in clawhammer as very quick hammer-ons or pull-offs (Example 2-74). The trick is to start your H or P as soon as you pluck the string, then linger on the hammered or pulled note throughout the remainder of its notated value. In the first instance of Example 2-74, strike fret 2, string 1 with M then immediately pull that string off. At the conclusion of the P, let open string 1 sound for the duration of its notated value (that is, one beat)..

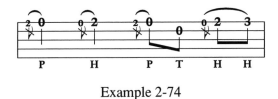

Example 2-74

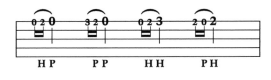

Example 2-75

69

Double grace notes are generally performed in clawhammer as a pair of super quick hammer-ons or pull offs, or as a combination of quick H's and P's, as shown in Example 2-75. The trick is play your pair of Hs or Ps (or combinations thereof) as soon as you pluck the string, then linger on the hammered or pulled note throughout the remainder of its notated value. In the first instance of Example 2-75, strike open string 1 with M, hammer quickly to fret 2, string 1, then just as quickly pull that same string off. At the conclusion of the P, let open string 1 sound for the duration of its notated value (that is, one beat).

It is extremely important that graces be performed with sufficient crispness so that the listener can plainly perceive which are the grace notes, and which are the full fledged notes that follow them. In other words, the melody should sound just as clearly comprehensible after you've added your graces, as when you play it unadorned.

Another way of thinking about grace and double grace notes is to relate them to triplets (cols. 2.6-8). Example 2-76 illustrates several triplets in clawhammer style, all of which make use of the same strings, frets and techniques as many of the graces in Examples 2-74 and 2-75. The first triplet, for example, is obtained via M-note, hammer-on and pull-off — exactly the same maneuvers used to perform the first double grace note in example 2-75. The only difference between the triplet on the one hand, and the double-grace-followed-by-quarter-note on the other, is in the time relationship between the notes involved. In the triplet, each note is even; in the double grace the first two notes are very quick, while the last note is long.

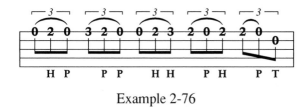

Example 2-76

The issue of how to best go about placing ornaments in a tune is discussed in detail in column 2.6.

Try double graces in this arrangement of the well-known Irish session-tune *Cooley's Reel*. You'll find other double graces in the arrangements for *Crooked Stovepipe, Chorus Jig and Gow's Lament*. You'll find single grace-notes in the arrangements for *Christmas Day in the Morning, Chorus Jig* and *Nine Points of Roguery*.

Cooley's Reel

Banjo Arrangement: Ken Perlman

Tuning: gDGBD

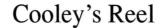

Arrangement © 1982 by Ken Perlman

70

Scottish fiddlers have been emulating piping ornaments since at least the mid-eighteenth century. Some such ornaments — such as single and double grace notes — could be transferred to fiddle virtually unchanged. Others were just too complex to be played on fiddle: the piper can build ornaments with all ten fingers, while the fiddler is confined to just four.

To serve in place of a whole battery of complex piping ornaments, Scottish fiddlers developed a bowing technique known as the *birl*. This technique, which is called *cuts* or *cuttings* in Cape Breton, involves three or four rapid bow alternations on the same pitch. (Example 2-77).

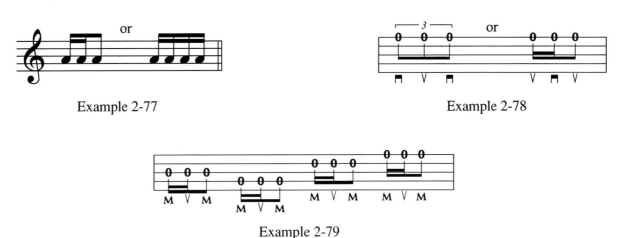

Example 2-77   Example 2-78

Example 2-79

Irish fiddlers came up with a somewhat different solution to the same problem. Instead of using extra bow-strokes to cover left-out pipe ornaments, Irish players developed a left-hand technique to serve this purpose. This maneuver — called an *Irish roll* — is performed by *slurring* several graces and full-fledged notes in a row (that is, playing them off the same bow stroke). Interestingly, since the 1920s players of fretted instruments in Irish music have employed plectrum-driven same-pitch triplets (in effect, birls) instead of rolls. (Example 2-78)

After much experimentation, I hit upon a method for playing birls and Irish rolls in clawhammer style. It involves

playing a triplet consisting of a conventional downstroke with M, followed by a wrist-driven upstroke (V) in which the string is caught with the underside of the M-finger. Finally, the string is plucked again with a conventional M-stroke. The entire technique is shown in Example 2-79.

MacNab's Hornpipe is also known as *Crossing the Minch* (the Minch is the body of water that separates the outer Hebrides from the Isle of Skye). It is used by budding Scottish fiddlers to perfect the birling technique, and it should serve a similar purpose for would-be clawhammer birlers. For the proper playing style of hornpipes, see column 3.2.

McNab's Hornpipe

Banjo Arrangement: Ken Perlman   Tuning: gCGCD (capo–2)

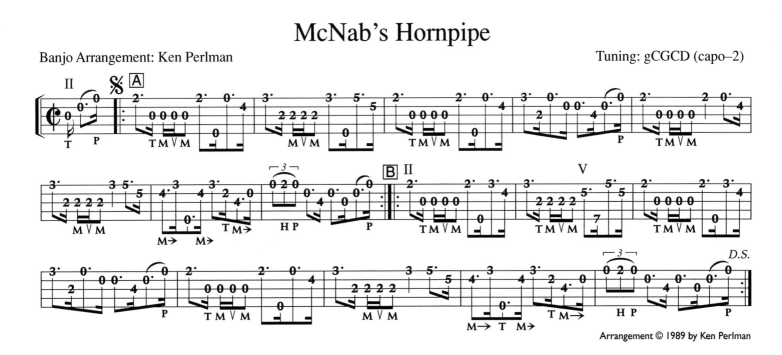

Arrangement © 1989 by Ken Perlman

3.1 Reels

As a banjoist, you've undoubtedly come across dozens of reels in your playing career. These include such well known tunes as *Hop High Ladies* (originally *Mrs. McLeod's Reel*), *Old Molly Hare* (originally a reel called *The Fairy Dance*), *Paddy on the Turnpike* (originally *The Old Reel*), *Turkey in the Straw*, *Dubuque* and *Blackberry Blossom*. Examples of a few popular reels tabbed out in this book are *Spoodis Skeery*, *Cooley's Reel*, *Hull's Victory*, *Lord MacDonald's Reel* (ancestor of *Leather Britches*), *the Flowers of Edinburgh*, *Sheehan's Reel*, *Green Meadow Reel* (ancestor of *Waynesboro*) and *Sally Gardens*.

Most reels have two repeated eight-measure parts—known respectively as A and B, low and high or coarse and fine. There is also an alternative structure that calls for a four-measure repeated A or low part followed by an eight-measure non-repeated B or high part (some reels appearing in this volume with this alternative structure are *Miss Lyall*, *Miss Johnson of Pittworth* and *The Black Mill*).

Generally, each reel measure contains eight eighth notes organized as two groups of four. For the purpose of providing rhythmic variety, a quarter note (or triplet) is sometimes substituted for a pair of eighth notes.

The term "reel" is descended from the old Anglo-Saxon word "rulla" (to whirl), and it once served as a generic term for any rural dance — particularly one in which participants wove about each other. There is also mention in Scottish judicial records dating to 1591 of a "reill or short dance" being performed by a group of women accused of witchcraft.

The musical form now known as the reel probably originated in Scotland some time in the late 17th or early 18th centuries. Probably the earliest definitive record we have of reel-tunes is the Drummond Castle Manuscript, transcribed by David Young for the Duke of Perth in 1734. The first published collection to include examples of the genre was Robert Bremner's *A Collection of Scots Reels or Country Dances*, published in Edinburgh in 1751. Reels probably began to trickle into Ireland by the mid-18th century and first appeared in Irish tune collections around the late 18th century.

Initially the reel musical genre was used to accompany a specific dance known as the Scotch Reel (Gaelic: *rhuidhleadh*).[1] The typical "set" for a Scotch Reel is made up of either three or four dancers. The dance itself consists of an alternation of two kinds of foot-work, which are known respectively as *setting steps* and *traveling steps*. Traveling steps are employed while dancers negotiate the outline of a circle, figure-eight or other geometric shape, the way figure-skaters might outline such a

shape in the "compulsory" portion of a competition. Setting steps are used to mark time between traveling figures.

The Scotch Reel dance spread to England and Ireland and it ultimately became quite popular in North America. The dance shows up on 18th century formal dance cards in Montreal and Québec, for example, and I've come across a comic account dating to the 1840s of Scotch reels being danced by local denizens in a rural Georgia cabin.

By the mid-18th century, reel tunes were being tapped regularly for use as accompaniment for Country Dances (now often called Contra Dances) and Cotillions. Later they were applied to accompanying Quadrilles and other, less formal square dances (see col. 9.20).

In North America, dancing to reels became so popular that the reel virtually eclipsed many other fiddle tune genres. Hornpipes, for example, pretty much disappeared as a distinct form, and those that were still played were *converted* to reels (see col. 3.14). The playing of jigs was also much reduced, and many of these 6/8 time melodies were also converted to cut-time (that is, reel-time) style.

If the reel format of eight eighth notes per measure presents a special challenge to the clawhammer banjoist it is one of phrasing. In the introduction to his *Kentucky Favorites* project Mac Benford observes that "unbroken strings of eighth notes" are "musically boring." To put this just a bit differently, I'd say that "strings of eighth notes are musically boring if they are unshaped." What this means is that musical passages need to be shaped, or "phrased" into distinct sub-melodies, each of which having a distinct origin and conclusion.

There are basically two issues here. First, how are phrases to be recognized? Second, once the phrases are determined, how do you bring them out?

The best way to determine phrasing is by listening to a given tune played by an accomplished fiddler or banjoist. Then memorize the tune and try to hear it in your mind exactly as that musician plays it. The phrases in the tune become apparent in the same way that the phrases of a song become apparent when you memorize it: as "breaths" in a melody.

As for how to bring phrases out on your instrument, this is a more subtle issue. I always think of it as an ever so slight shift in the weighting of the right hand that allows for a T-note or an M-note to be shaded so that it can be used to end one phrase or begin another.

---

[1] The adjective "Scotch" is generally regarded by the present-day inhabitants of Scotland as a derogatory term. The terms *Scotch Reel* and *Scotch snap*, however, are so well established — even among Scottish music and dance historians — that trying to avoid using them here would serve merely as a futile exercise in political correctness.

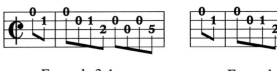

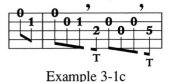
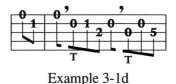

Example 3-1a	Example 3-1b	Example 3-1c	Example 3-1d

Just to give a few illustrations of this concept, Example 3-1 shows the same notes phrased in three different ways. Ex. 3-1a gives the unshaped melody. In 3-1b there is a breath (shown via a comma above the staff and a break in the beaming between notes) between the third and fourth pairs of eighth notes, paralleling the pattern initiated by the pair of pickup or upbeat notes. In 3-1c, there is a breath indicated prior to the *last*

eighth note of each eighth note group. In 3-1d there is a breath indicated after the *first* eighth note of each eighth note group.

Try some of these phrasing ideas out when you work through the tab for this well-known Irish reel, *Maid Behind the Bar,* also known as *Judy's Reel* and *Indy's Favorite.* I learned this version from fiddler Elmer Robinson of Woodstock, Prince Edward Island.

The Maid Behind the Bar

Banjo Arrangement: Ken Perlman

Tuning: gCGCD (capo–2)

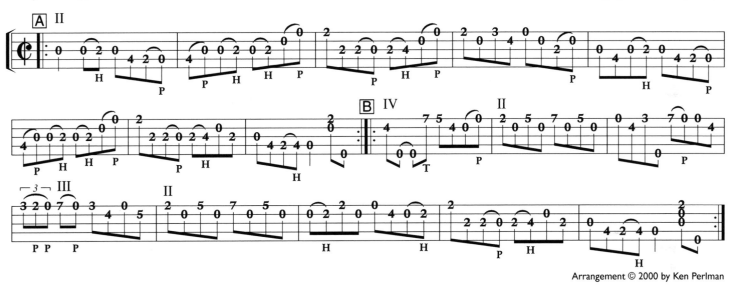

Arrangement © 2000 by Ken Perlman

3.2 Hornpipes

(Jan. '97)

The modern hornpipe seems to date to about the mid-18th century (in the 16th century, there was a completely unrelated family of dance tunes in 3/2 time also known as "hornpipes"). Authorities differ as to its origin but the modern hornpipe seems to have grown up as a slow to medium tempo musical form designed to accompany fancy step-dancing and clogging. It seems in particular to have been associated with agricultural regions in northern England, and — a bit later in the century — with the professional dancing stage. In terms of the latter, quite a number of famous hornpipes were composed for, or became associated with the stage acts of famous 18th-century dancers. Two notable cases in North America are *Ricketts' Hornpipe* (named for Samuel Ricketts, dancer and director of one of America's first traveling circuses) and *Durang's Hornpipe,* composed for dancer John Durang.

Most hornpipes consist of two parts. Each part has eight measures, and each part is played twice through before moving on to the next part.

Hornpipes have two beats per measure, and can be written with a time signature of either 2/2 (also called "cut time," the symbol for which appears in Example 3-2) or 2/4. Generally, each measure contains eight notes arranged as two groups of four notes each. From time to time, two of these notes can be replaced by notes of longer duration. If the time signature is 2/2, these notes in groups of four are written as eighth notes. If the time signature is 2/4, these notes are written as sixteenth notes. Example 3-3 shows how passages for hornpipes appear in both 2/4 and 2/2 time.

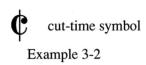

ℂ   cut-time symbol

Example 3-2

Example 3-3

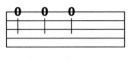

Example 3-4a

Example 3-4b

One "typical" feature of hornpipes involves the last measure of each part, which generally ends — for tunes written in cut time — with three quarter notes as shown in Ex. 3-4a (if the tune is written in 2/4, it ends with three eighth notes, as shown in Ex. 3-4b). Be a little wary of seeing this as a defining feature, however. There are hornpipes that don't have it, and other kinds of tunes that sometimes do.

In most North American fiddling traditions, hornpipes nowadays are played exactly the same as reels (for the purpose of this discussion, Southern "hoedown" tunes are also classified as reels). In other words the eighth or sixteenth notes are played fairly evenly, and the tune moves along quite briskly. This is as true of Nova Scotia and Ontario as it is of Kentucky and North Carolina. Some common examples of tunes generally played in this manner are *Fisher's Hornpipe*, and the aforementioned *Durang's Hornpipe*. Some hornpipes-played-like-reels that appear in these pages are *President Garfield's Hornpipe*, *Quindaro Hornpipe*, *Rickett's Hornpipe*, and *Upper Denton Hornpipe*.

In England, Scotland and Ireland (and among North Americans who emulate musicians from those areas) hornpipes are played quite differently from reels. First of all the *tempo* (speed) of performance is much slower (hornpipe tempos are quite variable even among various British and Irish traditions — they are played at a crawl for English country dancing and Morris dancing, they are played fairly briskly in the Irish tradition, etc). Not surprisingly, the major determinant for hornpipe tempo in

these traditions is the nature of the dance or dances that are being accompanied.

Second, the groups of eighth (or sixteenth) notes are played as "swing" instead of straight eighth (or sixteenth) notes. This is indicated in some tune-books by notating hornpipes in "dotted" fashion, as shown in Example 3-5. In other words, each pair of cut time eighth notes is presented as a dotted eighth plus a sixteenth (Ex. 3-5a). In 2/4 time each pair of sixteenths is presented as a dotted sixteenth plus a thirty-second note. (Ex. 3-5b). Both notations indicate that the first note sounds *three times* longer than the second.

This "dotted" notation is not exactly accurate. In actual performance of swing or "hornpipe-eighth" notes, the first note of each pair should sound only *twice* as long as the second note. This would be notated as a *triplet* with the first two notes tied together, as shown in Example 3-6a. This can be written more elegantly (in 2/2 time) as a quarter note plus an eighth note under a triplet bracket, as shown in Ex. 3-6b. In 2/4 time, it would be written as an eighth plus a sixteenth under a triplet bracket, as shown in Ex. 3-6c. To get the feel of swing eighths, count "1-&-a, 2-&-a" for each pair of notes, but play only on the number counts (1,2…) and the "a-counts." Each "&-count" is skipped.

In terms of timing, observe that you have four "swing-style" pairs of notes per measure. Make sure that you interpret these as two groups, made up of two swing-pairs each. The first note of each group is then accented, as shown in Ex. 3-7.

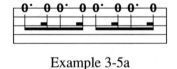

Example 3-5a

Example 3-5b

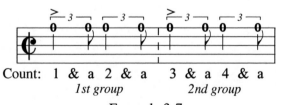

Example 3-6

Count: 1 & a 2 & a   3 & a 4 & a
1st group   *2nd group*

Example 3-7

74

In terms of interpreting such hornpipes in clawhammer style, no special adaptation must be made (after all, southern fiddle tunes are often also played with swing eighths, instead of straight eighths). Just use drop-thumbs, hammer-ons, pull-offs, and slides where appropriate.

Try the following tune, *The Leeds Hornpipe* in traditional British/Irish hornpipe-style. Some other tunes in these pages that are to be played in this manner are *Harvest Home Hornpipe, MacNab's Hornpipe* and *The Mariner*.

Leeds Hornpipe

Banjo Arrangement: Ken Perlman

Tuning: gCGCD (capo–2)

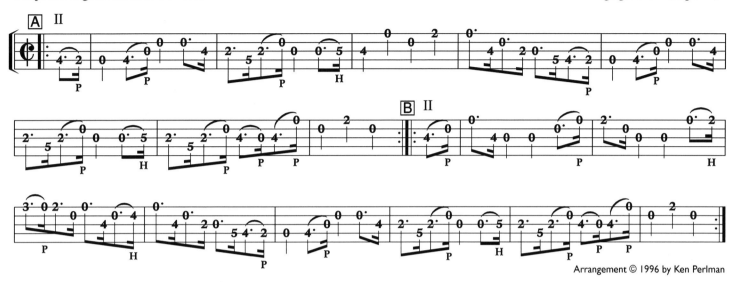

Arrangement © 1996 by Ken Perlman

3.3 Fast Dance Tunes That Aren't Reels (Plus a Word on "Hoedowns") (July '92)
3.4 Scotch Measures (Aug.'88)

If you're any kind of southern or Celtic fiddle tune fan, you've probably noticed that there are more kinds of dance tunes in the universe than jigs, reels and waltzes. This column is devoted to fast dance tunes in cut (or 2/4) time that don't qualify as reels.

Full-fledged reels are hard driving tunes in cut time that for the most part have eight eighth notes per measure. Longer notes (such as quarter notes) appear with some frequency, but their role is primarily as rhythmic accent. In addition these quarter notes are often highly decorated and they sometimes become the focus of such complex noting ornaments as the Irish roll, or the Cape Breton *cut* (col. 2.25). In most Celtic fiddling circles, the ability to play a good solid reel with appropriate feel and ornamentation is what separates the full-fledged players from the novices.

One element of confusion is that many of the "reels" you hear at an average dance are actually *hornpipes*. Hornpipes have the same basic structure as reels (eight eighth notes per cut time measure) and were originally played at much slower tempos with more of a "dotted" feel. As noted in column 3.2, however, in North America most hornpipes are now played in more or less the same fashion as reels.

There are many cut-time fast dance tunes played at modern dances that are neither reels nor hornpipes. The first indication that tells you that you are dealing with a different kettle of fish

is a decline in note density. In other words, you get melodies with a much higher proportion of quarter notes. Second, you don't get the same kind of drive to the bowing and the tunes take on a more bouncy, light-hearted character. Third, the rhythms become more varied. In other words, because there is now more of a mixture of different-length notes, there will be parts of the tune that have dense rhythms (full of eighth notes) and other parts that will have sparse rhythms (mostly quarter notes and even some longer notes). To bring out subtle rhythmic distinctions in musically dense reels and hornpipes takes considerable amounts of bowing skill. To bring out the rhythmic distinctions in these other fast dance tunes takes much less skill. For this reason most fiddlers start out by attempting to play the latter kind of tune.

There's no universally recognized name for this "less melodically dense" tune category, although I've seen the term *set tune* crop up more than a few times. The rationale is that these are melodies that can be used to accompany *set dancing* (an overall category that includes both square and contra dancing). Alternatively, some fiddlers on Prince Edward Island in eastern Canada call them *slow tunes* (with fewer notes to play, the fiddler's bow moves a bit slower for this kind of tune than it would for an average reel or played-as-reel hornpipe).

Be that as it may, we can take the "set-tune" category apart a little and look at some of the kinds of tunes that are likely to be found within it. One of its oldest inhabitants is a tune-variety called the *Scotch measure*. Scotch measures are cut-time dance tunes. Like reels, they are usually made up of two eight-measure repeated parts. Their special feature is that measures with lots of eighth notes tend to alternate with measures composed mostly of quarter notes. Generally, the odd-number measures of each part (first, third, etc.) are the ones with most of the eighth notes. The even number measures always start off with three strong quarter notes. Example 3-8 shows the first few bars of the Scotch measure *The White Cockade,* which clearly displays this alternating pattern.

As an aside, the first part of *Soldier's Joy* has the structure of a Scotch measure (Example 3-9), although I've not yet heard it suggested that the tune once belonged to this category.

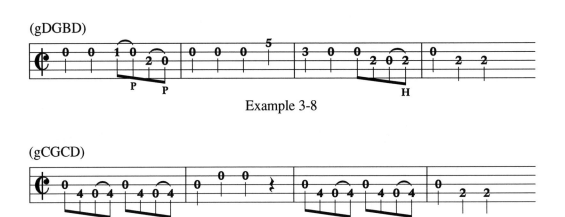

Example 3-8

Example 3-9

There are two Scotch measures in this volume — *The White Cockade* (which accompanies this column) and *The Dashing White Sergeant.*

Another easily recognizable — but less stylized — tune type that falls within the set-tune category is the *Irish* or *Kerry polka,* which hales from County Kerry in the south of Ireland. These are lively tunes formed from mixtures of eighth and quarter notes. This category got its name because the tunes were thought to resemble in spirit and musical structure some of the east-European polka tunes that swept through western Europe in the latter half of the 19th century. There are two Kerry polkas in this volume — *Scarteglen Polka* (which accompanies this column) and *Sean Ryan's Polka.*

Perhaps the largest group of non-reel fast dance tunes is made up of song melodies that have been adapted for use as dance tunes. Some examples you'll find in this book are *Darling Nelly Gray* (which accompanies this column), *Old Jim River, Old Joe Clark, Buffalo Gals* and *Angeline the Baker.* In some cases where a song melody was long enough to make only one part of a dance tune, a second part would be specially composed to go along with it. An example of this phenomenon is the Galax/Round Peak version of *Yellow Rose of Texas* (see my *Homespun Tapes* instructional series); another is *Sandy Boys* (pg.79).

There are also numerous North American tunes that were composed directly to serve as set tunes. Some North American set tunes in these pages that are more or less in the style of Kerry polkas are *Crooked Stovepipe* (which accompanies this column), *Tina's Schottische, Plaza Polka, Whelan's Breakdown* and *Judique Reel.* Alternatively, there are North American set tunes composed in the style of song melodies: one that appears in this book is *Maple Sugar.*

Some mention should also be made in this context of southern "hoedown" tunes: just how do they fit into all these tune categories? Basically, almost all southern hoedown tunes can be classified as *stylized* reels, hornpipes-played-as-reels or set tunes. By "stylized," I mean that the shape and character of the melodies have been put through a "lens" created by the tastes and preferences of generations of local and regional Southern fiddling populations. This has allowed certain characteristic turns of phrase and rhythmic treatments to creep into the music, giving it a distinctive sound and creating the impression that it is totally distinct from its Northern and Celtic counterparts. Some examples of hoedown tunes you'll find in this volume include *Sandy Boys* (which accompanies this column) *Puncheon Camps, Jay Bird, Ducks on the Pond, Waitin' for the Federals, Sally's in the Garden Siftin' Sand, Yew Pine Mountains, Over the Waterfall,* and *Dinah.*

Following are four examples of different kinds of set tunes, and one "hoedown." First is the Scotch measure *The White Cockade,* which was first published in 1782 under the title *The Ranting Highwayman.* (Be aware that this fairly active banjo setting somewhat camouflages the underlying Scotch measure structure, and that the key of the tune has been changed to C-major from the more customary G-major).

Second is the Kerry polka *Scarteglen Polka.* This tune is unusual in that it has three parts instead of the customary two, indicating that it was probably used for a specific dance with a 48-measure cycle.

Third is a banjo setting of the song-melody-converted-to-dance-tune *Darlin' Nellie Grey,* based on the playing of fiddler Johnny Morrissey of Newtown Cross, Prince Edward Island.

Fourth is the North American set tune, *Crooked Stovepipe,* which I learned from fiddler Reuben Smith of Blooming Point, Prince Edward Island. Observe the *double-grace* notes in Part A, meas. 7 and 8, and in Part B, meas. 6: these are explained in col. 2.24. Be aware as well that the second half of Part B, meas. 2 calls for fingering form #6 (see col. 2.17).

Finally, there's my version of Dwight Diller's arrangement of *Sandy Boys,* a hoedown he collected from the Hammons family of Marlinton, West Virginia. You might want to review the columns on syncopation and the skip stroke (1.12-13) before trying this one.

The White Cockade

Banjo Arrangement: Roger Rankin

Tuning: gCGCD

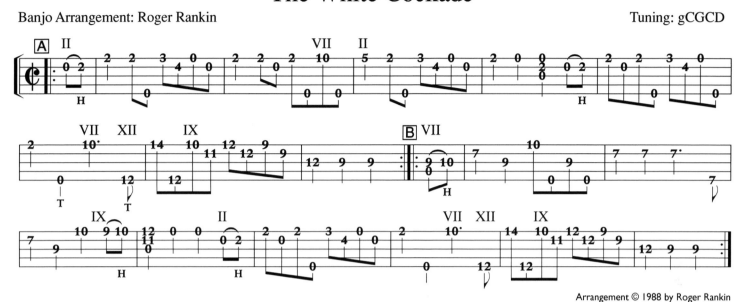

Arrangement © 1988 by Roger Rankin

Scartaglen Polka

Banjo Arrangement: Ken Perlman

Tuning: gDGBD

Arrangement © 1984 by Ken Perlman

77

Darlin' Nelly Grey

Banjo Arrangement: Ken Perlman

Tuning: gDGBD

Arrangement © 1994 by Ken Perlman

Crooked Stovepipe

Banjo Arrangement: Ken Perlman

Tuning: gDGBD

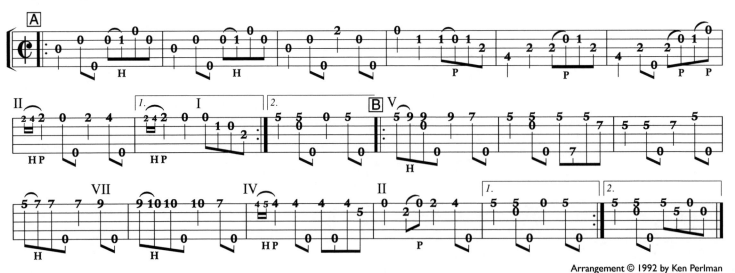

Arrangement © 1992 by Ken Perlman

78

Sandy Boys

Banjo Arrangement: Ken Perlman

Tuning: gDGBD (capo–2)

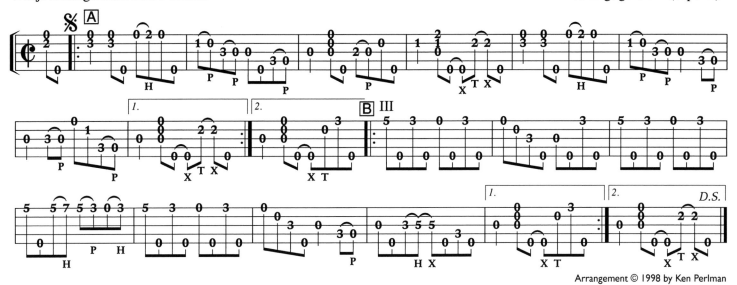

Arrangement © 1998 by Ken Perlman

3.5 Waltz Time
3.6 Waltzing the Banjo

(May '86)
(Feb. '99)

Somewhere along the line, it was decided that 3/4- or waltz-time was a problem for clawhammer banjo players. Why this determination was made is a mystery since there is no technical reason whatsoever why this should be the case!

In 3/4 time, there are three beats per measure, with quarter notes counting as one beat each (Example 3-10, meas. 1). Half notes count for two beats (meas. 2), dotted half notes count for three beats (meas. 3), eighth notes count for one-half beat each (meas. 4-5). So far, with the exception of the number of beats per measure, everything is exactly the same as for 4/4 time.

In 4/4 time as you know, quarter notes are generally played as single-string strokes or turned into single-string brushes. Whole notes, half notes and dotted half notes are replaced by combinations of quarter notes with brush-thumbs or single-string brushes. Eighth notes are obtained by drop-thumbs, hammer-ons, pull-offs or slides, and so on (these ideas form the basics of *arranging* tunes for clawhammer: see cols. 6.6-8).

Now, you won't find any whole notes in a waltz or other 3/4 time tune (they're just too big to squeeze into any one measure), but every other word in the above description applies just as much to 3/4 time as it does to 4/4 time.

Here's a few ideas to ease your transition to 3/4 time playing.

◆ Example 3-11 shows how by simple extension, your garden-variety "bumm-titty strum" can be turned into a 3/4 time figure. Just remember to accent the first beat of each measure, then count 1-2& 3- for the first measure, and 1-2&3& for the second measure.

◆ Example 3-12 shows how double thumb patterns can be modified to operate in 3/4 time. Again, accent the first beat of each measure, then count 1- 2&3& for the first measure, and 1&2&3- for the second measure.

◆ In Example 3-13, try playing single string brushes in a 3/4 time rhythm. For the sake of interest, the M-notes here describe an ascending and descending G-major scale. Accent the first beat of each measure, and count for each 1&2&3&.

◆ In Example 3-14, try playing H's and P's in 3/4 time. Once more, accent the first beat of each measure, then count 1&2&3&.

◆ Finally in Example 3-15, try mixing up the various techniques to create a 3/4-time phrase. Don't forget to accent the first beat of each measure, and count appropriately for each.

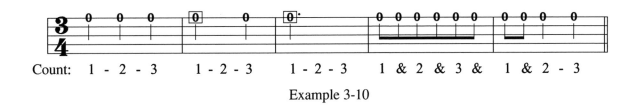

Count: 1 - 2 - 3   1 - 2 - 3   1 - 2 - 3   1 & 2 & 3 &   1 & 2 - 3

Example 3-10

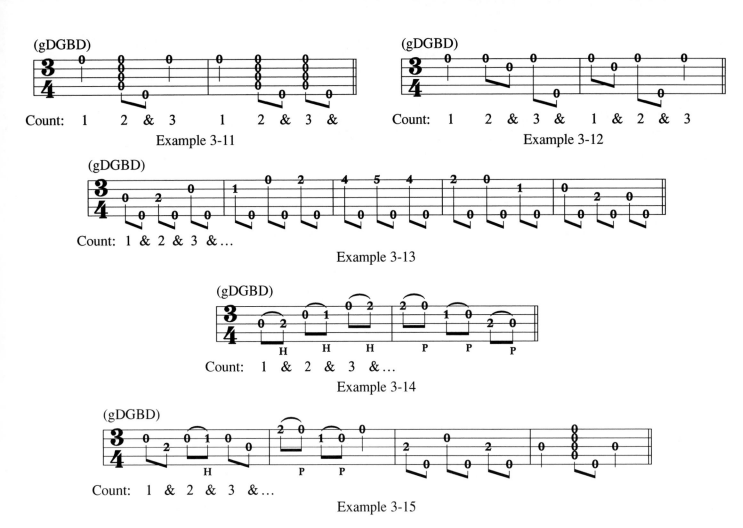

Count: 1   2   &   3   1   2   &   3   &

Example 3-11

Count: 1   2   &   3   &   1   &   2   &   3

Example 3-12

Count: 1 & 2 & 3 &…

Example 3-13

Count: 1 & 2 & 3 &…

Example 3-14

Count: 1 & 2 & 3 &…

Example 3-15

Black Velvet Waltz

Banjo Arrangement: Ken Perlman

Tuning: gCGCD

Arrangement © 1999 by Ken Perlman

Our next tune is *The Black Velvet Waltz*, which comes from Ontario. No one knows the original name of the tune: fiddler Ross Beyer learned it un-named from a cousin and decided to name it after a popular brand of Canadian whiskey. By the way, the original fiddle key is C, so you can play the setting uncapoed (if your favorite fiddler balks at playing in C it will probably work just fine in D: in which case just teach it to him or her with your capo up two frets). Some other waltzes or 3/4 time tunes in this book are *Country Waltz*, *Westphalia Waltz* and *Niel Gow's Lament*.

(Nov. '86)
(July '96)

3.7 Jigs and 6/8 Time
3.8 Jigs Revisited

Now that there are "news groups" and "L-groups" on the internet, friends are always keeping me abreast of the newest hot topics (for the uninitiated, these are electronic hang-outs where people who share an interest can place notices or conduct discussions via e-mail). In one recent interchange, apparently the discussion topic was jigs on the five-string banjo.

One banjoist inquired about the best way to investigate playing jigs in clawhammer style. He got a number of replies, about half of which offered helpful information about technique and tablature sources. Many of the other replies consisted of heated denunciations of the whole idea of playing jigs on five-string. These arguments could be summed up as follows: playing jigs on a banjo — especially a five-string banjo — can be regarded more or less as an "un-natural act" (I think this phrase was actually used). If you must play jigs on banjo, get hold of a tenor banjo and learn to use a plectrum. If against all dictates of reason you insist on trying to play jigs in clawhammer style, here's a couple of sources, etc., etc.

There's no denying that playing jigs in clawhammer style sometimes presents a challenge for even the dedicated player, but frailing jigs is not some newfangled innovation by a bunch of northern interlopers. Minstrel-style pickers in the mid 19th century considered jigs to be part of the standard banjo repertoire. In fact, nearly all instruction manuals for *stroke-style* banjo (as clawhammer was known at the time) included nota-tion for at least some 6/8 time tunes. Playing in 6/8 time is merely a lost art among contemporary clawhammer pickers.

I suspect that the absence of twentieth century examples of frailed jigs prior to the melodic era has more to do with the virtual disappearance of the genre from the Southern fiddle repertoire, than it has to do with the incompatibility of this genre with clawhammer style.

One intriguing possibility in this regard is that the genre may still have been around in the South at the dawn of the recording era in the early 1920s, but that jig performances were just not recorded by record companies on the lookout for material that would be regarded as distinctly "hillbilly" (see cols. 9.25-7).

What's the main problem with frailed jigs? Well, jigs are in 6/8 time. Tunes in 6/8 time have two beats per measure with each beat divided into three pulses (forget about the "6" part of 6/8: there are actually only two beats in a measure). The most characteristic rhythmic figure in most jigs then, involves group-ings of *three* notes (Example 3-16). Clawhammer picking, on the other hand lends itself most easily to notes that can be organized in pairs. Trying to fit clawhammer into a jig format, then, might be something like trying to fit a square peg through a round hole.

Example 3-16

Just as you actually can fit a square peg through a round hole if the peg is the right size, clawhammer style can be adapted to playing in 6/8 time with a bit of tweaking. The key here is that almost all clawhammer players already divide beats into three pulses quite frequently. In fact, this happens whenever swing eighth notes are played.

Almost all pairs of eighth notes played in Southern fiddle music — especially in the newer tunes being recorded by recent old time bands — are, in effect, swing eighth notes. In a swing eighth note pair, the first note is actually twice as long as the second note. Swing eighth notes are sometimes written in notation as a dotted pair (that is, a dotted eighth note plus a sixteenth-note), but a more accurate notation would be a modi-fied triplet grouping, or — more efficiently — a quarter note plus a single eighth note under a triplet bracket (review Ex-amples 3-5 thru 3-7 in col. 3.2). Try some swing eighth pairs in 4/4 time in Example 3-17. The count is 1-&-a, 2-&-a, 3-&-a, 4-&-a. Observe that notes are played only on the "number-counts" and the "a-counts." The "&- counts" are skipped.

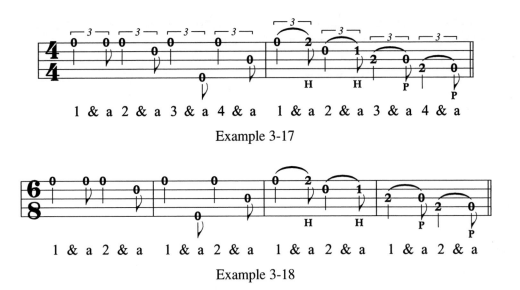

Example 3-17

Example 3-18

Now, there are two kinds of note combinations that occur most frequently in jigs — three note groupings (akin to "triplets" in 4/4 time) and two-note groupings. These two-note groupings are generally made up of a quarter note plus an eighth note (Example 3-18). In other words, they are exactly like swing eighths without the triplet bracket. What's more, they can be counted in exactly the same way (1-&-a, 2-&-a...), except that each measure now only has in effect only two beats. For each pair, the quarter notes are played on the "number-counts," and eighth notes are played on the "a-counts."

There are certain jigs that are made up primarily — or even exclusively — of these two-note quarter-eighth groupings. In the Irish tradition these tunes are known as *single jigs*. Any clawhammer player should be able to handle a single jig without any modification of technique whatsoever. In Example 3-19, try the first few bars of one of the best known single jigs, *Pop Goes the Weasel*. Note that dotted quarters count for three pulses (that is, one half-measure each).

(gDGBD)

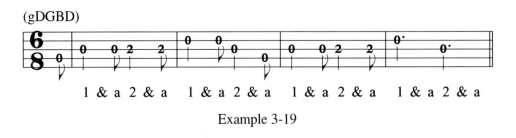

Example 3-19

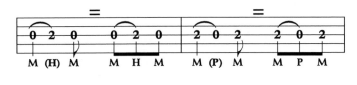

Example 3-20

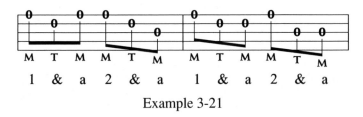

Example 3-21

Many three-note groupings in jigs can be obtained merely by adding hammer-ons and pull-offs to two-note groupings. The right hand then plays exactly the same thing as in a swing eighth pair, while the left hand provides a third note via some kind of slurring (that is, hammering-on or pulling-off). Example 3-20 shows two three-note groups created in this manner. In the first half of each measure, the quarter-eighth appearance is left intact and the H or P note is merely inserted between them; the second half of each measure shows how this maneuver would actually be written in 6/8 time tablature.

This leaves only a single modification of technique to master — namely a maneuver I often refer to as the Mary Tyler Moore stroke, or MTM (if you pick with your index finger, you

could think of it as the Indianapolis Technology Institute stroke, or ITI). In this technique, shown in Example 3-21, you merely add an additional down-stroke at the conclusion of a drop-thumb. Once again, the count is 1&a, 2&a, 1&a, 2&a, etc.

In general, right hand fingering for jigs is fairly obvious and doesn't need much special indicating. Here are the rules:

♦ Unless otherwise indicated, play all notes with M, *except* for the middle note of three note groupings, and 5th string notes.

♦ Unless otherwise indicated, use T to play the *middle* note of three note groupings as well as all 5th string notes.

Why bother playing jigs in clawhammer style, when using a plectrum might be easier? All I can say here is that frailed jigs have their own particular sound and esthetic. Moreover, there is a special satisfaction to be gained from exploring (or in this case re-exploring) frontiers. Just as food for thought, here are a few comparable arguments that could be made against a variety of musical and non-musical hobbies and pastimes: Why play pipe-tunes on the fiddle, when you can never recreate the ornamentation precisely? Why play ragtime on guitar, when it's so much easier on piano? Why improvise jazz leads on the stand-up bass when it's so much easier on saxophone, piano or guitar? Why bother having swimming competitions in the breast-stroke or butterfly when the crawl-stroke is so much faster?

Try your hand at a fairly simple and straightforward jig from the Canadian Maritimes, which on Prince Edward Island is called *John Dan MacPherson's Jig*. To get you started, I've indicated all the right hand fingering for the A part. See cols. 3.9-10 for two additional jig arrangements; still more 6/8 time tunes in this volume include *Chorus Jig, The Sailor's Wife* and *The Black Hoe.*

John Dan MacPherson's Jig

Banjo Arrangement: Ken Perlman

Tuning: gDGBD

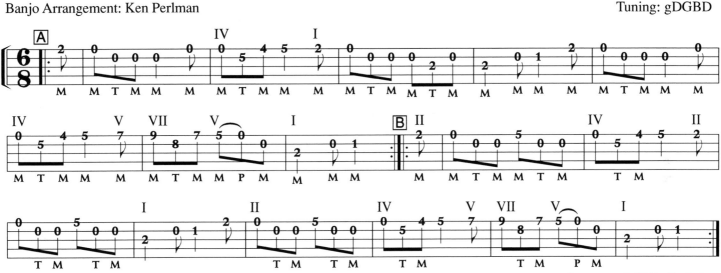

Arrangement © 1996 by Ken Perlman

3.9 Single Jigs
3.10 Happy-Go-Lucky Jigs from the Canadian Maritimes

(Mar. '87)
(June '92)

Strictly speaking, a jig is a jig. In other words, most Celtic based dance tunes in 6/8 time can be used to accompany most forms of traditional social dancing. Nevertheless, melodies that appear in jig time display a wide range of modes and moods, ranging from such well known "happy" tunes as *Haste to the Wedding and Smash the Windows* to such sorrowful tunes as *Banish Misfortune* and *The Sailor's Wife.* Happy or sad, jigs have been the subject of a number of attempts at categorization by various traditional music cultures.

Irish musicians recognize several kinds of jigs. 6/8 tunes made up primarily of three-note groupings — like *The Irish Washerwoman* or *John Dan MacPherson's Jig* — are known as *double jigs.* Those made up primarily of quarter-eighth combinations and dotted quarter notes — with maybe a few "three note groupings" thrown in for seasoning — are known as *single jigs* (review example 3-19 in cols. 3.7-8).

Single jigs are curious 6/8 time tunes that don't really sound very much like jigs. In fact, they don't much give the impression of being in 6/8 time either. I often find myself concentrating hard trying to figure out an unbelievably peculiar *double meter* tune (that is, one in 2/2, 2/4 or 4/4 time) when that sudden flash of inspiration hits: "Ah-ha! It's one of those (expletive deleted) single jigs!"

The reason that we Americans often find single jigs hard to recognize is our tendency to play straight eighth notes as swing eighth notes (review Examples 3-5 thru 3-7 in col. 3.2). Since we are already accustomed to hearing straight eighth note pairs transformed into quarter-eighth combinations, we can be easily confused when we encounter a tune made up of quarter-eighth combinations to begin with. So, if you're trying to figure out a relatively simple tune that seems to be in double meter but whose rhythm is driving you bonkers, try treating it as a single jig and see if that gets you anywhere.

Irish musicians also recognize two other categories of jig. One is known as a *slide*, and it's essentially a form of single jig with measures twice the normal length (there's an excerpt from a tune known as *O'Keefe's Slide* in Example 3-22; for the entire tab, see my *Homespun Tapes* audio instructional series).

Finally, Irish musicians recognize a kind of tune called a *slip jig* which, to confuse matters all out of hand, is in 9/8 time (Example 3-23 is excerpted from the slip jig *Rocky Road to Dublin;* for the complete tab see my book, *Basic Clawhammer Banjo)*. Many of you will probably be pleased to hear that slides and slip jigs are outside the scope of this book!

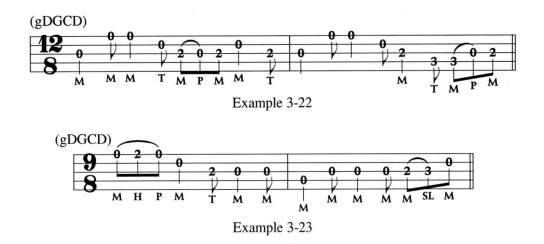

Example 3-22

Example 3-23

In the Canadian Maritime provinces (Nova Scotia, Prince Edward Island and New Brunswick), many fiddlers use the term *Irish jigs* to refer to double jigs. This reflects the common notion that jigs originated in Ireland, and that most commonly played jigs were developed in that country. As with most phenomena, the reality is a bit more complex. Although the form achieved its greatest expression and diversity in Ireland, even Irish authorities in the field of Irish traditional music such as Breandan Breathnach acknowledge that jig-like melodies originated in Britain. In fact, there are plenty of 6/8 time dance tunes with distinctly Scottish style melodies in 18th and 19th century Scottish tune books.

To hold in opposition to "Irish" jigs, Maritimes fiddlers also recognize a kind of tune known as the *Scotch jig*. Rhythmically, "Scotch" jigs tend to fall somewhere between single and double jigs, with notes about evenly distributed between quarter-eighth combinations and dotted pairs. Phrases in "Scotch" jigs are very well drawn but tend to be quirky. The melodies tend to be very un-Celtic, and in fact sound almost modern in character. By modern, I don't mean that they sound like contemporary pop music. Instead, they are reminiscent of early twentieth century music hall tunes, with sharply defined harmonies and frequent use of *accidentals* (that is, sharps and flats not in the key signature). Above all, these Scotch jigs are notable for their unalloyed high spirits — which is why I think of them as *happy-go-lucky jigs!*

In terms of origin, some Scotch jigs indeed derive from Scotland (appearing in the above mentioned Scottish tune books). Many others were locally composed in the Canadian Maritimes over the last few generations. I also strongly suspect that quite a number of these jigs are relics from the repertoire once used to accompany 19th century ballroom *quadrilles* (see column 9.20).

When putting together jig medleys for dance accompaniment or performance, fiddlers from the Canadian Maritimes usually mix Scotch and Irish jigs together for the sake of melodic and rhythmic contrast.

Christmas Day in the Morning

Banjo Arrangement: Ken Perlman

Tuning: gDGCD (capo–2)

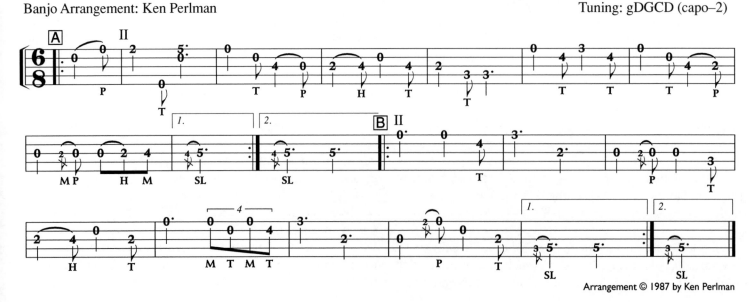

Arrangement © 1987 by Ken Perlman

Two tunes accompany this column. First is *Christmas Day In The Morning*, a single jig from Shetland. In Part B, measure 5, the four eighth notes are meant to be played in the space of a single 6/8 time beat. Remember that all notes are played with M unless otherwise indicated.

Next, "Tea Gardens Jig" is a "Scotch" jig composed by the great Cape Breton fiddler Angus Chisholm (it was apparently named for the Tea Gardens Chinese Restaurant in Sydney, Nova Scotia). Observe that I had to move the first two measures of part B up an octave in order to fit the section on banjo (see col. 2.19).

Tea Gardens Jig

Banjo Arrangement: Ken Perlman

Tuning: gDGBD

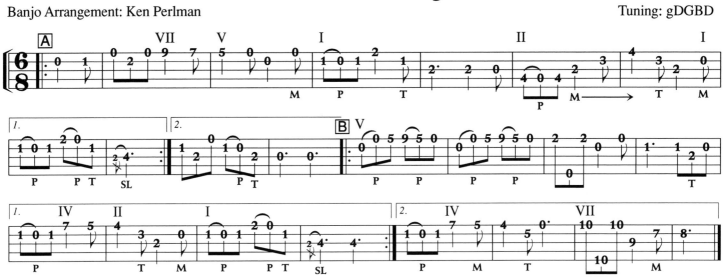

Arrangement © 1992 by Ken Perlman

3.11 Strathspeys

(Sept.'87)

Most dance tunes in the Anglo-Celtic tradition that are played nowadays can be categorized as jigs, reels, hornpipes, set tunes or waltzes. Scotland, however, boasts an additional kind of dance tune known as the strathspey (pronounced strath-SPAY).

I first encountered strathspeys in my early playing days while thumbing through the *1000 Fiddle Tunes*. The last few pages of the book contained dozens of strathspeys with titles ranging from the prosaic (*Lady Amy Stewart's Strathspey*) to the romantic (*The Maid of Isla*) to the ridiculous (*My Lady's Goon Has Gairs On't*). I remember trying in vain to play some of these tunes from the notation. After all, not only had I never heard a strathspey played, but I didn't even know what kind of recorded source to look for.

Over the years the picture filled in somewhat. First, I found out that strathspeys were Scottish tunes with an allegedly peculiar, somewhat irregular rhythm. Then, I heard many strange versions of strathspeys played by otherwise competent Irish and American musicians. These versions featured meters and rhythms that were so irregular that I was just about discouraged from further investigation.

Having finally heard many strathspeys played correctly by knowledgeable Scottish and Cape Breton musicians, I can at last reveal the nature of this mysterious tune category to the banjo players of the world.

To begin with, there are two common strathspey formats. Many strathspeys are made up of two non-repeated eight-measure sections. Others have a format of one repeated four-measure section, followed by a non-repeated eight measure section.

In terms of tempo and number of eighth-notes per measure (that is, eight), strathspeys resemble British- or Irish-style hornpipes (see column 3.2). One major difference is that while hornpipes are played in 2/2 or cut time (eighth notes organized as *two* groups of *four*), strathspeys are played in a true 4/4 time (eighth notes organized as *four* groups of *two*).

A good tempo for British/Irish style hornpipes is a metronome setting of about ♩ = 69 (half of each measure is played per click). A good speed for strathspeys a metronome setting of about ♩ = 132 (only *one fourth* of each measure is played per click).

Most strathspey eighth notes are written in the form of dotted pairs. A dotted pair is written as a dotted eighth-note plus a sixteenth-note, implying that the first note is three times as long as the second. In Scotland, dotted pairs are usually played pretty much as they are written. In Cape Breton, Prince Edward Island and other parts of Atlantic Canada where the tunes are still played in folk tradition, these notes are played so that the first note of a dotted pair is only *twice* as long as the second, becoming in effect a triplet with the first two notes tied, or a swing-eighth pair (review Examples 3-5 thru 3-7 in col. 3.2).

85

In terms of phrasing, each dotted pair in a strathspey is usually played so that the second note (that is, the note written as a sixteenth note) *leads on* to the first note of the *next* dotted pair (or whatever other kind of note occupies the *following* beat: see Example 3-24.) If you play your dotted pairs with the sixteenth note connected to the *preceding* dotted eighth (as is customary in hornpipe playing), the tune loses its character.

Example 3-24 shows how this "phrasing" behaves for both the Scottish and Cape Breton styles of strathspey playing. In 3-24a (Scottish style: notes as written), each sixteenth note leads on to the next dotted eighth. In 3-24b (Cape Breton style: notes shown as "quarter-eighth" pairs under triplet brackets), each eighth note leads on to the next quarter.

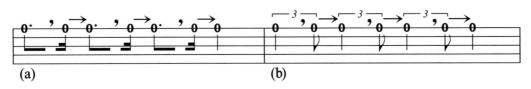

(a)   (b)

Example 3-24

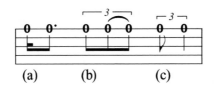

(a)   (b)   (c)

Example 3-25

Strathspeys often contain several different kinds of notes besides dotted pairs — most notably quarter notes, eighth-note triplets, sixteenth-note groups (see column 2.22) and a kind of note pair known as the *Scotch snap*.

Scotch snaps are essentially reverse dotted pairs. In other words, they are written as a sixteenth-note plus a dotted eighth-note (Example 3-25a). Again, in Scotland the pair is played more or less as written, but in North American traditions the second note of the Scotch Snap is only twice as long as the first

note. This yields a triplet with the last two notes tied (Example 3-25b), or — more "elegantly" — an eighth-quarter combination under a triplet bracket (Example 3-25c).

One way of elaborating a strathspey is by changing one or more dotted pairs to Scotch snaps.

Historically, strathspeys originated in the Strath Spey region of northeastern Scotland (that is, the Spey River Valley), in the mid-to-late 18th century. They were originally known as *strathspey reels* (reels played in the strathspey style), and are essentially slowed down, rhythmically elaborated adaptations of the reel form.

The Laird o' Drumblair

Banjo Arrangement: Ken Perlman   Tuning: gDGBD (capo–2)

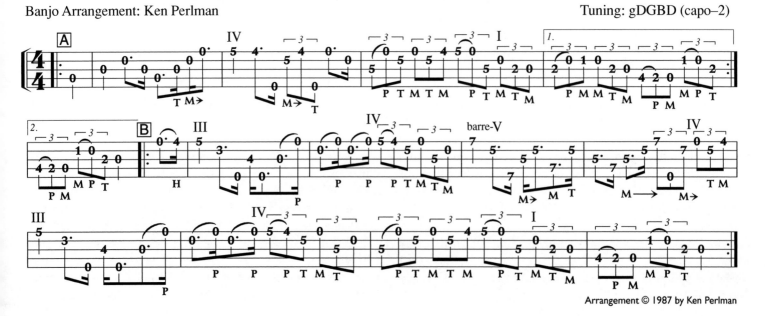

Arrangement © 1987 by Ken Perlman

One further note: most strathspeys do not in fact have an irregular meter and the four beats of each measure should progress with the same authority as the beats of any other Celtic dance-tune. Because there are often so many different kinds of notes intermingled, however, a musician who is unfamiliar with the form can easily make a given tune sound erratic by not being sufficiently careful and precise.

This being said, you should be aware that there are indeed some occasions when strathspeys are played in *rubato* (loose-rhythmed) style. First, there is a Scottish genre known as the *slow strathspey*, which is played in a manner approaching that of a fiddle slow air. Plus, there is a Scottish fiddling competition circuit in which strict rhythmic treatment of strathspeys is frowned upon.

You'll find Scotch snaps in the accompanying strathspey, *The Laird o' Drumblair* by famed fiddler James Scott Skinner (see Part A, meas. 1 and 3 and in Part B, meas. 1, 3 and 5). Given all the different ways in which triplets are obtained in this arrangement (MTM, MPT, MPM, MAT...), you'll probably want to review col. 2.8 before going ahead. There's one other strathspey in this book, *The Marquis of Huntley*.

3.12 Pipe Marches
3.13 Marches

(Dec. '87)
(June '93)

There's no mystery about how marches originated. They are musical pieces designed to make the members of an army keep pace with one another. In modern times, marches are pretty much confined to parade situations. In the not so distant past, however, they were actually used to set the pace by which troops approached or retreated from the scene of battle.

For the last century, American marches have been rather complex, almost orchestral affairs whose construction resembles that of late 19th century ragtime and light classical music. In fact, when most Americans think of marches, we think of John Philip Sousa's *Stars and Stripes Forever,* and his *Washington Post March.* Or perhaps we think of the various service-branch theme songs, like *The Marines' Hymn* and *Anchors Aweigh.* And we mustn't forget our various college fight songs in this regard. (Actually, I've been trying to forget my college fight song for some time!) But I digress.

Just as Sousa's music reflected the popular music of his own time (he was more or less a contemporary of famed ragtime composer Scott Joplin), the marches of earlier eras also echoed folk- and popular musical ideas. Another way of putting this is that many pre-Sousa marches pretty much resembled fiddle tunes or folk songs in terms of construction and melodic content. Haven't we seen heroic colonial troupes marching home from battle in countless films and cartoons to the strains on fife of *The Girl I left Behind*; or Civil War troops marching (somewhat anachronistically) to *Marching through Georgia* or *Jubilo*?

Of course, of considerable interesting to banjo players is the fact that the US Army fife and drum core was dominated throughout the middle third of the 19th century by a banjoist named Dan Emmett, who also put together the official Army music manual (see col. 9.19). Emmett, by the way, wrote *Old Dan Tucker* and — another tune later pressed into service as a march — *Dixie*.

In Britain, certain elements of the armed forces have employed bagpipers and bagpipe bands to supply march music for many years. The *pipe marches* they play come directly out of the Scottish musical tradition. As such, these marches are generally characterized by the same kinds of phrases, musical turns and approach to ornamentation as those found in Scottish dance tunes.

Scottish pipe marches have (as one would suspect) the same nine note range as the bagpipes. Starting at G above middle C, the pipes run more or less up the notes of the A-mixolydian scale, so that the entire pipes scale is G-(A-B-C♯-D-E-F♯-G-A). I say "more or less," because the C♯ is usually much flatter than what is found on a piano or orchestral instrument, while the D and G are generally somewhat sharper.

There are several kinds of march tunes composed for Scottish Highland Pipes, but probably the best known is the cut-time (2/2) march. Cut-time marches have four repeated eight-measure parts. The third part (A') is always a variation of the first part (A), while the fourth part (B') is always a variation of the second part (B). Usually the B' part has a lengthy "second ending" that opens with a musical "idea" not previously encountered in the piece. Generally, all four parts have the same two-measure *cadential* (ending) phrase.

Cut-time pipe marches resemble both hornpipes and strathspeys. Like hornpipes, there are usually eight eighth-notes per measure played as two groups of four with an accent on the first note of each group. Like hornpipes and strathspeys, most of these eighth-notes are played as dotted pairs (review Examples 3-5 thru 3-7 in col. 3.2). Like strathspeys, a certain number of dotted pairs are reversed, yielding Scotch snaps (review Example 3-25 in col. 3.11).

In Scotland, dotted pairs in pipe marches are usually played pretty much as they are written (with the dotted eighth note being three times longer than the following sixteenth note). In Cape Breton, Prince Edward Island and other parts of Atlantic Canada, the first note of the dotted pair is only *twice* as long as the second, becoming in effect a triplet with the first two notes tied, or a *swing-eighth* pair (review Example 3-7).

87

Don MacLean's Farewell to Oban

Banjo Arrangement: Ken Perlman

Tuning: gDGBD (capo–2)

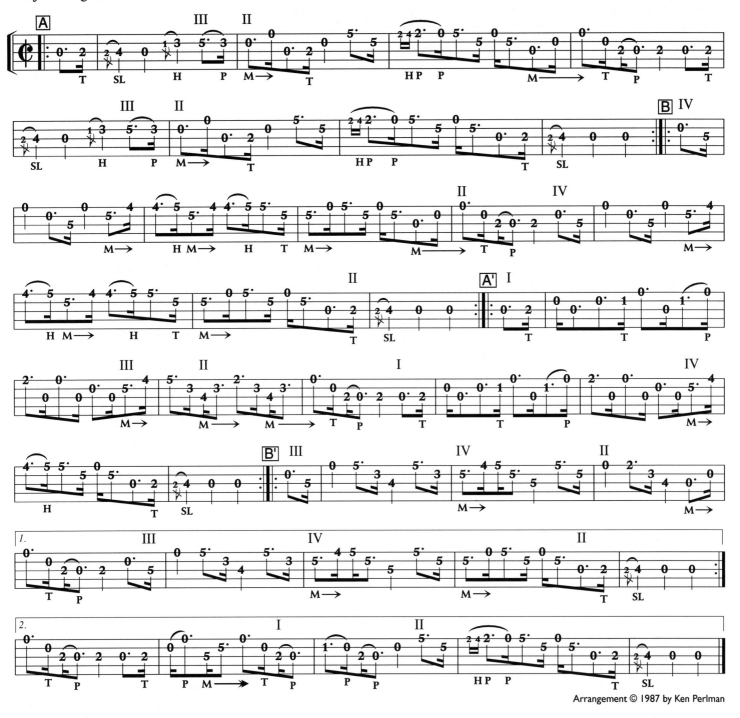

Arrangement © 1987 by Ken Perlman

Like strathspeys, dotted pairs in pipe marches are usually played so that the second note (that is, the note written as a sixteenth note) *leads on* to the first note of the *next* dotted pair (or whatever other kind of note occupies the *following* beat (review Example 3-24 in col. 3.11). If you play your dotted pairs with the sixteenth note connected to the *preceding* dotted eighth (as is customary in hornpipe playing), the tune loses its character.

Cut-time pipe marches are generally played at a speed that is somewhat faster than the tempo for hornpipes and strathspeys, but which is slower than the tempo for reels (c. ♩ = 92). They are played with a kind of overall loping pace: not surprisingly you'll get the right idea by imagining soldiers marching to it!

Beginning not long after their origin in the mid-to-late 19th century, many Scottish cut-time pipe marches made the trip across the Atlantic and began to circulate among fiddlers in the Canadian provinces of Nova Scotia and Prince Edward Island. Since there was little need for marches per se in this region, most of them got *converted* to reels (see col. 3.14). And indeed they make very good reels! (One example in this book of a march-converted-to-reel is *Pipe Major Christie of Wick*).

It took a post World War II Scottish-music "revival" movement — first in Cape Breton and later on Prince Edward Island — to renew interest there in playing pipe-marches in their original styles. And indeed there is now a new tradition of march composing in both provinces that has produced some really lovely tunes.

Accompanying this column is a cut-time pipe march called *Don MacLean's Farewell to Oban*, which I learned during a trip to Scotland in 1987. There's one other pipe-march in this volume, entitled *George V's Army*.

3.14 Tune Conversions

I've often told the following story concerning my visit in 1988 with two Scottish fiddlers: Angus Grant and Charlie MacFarlane of the Fort William, Scotland area. They had played several Scottish tunes for me, then informed me it was high time I reciprocated by playing an American one. For no special reason, I happened to pick the western Virginia tune

Green Willis. I played through the tune a few times, after which they exchanged glances and said, "We have a tune just like that one," and played it. The tune they played (which I later found out was called *The New-Rigged Ship),* was clearly the same tune, except for one important factor: it was a *jig.*

gCGCD (capo-2)

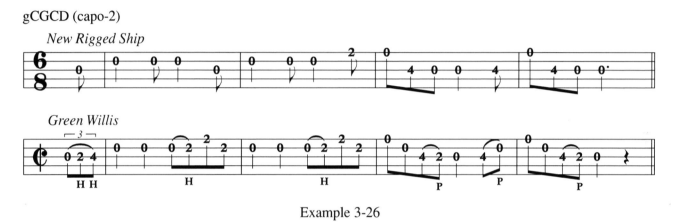

Example 3-26

gDGBD

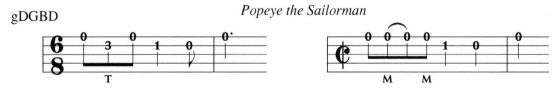

Example 3-27

What had clearly happened in western Virginia, then, was that this old Scottish tune — which dates according to *The Scottish Fiddle Music Index* to at least the late 18th century — had been transformed by traditional fiddlers from 6/8-time to cut-time (2/2). This immediately explains why *Green Willis* has such peculiar phrasing: when a melody is converted to a different *meter*, certain phrases fit neatly while others have to be squeezed or elongated. For example, when jigs (which have a maximum of six eighth notes to the bar) are converted into reels (which have a maximum of eight), there is a tendency towards elongation (Example 3-26 shows the first couple of bars for both tunes and illustrates how this elongation process operates). Another common example of elongation is the theme music for the animated cartoon *Popeye the Sailorman*. In early versions of the cartoon, the tune is a classic 6/8 time jig; in later versions, the jig phrases were stretched out to fit a 2/2 format (see example 3-27).

When the similarity between *The New Rigged Ship* and *Green Willis* became apparent, this naturally brought up the whole subject of converting melodies among tune-genres. According to both men, Scottish music was absolutely loaded with such *conversions*. In fact, Grant took a single melody called *Caber Feidh* (pronounced CAH-ber Fay, meaning "The Deer's Antlers"), and played it for me as a jig, reel, hornpipe, march and strathspey.

In traditional communities, one major reason for converting melodies in this way is that new tunes were often in short supply. Without recorded or broadcast music, and without the ability to read music, it simply wasn't that easy to come up with new material. So if you had a good tune committed to memory, changing its genre or metric format in essence gave you a brand new tune to play.

Another factor involved here is that from time to time an entire tune-genre will essentially die out in a given region, to be replaced by other genres. In the Canadian Maritime provinces (Prince Edward Island and Nova Scotia) for example, marches and hornpipes largely fell out of favor in the late 19th century. In the American south, jigs seem to have dropped from the repertoire at some point prior to the recording era. When a genre dies out in this way, musicians are left with a stock of melodies they can no longer use. Since new melodies are scarce, there is tremendous incentive to take melodies from the out-of-favor genres and convert them into genres that are still in frequent use. Consequently, fiddlers in the Canadian Maritimes converted many marches and hornpipes to reels, while Southern players converted quite a number of jigs to reels.

This discussion leads me to the night a few years ago when I was doing a gig for a folk club in Jackson, Mississippi.

Someone in the audience challenged me to do a tune that was a little bit Irish and a little bit bluegrass, and as I noodled around stalling for time it suddenly dawned on me that the quintessential Earl Scruggs bluegrass tune *Foggy Mountain Breakdown* could easily be squeezed into jig format. Not only this, but I later realized that in some ways the melody actually made more sense in 6/8 time than in its usual meter. So without further ado, I'll share *Earl's Jig* with you, which is guaranteed to get a raised eyebrow, if not a laugh from most audiences.

Observe that the symbol "ch" in the B-part denotes a *choke*, which means that a stopped sounding string is pushed along the surface of the fingerboard sufficiently to raise its pitch somewhat. Note also that a clawhammer version of this tune with its usual "metric" treatment appears in chapter 4.

Earl's Jig

Banjo Arrangement: Ken Perlman

Tuning: gDGBD

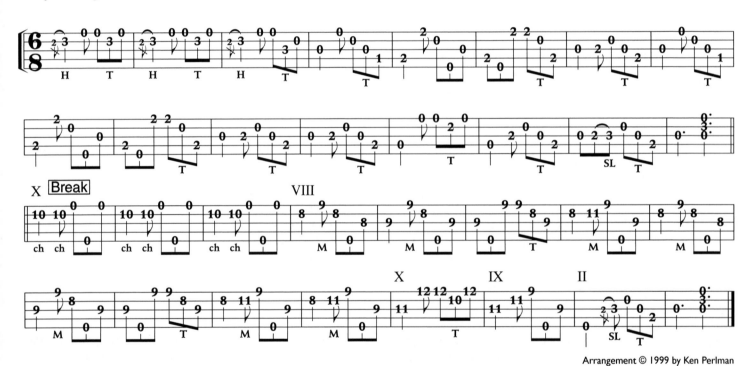

Arrangement © 1999 by Ken Perlman

3.15 The Importance of Phrasing

(Oct '90)

One of the factors that make fiddle tunes exciting to listen to is the intricate phrasing applied to them by master fiddlers. In fact, one compliment that could be paid to such a musician would be, "Gee, you could even make a C-scale sound interesting!"

To give you an idea about what is meant by phrasing, imagine picking up a fiddle tune collection and randomly choosing tunes to sight read. If you're like me, you'll play through ninety percent of them and say to yourself (while shrugging your shoulders, of course), "What's all the fuss

about? This doesn't sound like anything much at all!"). Written tunes will often, in fact, sound like just a collection of notes randomly assembled to fill space. Yet you know that at some time these tunes were part of a thriving tradition. And quite often when you hear the tunes played by a member of that tradition they sound just terrific.

It's true that sometimes book-versions of tunes are inaccurate. It's also true that quite often the "folk process" alters an original written version of a tune for the better. What most often makes a performed tune version come alive when a written

90

version falls flat, however, is that the former is usually well-*phrased* (or "shaped") by the player.

By shaping or phrasing I'm referring to the tunes within the tune, or less prosaically, to the small bits of melody that hang together within the melody as a whole. Another way of thinking of it is that phrases are small bits of melody (called *motives* by musicologists) that lie between breaks or breaths in the stream of notes that make up a tune.

Part of the process of learning a tune well involves sensing where the phrases lie and (perhaps) eventually coming up with new phrasing concepts that are uniquely your own. Quite often, I'll be listening to a master fiddler play a tune with which I've long been familiar and hear a new phrase or even a "phrase within a phrase" that I've never heard before. What's more, adding this new phrasing concept to my own rendition never fails to rekindle my interest in the tune in question.

One recent example is the tune *President Garfield's Hornpipe*, which I had known for years but never much liked. When I heard the exquisite phrasing used by Cape Breton fiddler Winston Fitzgerald, however, I instantly fell in love with the tune and spent several months perfecting it for clawhammer performance (it took four different fingering concepts before I came up with one that really worked).

Because the tune breaks or pauses ever so slightly at phrase divisions, a knowledge of where these breaks lie necessarily influences the method by which you obtain notes in your clawhammer arrangement. For example, in the B part of *President Garfield's* (see below) I was able to set the tune so that all the "upbeat" notes for many of the major phrases fell on the fifth string. Observe that the tune is arranged in its original key of B♭ (see cols. 5.6-8).

President Garfield's Hornpipe

Banjo Arrangement: Ken Perlman

Tuning: gDGCD

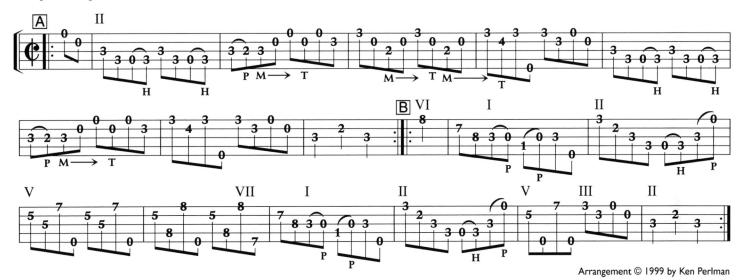

Arrangement © 1999 by Ken Perlman

3.16 The Construction of Fiddle Tunes

(June '91)

Each fiddle tune is made up of several melodic building blocks or *motives*. There is always an opening motive (which is usually relatively memorable), an answering motive (which balances off the opener) and a closing or *cadential* motive. There may also be *connecting* motives that stitch the tune together, and *secondary* motives, which serve as additional memorable musical bits within the tune.

Some of these various motives tend to move around from tune to tune. For example this month's tune *The Quindaro Hornpipe* (below), has an opening motive identical to that of the famous *Sailor's Hornpipe* (also known as *The College Hornpipe*). Connecting and cadential motives are particularly well-traveled, and the same ones might appear in countless tunes. Two extremely popular cadential motives appear in Examples 3-28a and b.

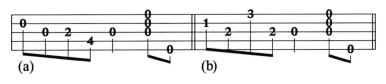

Example 3-28

91

If we dissect Quindaro, we get the following structure:

Part A

meas.
1-2. opening motive.
3-4. answering motive.
5-6. repeat of opening motive.
7-8. closing motive.

Part B

meas.
1. new opening motive.
2. repeat of preceding, at one scale step level higher.
3-4. repeat of answering motive of part A, which also serves as "answer" for part B opening.
5-6. secondary motive introduces new "memorable" musical idea.
7-8. closing motive, which ends identically to that of Part A.

For fun, why not look at a few tunes you know and take them apart in this manner? You can learn a lot about how the tunes behave, and about melodies in general. Having a clear idea of how a tune's motives inter-relate can clue you in to how to best perform it.

Quindaro Hornpipe

Banjo Arrangement: Ken Perlman

Tuning: gDGBD

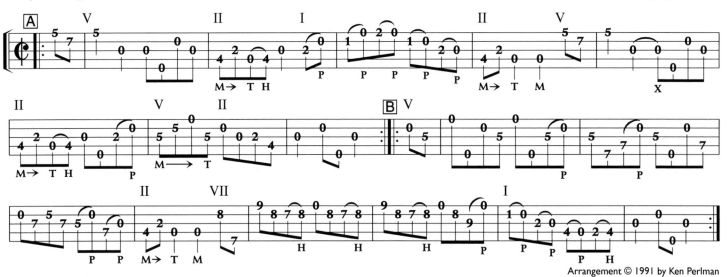

Arrangement © 1991 by Ken Perlman

Ken performing at Fox Valley Festival near Chicago with guitarist Ken Brown, Sept. '97
(Photo by Susanne Even)

CHAPTER 4: PLAYING ALL KINDS OF MUSIC

4.1 Composed for Clawhammer Tunes

(Sept. '84)

There have been dozens of tunes composed for bluegrass banjo over the last few decades, but there have been relatively few memorable tunes composed specifically for clawhammer since the close of the minstrel show era in the 1870s (one well-known composed-for-clawhammer piece from the traditional repertoire is *Last Chance*: see chapter 5). Most clawhammer pickers — whether their orientation is melodic or "traditional" — play a repertoire consisting primarily of fiddle tunes (that is, tunes composed for fiddle) and song accompaniments. Those who venture farther afield tend to play adaptations of tunes originally composed for such instruments as guitar, piano, Celtic harp, tin whistle, bagpipes, and so on.

When a piece of music is composed for a given instrument, the composer usually takes into account the strengths and weaknesses of that instrument. He or she tends to accentuate turns of phrase that are particularly resonant and easy to play, and to avoid those that are weak sounding or excruciatingly hard to play. When music composed for one instrument is adapted to another instrument, however, the strengths and weaknesses of the new instrument are very likely to conflict with those of the original instrument. In fact, passages that were virtually effortless on the original instrument may be extremely awkward on the new instrument. For example, nothing is more natural on a harp than running a single point of contact up and down a couple of dozen strings, thereby creating a run of about two dozen exquisitely resonant tones. Playing this exact sequence of notes at the same speed on, say a cello, is only within the realm of a virtuoso, and wouldn't sound nearly as beautiful.

Similarly, the basic versions of most fiddle tunes are not particularly challenging to play on the fiddle. All the notes usually fit into the first fingering position, and the required bowing is not especially advanced technically. On banjo however, the same series of notes might require a couple of dozen intricate and ingeniously planned maneuvers and several changes of fingering position.

Road to Mexico

By Ken Perlman

Tuning: gDGCD (capo–2 optional)

© 1984 by Ken Perlman

I for one would like to see more original clawhammer tunes composed by today's melodic and "traditional" pickers. Whether these tunes remain close to familiar fiddle tune format or stray far afield, they should above all be both banjoistic and "clawhammeristic." In other words, composers should stress maneuvers and turns of phrase that are strong and resonant on the banjo when it is played in clawhammer style. If we get a sufficient number of players involved in this we may see the evolution of a new form of music as dramatic and interesting as the bluegrass-banjo "breakdown."

To get the ball rolling, I'm offering an original tune of my own called *Road to Mexico* (I've recorded this as a solo piece on *Live in the UK*, and with a bluegrass-like ensemble on *Northern Banjo*). Part A is 16 measures long and explores many of the possibilities offered by alternate-string pull-offs in mountain minor tuning (g DGCD). Part B is eight measures long, and is based on two melodic fingering forms: meas. 1, 2, 3, 5 and 6 use form #2, while meas. 7 uses form #1 (see Example 2-73 in col. 2-23).

4.2 Dueling Bagpipes

Much musical innovation results from attempts by players of one instrument to imitate the sound of another instrument. Alternating-bass fingerstyle guitar picking, for example, originated from efforts to mimic the sound of ragtime piano. Similarly, cross-picking on the mandolin and guitar was developed by musicians eager to capture the rhythms easily available to bluegrass banjo players. Closer to home, much of the challenge of playing fiddle tunes in clawhammer style involves finding a way to play up-to-speed melodies and phrasings that are quite simple for fiddlers, but alas not for us.

One of the longest running relationships of this kind involves Highland bagpipes and Scottish fiddle, which have been sharing repertoire and ideas about ornamentation since the mid-18th century. Here are some features of bagpipes music that were adapted to Scottish fiddling, and through that to Irish and North American fiddling:

♦ *Repertoire*. Many piping tunes — such as pipe marches (see cols. 3.12-13) — were adapted to the fiddle outright.

♦ *Scale*. Pitches of the various notes on bagpipes are not identical in cycles per second to those found, e.g., on the piano or fretted banjo. Instead, in general some bagpipe pitches are somewhat flat or sharp relative to piano or banjo pitches (specifically the third and seventh notes of the scale are generally a bit flat, and the fourth note of the scale tends to be a bit sharp). Many Scottish fiddlers adopted these bagpipe pitches when noting, rather than conventional pitches.

♦ *Phrasing and Ornamentation*. Basically, the air running through the chanter is a steady stream. The only way that two successive notes on the same pitch can be played is to briefly break that stream by tapping an open hole or briefly releasing a stopped hole. The resulting short notes — which in essence are grace notes — may have started out as necessary evils, but they soon became regarded as ornaments that were desirable for their own sake. Similarly, pipers phrase their tunes by strategically stopping or directing the steady stream of notes through various noting and ornamentation patterns. When fiddlers began to play pipe-music, they also began devising ways to imitate both the sound of piping ornaments, and the highly distinctive sound of bagpipes phrasing.

♦ *Drones*. One obvious characteristic aspect of Highland piping is the use of *drones* (continuously sounding notes). Fiddlers imitating this feature adopted the practices of bowing double strings and using *double stops* (that is, two simultaneously fingered strings) in their playing.

Over the years, Highland bagpipers have also incorporated elements of the fiddle repertoire and approach. For example, many jigs, reels and other popular fiddle tunes have become part of the piping repertoire. In addition, elements of fiddle phrasing and ornamentation crept into piping technique.

Pipers have also borrowed ideas from other instruments. Of particular interest in this regard is the popular piping tune *Banjo Breakdown*, which offers us a piper's-eye-view of the banjo sound. Since the tune doesn't fall very naturally on 5-string, my guess is that the particular kind of banjo breaking down here was of the tenor (4-string) persuasion.

Observe that notes marked with a (v) symbol are to be played as upstrokes (see column 2.25). The tune is a *6/8 march*, and it will also help for you to review the concepts and techniques involved for playing in jig-time (cols. 3.7-10).

Banjo Breakdown

Banjo Arrangement: Ken Perlman

Tuning: gDGBD (capo–2)

Arrangement © 1988 by Ken Perlman

4.3 East Kentucky Fiddle Tunes

(Jan. '89)

The Southern old-time revival scene has been dominated for over two decades by players who emulate a very specific fiddling-banjo picking style from the Galax/Mt. Airy region on the Virginia-North Carolina border. This style — as represented by such well-known players as Tommy Jarrell and Fred Cockerham — features a highly exaggerated back beat, "swing" treatment of eighth notes akin to that found in bluegrass and jazz (review Examples 3-5 thru 3-7 in col. 3.2), and the overall primacy of rhythmic drive over melody. In fact, most Galax/Mt.

Airy melodies seem to be quite simple but their rhythmic interpretation is complex.

In recent years it has become increasingly clear that the Galax genre is far from the whole story of Southern old-time music. Moreover, it seems that most of the fiddling styles that grew up south of the Mason Dixon line before the dawn of recording share at least as much with Celtic fiddling as they do with Galax fiddling.

95

To begin with, not much of the fiddling heard on "hillbilly" recordings of the 1920s and 1930s (which represent a cross section of Southern fiddle genres of the period) particularly resembles the contemporary Galax sound. There's only a hint of swing-eighths and back-beat in these early recordings, and melody comes across at least as important as rhythm. Moreover, many regional British Isles fiddling styles, and Scots-Canadian styles (such as those of Cape Breton and Prince Edward Islands: see cols. 4.8-18) feature bowing accents which resemble the mild back-beat treatment of pre-Galax Southern fiddling.

Given that these ideas were running through my mind, it was particularly interesting to run into fiddler Bruce Green. Bruce is a Northeasterner who spent several years living among and learning tunes from traditional fiddlers in eastern Kentucky. The tunes Bruce picked up from these East Kentuckians seem to combine the tunefulness of Celtic tunes and the rhythmic drive of Galax tunes. Moreover, the East Kentucky playing style features many stylistic devices that are typical of British Isles fiddling. The difference is that some devices that are quite 4.4

prominent in, say, Scottish fiddling are extremely subtle in East Kentucky fiddling. For example, the double grace note which is a common ornament in Scottish music is made by distinct left-hand finger movements (see column 2.24). In east Kentucky fiddling, the player creates a similar — but less obvious sound — by briefly relaxing and reestablishing pressure on a stopped sounding string (interestingly, I have seen many fiddlers on Prince Edward Island use exactly the same technique). Similarly, as a syncopation device East Kentucky fiddlers play a subtle version of the Scotch snap (see column 3.11), which they accomplish by literally hammering-on to a sounding string.

Accompanying this column is *Ladies On A Steamboat*, one of the tunes Bruce Green picked up in East Kentucky. Bruce feels that it is closely related to *Sandy River Belle*, a connection which is perhaps most apparent in the B Part. Observe that measures 2 and 3 of the B Part are played from the fingering position shown in Example 4-1. For tabs of a couple of dozen other Kentucky tunes, see Mac Benford's excellent collection, *Kentucky Favorites*.

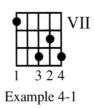

Example 4-1

Ladies on a Steamboat

Banjo Arrangement: Ken Perlman

Tuning: gDGBD

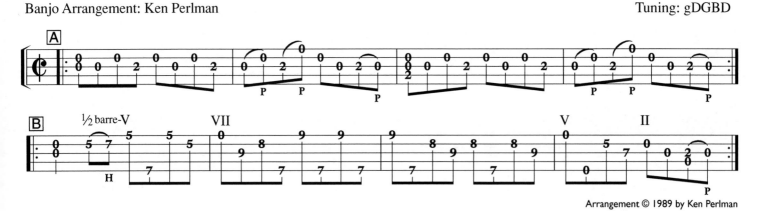

Arrangement © 1989 by Ken Perlman

Scruggs Picking, Clawhammer Style   (May '84)

This column is for all those clawhammer pickers who find themselves playing in a bar somewhere and get a request for *Duelin' Banjos* or *Foggy Mountain Breakdown*. Explaining that the requested tunes are representative of an entirely different style of banjo playing does about as much good as trying to get

rid of a charity-telemarketer by saying you gave at the office. Either the requester feels hurt and tries to stare you down with a sullen glare, or he goes on the offensive and impugns your competence with comments like, "Yeah, I know, that tune really is hard, isn't it?"

The one technique typical of bluegrass that is not easily performed in conventional clawhammer is the forward roll, shown in Example 4-2. Here the thumb (T) plucks one long string, the index finger (I) plucks the next higher string and the middle finger (M) plucks another still higher string. Finally, T plucks the fifth string and so on. This sequence can be reproduced in conventional clawhammer only by relatively awkward techniques like off-string pull-offs, shown in Example 4-3 (note that the off-string P's work just fine when all strings are open, and much less well when fretted strings are involved).

In col. 2.18, I discussed a technique called *clawhammer cross-picking*, which is a blend of ordinary drop-thumbing with one or more arpeggio (roll-like) strokes. Clawhammer cross-picking yields a similar sound to plectrum-based cross-picking styles on guitar and mandolin. Not only is this technique useful for playing nifty ragtime licks, but it also allows you to play the elusive forward roll with style and grace. Before proceeding, I recommend highly that you review col. 2.9 on arpeggios, and also take some time to go over the arpeggio exercises labeled B 1- 4 (col. 2.10). Then try the following routine: fret a conventional F-chord in G-tuning (shown in Example 2-47a in col. 2.16) and go through the specific right-hand patterns shown in Example 4-4 and 4-5. Then raise the F chord up to the second fret and repeat the patterns; raise the F chord up to the third fret and repeat the patterns again, and so on up the neck.

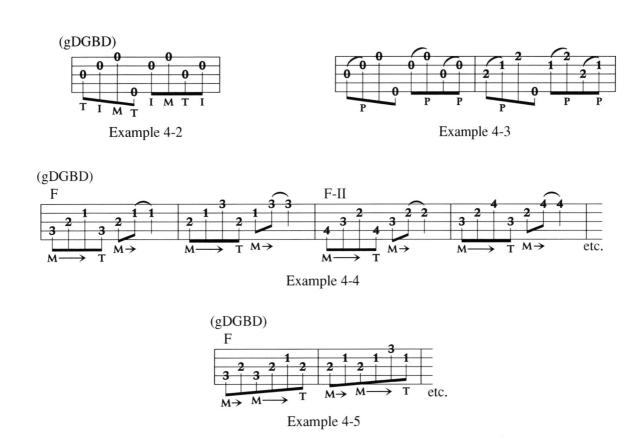

Example 4-2

Example 4-3

Example 4-4

Example 4-5

Once you can play these exercises quickly and fluidly, try *Foggy Clawhammer*. This arrangement combines forward rolls, Scruggsian licks and clawhammer approximations in such a way that it sounds pretty close to bluegrass-picking to the untutored ear. Performing it will appease the original requester, get the audience on your side, and impress any knowledgeable banjo fans in attendance with your versatility.

Here are some interesting features of the arrangement:

♦ *Grace hammer-ons.* This technique appears in measures 1, 2, 3 and 14. Start hammering on as soon as you pluck fret 2, string 2.

♦ *Delayed arpeggios.* Here, the forward progress of an arpeggio is interrupted by an intervening hammer, pull-off or slide. To get the right sound, pluck one string (say string 2) and rest heavily on the next higher string (string 1), keeping M firmly in contact with that string while the fretting hand performs an H, P, or SL on the lower string (string 2). Then continue your arpeggio.

♦ There are quite a number of "skips" here, indicated by an "X" in the tablature (see measures 13, 14, 16). You might want to review columns 1.12-13, which cover skips and syncopation.

In the break, note that all the string 2, fret 10 notes in measures 1, 2 and 3 are *choked* (symbol: ch). To perform a *choke*, push a stopped-sounding string *away* from your palm along the surface of the fingerboard in such a way that the pitch perceptibly rises (for string 4, you'll probably have to pull the string in towards the palm, since it can easily be pushed right off the fingerboard!).

Foggy Clawhammer

Banjo Arrangement: Ken Perlman

Tuning: gDGBD

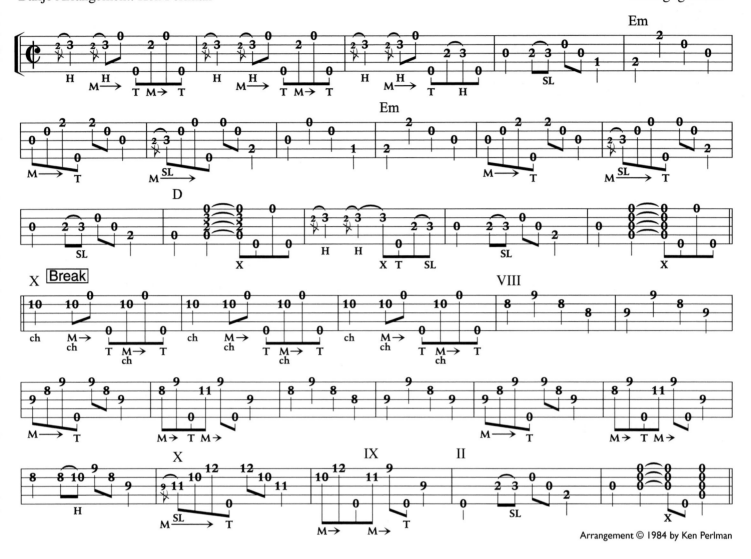

Arrangement © 1984 by Ken Perlman

4.5 Shetland Tunes
4.6 The New Idiom of Scottish and Shetland Fiddle Tunes

(Sept. '88)
(June '89)

The Shetland Islands lie some one hundred miles north-northeast of Scotland, and are accessible either by air or via a 10-hour ferry ride from Aberdeen. They were under the control of various Scandinavian countries until the 17th Century, and their approach to fiddling is still closely related to the hardanger (HAR-dan-gher) style of Norwegian fiddling.

Hardanger fiddles, which can be as ornately inlaid as any tree-of-life-design S.S. Stewart 5-string, have in addition to the customary four fiddle strings a complement of several sympathetic strings. These sympathetic strings run through the center of the fiddle bridge and sound when the ordinary strings are bowed. Much hardanger playing involves bowing the open adjacent string along with the melody string. Since the sympathetic strings sound along with the melody string and its open neighbor on every bow-stroke, the style is often referred to as *ringing strings*.

Contemporary Shetlanders play ordinary fiddles, but have retained many features of the ringing strings style — most notably the tendency to bow the open neighbor along with the melody string. In this regard at least, the result is a sound that is not unlike Appalachian fiddling.

Among today's best known Shetland fiddlers are Willie Hunter, Aly Bain (who plays with the Boys of the Lough) and noted collector/composer/teacher Tom Anderson. Mr. Anderson has published several Shetland fiddle-tune collections, such as *Da Mirrie Dancers, Ringing Strings* and *G' Us an A*.

I had a chance to speak with Mr. Anderson this past July when I spent a week observing at the Heritage of Scotland Fiddle Program, held at Stirling University near Edinburgh.[1] He indicated that, in addition to the hardanger influence, Shetland fiddling also features a strong Scottish component. This Scottish influence seems to divide into two eras. Before about 1900,

---

[1] Mr. Anderson passed away a few years after this column was written.

Scottish tunes and fiddling techniques were slowly and unconsciously assimilated into the Shetland repertoire. After 1900, the advent of radio and sound recording, along with the great popularity of Scottish fiddle-great James Scott Skinner, created great enthusiasm in Shetland for Scottish tunes and the Scottish sound.

Of course, Shetlanders absorbed Scottish tunes according to their own lights. According to Mr. Anderson, they never cottoned to the relatively slow pace of Scottish strathspeys and cranked the speed up on their victrolas to hear the tunes played more rapidly (strathspeys are discussed in col. 3.11). Consequently, strathspeys are now played much quicker in Shetland than in Scotland!

Another important musical influence was that of mid-19th Century Norwegian whaler men, who played a syncopated style of music similar to what we would recognize as the "old timey" sound. In fact, Mr. Anderson believes that these whaler men were in fact exposed to and influenced by American music.

Any description of Shetland fiddle music would be incomplete without also mentioning the new tunes, written during the last half-century by numerous composers. As was also the case in Scotland after 1930, many of these newly composed tunes were quite different from the older tunes in the repertoire. One major reason for this was the new-found dominance of the piano accordion in the dance music ensemble. Whereas the fiddle is primarily a melody instrument, the piano accordion is a harmonic instrument. Not only does the left hand have all those neat rows of chord buttons available, but the right hand has a row of easily accessible little black keys. Consequently, tunes written by accordion players or for accordion ensembles tend to be based upon chord progressions, and to feature a fair amount of *chromaticism* (extra sharps and flats). They also tend to include

a high proportion of passages where tunes just run up and down the scale (also easy-as-pie on the old squeeze-box).

Accompanying this column are two tunes. The first is the well-known, highly syncopated tune *Willafjord*, which is said to have been introduced there by Norwegian whaler-men. I've heard it played all over the U.K., and it has even crept into the repertoire at New England contra dances. In order to get the phrasing of the melody on banjo, I had to resort to a number of fairly unorthodox right-hand usages. Here are some of them:

♦ *M-T reversals* in Part A. measure 1. Play the first quarter note on string 3 with M, bringing T in contact with string 4. Play the next on-beat note (fret 4, string 4) with T. Play the following off-beat note (open 3rd string) with M and hold that note through the beginning of the next beat; T then falls in its "normal" place between-beats for the following note (open string 4). The same process is at work in Part A, measures 2, 3, 5 and 6 and in Part B, measures 1,3, 4 and 5.

♦ Part A measure 4. Follow a two-string arpeggio (from fret 5, string 4 to open string 3) with a *T-note pull-off* on string 4. This method is more fluid than trying to quickly come back with M to play string 4.

♦ Parts A and B, measure 7. Follow a three-string arpeggio (fret 4, string 3 to open string 2 then open string 1) with an ordinary drop-thumb at fret 4, string 2. This restores some ordinary M-T flow coming into the final measure of each part.

Following *Willafjord* is the tab for *Miss Susan Cooper*, a modern reel by accordionist Ronny Cooper. Observe in Part B, meas. 2 that a "Galax lick" has been adapted to obtain a particular sequence of notes.

Willafjord

Banjo Arrangement: Ken Perlman

Tuning: gCGCD (capo–2)

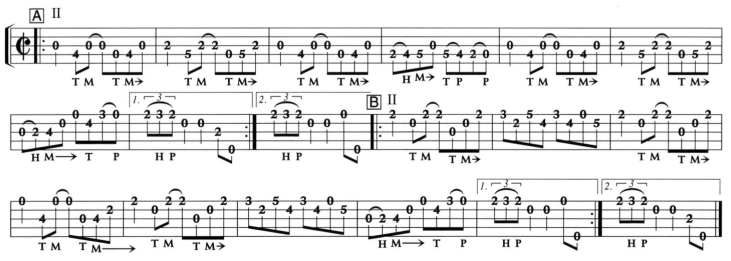

Arrangement © 1988 by Ken Perlman

Miss Susan Cooper

Banjo Arrangement: Ken Perlman

Tuning: gCGCD (capo–2)

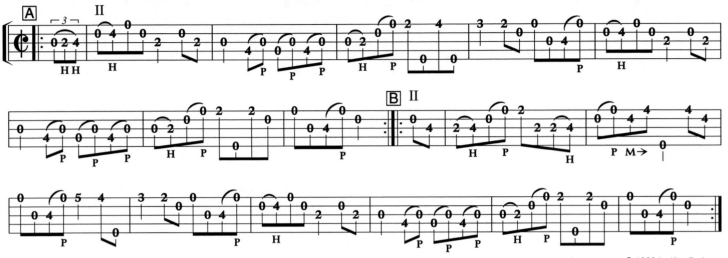

Arrangement © 1989 by Ken Perlman

4.7 The "Other" Old-Time Music: Canadian Fiddling

(Oct.'95)

Having just returned home from playing at a couple of Ontario festivals, I am more convinced than ever that clawhammer is ideally suited as both solo and accompaniment instrument for virtually all the traditional fiddle-music styles that still flourish in eastern Canada.

In terms of genuine musical traditions — that is, situations where tunes and skills are passed down within family and community — eastern Canada takes a back seat to no nation in the Western world. There are independent, active fiddling traditions in Newfoundland, New Brunswick, Cape Breton Island, mainland Nova Scotia, Prince Edward Island, Québec, and the Ottawa Valley of Ontario. If you add to the mix all sub-styles and regional variations (Prince Edward Island alone has several regional fiddling styles), the list is even more impressive.

On their home turf, much of this fiddling is referred to as *old-time music* (sound familiar?). Despite a myriad of differences among these various styles, there is a certain character or syncopation to the rhythm that they all seem to share. This syncopation is a bit different than that found in Southern old-time music, but it is nevertheless an ideal vehicle for clawhammer style. All it takes is a slight modification in the timing of the stroke — and presto! — the clawhammer picker becomes an integral (and indispensable) member of the Canadian old-time fiddle-tune ensemble.

A clawhammer player seeking to modify his basic stroke for Canadian old time music need go through no major contortions. If you just get a solid rhythm going that focuses on double thumbing and single-string brushes, you are more than half way there. The rest comes from really honing in on the fiddler and trying to *exactly* match his bowing rhythm with the rhythm of your banjo strokes. What seems to work for me is to actually keep my eyes focused on the fiddler's bowing hand. Somehow I find that this enables me to match his rhythm exactly.

A word of encouragement to Canadian clawhammerers: you have a whole world of indigenous fiddling out there to explore! Don't put down that banjo when the old feller down the road shows up at your Southern music jam and starts playing *Big John MacNeil*. Just join in and widen both of your horizons.

And you American banjo pickers, why not expand your repertoire (and that of your favorite local fiddler) with a few good Canadian tunes (well, make that a few *more* tunes — I'm sure you already know *St. Anne's Reel*).

Along with this column is tab for *Maple Sugar*, by the great Ontario fiddler of the last generation, Ward Allen.

Maple Sugar

Banjo Arrangement: Ken Perlman

Tuning: gCGCD (capo–2)

Arrangement © 1995 by Ken Perlman

4.8 Cape Breton Tunes

(Apr. '88)

Cape Breton is the Island portion of the Canadian province of Nova Scotia. It was heavily settled in the late 18th and early 19th Centuries by Scottish immigrants who brought their music with them. This essentially Scottish music has changed a bit over the years, but Cape Breton and Scottish fiddlers still share a similar repertoire. Some even consider Cape Breton fiddling to be a regional style of Scottish Fiddling.

Like their Scottish counterparts, Cape Breton fiddlers play airs, jigs, reels, marches and strathspeys. They also decorate their tunes with Scotch snaps (col. 3.11) and a variety of left-hand *grace notes* (col. 2.24). Yet, the overall sound of Cape Breton fiddling is substantially different from any of the major fiddling styles you can hear in contemporary Scotland. Probably the biggest difference is that Cape Breton fiddling is much more dance-oriented, and bowing accents are geared much more closely to dance rhythms. The bowing is substantially different as well: Cape Bretoners tend to use wrist driven *saw-strokes* (that is, one note per stroke) and to dig deeply into the strings, while contemporary Scottish fiddlers use more "slurring" (multiple notes per bow stroke) and a much lighter attack. What's more, imported Scottish tunes are often altered substantially by Cape Bretoners, and there are quite a number of tunes indigenous to Cape Breton that — at least until very recently — were not played in Scotland.

Some say that Cape Bretoners have merely retained a style of playing that was characteristic of fiddlers in Scotland at the time of major emigration to the Island. Others claim that internal evolution in Cape Breton and contact with musicians from such other immigrant groups as the French Canadians and Irish is

responsible for the differences. Whatever the explanation, Cape Breton fiddling is quite an exciting genre in its own right, and many tunes in its repertoire are both highly interesting and readily translatable to clawhammer.

I learned the accompanying tune *Chorus Jig* from the playing of John Campbell, a Cape Breton born fiddler who lives in Watertown, Massachusetts. I recently recorded it on my *Northern Banjo* CD.

Perhaps the most intriguing feature of this four-part jig — which with the capo is in the key of D mixolydian (D-E-F♯-G-A-B-C-D) — is that each part ends on the fourth note of the scale (G). Harmonically speaking, this G-note is an important part of the C major chord, which serves as the *dominant* chord of the key (see col. 6.10).

Another interesting note: around the beginning of the 19th century, some New Englander *converted* this melody from 6/8 into 2/2 or reel-time (see col. 3.14). The resulting version has been used ever since to accompany a famous North American contra dance known as *The Chorus Jig* (for the reel-version of *Chorus Jig,* see *Clawhammer Style Banjo*) .

One technical suggestion: Think of the *reverse quarter-eighth combination* in measure 4 of each part as being analogous to a Scotch snap (review Example 3-25 in col. 3.11). Just count this out triplet style (1-&-a, 2-&-a). Then allot the first note one count (that is, the "number-count"), and the second note two counts (the "&-count" plus the "a-count").

101

Chorus Jig

Banjo Arrangement: Ken Perlman

Tuning: gCGCD (capo–2)

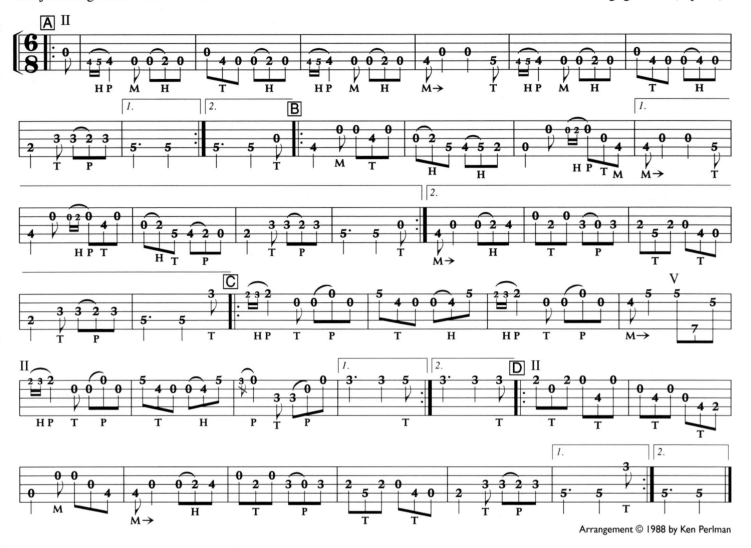

Arrangement © 1988 by Ken Perlman

4.9 Scottish and Cape Breton Medleys

(May '88)

Each fiddling tradition has its own ideas about medleys. In the Irish tradition, a medley usually consists of several tunes of the same type. The musician plays a number of reels in a row, for example, and varies the key, mode or feel from tune to tune to create interest. In the Scottish tradition, on the other hand, a typical medley consists of a variety of tune types, all of which are usually in the same key. One common Scottish medley — known as a *Scottish set*—consists of three tunes — a *pipe march* (cols. 3.12-13), a strathspey (column 3.11), and a reel (col. 3.1). Put a bit differently, the traditional Scottish fiddle medley starts with a moderate tempo, lopingly-paced tune, moves into a very abrupt, slower kind of tune that lends itself to elaborate ornamentation, and concludes with a fast, rousing, flat-rhythmed tune. Each tune in a Scottish set is generally played twice.

Cape Breton fiddlers also perform Scottish sets — a practice that they may very well have borrowed late in the 19th or early in the 20th century from the concert appearances or early recordings of Scottish fiddle great James Scott Skinner. They also play at least three other kinds of tune-agglomerations: medleys for square sets, medleys for step dancing, and performance medleys.

Square Sets is the Cape Breton style of square dancing, descended from 19th century *quadrilles* (see col. 9.20). In keeping with its quadrille ancestry, each complete square set dance is made up of a number of different segments or *figures*. Generally, there is different music for each figure, and a distinct pause between figures.

The original quadrilles danced in North America had five figures, but nowadays the number of figures that make up a given quadrille (or *square set)* varies with region. At Cape Breton dances in the Boston area, for example, they dance three figures. The first figure is done to jig accompaniment, the second figure is done to fast (non-dotted) hornpipes or slow reels, while the final figure is done to fast reels.

102

There is no standard length for square set figures, so the fiddler just keeps playing tunes until the *prompter* (their name for "caller") signals that the dance is about to end. For the first figure, a musician might have to play anywhere from two to four different jigs. For the second figure, it's usually two to four hornpipes or reels; for the third figure it would be several reels.

Cape Breton fiddlers do not merely throw their square set medleys together on the spot. As the tradition has evolved, each medley must feature tunes with the same key-note (although mode changes from major to modal are OK). More importantly, the tunes in each medley must fit together organically, and there must be no falling off of energy as transitions among tunes are made. Fiddlers spend years building up a repertoire of medleys for use in square sets, adding a tune here, dropping a tune there.

Similar principles of organization are employed to put together medleys designed to accompany *step-dancers* (cloggers). Step-dance medleys are made up of strathspeys, fast strathspeys (less notey strathspeys played up-tempo with fewer left-hand ornaments) and reels. The musician arranges his tunes so he can comfortably accelerate the tempo throughout. Again, the length of this medley is necessarily indeterminate (it goes on until the dancer cries "uncle"), but the musician who wishes to play for a step dance should have available at least seven to ten tunes that fit well together.

Performance medleys are an elaboration of the Scottish set in which elements of set-dance and step-dance medleys also come into play. Again, tunes are featured that share a common key center, but mode changes are permitted. There is a higher level here of crafting and tune-fitting than in the dance medleys, yielding a fairly intricate mosaic of contrasts and similarities, echoes and surprises. A typical performance set starts with a slow air, moves into a slow, intricate strathspey in a contrasting mode, and follows that with two or three additional strathspeys, each of which picks up the tempo slightly. A fast strathspey then serves as a pivot, preparing the way for the point in the medley of greatest excitement — namely the opening bars of the first reel. The medley then closes with three or four additional reels in various modes, the last of which is usually major.

The accompanying tune *Miss Johnson of Pittworth* seems to be fairly standard in the repertoire. I learned it from Cape-Breton born fiddler John Campbell of Watertown, Massachusetts, but I've also heard it on recordings by Cape-Breton born Joe Cormier of Waltham, Massachusetts and by the late great Cape Breton fiddler, Winston "Scotty" Fitzgerald. I recorded a version myself on the *Northern Banjo* CD.

Note that *Miss Johnson* is characterized by "short-form" reel-structure: a four-bar repeated A part, and an eight-bar non-repeated B-part. The tune is in the key of B♭, so you might want to consult cols. 5.6-8 before tackling it.

Miss Johnson of Pittworth

Banjo Arrangement: Ken Perlman

Tuning: gDGCD

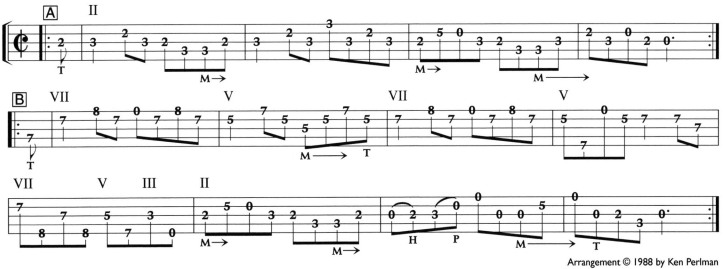

Arrangement © 1988 by Ken Perlman

103

Prince Edward Island is a long, narrow spit of land that sits in the Gulf of St. Lawrence, nestled in a crook made by the junction of the Canadian provinces of New Brunswick and Nova Scotia. Made up almost entirely of red sandstone, P.E.I. (which is itself an entire province) is characterized by flat or rolling country and countless miles of virtually uninhabited beaches. It is also a hotbed of fiddling.

The P.E.I. fiddling repertoire seems to have about a half dozen components. First, there are tunes that have come down in tradition from the mainstream Scottish repertory, which was collected or composed between the years roughly 1726-1900. Second, there are tunes that are commonly considered to be part of the New England repertoire, many of which are compiled in the famous *1000 Fiddle Tunes* book. Third, there are a considerable number of tunes composed locally or by recent composers from nearby Cape Breton Island such as Dan R. MacDonald and Jerry Holland. Fourth, P.E. Islanders play a substantial number of tunes often associated with the Irish repertory: some of these were assimilated from the original Irish population on the Island, while others crept into the repertoire via contemporary Irish or Cape Breton recordings.

There is a group of about two or three dozen "good old tunes" that has made up the core of the P.E.I. repertoire for generations. Included here are *Princess Reel, Farmer's Reel* (also known as *Golden Wedding*), *Paddy On The Turnpike, Lord MacDonald's Reel* (virtually identical to *Leather Britches*), *Pigeon on the Gatepost, Sheehan's Reel* and — two relatively recent additions — *Heather on the Hill* and *St. Anne's Reel*.

Fiddlers' oral histories describe a not-too-distant time when after a hard day of toil Islanders gathered together to play fiddle and dance till dawn at countless *house parties*. The fiddler was a crucial cog in his community: the liveliness of his playing made people want to dance, and the beauty of his tunes enriched their imaginations.

Tune and skills transmission were a family affair. If the young son of a fiddler showed interest in the instrument, the father would often hand the youngster his bow and lift him onto his knee. Then, he would encourage the child to work the bow on the instrument while he (that is, the father) noted a tune on the fingerboard. Meanwhile, Island women are said to have spent a good part of the day singing tune melodies to themselves while they worked, an activity that Islanders refer to as *tuning* or *jigging*. Consequently, tune melodies were always available for the up and coming player to tap into.

Many P.E.I. fiddlers report that they needed to hear a tune but twice to remember it in much of its detail. They describe awakening the morning after a dance to find a tune running through their minds with sufficient clarity so that they could easily find it on their instruments. As one might expect, this method of tune transmission led to a wide variety of *twists* (tune-variations). It's not so much that fiddlers have imperfect memories. Rather, it is considered important to only get the major *themes* of a tune on a note for note basis. As for the remainder, it is quite acceptable to reconstruct these passages according to one's own musical instincts. In practice then, no two fiddlers play a tune in exactly the same way, and certain phrases of particular tunes show tremendous variation from player to player.

As is the case on neighboring Cape Breton, most square dancing on the Island is descended from a 19th century social dance called the *quadrille* (col. 9.20). Like its ancestral form, each Island square dance is performed in either three or four *figures* or segments. Each figure requires a different kind of fiddle tune as accompaniment (although there was considerable disagreement among different communities about what kinds of tunes went with which figure). At some square dances, participants *step-dance* (clog) through the figures instead of walking through them.

Fifteen years ago, it looked to be a sure bet that traditional fiddling on P.E.I. would disappear. The onset of TV and pop culture had for the most part supplanted fiddle dances as the primary form of local recreation. Fiddlers were an aging population, and there simply were no young people taking up the instrument in a serious way.

Perhaps the greatest obstacle to developing young players at that time was adolescent peer pressure. Fiddling was seen as an activity that was only for the old folks. Consequently, promising youngsters were subjected to such a degree of withering scorn that they soon abandoned the instrument.

By the late 70s the decline of fiddling was sufficiently alarming that some Island fiddlers decided to do something about it. Several dozen of them founded the Prince Edward Island Fiddlers' Association, hoping both to put fiddling back in

---

[2] In the early '90s, I did an intensive research project on Prince Edward Island traditional fiddling, and wound up writing several columns on the subject — the contents of which are presented here in capsule form. Those readers who wish a fuller account of my P.E.I. project (or who wish to hear field recordings of the fiddlers I worked with) are encouraged to consult my tune book, *The Fiddle Music of Prince Edward Island*, its companion CD of field recordings, or the 2-volume CD set I produced for Rounder, entitled *The Prince Edward Island Style of Fiddling*.

104

the public eye, and to find some method for effectively passing on the art to a new generation.

Finding a new place for fiddling in Island life proved to be relatively easy. A number of annual fiddle festivals and concerts were organized at various locations around the Island. Taking the lead from the success of these larger festivals, many communities began organizing town-days and other celebrations, most of which featured performances by local fiddlers and stepdancers. By the mid-90s, weekly town *ceilidhs* (pronounced KAY-ley: Gaelic for musical evening) were also springing up all over the Island. All of a sudden, fiddling was news again!

Making sure that the art of fiddling would be passed down proved to be a more difficult task. Most fiddlers grew up in a milieu where formal instruction was not a part of life. As far as they were concerned, a youngster either had the *gift* for fiddling — and would learn on his own — or he hadn't. Moreover, most older fiddlers felt that if you couldn't read music (and most of them couldn't), you had nothing to offer a novice.

Fiddle-teaching programs, such as the one set up by the fiddling Chaisson family of Bear River in northeastern P.E.I., have done much to counteract this state of affairs. After a rocky start, these programs took hold and by the end of the 90s everywhere you looked in certain parts of the Island there were fine young players to be seen. So the tradition is safe, at least for the next generation!

Accompanying this column is a banjo arrangement for what is probably the quintessential PEI fiddle tune: *Lord MacDonald's Reel*. This tune originated in 18th century Scotland, and has since circulated throughout Britain, Ireland and North America. In the American South, it is known as *Leather Britches*. This version is based on the fiddle playing of Peter Chaisson, Sr. of Bear River; I recorded it on my *Island Boy* CD.

Incidentally, there are quite a number of other tunes tabbed out in this book that I learned from Prince Edward Island fiddlers, and which I have also transcribed into standard notation for *The Fiddle Music of Prince Edward Island*. These are marked with an asterisk in the Index of Tunes.

Lord MacDonald's Reel

Banjo Arrangement: Ken Perlman

Tuning: gDGBD

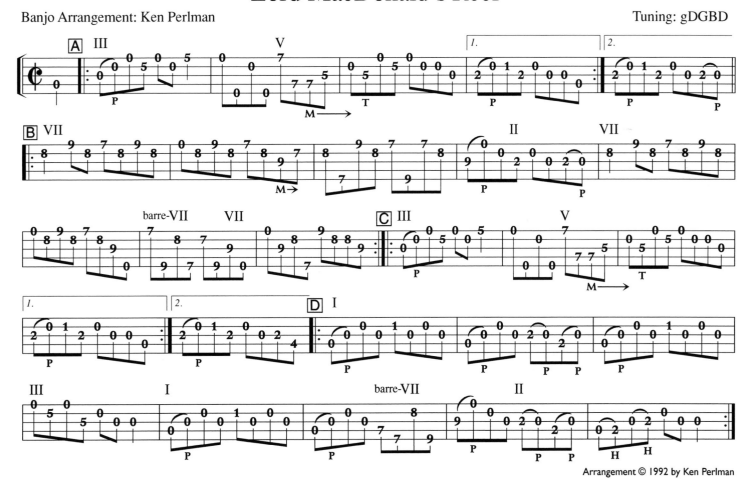

Arrangement © 1992 by Ken Perlman

"That's piling on the bois sec!" This cry is how members of Prince Edward Island's Acadian French community describe a really hot musical session. Literally, the expression *bois sec* (which they pronounce "boo SECK") means dry wood, or kindling. The implication is that the session is so hot that a large fire is imminent.

P.E.I. was originally settled by the Acadian French, who were unceremoniously expelled when the island entered the British sphere of influence. Some Acadians moved back to France, some moved to Louisiana (later becoming known as *Cajuns)*, and a very few (about 30 families) remained or were eventually allowed to return. Most of the Island's Acadian population is descended from those original 30 families. Among those 30 are the names borne today by some of P.E.I.'s most prominent fiddling families: the Gallants, the Arsenaults, the Chaissons, the Longaphies and the Cheveries.

In King's County — the eastern-most part of the island with the most Scottish influence — most Acadian French have intermarried and assimilated with their neighbors. On the western side of P.E.I. known as Prince County, however, many Acadians have retained their language, their customs, and their separateness from the surrounding Anglo population. The fiddlers in this part of the island also play the Scottish and Irish tunes that make up the general island repertoire, but they have their own way of playing them. They also use a distinctive two-footed tapping routine to keep time.

Perhaps the most prominent Acadian fiddler in Prince County is Eddy Arsenault of St. Chrysostom. A lobster fisherman by trade, Mr. Arsenault has had many offers to take his act on the road, but he prefers to stay peacefully at home. He has a brother who plays guitar, two sons who play fiddle, and a

daughter — Helene Arsenault Bergeron — who is one of the best Acadian step dancers on the island. He is also noted for his modesty ("It is not I who am the great fiddler, it is you...") and for passing on the "piling on the bois sec!" expression to this banjoist.[3]

One technique that Acadian fiddlers frequently make use of is what might be called a "suppressed" bow stroke, which is analogous to the M-skip technique used in clawhammer (see cols. 1.12-13). In a skip, you make as if to hit a string but don't actually strike it. Consequently, the note *preceding* the skip is emphasized by the absence of the skipped note. This conveys to the ear the notion that this preceding note has been accented (that is, syncopated).

In essence, the Acadian fiddler is doing the same thing. He doesn't "skip" a bow stroke, but he undergoes some action so that the sound of that stroke is suppressed. This in effect causes the preceding note of the tune to sound stressed or syncopated.

There seem to be two varieties of suppressed strokes. In one, the fiddler plays a neighboring drone string instead of the melody string, causing the melody to momentarily drop from sight. In the other method, the fiddler bows the melody string but damps out its sound — either with the left hand or by changing the attack of the bow so it produces a "splat" rather than a clear tone.

The most common places for this to appear is either in a *Turkey in the Straw*-type syncopation (Fig. 4-6), or at the beginning of a four-note eighth note grouping (Fig. 4-7). Observe that the suppressed note is shown by placing an "X" *on the staff.*

Example 4-6

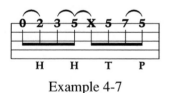

Example 4-7

To translate the suppressed stroke into clawhammer, I tend to damp the note out with the left hand — either by relaxing pressure on the string or (if the string is open) by tapping it with the flat of a fretting-hand finger.

The accompanying tune is *Reel du Cordonnier* (Cobbler's Reel), which is from the playing of Louise Arsenault of Mont

Carmel, P.E.I. The tune is also played in Québec, generally in medley with another tune called *Reel du Pendu* (Hanged Man's Reel). Note that the "v" symbols indicate an upstroke of the M finger (column 2.25); the new element here is that the v-stroke is *not* part of a birl or triplet. Observe also that Part B, meas. 1 and 3 employs fingering form #6 (see Ex. 2-51 in col. 2.17).

---

[3] Helene Arsenault Bergeron and her brother Albert now work together in the well known touring group, *Barachois.*

Reel du Cordonnier

Banjo Arrangement: Ken Perlman

Tuning: gDGBD

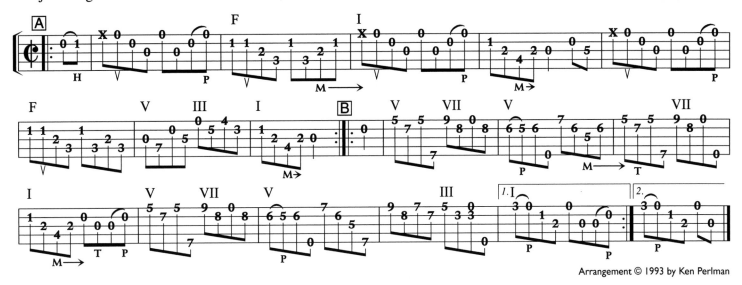

Arrangement © 1993 by Ken Perlman

4.19 Guitar Pieces on Banjo

(Feb. '90)

Taking on pieces designed for guitar is another fruitful endeavor for the dedicated melodic player.

In 19th Century America, playing "parlor" guitar was a highly popular musical pastime. A style of picking evolved that resembled both modern Travis-picking and Mississippi John Hurt-style country blues. In the latter part of the century, many popular parlor-guitar tunes were adapted to classic (fingerstyle) banjo, and eventually some of the best-known parlor-guitar tunes entered that muddy stream we call the "folk process."

One such tune is *Spanish Fandango*, which was played by parlor-guitarists in open-G tuning (probably explaining why this guitar tuning is sometimes called "Spanish tuning"). Mississippi John Hurt recorded a guitar version called *Spanish*

Flangdang, while numerous other folk-banjoists and folk-guitarists have also recorded versions of the tune. Around 1970, John Burke published a fingerstyle banjo tab for *Spanish Fandango* in his book, *Old Time Fiddle Tunes for Banjo*.

Marjorie Skora of the Chicago area recently came up with this clawhammer version of the tune and uses the arpeggio technique (column 2.9) to capture the cadence of fingerstyle guitar. Observe that the "curvy" vertical line in Part A, meas. 1 and 5 indicates a *broken chord*. Think of this as a clawhammer roll (col. 2-11) without the 5th string component.

Observe that the tuning used here is *open C*, or gCGCE. To get open C tuning from double C, tune up string 1 to match *fret 4, string 2*.

Spanish Fandango

Banjo Arrangement: Marjorie Skora

Tuning: gCGCE (capo–2 optional)

Arrangement © 1990 by Marjorie Skora

Roy Patchell of Lexington, Kentucky sent in this tune entitled *Dona Nobis Pacem* (Give Us Peace). As you can see from the tab, this tune is accessible to anyone who can brush-thumb, drop-thumb and hammer-on. Here's what Roy has to say about it:

"This arrangement is a round for (up to) three banjos. The piece was originally written by Palestrina, a 16th Century Italian composer noted for his large output and expert use of *polyphony* [music in which several melodies are inter-weaving simultaneously]. Excerpts from his compositions frequently appear in modern music textbooks as examples of counterpoint. *Dona Nobis Pacem* was originally a vocal round, but it works quite well in the clawhammer idiom as a banjo round.

"*Dona Nobis Pacem* is played in the usual way rounds are performed. That is, the first banjo begins the piece at the beginning and plays straight through. When the first banjo reaches the point marked with an asterisk (*) the second banjo starts to play from the beginning. The third banjo begins to play from the beginning when the first banjo reaches the point marked with two asterisks (**). Rounds are usually played completely through three times by each player, but the length can be altered to suit performers' tastes. The piece can be played as a solo, a duet, or a trio."

You might want to review the section on playing in 3/4 time (cols. 3.5-6) before proceeding.

Dona Nobis Pacem

Banjo Arrangement: Roy Patchell

Tuning: gDGBD

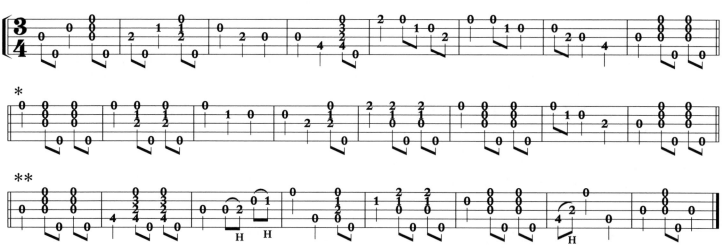

Arrangement © 1990 by Roy Patchell

4.21 Mike Seeger's "Rollin' & Tumblin' Blues"   (Feb. '00)

"Rollin' and Tumblin'" is an extraordinarily ingenious banjo-setting. Essentially, Mike Seeger takes a relatively small number of simple elements and creatively combines them to effectively render a full-fledged Delta-style blues — a genre which is for the most part quite foreign to mainstream clawhammer.

When I say "simple" elements, I mean that the entire piece can pretty much be played with one finger of the left hand (well, there might be a couple of places where using two fingers might be helpful). On the other hand, the use of these elements to produce or suggest intricate syncopated rhythms is nothing short of brilliant, and Mike's execution of these rhythms is sharp and flawless.

One adaptation that Seeger made to the banjo's lack of sustain was to arrange the piece in "double-time" format (see cols. 6.7-8). In other words, what would be a standard "12-bar blues" on guitar, becomes for all intents and purposes a 24-bar blues on banjo. Since the tempo for these 24 bars is twice the rate as for the guitarist's 12 bars, however, a vocalist working with the banjo version performs at exactly the same speed as one performing with the slower-moving guitar version.

To maximize the "bluesy" feel of the arrangement, Mike uses a fretless skin-head instrument with a gourd pot and strings tuned down about half a step from standard. You won't get the same kind of sound with a fretted instrument, particularly one with a substantial tone ring and tightly cranked plastic head like my Vega Tubaphone. On the other hand, if you tune your "cranked" instrument down at least a full step from standard — and perhaps even loosen the banjo-head a bit — you can get a better approximation of his sound.

Since Mike was playing a fretless instrument, he was able to play "blue-notes" (that is, notes falling in between the pitches of two adjacent frets) without having to choke (bend) the strings. This can't really be shown too well in fretted-instrument tab, but you should be aware of the following:

♦ Many of the notes at strings 1 and 4, fret 3 (F-natural) are actually a bit higher than notated, but not so high as the next higher fret (F-sharp).

♦ Many of the notes at fret 3, string 3 (B-flat) are actually a bit higher than notated, but not so high as to be the equivalent of the next higher fret (B-natural).

♦ Many of the notes at fret 4, string 3 (B-natural) are actually a bit lower than notated, but not so low as the next lower fret (B-flat).

If you're playing this piece on a fretless instrument, make sure you listen carefully to the recording to get closer to the exact pitches that Mike uses. If you're playing on a fretted instrument, you might want to choke the F-naturals and B-flats a bit, or play the B-naturals as choked B-flats.

Another feature of this arrangement that doesn't show up in tab too well is slide-duration. In the tab, some of Seeger's slides are described as quick or ornamental slides, and others show up as even slides (see col. 1.9). On the recording, many of these slides are actually somewhere in between these two extremes: listen and adjust the duration of your slides accordingly.

An *off-beat slide*. In measure 19, an even slide is initiated between the beats by a T-note (this is analogous to off-beat H's and P's: see col. 2.12). As you perform the slide bring T back into contact with the fifth string, then strike that string at the time called for in the tab.

Rollin' and Tumblin' Blues

Banjo Arrangement: Mike Seeger

Tuning: gDGBD

Arrangement © 1988 by Mike Seeger; Tablature © 2000 by Ken Perlman

4.22 Swedish Tunes

(Jan. '88)

More and more in recent years, fiddle tunes drawn from the Swedish tradition are creeping into the contra-dance repertoire. Just about every fiddle-tunes scene in the country has at least one picker who is seriously into Swedish tunes. Many of the tunes fit quite nicely on the banjo, and the genre presents a whole new area for clawhammer exploration.

I don't pretend to be an expert on Swedish fiddling, but I have spent some time playing with Swedish-revivalist pickers and have thereby gained enough of a feeling for the style to at least take a stab at a couple of tunes. In the Boston area, I've had a chance to listen to Matt Fichtenbaum, who plays both fiddle and nickelharper (a Swedish keyed fiddle: sort of a bowed hurdy-gurdy). And on my recent U.K. tour, I spent some time with ex-New Lost City Rambler Tom Paley, who has been heavily into Swedish style fiddling for some years now.

I taped a few Swedish tunes from Tom's playing, and started trying to learn some of them soon afterwards. At first, I was convinced they would never work on banjo, but after a lot of listening and experimentation I found I could put together some pretty nifty Swedish-tune banjo settings.

Most Swedish tunes seem to use the same scales and time signatures as Celtic and American fiddle tunes. They are also built for the most part of two repeated eight-measure sections. What may take some getting used to is the fact that in Swedish tunes the phrases sometimes start and end at what to us might seem weird points in a tune (for more on phrasing, see column 3.15). In Southern US or Celtic music, the major phrases of a tune almost always start on the downbeat (first beat of the measure) or on the note or series of notes leading into that downbeat (called the *upbeat*). In some Swedish tunes, however, the first major phrase can begin *after* the first measure downbeat (the latter serving merely as a place-keeper). Phrases then continue in this "out-of-phase" manner throughout an entire part. Even if the tune later returns to a more conventional approach to phrasing, the fact that the tune started off the way it did can leave us scratching our heads.

This month's selection, *Jentland Tune* (pronounced "Yentland") is from the playing of Tom Paley. It's in 9/8 time,

so those of you who have attempted Irish slip jigs should have no problem (this might be a good time to review cols. 3.7-8 on 6/8 time tunes). Remember to think of each 9/8 measure as being made up of three beats, each of which is divided in turn into three pulses or sub-beats. A beat is then be filled by three eighth-notes, a quarter-note plus an eighth-note, or by a dotted quarter-note. For ease of communication, I refer to notes in the first third of a 9/8 measure as "beat 1," notes in the second third of the measure as "beat 2," and notes in the last third as "beat 3."

Looking at *Jentland*, the first phrase of Part A starts on the *second* beat of the first measure (the preceding upbeat and downbeat are just place-keepers), and runs through the second beat of measure two. The second phrase runs from beat 3, measure 2 through the first quarter note of measure 4. The third phrase runs from the first eighth note of measure 4 through the first beat of measure 5. The fourth phrase (identical to the first phrase) runs from the second beat of measure 5 through the second beat of measure 6. The fifth phrase runs from beat 3 of measure 6 to the end of the part.

In Part B the first phrase starts conventionally on the upbeat of the first measure, and goes through the first beat of meas. 2. The second phrase runs from beat 2, measure 2 to the first quarter-note of measure 4. The third phrase runs from the first eighth-note of measure 4 to the last quarter-note of measure 4. The fourth phrase runs from the last eighth note of measure 4 through the first beat of measure 6. The last phrase runs from the second beat of measure 6 to the end of the part.

This particular tune uses two unusual scales. Part A is in an altered hexatonic D-Modal scale (D-E-F-G-A-C#-D). The first and fourth phrases of Part B seem to be in D-Lydian: (D-E-F#-G#-A-B-C#-D), while the rest of the part uses the same scale as Part A.

Jentland Tune

Banjo Arrangement: Ken Perlman

Tuning: gDGCD

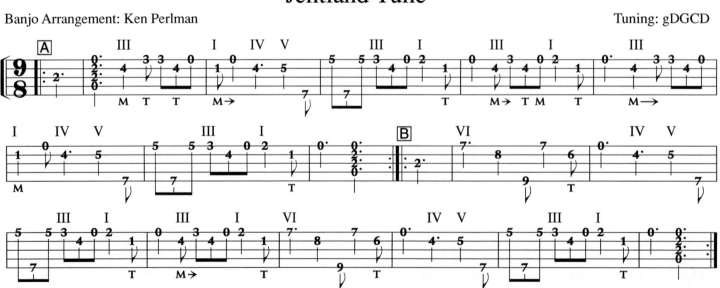

Arrangement © 1988 by Ken Perlman

110

Klezmer music is an urban-generated blend of Jewish music, east-European folk music, and North American jazz that flourished in the 1920s and 30s. It featured various instruments that were also popular in contemporary jazz ensembles, such as clarinet, saxophone, violin, and accordion.

As with many other kinds of ethnic music, klezmer has for the last decade or two been subject to a revival among urban, educated people from a variety of backgrounds. As one might suspect, there is a lot of overlap from the bluegrass, old-time and contradance music scenes on the one hand, and the klezmer

Romanian-Bulgarish

Banjo Arrangement: Ken Perlman

Tuning: eCGBD

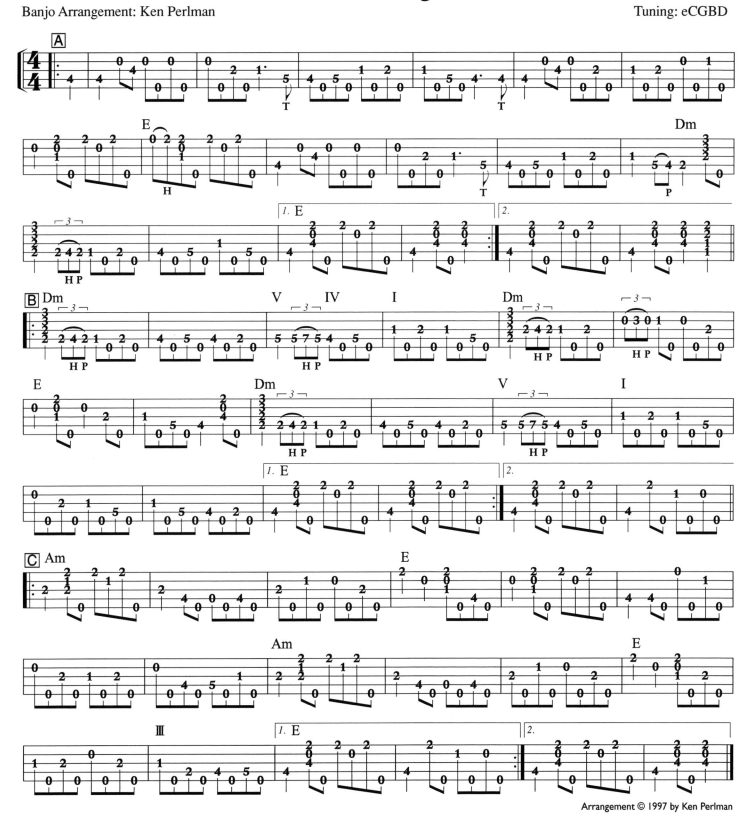

Arrangement © 1997 by Ken Perlman

111

scene on the other. Mandolinists David Grisman and Andy Statman, for example, are especially noted for their forays into the world of klezmer. Clawhammerist Henry Sapoznik — who appeared on the old *Melodic Clawhammer Banjo* LP (Kicking Mule Records) — is leader of a renowned contemporary klezmer ensemble called Kapelye (kuh-PEL-yeh). Fiddler David Brodie (who put together the *Fiddler's Fakebook* series of tunebooks) played for years in a Boston-based group called Klezmer Conservatory. And the list goes on.

Needless to say, 5-string banjo has not been an overly featured instrument in these klezmer-revival ensembles (Sapoznik plays either tenor banjo or fiddle during Kapelye performances). Every once in a while, however, a picker of the "5" does take a stab at coming up with an effective bluegrass or clawhammer arrangement suitable for performing with a bunch of klezmorim (klez-mor-EEM, as players of the style are known). In the clawhammer world, these arrangements have become frequent enough so that the name *klezhammer* has been coined to describe them.

When I was at the Maryland Banjo Academy not long ago, Washington-area clawhammerist Wendy Morrison — an active klezmorim herself on squeeze box — suggested that I might want to take up klezhammer as a new project. She even xeroxed me some sheet music for a couple of popular klezmer tunes, including *Romanian-Bulgarish*, which is featured with this column.

At any rate, I thought I'd give these tunes a crack. After a bit of experimentation I came to the conclusion that although the rhythm, phrasing, and style of syncopation are quite different than in old time or Celtic music, much of what's going on in klezmer can be handled via conventional clawhammer techniques.

The tuning I've selected for this key of E tune is a modified standard-C tuning, namely eCGBD. To obtain it, go to standard-C (gCGBD) and tune the fifth string down to match fret 2, string 1.

The scale in use may sound strange to the American ear but it is quite common in Eastern European folk music. In terms of the modal system, it is closest to the *Phrygian Mode*, which (assuming an E key-center) has a scale of E-F-G-A-B-C-D-E. The G is always played sharp, however — and the C is sometimes played sharp (particularly in the low register) — so the actual scale is E-F-G♯-A-B-C/C♯-D-E. Harmonically, having F-natural and G♯ in the same scale produces some unusual chord combinations. The tonic or primary chord for the piece is E-major, with secondary chords F, Dm and Am. If I had to select a "dominant" chord (the equivalent to D or D7 in the key of G), I'd have to go with F or Dm.

4.24 Calypso Clawhammer   (Apr. '91)

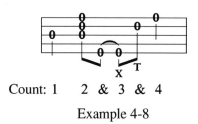

Count: 1   2 & 3 & 4

Example 4-8

In a recent letter, Ken Jennings of Eugene, Oregon describes how he developed an effective clawhammer method for playing calypso tunes. For those of you who were not yet around in the late 50s when Harry Belafonte and other calypso performers ruled the airwaves, this genre originated in Jamaica and was characterized by three-chord harmonies, simple catchy melodies and frequent syncopations. Its popularity was due in part to its resemblance to the style of American folk music performance presented at the time by such popular groups as the Weavers and the Kingston Trio. The influence of the calypso sound lasted at least through the late 1960s, as can be seen by such recordings as the Beach Boys' *Sloop John B* (which was initially recorded in the early 50s by the Weavers).

What seems to define the calypso style is the characteristic rhythm shown in Example 4-8, which features a syncopation (that is, an "unexpected" stressed note) half way between the second and third beats. This note is then tied over (held) through the first half of the third beat. To perform this in clawhammer, do an ordinary skip stroke at the conclusion of the second beat, but instead of bringing T into contact with the fifth string, bring it into contact with the second string (ready to perform a drop thumb). You might want to review cols. 1.12-13 before proceeding.

Try your hand at the well-known calypso tune *Jamaica Farewell*. This song was a major Tin Pan Alley hit in the 1950s and was popular in folk circles well into the 1960s. Here are two pointers:

◆ Part A, first ending. Use M twice in a row at the beginning of the measure and hold the second M-note (fret 1, string 2) through the beginning of beat two. Between beats two and three, use M again on open string 1 (followed by a skip stroke).

◆ Part B, measure 1. Hold the drop-thumb note (open string 2) through the beginning of beat three. Then at the conclusion of the skip-stroke, use T on the fifth string.

One accompaniment pattern suggested by Ken Jennings is none other than the rhythmic figure shown in Example 4-8. Just repeat this same lick over and over with the right hand and plug in chords as appropriate.

Jamaica Farewell

Banjo Arrangement: Ken Jennings

Tuning: gDGBD

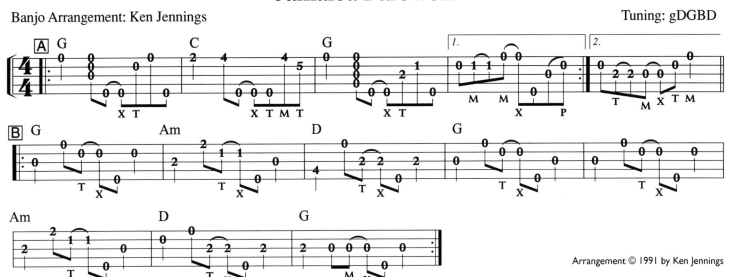

Arrangement © 1991 by Ken Jennings

4.25 Hungarian Bagpipe Tunes

(May '89)

Much Hungarian folk music is about as far away as you can get from the old-timey/Celtic idiom and still be European. One Hungarian genre that sounds at least somewhat familiar to at least this banjo player's ear is the *dudanota*, or bagpipe tunes. Like the Scottish Highland pipes, the Hungarian bagpipe or duda (rhymes with Buddha) plays a mixolydian scale (equivalent to a major scale with a flat seventh note; i.e., C-D-E-F-G-A-Bb-C). The range of the duda is confined to a single octave, however, while that of the Highland pipes is an octave plus a lower seventh note (see cols. 3.12-13 and 4.2).

Most dudas have but a single reed in the chanter (the part of the bagpipe that has the fingering holes). This gives them a

sweet, mellow sound analogous to the Northumbrian smallpipes, or even the clarinet. Highland pipes have a double reed in the chanter, giving them a harsher, more plaintive tone analogous to that of the oboe.

Unfortunately, the art of duda-playing is rapidly passing from the scene in Hungary, and most of the better performers can only be heard on record. Hungary does have a long history of folk-tune collecting, so it is relatively easy to obtain copies of quite a number of well-preserved performances. If you are interested in tracking down a recorded source, I'd suggest checking your websites under *Hungarian Instrumental Folk Music*.

Hungarian Dudanota

Banjo Arrangement: Ken Perlman

Tuning: gDGCD

Arrangement © 1989 by Ken Perlman

I managed to find at least one dudanota that seems to work well on banjo, and tabbed it out to go along with this column. I chose mountain minor tuning (rather than open G) because the suggestion of a strong major sound would be foreign to the tone-quality of the duda. The recording I listened to offered no name for the tune so alas, neither can I.

4.26 French Hurdy-Gurdy Tunes

(Jan. '99)

The hurdy-gurdy repertoire pretty much occupies the same niche in France as does the fiddle tune repertoire in English-speaking countries. Like fiddle music, it has been the focus of a revival and enthusiasts congregate at major festivals and competitions to jam and soak in the atmosphere. Try your hand at *Schottische á Eric Montbel* (Eric Montbel's Schottische), a contemporary French hurdy-gurdy tune arranged for banjo by a student of mine from Waltham, Mass. named Linda Abrams. Linda learned it from her hurdy-gurdy playing neighbor Nina Bohlen, who had picked up the tune at a festival in Washington State. It should be played at a moderate tempo.

Schottische à Eric Montbel

Banjo Arrangement: Linda Abrams

Tuning: gDGBD

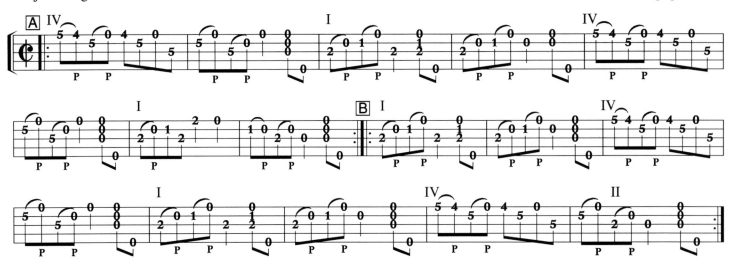

Arrangement © 1999 by Linda Abrams

Ken at Glen Coe, Scotland, during first UK tour, May '87
(Photo by Rob Mairs)

5.1 Original Waltz in Cumberland Gap Tuning

(Nov '88)

Cumberland Gap or "Bead Tuning" (f♯BEAD) offers some unusual tonal territory to the clawhammer picker. Although it is usually employed to play simple tunes in D major (see the chord diagrams in Example 5-1), the tuning itself seems to belong to no one key in particular.

To obtain Cumberland Gap tuning from G or double C tuning:
- Tune string 2 down to match the pitch of fret 2, string 3
- Tune string 3 down so that its fifth fret matches the *new* pitch of open-string 2
- Tune string 4 down so that its fifth fret matches the *new* pitch of open-string 3
- Tune string 5 to fret 4, string 1

Two Rivers

By Larry Unger

Tuning: f♯BEAD

Arrangement © 1988 by Larry Unger

One interesting feature of Bead tuning is that strings 2 through 4 are dropped substantially below their normal pitches. Not only does this increase the proportion of low overtones, but the slackness of the strings gives the instrument a "loosy-goosy" sound that harks back to the early days of banjo playing (cols. 9.3-4). Bead tuning is also of special interest to banjoists who also play guitar, since the banjo's four long strings are tuned in the same relationship to one another as the four lowest guitar strings. Consequently, the bottom four strings of any guitar chord form can be directly transferred to the four long strings of a Bead-tuned banjo. The pitch of each transferred chord is a fourth lower than the corresponding guitar chord. So, the bottom four strings of a G-chord on guitar becomes the standard D-chord form on a Bead-tuned banjo, the bottom four strings of a C-chord on guitar becomes the standard G-chord form on a Bead-tuned banjo, and the bottom four strings of a D- chord on guitar becomes the standard A chord form on a Bead-tuned banjo (compare the guitar chord "shapes" in Example 5-2 with the banjo shapes in 5-1).

115

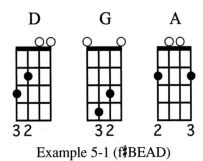

Example 5-1 (f#BEAD)

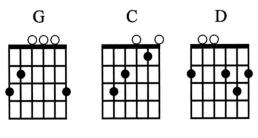

Example 5-2

Boston-area teacher/performer Larry Unger has written an interesting waltz for banjo in Bead tuning called *Two Rivers*. By avoiding most of the tuning's cliches, he has come up with a very original exploration of its possibilities. Review columns 3.5-6 on playing in 3/4 time before proceeding.

He uses a few unusual techniques in the piece.

♦ *Part A, measures 12-13*: Hold the P-note in measure 12 (fret 7, string 1) until after the open fifth string note in measure 13. Then use the holding finger to pull off string 1.

♦ *Part B. measures 9-10:* Using T on the open fifth string at beat 2, "displace" M a half-beat to the right. Using M, start an "off-beat" P from fret 12 to fret 9, string 1 and hold on to fret 9. This P has once again displaced M to a between-beats location, but what you are asked to do here is just a single-string brush that crosses the measure line. Once you have played your drone string, you can then pull off fret 9 with the holding finger.

♦ *Part B, measure 11*: This 3/4 time measure is broken up into two three-note Galax-licks. Play your first two string arpeggio plus fifth string note on the downbeat, then start the second arpeggio a half beat after the first fifth string note sounds.

5.2 Last Chance Tuning   (Dec '97)

This is a transcription of Reed Martin's arrangement of *Last Chance*, which appears on his recording entitled *Old-Time Banjo*. The tuning here is fDFCD, often referred to as "*Last Chance* tuning."

To obtain it from mountain minor (gDGCD):
♦ Tune string 3 down to match fret 3, string 4.
♦ Then tune the fifth string down to match fret 3, string 1.

Last Chance

Banjo Arrangement: Reed Martin   Tuning: fDFCD

Arrangement © 1997 by Reed Martin; Tablature © 1997 by Ken Perlman

I have tabbed out the full 16 bars of the A part in order to show some of Reed's variations. You might want to review cols. 1.12-13 on skip-strokes and syncopation before trying the tune. Just playing this arrangement is actually fairly straight forward; playing it up to Reed's tempo, on the other hand, is another matter entirely!

Incidentally, you might want to check out some of the other unusual tunings used or described in this book, such as gGDGD (col. 2.2), gCGCE (col. 4.19), eCGBD (col. 4. 23), fCFCD (col. 5.6-8), aDGBD (col. 5.9) and gCGCC (col. 9.1-2).

5.3 Playing Tunes that Change Keys

(Apr. '97)

There are lots of fiddle tunes that change keys mid-stream. There's a whole genre in fact of Southern tunes called *cotillions* where this happens all the time. Take two tunes in this book, for example. *Richmond Cotillion* has an A-part in D major and a B-part in A major; *Flying Cloud Cotillion* has an A-part in G major, and a B-part in D-major.

In other tunes, there might be a switch to the relative minor between parts. Probably the best-known tune that does this trick is *Temperance Reel* (see my *Melodic Clawhammer Banjo* book), which has an A-part in G major and then switches to the minor-like E Dorian mode for most of the second part. (strictly speaking, this is not a relative minor switch because there's also a shift in scale — Dorian calls for a C♯ instead of a C-natural — but sometimes it helps not to get too technical).

What goes on in a true shift from major to relative minor (or the reverse) is that the key center changes but the scale (set of pitches used) remains the same. There are other such shifts that can occur in a tune as it moves between different *modes* (Dorian, Mixolydian etc.). One common example is the tune *Old French* (see my *Melodic Clawhammer* book) whose A-part is in D-major (scale: D-E-F♯-G-A-B-C♯-D), but whose B-part shifts to A-mixolydian (scale: A-B-C♯-D-E-F♯-G-A). Observe that the pitches remain the same, but the starting and ending points change.

Finally there's the situation where the key-center remains the same from part to part, but the scale shifts — in essence creating a new mode with the same key-center. One common southern tune where this occurs is *Kitchen Girl* (also in *Melodic Clawhammer*). Both parts of the tune are what is commonly referred to as *modal*. Those who are familiar with the tune, however, would no doubt agree that the lower, "slinkier" part of

the tune is a little more modal than the higher part. In fact they would usually tell their guitar player to use A-*minor* and G-major chords for the low part, but A-*major* and G-major chords for the high part. What's actually going on is that the tune shifts from the A-*Dorian* mode (A-B-C-D-E-F♯-G-A) to the A-*Mixolydian* mode (A-B-C♯-D-E-F♯-G-A).

In all of these situations, the clawhammer player must play about half the tune without the advantage of being in a friendly tuning. Let's look at some adaptations that can be made to help this task along.

Probably the easiest situation described above is the one presented by tunes like *Kitchen Girl*. Example 5-3 shows a scale exercise in gDGCD tuning for the Dorian mode (5-3a) and for the Mixolydian mode (5-3b). Note that these two scales are quite similar. In fact, for tunes played by the fiddle in A there is only one spot that you need to watch: namely the 3rd fret (Dorian) vs. the 4th fret (Mixolydian) on the 3rd string.

Although the notes being played are the same when you shift into a relative minor (or major), the manner in which they relate to each other changes significantly. Consequently, the sound of some open strings may no longer reinforce the underlying harmony. Let's say we are going to play *Temperance Reel* in G-tuning (gDGBD). We breeze through the A part, hit the B and all of a sudden the notes begin to move in different patterns (we can help this state of affairs some: try the E-Dorian scale exercise in Example 5-4). What's more, the fifth-string is no longer helping as much. This is because the G-note (the strongest pitch of the G-major scale) isn't nearly as important in the E-minor or E-Dorian scales. In other words, it simply isn't as good a drone.

gDGCD (Dorian)

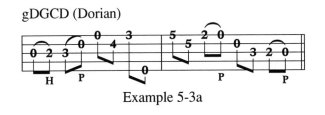

Example 5-3a

gDGCD (Mixolydian)

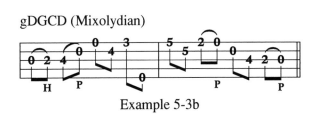

Example 5-3b

gDGBD (Dorian)

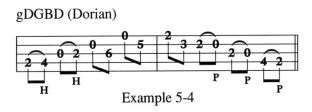

Example 5-4

117

gDGBD (Key of D Major)

Example 5-5

gCGCD (Key of G Major)

Example 5-6

gCGCD (Key of F Major)

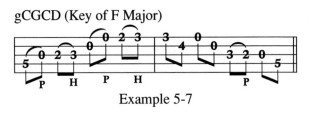

Example 5-7

Other shifts in key center can be quite tricky to accomplish effectively. The only help here is to become familiar with, and practice patterns of notes for various scales in different tunings. In example 5-5, try a scale exercise for playing in the key of D major in G-tuning. Example 5-6 gives a G-major scale exercise for double C tuning. Finally, example 5-7 shows an F-major scale exercise for double-C.

It should be noted that choosing a "friendly" tuning is essential to coming up with an effective banjo arrangement. If you had tried to play *Kitchen Girl* capoed up in open-G tuning (gDGBD), for example, you might have found yourself gling mightily because the open second string (B) is not part of the G-Dorian mode. When it comes to tunes that shift key center, it is important to try the tune each way. In other words (assuming a second fret capo), you must decide if a tune that shifts from D major to A major is easier to play out of a C-tuning or a G-tuning.

Accompanying this column is *Judique Reel*, named for Judique [pronounced: JOO-dik], Nova Scotia. It shifts from A-major in the first part to D-major in the second. The tab is in G-tuning (capo-2). After you learn the tune, try it in double-C tuning and see which one works the best for you.

Judique Reel

Banjo Arrangement: Ken Perlman

Tuning: gDGBD (capo–2)

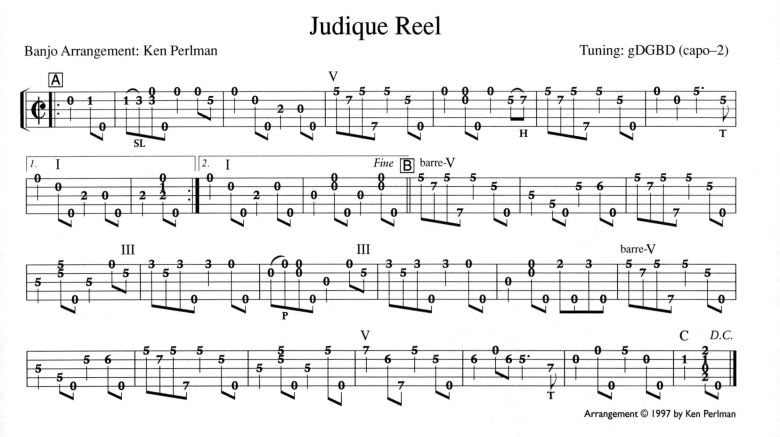

Arrangement © 1997 by Ken Perlman

On blues harmonica, it is customary to play Key-of-E blues on an A Harp (that is, a harmonica tuned to an A Major scale), Key-of-A blues on a D Harp, Key-of-D blues on a G Harp, and so on. Blues harp players refer to the process of performing in one key on a harmonica tuned for another key as "playing cross-harp."

On banjo, we find it necessary now and again to play a tune in one key while employing a tuning designed for another key. Obviously, a nifty name for this process could be *playing cross-tuning*.

There are a few situations where playing cross-tuning might be a necessary or desirable step:

♦ *Key or Mode Changes within the Same Tune*. This was discussed in col. 5.3.

♦ You may wish to play a medley of two or more tunes in different keys or modes. When fiddlers play a medley, they often shift key and/or mode from tune to tune to create interest. Common shifts (using tunes in this book as examples) are from G Major to D Major (e.g., *The Flowers of Edinburgh* to *Willafjord*); D major to A Major (e.g., *Rickett's Hornpipe* to *Dinah*) and, particularly in Irish music, D Major to the E-Dorian mode (e.g., *The Maid Behind The Bar* to *Cooley's Reel)*. Obviously, if you play a medley of two tunes in two different keys or modes, one of them has to be played cross-tuning.

♦ Achieving total flexibility. Every banjo picker knows how much of a pain retuning your instrument can be, and — while some deal with this issue by showing up at a gig with several different banjos — being able to play cross tuning could sure make one's job a lot easier. I have met a few players who claim

that they play everything out of a single tuning, usually double C. I even once met a fellow who dealt with this issue by having an instrument built with a neck that had a tenor-banjo scale length, but also had a fifth string. Since he tuned the banjo in fifths like a tenor (CGDA or GDAE), it allowed him as much flexibility as he could want. I doubt, however, if such an arrangement would feel right to most frailers.

Speaking of the fifth string, you're probably wondering what you do with it when playing cross tuning. Well, actually you can do all kinds of things depending on the particular relationship between the cross key on one hand, and the pitch of the open-5th on the other. Sometimes the fifth string can be used for melody, or for an interesting "dissonant" accent. Sometimes the fifth string is actually part of the tonic, or "key-chord" of a cross key. For example, when you play in the key of E-Dorian out of G-tuning, the fifth string is indeed a note in the key-chord E-minor. Similarly, when you play in E♭ out of double C-tuning, the fifth string is a note in the key-chord E♭ major. Alternatively, certain "subsidiary" but important chords in the cross key might go with the fifth string. For example, if you're playing in the key of F out of a C-tuning, the open fifth string can be used freely whenever you play the *dominant* chord, or C major. Or, if you're playing in B♭ out of mountain minor, you can hit the fifth string whenever you use the *sub-dominant*, or E♭ chord (col. 6.10 discusses some aspects of chord theory).

Example 5-8 shows the location for notes in a number of scales as they appear cross-tuning in open G-tuning. Example 5-9 shows the same information for double C-tuning (gCGCD), while Example 5-10 deals with mountain minor (gDGCD). Note that a capo at the second fret raises C scales to D, G scales to A, and so on.

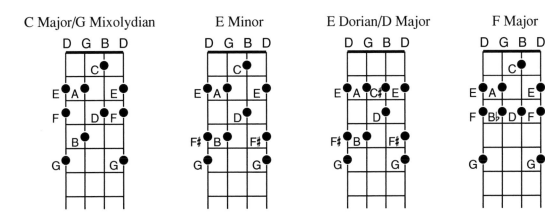

Example 5-8 (gDGBD)

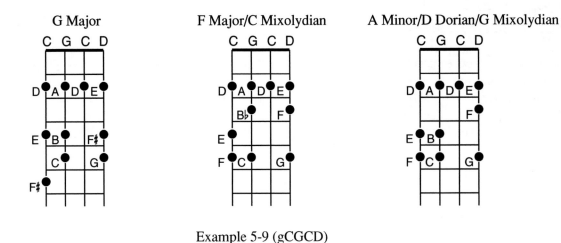

Example 5-9 (gCGCD)

Example 5-10 (gDGCD)

Accompanying this column are a series of exercises that offer a feel of how certain cross keys work in the three most common tunings. Exercises E-1a and E-1b illustrate how to play in D-major and E-Dorian out of G-tuning. Exercises E-2a and E-2b show how to play in F-major and B-flat major out of mountain minor. Exercises E-3a and E-3b illustrate how to play in F-major, D-Dorian and E♭ major out of double C.

Some tunes in this book played cross-tuning include *President Garfield's Hornpipe*, *Miss Johnson of Pittworth* and *Janet Beaton* (these three tunes are in B♭, and are arranged cross-tuning out of mountain minor). Another tune set cross-tuning is *Hull's Victory*, which is played in E♭ from double C tuning (the tune is in F, counting the capo).

Exercises E1–3

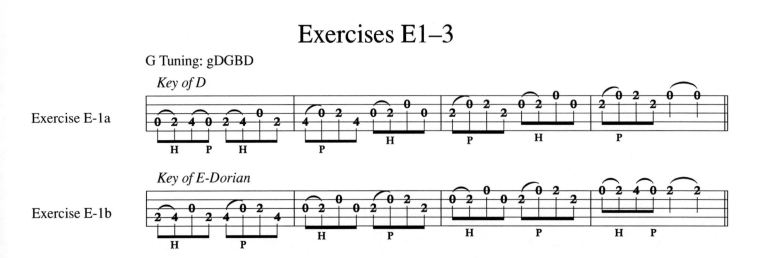

120

C Tuning: gDGCD

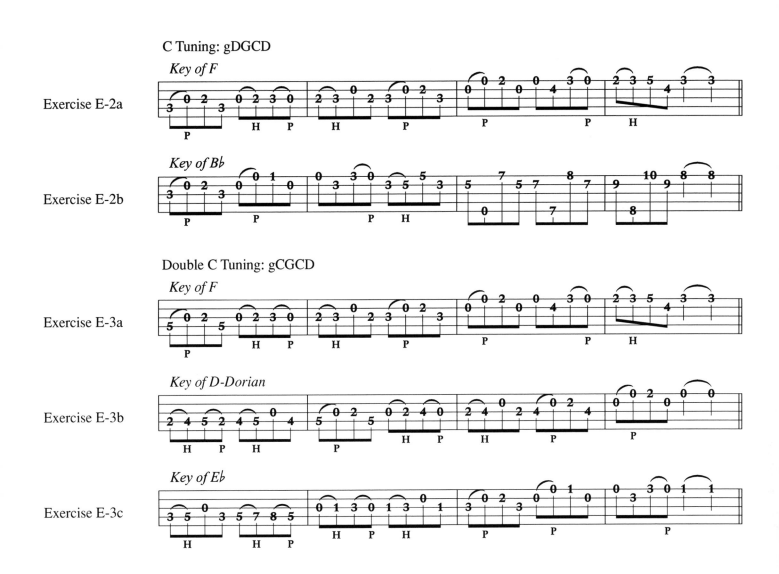

5.6 Playing in B♭ and Other Flat Keys   (Dec 88)
5.7 Playing in E♭   (Aug '89)
5.8 Playing in F   (Mar '88)

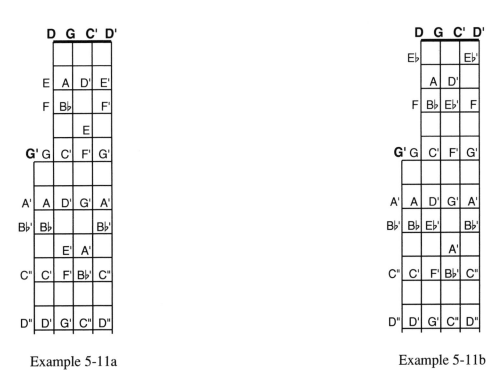

Example 5-11a   Example 5-11b

In July of 1988, I spent a week observing classes in Scottish fiddle playing at Stirling University in Stirling, Scotland. Coming out of an American scene where most tunes are in D, G and A, I was surprised to find a significant portion of the mainstream Scottish repertoire in the keys of F, B♭ and E♭. Two instructors in particular — Ian Powrie and Alastair Hardie — took special pains to show their classes how to adapt ordinary first-position fiddle fingering patterns to playing in the flat keys. It soon became clear that handling tunes in F and B♭ wasn't a heck of a lot harder for the average fiddler than dealing with tunes in D and G. In the process I also became aware that the Scottish flat-key repertoire contained some really exquisite tunes!

Until then, I had usually dealt with B♭ or E♭ tunes by transposing them to G or C respectively, and capoing up to the third fret. For tunes in F, I used a C-tuning and capoed up to the fifth fret. As a result of my Stirling experiences, however, I've been rethinking my flat-key strategy. Let's first look at how the key of B♭ can be handled. Then we'll turn our attention to E♭ and F.

Many B♭ tunes can be arranged for banjo very successfully using ordinary mountain minor tuning (gDGCD). This tuning has been customarily employed for tunes in the G-Dorian mode (G-A-B♭-C-D-E-F-G). The notes that make up this mode can be obtained at the fingering positions shown in Example 5-11a (review also Example 5-3a).

Tunes that are in G natural minor (also known as the Aeolian mode: G-A-B♭-C-D-E♭-F-G), are also often played in this tuning. The notes that make up G-Aeolian can be obtained at the fingering positions shown in Example 5-11b. As you can see, G-Aeolian and G-Dorian differ from each other by only a single note. Specifically, E is flat in Aeolian, but natural in Dorian.

Now, B♭ major and G-Aeolian/natural-minor are *relative* scales. In other words, they are made up of exactly the same notes. The only difference between them is in the tonic or key center. (B♭ is the most important note in B♭ major; G is the most important note in G minor/Aeolian). So, the notes for both scales are found at exactly the same points on the banjo neck (that is, the ones shown in Example 5-11b).

The upshot here is that if you can play G minor tunes from mountain minor tuning, you should also be able to play B♭ major tunes in mountain minor. Moreover, all open strings in the tuning (g, D, G, C and D) are in the B♭ scale, and the overtones that are characteristic of the tuning seem to adequately support a B♭ tone center.

The only difficulty here is that the fifth string tuned to G may give your B♭ major tunes a little too much of a minor cast. In other words, a continually sounding high G with this gamut

of notes implies G minor/Aeolian to the ear. If this bothers you, try tuning the fifth string down to F or up to B♭.

Playing in the key of F Major has long been a problem key for clawhammer pickers used to playing in C- and G-based tunings. To begin with, capoing is rarely helpful. If your banjo is in G tuning (gDGBD) you'd have to capo up to the tenth fret to get F. In any of the common C tunings, you'd have to capo up to the fifth fret to get F. (Fifth fret capoing is not undesirable in itself, but you'd probably have to install a fifth string capo or extra railroad spike in order to tune the fifth string up to match the capoed long strings.)

One solution to the capoing dilemma is tuning the entire banjo to an F tuning. You could, for example, tune each string in G tuning (gDGBD) down a full step to fCFAC. This works theoretically, but in practice the process of tuning five wayward banjo strings a full step in the same direction is a major project. Another possibility is an F tuning sometimes known as Sandy River Belle Tuning (fCFCD). This has the advantage of being easy to reach from Double C Tuning (gCGCD) as follows:

♦ Tune the third string down to match the pitch of fret 5, string 4 (F below middle C)

♦ Tune the fifth string down to match the pitch of fret 3, string 1 (F above middle C)

There are some disadvantages to fCFCD, however. First, it's yet another tuning to become familiar with. Second, with the exception of certain tunes with a strong Pentatonic flavor like Sandy River Belle and Rambling Hobo, fiddle tunes just don't seem to note very conveniently in this tuning. Third, many chords you'll need in the tuning are inconveniently fingered.

A more effective way to go is play F tunes "cross tuning." In other words, play the notes in F, but use a conventional or slightly modified C or G tuning. To this end, review Example 5-9 in col. 5.4-5 to see where F-major scale-notes fall in double-C tuning (gCGCD), and review Example 5-10 to see where F-major scale-notes fall in mountain minor tuning (gDGCD).

There is still another possibility that occurred to me not long ago. I had been aware that double C Tuning (gCGCD) was pretty much as effective for C minor tunes as for C major tunes (with capo at second fret: D minor and D major tunes). I realized that since E flat major had the same notes as C minor, I could probably play E flat tunes in double C tuning. Moreover, since the note G is in the E♭ major chord, I wouldn't even have to retune the fifth string. And, since E♭ major capoed at the second fret becomes F major, I could segue from a D tune to an F tune without retuning! Example 5-12 shows where E flat scale notes fall in double-C tuning, which become key of F scale notes when you capo at the second fret.

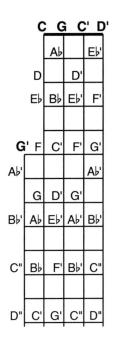

C	G	C'	D'
	A♭		E♭'
D		D'	
E♭	B♭	E♭'	F'
G'	F	C'	F'	G'
A♭'			A♭'
	G	D'	G'
B♭'	A♭	E♭'	A♭'	B♭'
C"	B♭	F'	B♭'	C"
D"	C'	G'	C"	D"

Example 5-12

Two tunes accompany this column. The first is *Janet Beaton*, a Cape Breton jig in the key of B♭, which I've arranged "cross tuning" in mountain minor (review cols. 3.7-10 on playing jigs). I learned it from Ludger LeFort, a Cape Breton fiddler who lives in Waltham, Massachusetts. The second is *Hull's Victory*, a contra dance tune usually played in F. I've arranged it in the key of E♭ out of gCGCD tuning: a capo placed at the second fret yields F and allows the tune to be "medleyed" with any key of D tune you choose.

Janet Beaton

Banjo Arrangement: Ken Perlman

Tuning: gDGCD

Arrangement © 1988 by Ken Perlman

123

Hull's Victory

Banjo Arrangement: Ken Perlman   Tuning: gCGCD (capo–2)

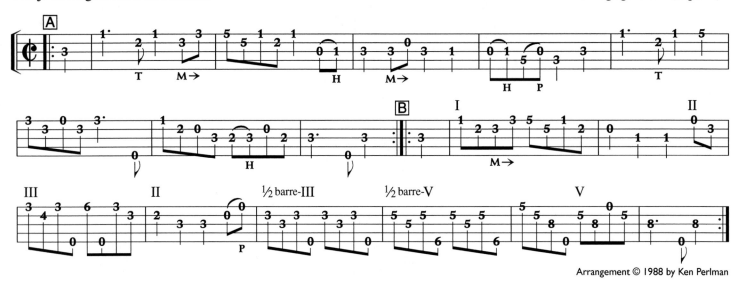

Arrangement © 1988 by Ken Perlman

5.9 Playing in A out of G-tuning   (Apr. '00)

Recently, a friend of mine from Syracuse, New York named John Rossbach played me a ditty he had just penned on the mandolin called *The Gemstone Reel*. I expressed a liking for the tune, which was more or less in the key of A-mixolydian (like A-major but with a flat-seventh scale note), and tried to play it as I normally play tunes in that key: in G-tuning capoed up to the second fret, and with the fifth string capoed up to match.

After I'd tried it that way for a while, John showed me how Karl Lauber, the banjoist in John's Chestnut Grove bluegrass band, played the tune. It seems that Lauber used an uncapoed-G tuning with only the fifth string capoed or tuned up to A. In other words, he was playing the key of A *cross-tuning* out of what was essentially open G tuning.

I tried the tune this way clawhammer style, and damn if it didn't suit the tune perfectly. Before you try the tune, try just a scale to see how the key of A-mixolydian operates out of G tuning. Let's get into the tuning to begin with: conventional

G tuning with the fifth string tuned up to match the pitch of fret 7, string one (or, put the string into a railroad spike or fifth-string capo at the seventh fret).

Example 5-13 illustrates an ascending and descending octave scale, followed by a series of notes down and back on the third and fourth strings, beginning and ending on the note A (fret 2, string 3). Example 5-14 shows a more complex run, which starts with an arpeggio (roll-like) motion (review col. 2.9), then continues with combinations of open M-played notes with up-the-neck fretted thumb notes (review col. 2.13).

Some hints: Part A, meas. 1 starts with a three-string arpeggio followed by a drop thumb. In Part B, meas. 2 the fifth string at its A-pitch clashes with the G-chord harmony at that point, so the drone is provided by a thumb-played third-string note. In part B, meas. 4, the fifth string note is tied over, and the thumb gets its next note as a drop thumb (review cols. 1.12-13).

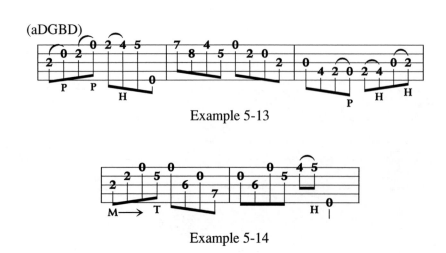

Example 5-13

Example 5-14

124

Gemstone Reel

By John Rossbach

Tuning: aDGBD

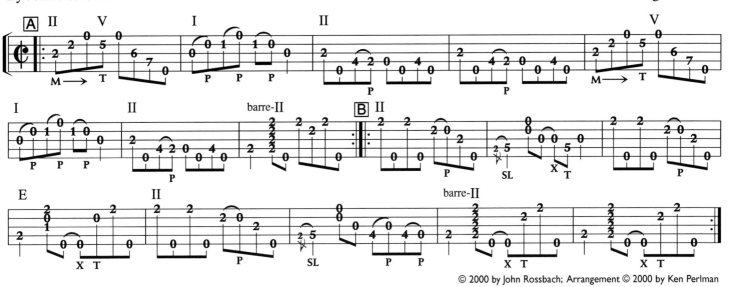

© 2000 by John Rossbach; Arrangement © 2000 by Ken Perlman

Ken with vocalist Marybeth Lahr, c.1978. The duo played Irish pubs in the New York City region.

CHAPTER 6: LEARNING, ARRANGING AND BACKUP

6.1 Learning by Ear   (Dec. '94)

A couple of readers have written in of late with questions about playing by ear. One reader wanted some tips on how to go about the process. The other wanted to know if it was even OK to go about learning tunes in this manner, as opposed to learning from tab or sheet music.

Let's deal with the second issue first. Not only is learning tunes by ear OK, but it is infinitely preferable to learning tunes from either sheet music or tab. When you learn by ear, you generally pick up a host of stylistic nuances that are impossible to glean from a written version. Written music or tab can be an aid to learning by ear, but they can never entirely substitute for it.

I almost always start with a version of a tune by a player I admire. I then learn that version by ear as completely as possible, gradually modifying it over time to suit my own taste and musical idiosyncrasies. Only when this process is complete does the arrangement get tabbed out.

This being said, what's the best way to learn by ear? Well, the very best way is to play at lots of music sessions with the same group of people. Since a given group tends to play more or less the same cadre of tunes at each session, you generally have a good opportunity to hear those tunes sufficiently to commit them to memory. Alternatively, a tune recorded on tape or CD can be replayed sufficiently to impress it on memory.

This last process is much easier now than it used to be. When I first took up guitar and banjo, I would take an LP and slow it down to the 16-RPM setting, then play it over and over until I got the sequence of notes I wanted. The downside was that after a few passes through, the cut was forever ruined by over-hasty needle placement. Nowadays you can replay your CDs endlessly without harm. What's more, some cassette recorders — such as the Marantz model PMD-201 — play at half speed (an octave down) with a flick of a button, and some even higher-tech devices and computer programs available today allow you to play tunes back at slower speeds without any pitch-change at all.

Once a tune is selected, there's the matter of picking it out on your instrument and coming up with a playable arrangement. Picking the tune out is really just a matter of perseverance. Make sure your banjo is in tune with the recording and plunk along with it until you are pretty sure you're in the same key. Once the key-note is established, proceed to hunt and peck for the melody notes until most of them come along.

Finding a playable arrangement is mostly a matter of experience. If you've never done this before, I suggest you start small. Try coming up with an arrangement for something on the order of Yankee Doodle: don't make your first project some complex tune like *Beaumont Rag* or *Leather Britches*.

For detailed instructions on arranging tunes for clawhammer, see cols. 6.5-9.

6.2 Picking Up Unfamiliar Melodies   (Nov. '99)

One of my students recently asked me how he could improve both his ability to sight-read standard music notation, and his ability to pick up unfamiliar melodies on the fly during jamming situations. I had to think about this a minute, since to me both activities have been fairly instinctive throughout much of my playing career.

What I finally came up with, is that I tend to work off familiar melodic "patterns" — ways of organizing melody that are so habitual that I can obtain them instantly whenever they occur in a tune. It also occurred to me that certain aspects of my childhood piano-lesson days (you know, those times when you asked for a guitar but were assured that the only way to get one was to take piano lessons for umpteen years) were probably to a great degree responsible for helping me develop these kinds of skills. By this, I mean that regularly performing certain kinds of exercises — such as scales, arpeggios, and combinations of the two — had probably created a mental set that was conducive to being able to break down melodies systematically, thereby making it easier to function in unfamiliar situations.

Essentially, melodies are pleasing combinations of two kinds of musical movement: *scalar motion* (that is, moving among contiguous notes one at a time) and *leaps* (movement that involves skipping one or more scale notes). If we can perform exercises that focus on each kind of activity and somehow transfer that to clawhammer banjo, this should ultimately be quite useful in helping to develop the right "melodic" equipment.

Let's start with an ascending and descending eighth-note G-scale in G-tuning (Example 6-1). Note that I've gone a little bit above the octave on the way up and a little bit below the key-note on the way down. This is to extend the range of easily obtainable notes in both directions. Using this G scale as a template, it would also make sense to try playing other scale exercises in the same tuning, and also to devise scale exercises for other tunings.

One of the more common "leaps" found in music is the *arpeggio,* or movement from point to point *in a chord* (not to be confused with the arpeggio *technique* described in column 2.9, which refers to movement from *string to string*). Since fiddle tunes often contain arpeggiated passages (that is, phrases made up of notes that outline the shape of a chord) it makes sense to also try some arpeggio exercises in clawhammer style. One such exercise is shown in Example 6-2. Again, try making up others in G-tuning for yourself, or try adapting this idea to create similar exercises for other tunings.

In practice, it is relatively rare to encounter purely scalar or chord-arpeggio passages in fiddle tunes. Much more likely are phrases made up of combinations of the two: for example a leap up from one note to the next note in a chord, followed by a "scalar" (tone by tone) descent. Alternatively, you could have a scalar ascent followed by a leap downward. Exercises focusing on each of these patterns appear in Examples 6-3 and 6-4. Or, try a series in which you leap up three notes, then return to

the original note by scale steps (Example 6-5). Observe that these exercises are quite similar to those used to prepare you for clawhammer *improvisation* (column 2.4). The melodic fingering forms discussed in cols. 2.16-17 are also designed to express the same musical ideas.

Try coming up with additional exercises that cover other commonly encountered patterns.

I know that doing exercises is not the favorite pastime of most banjo pickers, and there's no doubt that playing exercises certainly can be boring when time is limited and there are so many good tunes around to learn. But the main object here is to use exercises to achieve a better mental focus on the instrument. Since the mind is actively engaged, the process can actually be stimulating. Ultimately, it's just a matter of how much you want to acquire these skills. After all, there's no reason why the banjo shouldn't be treated as seriously as the piano!

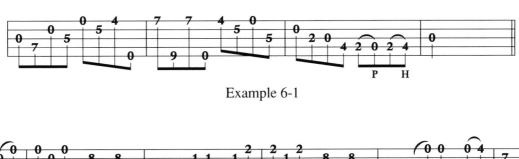

Example 6-1

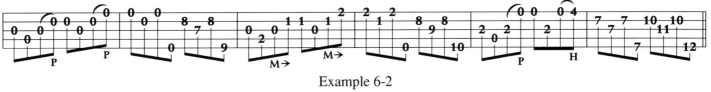

Example 6-2

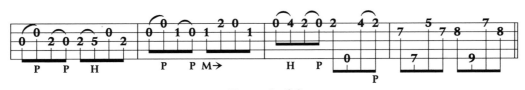

Example 6-3

Example 6-4

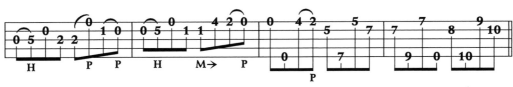

Example 6-5

127

One fine June day a few years ago, when I was on tour in England, my host of the moment took me along to a small old-timey music session in the nearby city of Leeds. The local group of pickers were pretty well up on the current crop of old-time Southern favorites, and we quickly ran through a number of those. Then we got on to a few numbers that were more in the Scottish/Irish vein. Finally someone leaned over to the fiddler and said, "I bet Ken hasn't heard *The Leeds Hornpipe*." He was right, I hadn't heard it, and as they say over there, it was a *cracker* (i.e., a really good tune)!

I didn't have a tape recorder handy, so I whipped out a sheet of paper and asked the fiddler to play the tune. Because I was familiar with the *fiddle scale*, (the way a players fingers must be placed on the instrument to produce the various notes) the tune was a cinch to learn and subsequently commit to writing. Whichever notes I couldn't quite get by ear, I could discern by watching the spots where his fingers pressed the strings down.

Most of you I'm sure are aware that watching the guitar player's fingers can make a banjoist's life easier. Specifically, each guitar chord has a certain fingering shape, and watching how these shapes succeed each other can give an immediate picture of a tune's harmony. In fact, I highly recommend that every banjo player learn enough guitar to be able to recognize

all the common chord positions as they are played. Believe me, you won't regret it!

Similarly, knowing fiddle fingerings gives you two kinds of information. First, you can get the key of the tune by watching the fiddler's fingers. The method here is relatively easy — you just see where he or she is *stopping* [pressing down] the strings *when the tune sounds final*. That's usually the key note of the tune.

What's more (as previously mentioned), you can actually pick up sequences of notes from the fiddler "on the fly."

The best way to begin your understanding of fiddle fingerings is to learn the mandolin fretboard (mandolins have the same tuning and string length as fiddles, but luckily for us, they have frets). Let's look at a diagram of the mandolin fingerboard, shown in Example 6-6a. Before we begin our discussion, you need to be aware that mandolins have four strings (each string is actually doubled, but for the sake of simplicity I'll refer to each set or *course* as a single string), with each string tuned to the *seventh fret* of its lower neighbor. These strings are tuned (from low to high) to G, D, A and E. You should also be aware that most fiddle tunes have a *range* that ascends no higher on the instrument than the seventh fret.

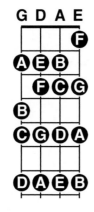

MANDOLIN FRETBOARD

Example 6-6a

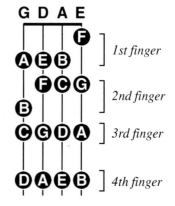

VIOLIN FINGERBOARD

Example 6-6b

Let's look first at the fourth string, which is tuned to G. You get A at fret 2, B at fret 4, C at fret 5 and D at fret 7. Generally speaking A is played with the first finger, B with the second, C with the third and D with the fourth. For tunes with a C♯, the third finger is stretched out further to fret 6.

Let's look at the third string, tuned to D. You get E at the second fret, F at the third, G at the fifth and A at the seventh. Here, E is played with the first finger, F with the second, G with the third and A with the fourth. For tunes with an F♯, the second finger is stretched out further to fret 4. For tunes with a G♯, the third finger is stretched out further to fret 6.

On the second string (tuned to A), you get B at the second fret, C at the third, D at the fifth and E at the seventh. Here, B is played with the first finger, C with the second, D with the third and E with the fourth. For tunes with a C♯, the second finger is stretched out to the fourth fret.

On the first string (tuned to E) you get F at the first fret, G at the third, A at the fifth and B at the seventh. Here, F is played with the first finger, G with the second, A with the third and B with the fourth. For tunes with an F♯, the first finger is moved up to the second fret; for tunes with a G♯, the second finger is stretched out to the fourth fret.

Once you become familiar with the mandolin fingerboard, and with mandolin fingering (it's probably worth getting hold of an inexpensive mandolin to practice on), it's easy to associate notes — not only with certain frets — but with certain fingers. In other words (looking across the instrument from the fourth to the first string) the first finger *always* plays A, E, B or F/F#; the second finger *always* plays B, F/F#, C/C#, or G/G#; the third finger *always plays* C/C#, G/G#, D or A; the fourth finger plays D, A, E or B.

When you have made the association of certain fingers with certain notes, you can make the transition to understanding the fiddle fingerboard, which has no frets. This is shown in figure 6-6b. Looking across the strings again from fourth through first, the first finger *always* plays A, E, B or F/F#; the second finger *always* plays B, F/F#, C/C#, or G/G#; the third finger *always plays* C/C#, G/G#, D or A; the fourth finger plays D, A, E and B. If you can picture the fiddlers' movements in this way, it is that much simpler to pick up the notes that he or she is playing.

Tab for *The Leeds Hornpipe* appears in this volume along with column 3.2.

6.4 Learning from Tune Books and Other Sources

(June '87)

Let's say you've scoured every clawhammer banjo-tab collection known to man and the one tune you really want to learn is just not to be found, Or you've more-or-less mastered most of the banjo tabs you could lay your hands on and are thirsting for new material, What next?

If you can read music, fiddle-tune collections are an obvious source for new material. The process is simple: you merely "read" the notes for a given tune on your instrument and gradually work out an effective arrangement, You have the option of working with familiar material (i.e., tunes you have heard before), or of *sight-reading* tunes at random until you find ones you like. If you use books as a tune source, remember that you may have to do some *transposing* (key changing). After all, many D tunes are played on banjo in C capoed at the second fret, many A tunes are played on banjo in G capoed at the second fret, and so on.

Some well-known or comprehensive fiddle-tune books are:[1]

♦ David Brodie, *The Fiddle Tune Fake Book* (Music Sales)
♦ R.P. Christeson, *The Old Time Fiddler's Repertory* (University of Missouri Press)
♦ Kate Dunlay, *Traditional Celtic Violin Music of Cape Breton* (Mel Bay)
♦ [James Spiers Kerr]. *Kerr's Collection of Merry Melodies for the Violin*
♦ Keith Norman MacDonald, *The Skye Collection*
♦ Capt. Francis O'Neill, *O'Neill's Music of Ireland*
♦ Stacy Phillips, *Traditional American Fiddle Tunes* (Mel Bay)
♦ Ken Perlman, *The Fiddle Music of Prince Edward Island* (Mel Bay)
♦ *The Roche Collection of Traditional Irish Music* (Ossian Publications)
♦ [Wm., Bradbury Ryan] *1000 Fiddle Tunes* (now available through Mel Bay as *Ryan's Mammoth Collection*)
♦ Susan Songer, *The Portland Collection* (private printing)
♦ James Stewart-Robinson, *The Athole Collection*

There are several disadvantages to learning unfamiliar material from fiddle-tune collections. First there is the accuracy question. Just how close to what musicians actually play is the series of notes on the page in front of you? All too often the answer to this question is, "not close enough!"

Fiddle tunes may be structurally and harmonically simple, but they are melodically complex. The structure is elementary — most often two repeated eight measure sections. The harmony is usually confined to a few basic triads (triads include such basic chords as C, G, Am and so on). But the melodies are often both beautiful and memorable — despite the fact that the composer only has somewhere between 75 and 125 notes to make a statement.

No one would ever think of changing even a single note of a famous symphony, yet symphonies are made up of thousands upon thousands of notes and the alteration of a few here or there would most likely go un-noticed. But many tune-book compilers think nothing of presenting written versions of fiddle-tunes that differ substantially from actual played versions. After all, if a tune only has 100 notes, it only takes a few inaccuracies to make the whole piece fall apart.

I am not implying here that there is one and only one version of a given fiddle tune. There are certainly legitimate regional and even personal variations. Each fiddle tune worthy of the name, however, has at least a couple of unique memorable phrases that immediately identify it and that have the power to send the true fiddle-tune aficionado into swoons of ecstasy. The effect of these phrases — I'll call them *signature phrases* — depends on a fairly exact sequences of notes.

It is quite a detailed process for the notater to get these exact sequences correctly, and it is all too easy to get them a little bit wrong. And, if you get the signature phrases of a particular tune wrong, it can sound "tuneless" when played through.

---

[1] In recent years it has also been possible to down-load tunes off the internet. For example, I am assured that the entire contents of *O'Neill's Music of Ireland* is available on line.

Tunebooks can also err on the side of including too many notes. Some books include so many triplets and ornaments, for example, that the basic melodies of many tunes are obscured.

Another problem with tune-books stems from that old saw about a little knowledge being dangerous. For example, whoever did the music notation for *O'Neills Music of Ireland* obviously knew about major, melodic minor and harmonic minor scales, but they must have had little notion of the modes. In order to make modal tunes fit in with their musical "knowledge," therefore, they simply introduced sharps, flats and naturals into written versions — even though these *accidentals* were not present in played versions.[2]

At any rate, tune-books are most helpful when used in conjunction with other sources. Let's say you have a portion of a tune running in your head from listening to a recording or live performance. Consulting a written version can then help you get the rest of the tune down. Most importantly, having already heard the tune, you are in a position to judge just how good the written version is.

Of course, the very best sources for correctly played tunes are live musicians or professionally recorded tapes and CDs of fiddle music (see cols. 6.1-3).

6.5 The Arcane Art of Arranging

(Mar. '85)

Arranging is the art of making a melody playable on an instrument or group of instruments. An arrangement can be excruciatingly simple — just a bare-bones melody — or highly complex, complete with harmony, counterpoint, improvisation, syncopation, ornamentation, and so on.

No matter how far you progress in mastering material arranged by others, you will never be considered a full-fledged artist in your own right unless you start arranging and performing your own material. And the earlier in your playing career you begin experimenting with the arranging process, the sooner you will be able to make the quantum leap from student to artist.

The art of arranging is very much like the art of expository (non-fiction) writing. You can teach students the alphabet, spelling, vocabulary, grammar, punctuation and syntax, but you can't teach them directly how to write. Instead, subjects for compositions are assigned, like "What I Did On My Summer Vacation," "My Favorite Career," and "Why I Want To Win the State Lottery." When assignments are completed, they can be corrected for obvious errors, and suggestions for improvement can be made. As each student advances in age and experience, their assigned compositions generally improve both technically and stylistically. As a result, after twelve to sixteen years of schooling most of us are capable of writing coherently on a variety of subjects.

Similarly, you can teach pitch, rhythm, theory, harmony, counterpoint, syncopation, ornamentation and dozens of playing techniques, but you can't directly teach arranging. You can only make assignments, correct mistakes and offer suggestions. In the several years required to master the arranging process, a student goes from picking out a note-for-note version of *Skip To My Lou* to making up his or her own arrangement for *Dill Pickle Rag*, complete with several variations.

The key to the last sentence is the words "several years." Despite our natural tendency towards impatience, students have

to accept that their first arranging efforts will result in some pretty basic, unexciting stuff. Developing a unique, recognizable arranging style requires countless attempts and experiments, not to mention quite a bit of seasoning.

Having said this much, let me offer a few pointers for getting started arranging your own material. Once you get the hang of it, I'm sure you'll find it one of the great joys associated with playing music.

◆ *Get started early.* Don't wait until you're a technically adept player to start arranging your own stuff. You'll find it much harder to accept the minimal level of your first efforts and too easy to continue just learning other peoples' work. Start adapting material to your instrument as soon as you master brush-thumbing and a few basic chords. The best tunes for first attempts are simple melodies you've known since childhood, such as *Yankee Doodle, This Old Man, O Susannah, Camptown Races, Sweet Betsy From Pike, When The Saints Go Marching In, Skip To My Lou* and the two dozen or so most popular Christmas carols. For best results, put your banjo in your favorite tuning and pick out the melody for a given tune by ear. Then pick out the harmony (that is, the chords for the tune) by ear. Finally, try putting them together by ear.

◆ *Don't be too self-critical.* Mozart may have written a symphony at the age of six, but most human beings (including most of those later called geniuses by history) require years of effort at a particular art or discipline before their talent begins to shine through. Your first several dozen efforts will probably not impress anybody, and they are even less likely to be comparable to what you hear on records. Don't let this discourage you! Just try to enjoy the process of arranging for its own sake, and somewhere down the line you may discover that you have developed a knack or even a great talent for it. If you give up early in the game because of unrealistic self-criticism, your talent will certainly never manifest itself.

---

[2] According to a biographer, Capt. Francis O'Neill was himself virtually musically illiterate: most of the notation for his book was actually done by a number of others, notably an associate named James O'Neill (no relation).

♦ *Emulate your favorite musicians.* As I developed technically as a guitarist and banjo player, I spent much of my practice time trying to copy the playing styles of my favorite artists. When a new song came to my attention that I wanted to learn, I patterned my arrangement style after those of my heroes. Copying the styles of established artists gives you a secure place to start. And, since no exact copy of someone else's style is possible, it gives you a chance to be creative despite yourself!

♦ *Steal everything you can.* Whenever you learn a new piece arranged by someone else, ask yourself, "What do I like about this piece?" and "What special licks and techniques are used?" Above all the question is, "What can I take from this arrangement to make my own arrangements better?" If you like a particular break, see how you can fit it into one of your arrangements; if you like a given series of ornaments, see how you can use the same series in another tune; if you like a particular syncopation, see how it can work for you elsewhere, and so on. Since everyone likes to be quoted, the artists you borrow from won't be offended. After all, "Imitation is the sincerest form of flattery!"

♦ *Keep your arrangements abreast of your technical development.* As your playing improves, try to keep your arrangements up to date. When you learn to drop-thumb, for example, try to work drop-thumbing into some of your already existing arrangements. The same goes for every new technique you learn.

Always make sure you understand how each new technique is used to enhance someone else's arrangement, then attempt to apply that understanding to one of your own.

♦ *Arrange to Your Strengths.* Bear in mind that people who write tabs (myself included) always play to their own strengths. Yes, I'm always looking for a particular sound and phrasing, but I'm also looking for something that comes naturally to *me*. When I was starting out, it was a major step forward to discover that it was perfectly OK to re-configure a troublesome passage in someone else's arrangement. The upshot here is that you should craft your arrangements to suit your own style of playing.

♦ *Ask accomplished arrangers for help.* Don't be too proud (or shy) to ask for help in your arranging efforts. Outside input can be invaluable in guiding your development. If you are taking lessons, you already have an obvious person to turn to. If not, try to corner (or schedule occasional lessons with) accomplished players that live in or pass through your area. Or, try attending festivals that feature clawhammer artists and ask for advice in a quiet moment.

♦ *Organize a self-help group.* If you know several other players at about your own level who live nearby, why not meet periodically for a session of airing out and constructively criticizing each other's arrangements?

6.6 Arranging by Formula

(June '85)

My first column on arranging stated my general philosophy on the subject, but I didn't really offer any concrete hints. So if you've never arranged anything for clawhammer before, or you have only the foggiest notion of how to go about it, the suggestions that follow are for you. The place to start is the melody of the tune. Pick out the melody on your banjo in as basic a version as you can. (If you can read standard notation, a printed version of the melody is acceptable).

Many of you may complain at this point that you have no ear, but I say to this idea, "Fiddlesticks!" Anyone who appreciates music enough to want to play an instrument has an OK ear and is perfectly capable of picking out a simple melody. If you don't believe me, try picking out the melody to Yankee Doodle in open-G tuning (Hint: the first note is the open third string).

Then, work out the chords that go along with the tune, (or obtain them from a printed source or musician friend). Once you have the melody and chords you are still left with the problem of combining them and making the result sound like banjo music. Now, to make banjo music, you have to learn to think like a banjoist. I've found that the best way to get my students to think "banjoistically" is to have them first learn to arrange by formula. Taking for a first project a *lead sheet* (that is, a version consisting of just melody plus chord symbols) for *Grandfather's Clock*, here's Perlman's patented arranging formula for fearless frailers:

♦ *Step 1.* You can, at the most basic level, simply play all quarter notes with the M finger (for other possibilities, see steps 6 and 7).

♦ *Step 2.* Take all half notes in the melody and change them to a quarter note plus a brush-thumb (that is, a bumm-titty strum) on the appropriate chord, as shown in Example 6-7a.

♦ *Step 3.* Take all of the dotted half notes in the tune and change them to a quarter note followed by a brush-thumb, followed by another quarter note, as shown in Example 6-7b.

♦ *Step 4.* Replace some whole notes with two bumm-titty strums, as shown in Example 6-7c.

♦ *Step 5.* Replace other whole notes — particularly those tied over to notes in another measure — with a bumm-titty strum plus a hammer lick, as shown in Example 6-7d.

♦ *Step 6.* For added interest, change some pairs of quarter notes into a hammer-on or pull-off plus brush-thumb, as shown in Example 6-7e.

♦ *Step 7.* For still more interest, add drone notes to some quarter notes, as shown in Example 6-7f (see also cols 2.1-3).

KIND OF NOTE   BECOMES:

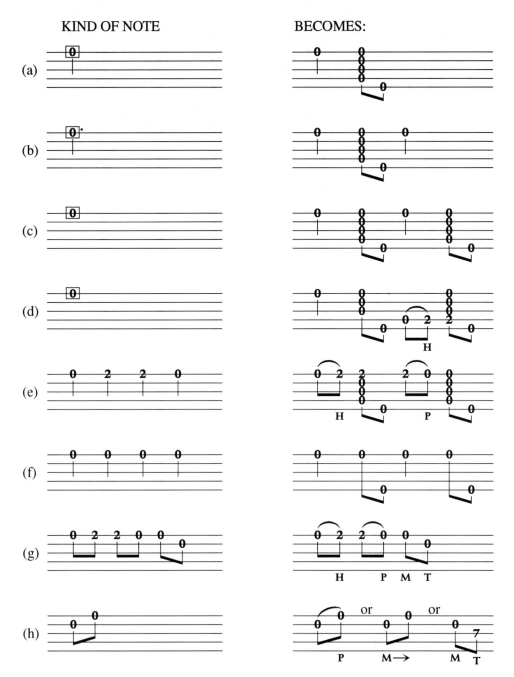

Example 6-7

Taking just these elements, I've put together an arrangement of *Grandfather's Clock* that is at least respectable as a banjo piece. I'm convinced you can do the same with this or with most other simple tunes. For ideas on how to spice up a simple arrangement such as this one, review columns 1.12-13, paying particular attention to how the syncopated version of *Buffalo Gals* was put together.

For more complex melodies with lots of eighth notes, remember that in many cases the way in which notes fall on the instrument dictates which technique will be most effective to play them. As illustrated in Example 6-7g, a pair of ascending eighth notes on the same string usually calls for a hammer-on, a pair of descending eighth notes on the same string usually calls for a pull-off, a pair of descending eighth notes on adjacent strings generally calls for a drop thumb, and so on (see cols. 1.2-3 and 1.7). Alternatively, two ascending eighth notes on adjacent strings (Example 6-7h) can call for a variety of techniques, such as off-string hammer-ons or pull-offs (col. 1.8), arpeggios (col. 2.9), and up the neck fingering patterns (cols. 2.16-17).

132

Grandfather's Clock
Lead Sheet

Banjo Arrangement: Ken Perlman

Tuning: gDGBD

Arrangement © 1985 by Ken Perlman

Grandfather's Clock
Banjo Arrangement

Banjo Arrangement: Ken Perlman

Tuning: gDGBD

Arrangement © 1985 by Ken Perlman

By far, the lion-share of writing that has been done in this column has been devoted to playing fiddle tunes on banjo in clawhammer style. Why so much attention on fiddle tunes? Much of this comes from the way players thought about the banjo back in the early 70s when I took up the instrument. At that time Pete Seeger's influence was still paramount, and most open-back banjo playing you heard involved song arrangements and song accompaniment. Playing fiddle tunes at that time was a novelty. Since everyone already knew how to play songs on the instrument, it seemed that the aspect of banjo that needed most attention was tunes-playing.

Nowadays, I think the situation has reversed itself to some degree. There are plenty of tunes-tabs around (many of them, in fact, are mine), but there really aren't too many available tabs for vocal numbers. In fact, when players new to the banjo look for song-accompaniment models these days, they are sometimes at a loss for where to turn.

This subject came up recently when I got a call from an Ohio banjoist who was having trouble adapting the Australian song *Waltzing Matilda* to clawhammer. There was one part that just wouldn't come out right. I asked him to tab out his attempt and fax it to me along with the sheet music. Once I got his tab, the problem was immediately clear. Basically, he had intermingled two *metric* approaches to song material: *straight-time* and *double-time*. This has happened often enough with my own students so I can probably point to this as a major pitfall when arranging simple melodies. You must keep these two different approaches sorted out or it results in confusion.

In *straight-time*, you play at exactly the same rate that the melody moves. When there's a quarter note in the melody, you play a quarter note; when there's an eighth note, you play an eighth note, and so on. For notes longer than a quarter note, you generally fill in with some combination of notes and brushes, (see col. 6.6). The reason for all this filling in is that the sound of the instrument dies away very quickly after being struck. Long notes are therefore extremely uninteresting.

Straight time is most appropriate for song melodies when you want to create a gentle, relatively sophisticated rendition.

In *double-time* (Example 6-8), you actually play *twice as fast* as the melody progresses. Every eighth note in the melody becomes a quarter note in your arrangement (6-8a), every quarter note becomes a bum-titty strum (Example 6-8b), while every half note becomes two bum-titty strums (Example 6-8c). In order to keep the melody progressing at a normal rate, however, you must perform the arrangement at double-speed. The advantages to double-time playing are two-fold:

♦ The playing is much faster than in straight-time. This is often regarded by audiences as more compelling or exciting than straight time.

♦ You are able to reduce nearly all banjo maneuvers to a few basic techniques. You don't have to worry too much about hammer-ons, pull-offs, drop thumbs, or other more complex maneuvers.

Double-time treatments were popularized by Pete Seeger, especially in such "novelty" numbers as *The Goofing Off Suite*. In that well-known medley, he plays a number of famous themes in double-time, such as Beethoven's *Ode To Joy*. Example 6-9a shows the basic melody for the first few bars of *Ode to Joy*, while 6-9b shows the same melody arranged double-time for clawhammer.

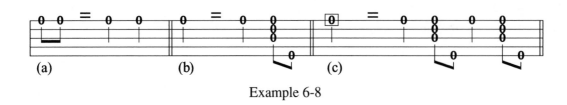

(a)   (b)   (c)

Example 6-8

Example 6-9a

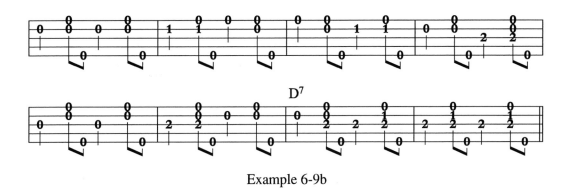

Example 6-9b

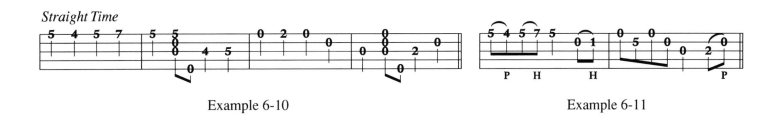

Straight Time

Example 6-10   Example 6-11

One example of a double-time arrangement in this book is Mike Seeger's *Rollin' and Tumblin' Blues* (col. 4.21).

As I noted above, intermingling straight- and double-time playing tends to create confusion. In fact, what my Ohio correspondent had done was play the first several bars of each verse in double-time, while attempting to play the last couple of bars in straight-time.

Now, a sophisticated player can indeed mix straight- and double-time segments of an arrangement to advantage. One strategy would be to play the tune a few times through in straight time, then move into double time to create more excitement. Or you can perform in straight-time when singing, then move into double time for a break. Straight- and double-time can actually be intermingled within the same verse but this is an *extremely* sophisticated approach and should only be attempted by the very advanced player.

There's still another approach to song arrangement, which could be called *half time*. In this case, the banjo player in essence is devoting *half* the time to the tune as was present in the original melody. In other words, every half note in the original tune becomes a quarter note; every quarter note becomes an eighth note; every eighth note becomes a sixteenth note, and so on. In Example 6-10, the first few bars of the famous folk song, "Golden Vanity" is shown in straight time. Example 6-11 shows the same melody in "half time." Note that in half time style the number of bars needed to play the same amount of melody is actually cut in half.

This timing approach on banjo can effect the style of attack quite dramatically. Instead of using mostly single string strokes and brush thumbs to play melody, for example, the new method of choice can feature a combination of drop-thumbs, hammer-ons and pull-offs.

When creating any arrangement from music notation, it is important to bring to bear previous experience with the piece in question, or (if you've never heard it before) previous experience with its genre. In other words, when interpreting a score it helps to know the customary playing speed and overall feel for a ballad, a sea chantey, an agricultural work-song, a cowboy song or anything else you might encounter.

6.9 Clawhammer Duets   (Sept. '83)

One of the first recorded note-for-note clawhammer duets was the version of *Green Willis* performed by Bob Carlin and Henry Sapoznik on the *Melodic Clawhammer Banjo* album (Kicking Mule #209). The effect was quite unusual, not to mention pleasing to the ear, and I'm sure many of you would like to know how to construct similar duets of your own.

Although note-for-note duets can be constructed by trial and error, your job will be a lot easier if you make use of some elementary principles of harmony. As you probably know, the building blocks of chords are musical entities called *thirds*. A third consists of any pitch, plus the pitch two "letters" higher or lower than the first pitch. For example: C-E is a third (E is two letters higher than C), as are G-B, D-F, and F-A. Alternatively, C-A is a third (A is two letters lower than C) as are G-E, D-B, and F-D. The higher note in a third is said to be a *third above* the lower note. Conversely, the lower note in a third is said to be a *third below* the upper note.

Within the context of a given scale, any melody note can be *harmonized* by playing a note that is a third above or a third below that melody note. And if every note in a tune is harmonized, the result is a note-for-note duet. In other words, you can construct a simple but effective note-for-note duet by merely putting together a part that is exactly a third above, or a third below the melody line.

Example 6-12 shows the C-major scale: first with third-above and then with third-below harmonies. The top staff shows tablature melody while the bottom staff shows tablature harmony. Observe that the note C can be harmonized by the note E (third above) or A (third below). The note G can be harmonized by B (third above), or E (third below), and so on. Example 6-13 shows the G-major scale in G-tuning with third-above and third-below harmonies.

(gCGCD)

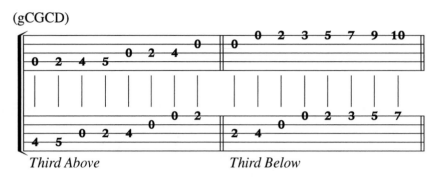

Third Above   Third Below

Example 6-12

(gDGBD)

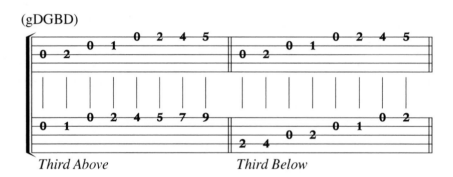

Third Above   Third Below

Example 6-13

It isn't necessary — or even desirable — to be absolutely consistent when you construct your duet part. For one thing, you don't have to stay exclusively a third above — or a third below — the melody throughout the entire tune. In most of the clawhammer duets I've heard, the harmony part stayed a third above the melody for most of the tune, but dipped to a third below on at least a few occasions. Plus there are a few instances where — in order to produce a note-for-note harmony that is compatible with the underlying chords — you have to depart somewhat from a strict third-above/third-below approach.

Of course, the final arbiter is your ear. Test out your harmony while a friend plays the melody. If you don't know any nearby clawhammer players, try recording the melody part on a cassette tape or mini-disc player at slow speed, then play your harmony part against the result.

Rick McCracken of Idaho Falls, Idaho sent in the *Rickett's Hornpipe* duet presented here. For the melody, Rick used one of my published versions of the tune. This is shown in the top staff. Rick then constructed a harmony more or less according to the principles outlined above. The harmony is shown in the bottom staff.

Let's analyze the harmony for Part A. In measures 1, 2, 4, 5, 6 & 8 (with a couple of exceptions) Rick's harmony is exactly a third above the melody. One exception is the fourth note of measure 1, where in order to maintain a C-chord harmony, a C-note (open string 2) was used instead of the third-above B note (fret 4, string 3).

In measure 3, the first half is a third below the melody while the second half is a third above the melody. Measure 7 is a third below the melody. In Part B, measure 7 is also a third below the melody. The rest of Part B is based on a third-above the melody approach.

Remember when constructing your harmony parts that the same pitch can occur in a number of locations on the fingerboard. In double C-tuning, for example, the pitch G above middle C can be found on the open fifth string, at fret 5, string 1, fret 7, string 2, fret 12, string 3 and fret 19, string 4. Similarly, the pitch middle-C occurs on the open second string, fret 5, string 3, fret 12, string 4, and so on.

136

Rickett's Hornpipe Banjo Duet

Banjo Arrangement: Ken Perlman & Rick McCracken

Tuning: gCGCD (capo–2)

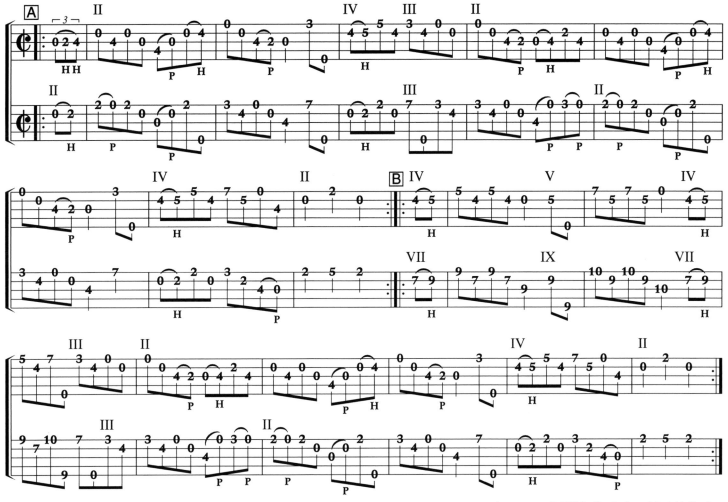

Arrangement © 1983 by Ken Perlman & Rick McCracken

6.10 Backup (and the Rudiments of Chord Theory)

(Jan. '84)

I never dreamed that I'd find myself writing a column on this subject. After all, until the melodic clawhammer movement appeared on the scene, clawhammer playing in this century was almost exclusively a back-up style. In fact, the main reason-for-being of the original Kicking Mule *Melodic Clawhammer* album and my own *Melodic Clawhammer* book was to demonstrate that it was indeed possible, even desirable, to play intricate melodies in clawhammer style.

A number of years have passed since the *Melodic Clawhammer* book and record first appeared, and there has been a slow but increasingly significant change in the way that many student pickers go about learning clawhammer. More and more players are honing their skills by learning tunes from published melodic tablatures. When faced with a situation where back-up must be played, many of these players feel lost. We may be moving from an era where pickers played back-up almost exclusively to one where many pickers do not know how to go about constructing an effective accompaniment.

With this in mind, I'll try to give a few simple rules for creating a back-up part.

Effective back-up starts with determining the key. If your printed source doesn't have the information, and your musician friends don't know it, you can usually find the *tonic* (key-note) by locating the very last note of the tune. In other words, if a tune ends in A, it is almost always in the key of A; if a tune ends in D it is almost certain to be in the key of D, and so on. For fiddle tunes, your job is simplified by the fact that most tunes are in just a few keys (pg.138).

The next step is finding the correct *mode*. Most of us are sufficiently familiar with the major scale (Do- Re-Mi-Fa-So-La-Ti-Do) to recognize when a tune is in a major key. About 75-80% of all fiddle tunes are major. Most major-key fiddle tunes are in three keys: D major, G major and A major. Sometimes you'll also encounter C-Major, F-Major or B♭-major tunes.

137

Mixolydian-mode tunes sound like major tunes in which there is something strange happening in the La-Ti-Do area. Specifically, the seventh note of the scale (Ti), is *flat* (lowered) one-half step relative to a major scale. Mixolydian scales you're likely to encounter in fiddle tunes are C-mixolydian (C-D-E-F-G-A-B♭-C), G-mixolydian (G-A-B-C-D-E-F-G), D-mixolydian (D-E-F♯-G-A-B-C-D) and A-mixolydian (A-B-C♯-D-E-F♯-G-A)

Tunes that sound "minor" are either in the *Aeolian* or *Dorian* modes. Dorian scales found frequently in fiddle tunes are D-dorian (D-E-F-G-A-B-C-D), A-dorian (A-B-C-D-E-F♯-G-A) or E-dorian (E-F♯-G-A-B-C♯-D-E). Aeolian scales commonly found in fiddle tunes include D-aeolian (D-E-F-G-A-B♭-C-D), A-aeolian (A-B-C-D-E-F-G-A), and E-aeolian (E-F♯-G-A-B-C-D-E).

Once you've established the key and mode for a particular piece of music, you need to know the chords that can be used to harmonize that key and mode. The basic chords used most frequently to accompany fiddle tunes are three-note entities called triads. I don't have the space here to go deeply into chord theory but let me just say that each scale note (numbered I through VII) is assigned a specific triad. Example 6-14 shows the triads assigned to each of the scales mentioned above. Observe that for each scale category, the kind of chord found on a given *degree* (scale number) is constant from key to key. In other words, the triad assigned to the fifth degree of a major scale is always major; the chord assigned to the second degree of a Dorian scale is always minor, and so on.

MAJOR KEY

	I	II	III	IV	V	VI	VII	VIII
C	C	Dm	Em	F	G	Am	B°*	C
G	G	Am	Bm	C	D	Em	F♯°	G
D	D	Em	F♯m	G	A	Bm	C♯°	D
A	A	Bm	C♯m	D	E	F♯m	G♯°	A

MIXOLYDIAN KEY

	I	II	III	IV	V	VI	VII	VIII
C	C	Dm	E°	F	Gm	Am	B♭	C
G	G	Am	B°	C	Dm	Em	F	G
D	D	Em	F♯°	G	Am	Bm	C	D
A	A	Bm	C♯°	D	Em	F♯m	G	A

DORIAN KEY

	I	II	III	IV	V	VI	VII	VIII
D	Dm	Em	F	G	Am	B°	C	Dm
A	Am	Bm	C	D	Em	F♯°	G	Am
E	Em	F♯m	G	A	Bm	C♯°	D	Em

AEOLIAN KEY

	I	II	III	IV	V	VI	VII	VIII
D	Dm	E°	F	Gm	Am	B♭	C	Dm
A	Am	B°	C	Dm	Em	F	G	Am
E	Em	F♯°	G	Am	Bm	C	D	Em

* °= diminished

Example 6-14

The chord built on the first degree of any scale is known as the I-chord or *tonic*. The tonic triad appears most frequently overall, and it is particularly likely to show up at the beginning, middle and end of a fiddle tune part. The next most important chord in any key is the *dominant* triad, which tends to appear just *before* the middle and end of each part. For major keys, the dominant triad is assigned to the *fifth* scale degree. For modal keys, the dominant is often assigned to the *seventh* scale degree. The third most important chord for most modes is the *subdominant* chord, which is assigned to the *fourth* degree of all scales. The triads assigned to other scale degrees also appear from time to time in tune harmonies.

The notes appearing in each passage of a tune either determine or hint at the proper chord to use for harmony. If you're lucky, the notes of the passage will actually "spell-out" a given chord. Otherwise, the passage might suggest a number of chords, and you must make an educated guess as to which chord is best. If your best guess doesn't sound right to you, try the other chords assigned to that key until you find the best fit possible.

Bay of Fundy
(with Backup Parts)

Banjo Arrangement: Ken Perlman

Tuning: gCGCD (capo–2)

Arrangement © 1984 by Ken Perlman

Let's look at the top staff of the accompanying tune, *Bay of Fundy*, which gives the melody. Both parts, A and B, end on the note C, indicating that the tune is almost certainly in some C-key (fiddlers play the tune in D, so remember to capo–2 when playing with others). The overall sound of the tune is major-like, but observe the tell-tale Bb in Part A, measure 3, indicating that at least part of the tune is in C-Mixolydian. The B-naturals appearing in Part A, measure 8 indicate that this portion of the tune is in C-Major. Part B is in the key of C-Major throughout.

The first couple of measures of Part A contain lots of C's, E's and G's, indicating a tonic C-triad harmony (C-E-G). The next two measures have plenty of F's, D's and a B♭, making the Mixolydian dominant B♭ triad (B♭-D-F) an obvious choice. Measures 5 and 6 return to a C chord. Measure 7 starts with an ambiguous series of notes that sound best to me when harmonized by the sub-dominant F triad (F-A-C), then returns to a tonic C triad. Measure 8, which has a B natural in its first group of notes, calls out for a Major-dominant G triad (G-B-D) before finishing on a tonic C-triad.

In Part B, measures 1, 4, 5 and 8 spell out a tonic C triad, while measures 2 and 6 spell out a sub-dominant F-chord. Measures 3 and 7 strongly suggest a dominant G chord.

Once you know the chords, creating a simple back-up is merely a matter of knowing a few easy-to-play rhythmic patterns. Several patterns are presented in the middle staff of *Bay of Fundy*. In Part A, measures 1, 3 and 7, and in Part B, measures 1, 2 and 3, my back-up consists of a bumm-titty strum plus a double-thumbing group (single-string brush plus drop-thumb). In Part A, measures 2 and 6, and in Part B, measure 4, the back-up is a double-thumbing group followed by a bumm-titty strum.

Part A, measure 4 has an accompaniment of two bumm-titty strums; Part A, measure 5, and Part B, measures 5-7 are accompanied by two double-thumbing groups, and so on. It's obvious that there are dozens of potential patterns of this kind and that you can easily compile a number of them to use as an accompaniment repertoire.

Creative accompaniment usually involves a hodge-podge of different approaches and cannot be taught by formula. It's an art that usually requires a great deal of playing experience to master. The bottom staff of *Bay of Fundy* offers some suggestions as to how a creative accompaniment can be constructed. In measures 1, 2, 5 and 6 of Part A, I accompany the tune by loosely paralleling the form of the melody without hitting all the notes. In measures 3, 4, 7 and 8, I use standard melodic licks to create a counter-melody, thereby adding texture.

In Part B, measures 1, 2, 5 and 6, I play a note-for-note duet (see column 6.9). In measures 3, 4, 7 and 8, I use standard melodic licks for counter-melody.

I recorded *Bay of Fundy* with a few variations (breaks) on my *Devil in the Kitchen* CD.

6.11 Backup Revisited   (Feb. '91)
6.12 Backup Re-revisited   (July '93)

Most fiddle tunes can be effectively accompanied by two or three chords. Knowing *when* to change these chords, however, takes a great deal of familiarity with the style. In fact, I have seen accomplished guitar players (yes, bluegrass guitar players too!) totally baffled by the changes of what I regarded as an absolutely conventional fiddle tune. This is not said to discourage the attempts of the novice, but rather to sensitize him or her to the issues involved. Once you get the feel of fiddle tune harmony, the tune itself virtually calls out to you not only when the next chord change arrives, but what it is!

Once you know the chords (see col. 6-10), effective back-up consists of setting up a rhythmic pattern (or a series of rhythmic patterns) that is compatible with the *meter* of a given

song or tune. The term meter refers roughly to the number of beats per measure in a given musical piece. In practice, the meters you're most likely to encounter are 2/2, 2/4, 4/4, 3/4 and 6/8.

The most common meters by far in contemporary usage are those that call for two or four-beats per measure. Such tunes include hoedowns, marches, reels, hornpipes, strathspeys, Irish polkas, rags and countless varieties of songs from both the American and Celtic traditions. Although two and four-beat meters are technically quite distinct, they can be treated from a back-up point of view as more or less the same thing. I'll give two rhythmic accompaniment patterns that work for two and four-beat meter tunes.

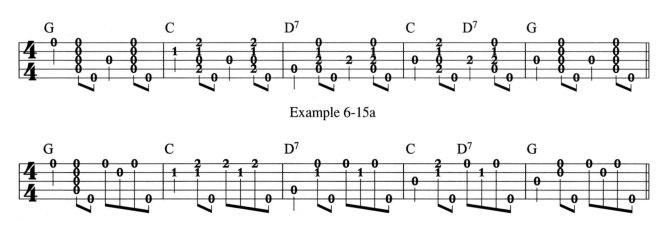

Example 6-15a

Example 6-15b

140

Example 6-15a shows a very basic accompaniment pattern (namely two bumm-titty strums per measure). Observe that you can use any note in the chord for any given quarter-note in the strum. If two chords evenly divide a measure, merely play one bum-titty strum for each.

A more advanced pattern for two and four-beat meter tunes is shown in Example 6-15b. Here, each measure is filled by one bum-titty strum (with light brush), plus a double-thumbing sequence. Again, any note in the chord can be played at any point in the strum, so long as you keep the rhythm going.

Note that you'll have to adjust the rhythm of the patterns a bit to suit the playing style of whomever it is you're accompanying. For example, it is quite rare for a fiddler to play eighth-

notes exactly evenly. Generally, the first note of each eighth-note pair is somewhat longer than the second note. You must determine by ear the exact relationship between notes in the eighth-note pair, and adjust your attack so that you blend in.

Tunes in three-beat meters (such as 3/8 and 3/4 time) include waltzes, many fiddle airs, and a significant percentage of songs from both American and Celtic traditions. Example 6-16 shows two effective approaches to 3/4 time accompaniment. In Example 6-16a, each measure is filled by a quarter-note plus two brush-thumbs (more or less an extended bumm-titty strum). A somewhat more elegant pattern for three-beat meter tunes is shown in Example 6-16b, where the three beats are filled up by a combination of single-string brushes and drop-thumbs.

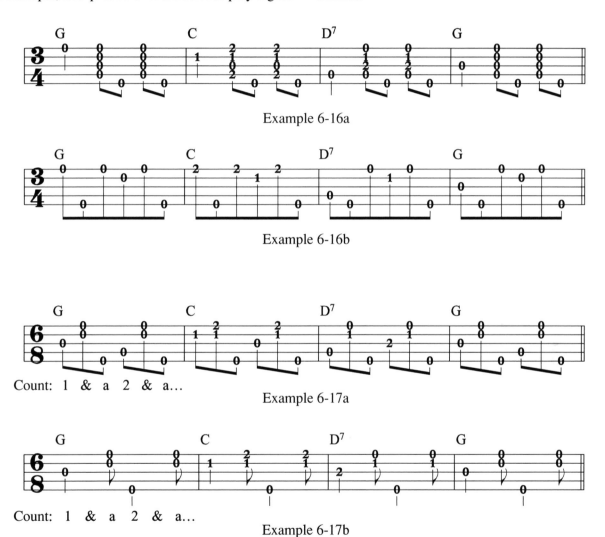

Example 6-16a

Example 6-16b

Count: 1 & a 2 & a...
Example 6-17a

Count: 1 & a 2 & a...
Example 6-17b

6/8 time is considered a *double compound meter* (6/8 tunes have two beats, with each beat divided into *three* pulses). Tunes in 6/8 time include jigs, some marches, some fiddle airs, and again, a significant percentage of songs from the American and Celtic traditions. Example 6-17 shows two effective approaches for double-compound meter tunes. Example 6-17a is more or less a compressed bum-titty strum. Example 6-17b shows a less notey pattern.

Keeping a rock steady beat is of course a must when playing backup. Nothing is more frustrating for a lead player than the feeling that the accompanist is pushing him to play faster, or is consistently lagging behind. On the other hand, a backup player's steadiness must be tempered by having enough sensitivity to follow the soloist should he or she falter or shift tempos. In other words, if the soloist changes speeds you must follow along. If the soloist stumbles, your job is to keep the beat rolling along so that the miscue is less noticeable.

141

Later on, there are many elements that go into what might be termed sophisticated backup. For example, to avoid conflicts with other instruments, you may wish to learn a number of positions around the neck for each chord (see col. 2.16). This gives you the option, for example, of selecting chord positions in the lower ranges when you play with a high pitched instrument like the mandolin. Alternatively, you would be able to use chord positions up the neck when playing with instruments like the piano, which tends to dominate the low and mid-ranges.

6.13 Backup: Coming Full Circle

(Dec.'93)

Those of you who are devotees of this column know that one of my pet peeves is the notion that clawhammer banjo should rarely if ever be used in a primarily melodic role. This seems to be a dearly held axiom of what might be called the right wing of old time music movement. A corollary of this belief is the notion that you can't play the full melody of a tune in clawhammer style without sacrificing most of its rhythmic drive and nuance. Needless to say, I disagree strongly with this point of view and have always maintained that melodic playing can also be highly rhythmic. Indeed, I feel that it must have full rhythmic drive and nuance to be considered *good* melodic playing.

The melodic style of clawhammer is essentially a method of *soloing* in clawhammer style. Because it is a method of soloing, however, it does not follow that its practitioners are *unable* to play fiddle backup. On the contrary, melodic players should be — and often are — adept at playing behind the fiddle. Moreover, the enhanced technical skills that make melodic playing possible allow for the development of new creative approaches to fiddle-tune backup.

This being said, there is no arguing that the "traditional" approach to clawhammer is the best *point of departure* for melodic players who want to study the art of fiddle-tune backup. By all means, get hold of every old-timey tape and CD you can, and listen to the banjo player. Go to every concert and festival you can that features old time music, and watch the banjo player. Don't just sit around learning tabs, even if they're *my* tabs.

The "traditional" approach to clawhammer is effective as a backup technique because it aims for a total unity between banjo and fiddle (with banjo in the support role). To this end, it provides a strong rhythmic attack, so that notes come off banjo and fiddle *with exactly the same rhythmic flavor and accents.*

As you know, a typical 4/4 or 2/2 time fiddle tune is made up primarily of streams of eighth notes. In "traditional" backup the idea is that everywhere the fiddler plays an eighth-note, the banjoist should also play an eighth note. When the fiddle plays longer notes (that is, quarters and halves), the banjo continues with a steady eighth-note attack. Now, the traditional clawhammer player does not attempt to play the entire melody: the fiddle is already doing that. Instead, he or she tries to get whatever notes come easily and strongly with basic clawhammer techniques. Those passages that are not played note-for-note are filled in with harmonically compatible double thumbing, hammer-ons, and pull-offs or with easily accomplished counter-melodies. When a really accomplished traditional picker plays with his regular fiddler, the effect is electric. You often can't tell he or she isn't playing the entire tune unless you know what to look for or you record it and slow it down!

What can the melodic player learn from the traditional player? What can he or she add to the mix? You ask age-old questions, grasshopper! Seriously, I think some answers can be offered. First, the notion of molding your attack and note production to the fiddler so that your notes come out precisely as his or hers is extremely important. Second, the notion that you *don't* have to play the melody all the time needs to be stressed. After all, as stated above, the fiddler is already doing that. And third, remember that you can match the melody note for note in certain passages — where it comes out particularly strong and clear on your instrument — and play harmony or counter-melody backup for other passages.

What the melodic player can bring uniquely to the mix is that he or she has presumably vastly expanded the range of what is easy to play in clawhammer style. Therefore, much more complex passages can be played strongly and rhythmically on a note-for-note basis. This being the case, melodic players should ultimately provide stronger and more flexible backup than their "traditional" counterparts.

I had many of these thoughts last summer while I was whiling away many a pleasant evening by "having a few tunes" with members of the Chaisson family of Bear River, Prince Edward Island. I was paying close attention to Kevin Chaisson the pianist, and was attempting to determine what he was doing. It turned out that he — along with many contemporary Cape Breton pianists—employs an approach to fiddle tune accompaniment not unlike that employed in "traditional" clawhammer. In other words, he chords some of the time, but he also plays certain strategic passages out on a note-for-note basis under the fiddle. So as I began to experiment with this approach as a potential style for accompanying Cape Breton and Prince Edward Island tunes in clawhammer, it occurred to me that in a way I had really come full circle and "rediscovered" traditional clawhammer fiddle tune accompaniment style.

Try some of these back-up ideas for a Cape Breton tune called *The Dismissal,* which I recorded on my *Island Boy* CD. The top staff show the melody as it would be played on banjo. The bottom staff shows an accompaniment that blends melody, counter-melody and chording. The passages I play note-for-note in the backup part are those that seem to ring out best with the fiddle playing over them.

The Dismissal
(with Backup Part)

Banjo Arrangement: Ken Perlman

Tuning: gDGBD

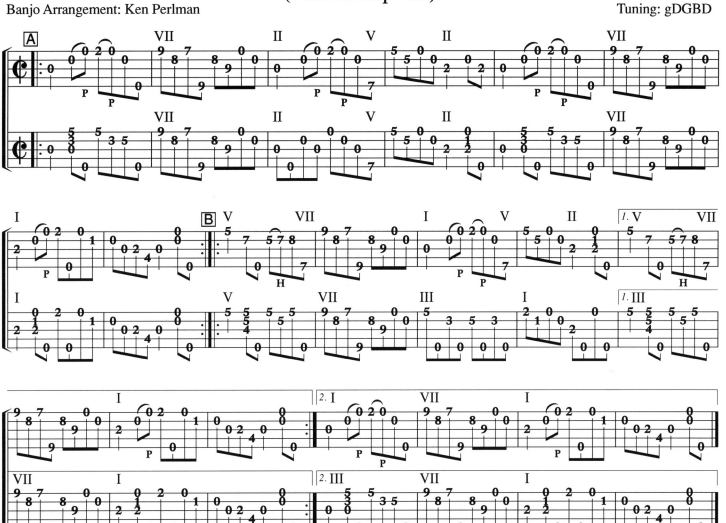

Arrangement © 1993 by Ken Perlman

Ken plays a duet with tenor banjoist Mick Moloney during Banjo Workshop at the Pennsylvania Folk Festival (Chambersburg, PA), c.1981. At left are Larry Marschall and Debby McClatchy.

CHAPTER 7: THE INSTRUMENT

7.1 Instrument Specifications (Excerpt from Ken Perlman interview)   (May '82)

BNL: What kind of banjo are you playing now, and have you set it up in any special way which may be of interest to readers?

KP: I actually went out and had a banjo custom built to suit my style. I wanted an instrument that could project well and have excellent tonal response over its entire range. At the same time, I wanted low action over the entire fingerboard so I could play up the neck on all strings. And, I wanted a short scale (a nut-to-bridge scale length of 26¼") so that my fingers could easily stretch out to perform all those fretted hammer-ons and pull-offs that I do. I got hold of an old 10¹⁵⁄₁₆" Vega Tubaphone pot which I knew had the potential for the type of sound I wanted, and I had the Arthur E. Smith Banjo Company of Shelburne Falls, Massachusetts build a neck to my specifications. One of the main features I asked for was a greater angle than is ordinarily the case for most modern frailing banjos (17½° between peghead and fingerboard). This puts tension on the strings — allowing greater projection — without making it necessary to have high action up the neck. To ensure wide uniform spacing between all strings above the fifth fret, I had the neck and fingerboard built slightly wider than normal (1¼" at the nut; 1¹⁵⁄₁₆" at the heel).

And, I had the pip set in at the very edge of the fingerboard so that the fifth string would come into the bridge at the same angle as the long strings.

I also had the builder make sure to allow each fret wire to run virtually to the end of the board before beginning to file it off (you can easily lose ¼" of your string-spacing through over filing of fretwire ends). Another important feature was having the builder shape the back of the neck in an extremely shallow, perfectly symmetrical curve (almost like an electric guitar neck), so that I could comfortably play with my thumb behind the neck as a classical guitarist does. (By symmetrical, I mean that both the narrow and the wide portions of the neck were symmetrical around their own axes). Incidentally, I generally use medium gauge strings, a ⁹⁄₁₆" bridge, and, to give the strings a little extra pop, a Kirschner tension tailpiece.

One other feature that I asked for was an inlayed marker at the 14ᵗʰ fret rather than at the more customary 15ᵗʰ fret. Since I often play fiddle tunes and fiddle-tune backup capoed up two frets, this feature clearly marks out the capo-2 octave fret.[1]

7.2 The Importance of Good Banjo Set-Up   (June '99)
7.3 Excerpt from Ken Perlman interview   (May '82)

Most clawhammer players are unaware just how important good-set up is. Such issues as truss rod maintenance, string action, height of strings off the head, state of bridge and nut-slots, state of the frets, state of the bridge, level of head tension and firmness of the joint between pot and neck all have a significant effect on banjo sound and playability.

Having an action much higher than is ideal, for example, makes every fretting movement harder than it needs to be. Generally, nut slots that are too high make stopping the strings on lower frets difficult and also make hammering and pulling off problematic. A bridge that is too high makes up the neck playing hard.

Alternatively, you can have your nut and bridge at exactly the right height and still have string-action problems if your fingerboard *bows* (becomes concave).

Your banjo sound can also be adversely affected by other set-up problems. *Buzzing* results from having an action that is too low. Generally, this is caused by nut slots or bridges that are set too low. In addition, unevenly worn frets or nut- and bridge-slots that are too wide can also produce fuzzy tone or even buzzing.

Again, you can have your nut and bridge at exactly the right height and still have buzzing if your fingerboard *back-bends* (becomes convex). Incidentally, before you get worked up about a buzzing problem make sure your banjo-head is tightened to its ideal level (a loose head allows string-tension to push bridge and strings too far downward).

As a clawhammer player, you should also be aware of the importance of having an adequate string height off the head. Lately, I've seen too many old time banjos sent out of the factory with strings set much too close to the head. Consequently the average player has no room to give the right-hand thumb purchase on the strings.

All this points to the importance in one's playing life of a good set-up and repair-person, or — since these are all too rare — of learning how to do your own set-ups and minor repairs. I remember when I was starting out, music-store people were always telling me that nothing could be done about the action when it was patently clear that something could be done. In fact, one music store in New York City had a sign posted, "Will everyone who wants their action as low as possible without buzzing please leave!"

---

[1] I asked for most of the same features recently when I had another instrument built for me by Ome Banjos of Boulder, Colorado (a "Renaissance" model to be precise).

When I became known as a performer and teacher on the other hand, I found it interesting that all those supposedly "impossible" action adjustments suddenly became possible.

At any rate, here's a few tips and suggestions on how to get the most out of your banjo.

♦ When you first get the instrument (or if you've never had this done before), have the bridge and nut adjusted to proper height, which actually is — notwithstanding the aforementioned New York store — "as low as possible without buzzing." Of course, ideal height here depends to some extent on playing style, since those who hit the strings harder require a slightly higher action than those who play with a less aggressive attack. Again, before you do this you'll want to tighten up the head to get a true picture of the actual state of the action.

♦ For a still finer tweaking of the action, you may find that you need to have a *fret-job* or a *truss-rod adjustment*. In a fret job, badly worn fret-wires are replaced and fret-wire surfaces are filed so that they line up without obvious high spots. Adjusting the truss-rod (a real pain for instruments like mine that require removal of the neck to get at the rod) straightens out concavity or convexity in the fingerboard. Both of these processes allow for a much lower action without buzzing than would otherwise be the case.

♦ Most vintage banjos do not have adjustable truss rods, so for them adjusting concavity or convexity in the fingerboard usually requires removing fretwires and resorting to a file (don't try this yourself unless you're an expert).

♦ In the process of adjusting bridge- and nut-heights, attention should also be paid to slot width. Having slots that are too wide or filed in the wrong shape creates fuzziness of sound.

♦ Avoiding fuzziness is another reason to have your frets checked. Frets with ridges worn into them by string pressure over time should be smoothed out or replaced (avoiding such wear, by the way, is an excellent argument against leaving your capo on the instrument when the latter is not in use).

♦ Speaking of bridges, they tend to break down after anywhere from a couple to a few years of use. One common problem is that string pressure against a wooden bridge sitting on a flexible membrane (like a banjo head) tends to make it swaybacked. Replacing your bridge periodically, therefore, is a good habit to establish.

♦ If the height of the strings off the *head* is too low for right-hand comfort, the neck/pot joint can be adjusted to allow the neck to sit up a little higher vs. the pot. This permits the neck action to remain the same while the pot-action increases. Alternatively, the same effect can be achieved by adjusting the *angle* at which neck meets pot.

Above all, be aware that you don't need a superb instrument to play complicated tunes: just a well set up one. In fact, most cheap or moderately priced banjos can be set up adequately and many of my students have played — without any significant learning handicap — Stewart-MacDonald kit banjos, or mass produced Japanese bluegrass banjos from which the resonators had been removed.

7.4 Bridge Alterations & Tone (Harmonics and the Overtone Series) (July '87)

Setting up violin bridges properly has been a fine art for two or three centuries, but installing banjo bridges has — at least in recent years — been more or less a haphazard affair. Most pickers merely buy a stock banjo bridge — the three post maple bridge with grafted ebony crown seems to be pretty much standard these days — adjust its height some for desired string action and install it directly on their instrument. Most pickers don't realize that they can dramatically improve the tone of their banjo via slight alterations in over-all stock-bridge shapes.

When a string is plucked, a complex series of events is touched off. Not only does the string vibrate as a unit — producing a tone called the *fundamental* — but it also vibrates in various fractions of its length. The tones produced by these vibrating fractions of strings are called *harmonics* or *overtones*.

When you pluck the banjo third string in G tuning, for example, the fundamental produced by that string vibrating along its entire length is G below middle C. In addition to vibrating as a unit, however, the string also vibrates as two halves. Each of these halves produces an overtone (or harmonic) whose pitch is one octave above the fundamental, or G above middle C. You can hear this tone — known as the *first harmonic*

— by touching (but not pressing down) a string over the wire bordering the upper end of fret 12 (a point that exactly divides the string in half), and then plucking that string.

The string also vibrates in thirds, and each third produces an overtone (or harmonic) whose pitch is an octave plus a perfect fifth interval above the fundamental, or two D's above middle C. This overtone — called the *second harmonic* — appears if you pluck a string that is touched over the wire at the upper end of fret 7 (the point that is one-third of the way from nut to bridge).

The *third harmonic*, which results from the string vibrating in fourths, is two octaves above the fundamental, or two G's above middle C. You can hear it by touching the plucked string over the wire at the upper end of fret 5 (one fourth of the way from nut to bridge).

The *fourth harmonic* results from the string vibrating in five equal sections. It is two octaves plus a major third interval above the fundamental, or two B's above middle C. You can hear it by touching the plucked string above the wire at the upper end of fret 4 (one fifth of the way from nut to bridge).

The process goes on and on, but you get the idea. The collection of overtones (or harmonics) which appears along with the fundamental when a string is plucked is called the *overtone series* for that string. And, the relative strengths and weaknesses of each point on the overtone series determines the *timbre* (tone quality) of each string. So, banjos which are perceived as shrill or trebly probably are strong at the upper end and weak on the lower end of the overtone series, while banjos perceived bassy or tubby probably have the opposite condition. Most banjos fall somewhere in between, but each has its quota of strong and weak points in its overtone series.

Most of you have already had some encounters with the overtone series. When you alter the spot on the string where you strike, change the shape of your picking nail, or doctor the angle of your attack to get better tone, you are trying to coax a more desirable overtone series out of your instrument. In other words, each of these alterations tends to strengthen certain harmonics and weaken others.

Altering the shape of the bridge is another way to affect the overtone series. Specifically, thinning the bridge-body and crown on both sides, so that the strings are resting on a less massive cross-section, tends to strengthen high overtones and eliminate tubbiness. Leaving the bridge at its full "stock" dimensions or even installing a more massive bridge (such as a compensated bridge) will tend to strengthen low overtones and eliminate shrillness.

Experimenting with various bridge thicknesses at the crown cross-section is certainly an excellent way to obtain the very best tone your banjo is capable of producing. Obtain several stock three-post bridges, then shave varying amounts off the sides of each bridge-body and crown using sand paper, a wood file, or a belt sander. Having adjusted each bridge for optimal action, try each in turn for several days on your instrument. You can then determine which crown cross-section thickness yields optimal tone for your banjo.

7.5 "Tilted" vs. Compensated Bridges, Placing a Bridge (response to a reader)   (Feb. '96)

The procedure for setting a bridge in place requires that you match the *first harmonic* on each string (that is, the one obtained at the twelfth fret: see col. 7.4) with the note obtained by stopping that string at the twelfth fret. If the fretted notes are sharp relative to the harmonic, string lengths are too short and the bridge must be moved back towards the tailpiece; if the fretted notes are flat relative to the harmonic, the string lengths are too long and the bridge must be moved towards the neck.

Compensated bridges take into account the fact that the ideal scale length for each string is slightly different. Thinner strings require a slightly shorter scale length to make the frets sound true than do thicker strings, and vice versa. I deal with this on my own instrument by *tilting* the bridge. In other words, the bridge sits significantly closer to the neck where the first string rests, than it does where the third or fourth strings rest (put another way, the first string length is somewhat shorter than either the third or fourth string lengths).

The problem here is the fifth string, which is just as thin as the first, but located in such a way that tilting the bridge allots it too long a scale length. A number of commercial bridges have been developed to deal with this situation, most notably the Shubb compensated bridge and the Moon bridge.

The Shubb bridge is made with five distinct levels for strings to rest on, each supposedly at ideal length. The main problem is that it is fairly massive. Personally, I find that the excess mass soaks up a lot of high end overtones and makes banjos sound tubby.

The Moon bridge is bent into a crescent shape (hence the name) and serves the same purpose as a the Shubb bridge without adding the extra mass. It theoretically should be the ideal choice, but I wonder if it transmits sound as effectively as a standard straight bridge. After all, there must be some reason why countless generations of luthiers have designed stringed instruments with straight bridges and saddles.

7.6 On String Gauges (response to a reader)   (Aug. '92)

I have tended to use medium gauge strings on my banjos, but I have observed that each kind of banjo calls for its own ideal string weight. For example, Whyte Laydies and S.S. Stewarts, which have lighter construction than tubaphones, seem to sound better with light gauge strings. I tend to play instruments with relatively massive tone rings, such as Vega tubaphones and Omes. I've often felt it has a lot to do with the tension on the strings relative to the weight and responsiveness of the tone ring

(if any). At any rate it's certainly an individual decision based on sound quality vs. ease of playing.

Sometimes it's not a bad idea to experiment with the gauges of individual strings (for example try a .022 or .024 fourth string instead of the standard medium-gauge .023). Don't necessarily be satisfied with the standard "light" and "medium" settings just because they each come in a neat package!

7.7 Designed for Clawhammer Banjos

When I was interviewed for BNL in May '82, I spoke at length about banjo design and specifications. My emphasis was on neck design and set-up fine points. I was unable to discuss much about tone production because pot and tone-ring technology has been virtually static since the 1930s. What's more, there have been no systematic attempts to produce improvements in *made-for-clawhammer* pots since the 1870s.

Now, a properly set up Tubaphone, Whyte Laydie, Bacon, Stewart or Orpheum original or conversion 5-string has a pretty good sound for clawhammer. The pots and tone-rings of all these banjos, however, were designed for classic banjo style (which features bare-finger picking and gut/nylon strings). Similarly, the pots and tone-rings of most Paramounts, Bacon & Days and Gibsons were designed for tenor or plectrum banjo styles.

Since the clawhammer method of attacking the strings is fundamentally different from the one employed for fingerpicking and flatpicking, it seems pretty obvious that it calls for a highly different style of pot and tone-ring construction.

When the M finger strikes the strings, for example, it is moving downward in an arc-like trajectory, producing a tone that has a very high component of overtones. If you play fretted notes way up the neck, these overtones can become so powerful that the fundamental seems to disappear — creating some pain-in-the-you-know-what dead spots. When the bare thumb plucks the strings, however, you are faced with the potential of a highly different set of tone qualities. Any attempt at building made-for-clawhammer pots should address such issues.

Another problem we clawhammer pickers face is lack of projection. The bluegrass banjoist has his Mastertone or Stelling, the mandolin player his Lloyd Loar F-5. What do we have that can compare? In order for clawhammer players to be taken seriously in band settings we need specially designed instruments that will cut through anything — at all registers — when addressed with a clawhammer attack. Such instruments should be especially responsive to fretting hand maneuvers like hammer-ons, pull-offs, and slides. [2]

7.8 Banjos That Are Born Not Made

In a recent column, I bemoaned the lack of recent progress in made-for-clawhammer pot design. A couple of weeks ago, I received an extremely interesting letter from Scott Didlake, head of a company called Kalanda Banza, which is located in Crystal Springs, Mississippi. I'd like to share with you some excerpts from this letter:

"My little banjo company is in fact trying to develop banjos which are in a sense made-for-clawhammer. These of course are calabash gourd banjos, which was the original southern form of the instrument before it moved up North and became an industrial product. These banjos are grown, not fabricated, and making 'good ones' is strictly an agrarian question.

"We are concentrating on building the original gourd form of the instrument, and trying to create a new calabash banjo that would be suited for, strangely enough, both clawhammer music and what I call 'post-bluegrass banjo' music

"Recent research into drawings of the early banjoists has convinced me that a lot of white minstrels, and not just blacks on plantations, either played real gourd banjos, or wood-chamber banjos directly modeled on original calabash designs.

"As for the gourd, I know now from experience in building that, with tackhead construction, they can be vastly superior to the rim banjos used by the early minstrels. In fact, the only explanation for the coming of rim banjos is that they were made by Northern, urban, industrial makers who could not get calabash gourds. Southern black banjo makers apparently knew how to make drum rims, but they always, from accounts, made banjos from gourds. I am convinced that these instruments were in no sense 'primitive,' but resulted from a lost art.

"The secret is getting the 'right' gourds. There are gourds and then there are *gourds*. Some gourds are actually harder and stronger than rock maple: I kid you not! But getting the right gourds is very difficult. We are solving this problem now by cultivating our own calabash gourds. Wish our crop of banjos well!"

Incidentally, the calabash gourd plant roughly resembles a zucchini plant (a *courgette* to our British readers), to which it is distantly related. Who says banjos don't grow on vines? [3]

---

[2] Since this column was written, a few banjo-makers have begun to address these issues, but much work still needs to be done.

[3] Scott Didlake passed away in the early 90s. Many of the ideas he espoused about gourd banjos, however, have been taken up by such modern banjo builders as George Wunderlich and Bob Flesher.

For years I more or less ignored the whole issue of amplification. After all, the banjo is pretty loud all by itself, isn't it? Basically, I felt that my amplification problem was solved when I got my first (Vega) tubaphone. And it was, to a certain extent. If I needed a little more volume at a small concert or during a jam session, all I had to do was play a little harder. If I was playing in a larger hall, the house microphone provided more than enough "oomph" for my purposes.

In fact, there were certain circumstances where neither the natural tubaphone sound nor even the house microphone did the job, such as out-door solo concerts and festivals, band-work, and dances.

For outdoor concerts and festivals, the major issue is *presence* rather than mere loudness. The sound must be focused enough to grab the listener — otherwise attention wanders and you've lost your audience. This is particularly true for performers whose appeal is dependent upon the audience being able to closely follow an intricate melody line. No matter how loud you make a P/A system, there is a tendency for microphone-generated sound to dissipate and become fuzzy in both outdoor and large indoor venues.

For band work and dances you run into a slightly different problem. Here the banjo player is often the victim of the particular sound-quality of his or her instrument. Up close, the banjo is quite loud compared to many other instruments. As the distance from the banjo increases, however (and somebody could probably plot this on a graph if they had nothing better to do on a Sunday afternoon), both loudness and presence decrease fairly precipitously. The fiddle has just the opposite sound-character. It doesn't seem quite so loud up close, but it sure *projects* well (in other words, it's no accident that so many cultures feature the fiddle as the primary dance-music instrument).

Since the banjo is loud up close, sound engineers in general tend to place the banjo setting on the P/A system fairly low relative to other instruments. *They* can hear you just fine, but as it turns out all too often the audience or dancers cannot. This leads to the constant refrain one hears in such circumstances, "Gee I saw your fingers moving, but I really couldn't hear the banjo especially well."

Bluegrass banjoists theoretically face the same problem but (1) their banjos are *a lot* louder, (2) their use of fingerpicks aids substantially in projection, and (3) they often have more assertive personalities than do clawhammer players, and hence tend to have more control over P/A volume.

I have tried various solutions to the amplification problem over the years. I was probably among the first to try a Barkus-Berry transducer on a banjo back in the 70s, but the sound was if anything less *present* than the straight miked sound. In the early 90s, I tried using a new-generation Fishman transducer which had been designed for harp. This was a great improvement on the 70s Barkus Berry, but it still didn't really do the trick.

When I originally wrote this column, I had great hopes for one of Fishman's banjo-specific transducers, which was a black cylinder that fit right under the banjo head and fastened around the draw-stick or metal connecting rods. With this apparatus, you got pretty good projection and you could be loud at a distance without being perceptively louder to your band-mates. Unfortunately, to work properly the device had to sit so close to the underside of the banjo head that it had a dampening effect when the instrument was played acoustically. Plus, the pick-up seemed to give the instrument a fairly harsh sound, no matter where you placed it.

To date, I have not completely solved the banjo-miking problem. For dances and other occasions where good tone is less important than projection, I am currently using one of those tiny *contact* mikes (the kind used these days for drums and saxophones) that clip inside the instrument: if you go this route, you'll need to experiment to determine the best location for maximum tone and projection. In concert situations, there are certain *cardioid* mikes — like the Audio Technica C-1000 — that seem to be particularly effective in terms of both sweetness and presence.

CHAPTER 8: CLAWHAMMER MISCELLANY

8.1 Never Listen To What "They" Say

(Apr. '86)

When I first started playing clawhammer banjo, I encountered a continuous chorus of nay-sayers. Among many prophecies of doom were statements like: "You can't frail that tune," "Jigs are unfrailable," "You can't play that lick in clawhammer style," "You're not supposed to play the melody," and "You're not supposed to fret the fifth string!"

Fortunately for my development, I took each of these comments as a challenge. I just had to go home and prove these "nattering nabobs of negativity" (remember Spiro Agnew?) wrong. So I worked out how to play jigs, reels, hornpipes, rags, bluegrass licks and whatever else caught my fancy. Some years later I found out that the old minstrel pickers had worked out a similar approach to clawhammer playing over 150 years ago, and that succeeding generations of banjo players had merely "forgotten" how to use the style to its utmost (see cols. 9.3-4).

What I am driving at here is that I want to encourage all of you to follow every banjo-oriented whim, no matter how wild. Above all, don't take any authority as the last word on whether something can be accomplished, even if that authority is me!

8.2 Is Anatomy Destiny?

(Aug. '85)

I was down near Washington, D.C. in early June to play at a small festival in Herndon, Virginia. My gig was over early in the afternoon so I had lots of time to drive over the Maryland line to Glen Echo Park, where the Washington Folk Festival was in full swing.

I was particularly happy to run into clawhammerist-extraordinaire Reed Martin there, and we took about an hour or so to play some tunes together and trade licks. I don't remember exactly how this came up, but for some silly reason we decided to compare hand sizes. Reed's hand dwarfed mine by at least the length of a full joint, and I have relatively large hands! Upon further examination, it turned out that our fingers were exactly the same length (though his were much thicker), but his palm was substantially larger and more massively muscled than mine.

Later on, this set me to thinking how the general construction of a person's hand can influence their playing style. In one sense, the answer is obvious: someone with exceptionally small hands might be discouraged from taking up the banjo in the first place, while a person with large hands probably has some innate advantage. But I was thinking about more specific features.

Watching Reed's fretting hand while he plays, I've always been struck by how easily he manages to handle a four fret stretch with only three fingers, and also by the tiny amount of movement his fingers require to execute the most demanding series of triplets and grace notes. Knowing Reed — who prides himself on being a purely instinctive player — I doubt that he spent years working on long stretches and efficient finger movement. These are skills that probably came quite naturally to him. And, considering that many of the small muscles responsible for moving the fingers run through the palm, it seemed reasonable to theorize that at least some features of Reed's playing style is attributable to his unusually massive palms.

For many players, however, unusual hand features are often the source of problems. I am afflicted, for example, with "hitch-hiker's thumb." When I fully extend my thumb, the first joint (the one that has the nail) is virtually at right angles to the mid-joint. This made adaptation for my right hand to the basic clawhammer stroke quite difficult at first, to say the least. Eventually, I worked out a compromise where during drop-thumbing and fifth-string plucking, my attached and middle joints are fully extended but my first joint is bent slightly inward. This creates a certain unavoidable amount of "wiggle" in the thumb when I play, which students with different kinds of thumbs should, of course, not try to emulate.

Over many years of teaching, I have encountered many other troublesome hand features. Here are just a few of them:

♦ unusually small fingers
♦ unusually thick fingers
♦ thumbs that when fully extended form a right angle between mid-joint and attached joint
♦ thumbs that do not extend fully
♦ exceptionally weak, or insufficiently independent third or fourth fretting-hand fingers

All of these and dozens of other anatomically based difficulties can certainly be overcome with extra practice and/or plain old Yankee ingenuity. Sometimes we can make an instrument adapt to us, and sometimes we must adapt to it. In either case, we grow considerably as musicians by overcoming our handicaps.

Sometimes a handicap on one end of things prove beneficial elsewhere. For example, my hitch-hiker's thumb proved an advantage on the fretting-hand side of things, because it provides a convenient spot on the joint-bone for the banjo neck to rest.

Alternatively, students can learn to overcome their disadvantages. Those with small fingers can work hard on developing stretching ability or they can even have smaller-scale instruments built for them. People with thick fingers need to work on precise fretting finger placement. They can also have their nut and bridge notches spaced wider apart, or even purchase instruments with wider fingerboards. People with weak or insufficiently independent fretting hand fingers need to work extra hard on developing strength and independence.

Here are some thoughts about banjo teaching (and learning) that flow out of this discussion :

♦ Teachers should make the student aware of troublesome anatomical features, and help him or her overcome them.

♦ Students should be allowed to evolve into their ultimate hand positions over a period of time so that their particular mix of strengths and weaknesses can reach a workable equilibrium.

♦ Students should *not* necessarily copy exactly the hand positions of well-known players. Who knows what unusual anatomical features led a particular artist to evolve a given hand position? Think how many thousands of would-be classical guitarists ruined their hands over the years by attempting to exactly copy the contorted hand positions of Andres Segovia — a man who must have been blessed by exceptionally strong wrist tendons.

8.3 The Agony of De-hands (Sept. '95)

It is a rare picker over thirty and playing at least ten years who has never experienced some sort of ache or pain in his or her hands. Most hand pain is merely fatigue and goes away in a day or two, but some is more problematic. Here are some helpful hints on what to do when your hands act up.

The most important thing to remember is that pain is nature's way of telling you there is a problem. Trying to be a tough guy or gal and ignoring hand pain entirely is a sure way to develop a problem severe enough to threaten your musical career. In fact, unless you have a big gig coming up or a non-postponable recording date, the first thing to do when you experience hand pain is to back off from your instrument and rest that hand until the pain subsides.

In many cases, hand pain is related to inefficient hand-usage. In other words, something you are doing while you play is putting excessive stress on your hands. This might be a life-long habit or an alteration you've made recently (and sometimes unconsciously) in your playing style. Perhaps the best way to identify and eliminate the offending element is to spend some time with a good banjo teacher. Alternatively, you might try playing in front of a mirror. Sometimes watching yourself play is the quickest method to identifying problem areas in your technique.

Sometimes hand pain has its roots in non-musical activities. A frequent culprit of late is computer-keyboard use. Other irritants include manual labor or crafts, weight-lifting or Nautilus training, and writing. Here the non-musical activity may be the actual irritant, while banjo playing is merely the precipitating incident for hand pain. In this case, you may then need to either modify the offending activity or — if at all possible — eliminate it entirely from your daily regimen.

If pain persists, you may ultimately need to consult a physician. Fortunately, the usual things that can go wrong — tendinitis, sprains, muscle spasms, nerve irritations — are treatable with a combination of rest, ice pack or heat application, and mild anti-inflammatory drugs like aspirin or ibuprofen.

One fruitful line of medical research that is in the course of being developed surrounds what is sometimes referred to as *Repetitive Stress Injury (RSI)*. As the name implies, there are all sorts of problems that can result from overuse of certain joints and muscles. Treatments that are on offer following an RSI diagnosis include ergonomic revamping of habitual activities, daily stretching and strengthening exercises, therapeutic massage and ultra-sound treatments.

8.4 Care of the Picking Nail (response to a reader) (Apr. '85)

For good clawhammer tone, the nail of the picking finger only has to be grown about one-eighth of an inch past the edge of the fingertip — a length that will barely be noticed and is not likely to get in the way of most activities.

Once you grow your nail out, be sure to keep it in a semi-circular shape, and remove any rough edges with a good quality nail file ("diamond files" are far superior to both all-metal cross-hatched files and emory boards for shaping purposes). At times I also further refine the nail shape with #500 or 600 wet-and-dry carbide paper.

Those of you born with soft fingernails take heart! My own picking nail always wore itself down to the quick for the first few years I played, until at last I hit on the following two nail protection methods:

1. I paint nail conditioner/thickener on my picking nail a few times a week, making sure to coat *both* sides of the nail.

2. I wear a piece of Scotch tape as a protective coating over my picking nail. I tuck one edge of the tape under the nail-tip, and make sure the other end extends down to the cuticle, but *no farther* (if the tape goes past the cuticle, it will quickly pick up moisture from the skin lose its ability to adhere).

For those whose professions or other interests preclude growing a picking nail to a length that is ideal for clawhammer, never fear! You can indeed become a good clawhammer picker without growing the nail out. You'll just have a somewhat different tone — softer and more subtle — from those who do play with nails (a callus eventually forms on the nail-less picking finger that serves as a semi-hard point of contact between finger and string).

If you can't grow a nail and still want or need the extra projection a grown-out nail provides, try the following strategies: wear a backwards fingerpick, use double stick tape to paste on an artificial "press-on" nail, or attach a bit of flat plastic (for example, a piece of flatpick) to your fingertip with a length of cloth tape. Some pickers have also had good luck with the paint-on artificial nails obtainable these days at "nail salons."

8.5 The Joy of Picking With Others

(Jan. '90)

When I was starting out on banjo, I spent nearly three years as just a closet frailer. I practiced a lot and learned a few tunes really well, but I never tried to find other musicians to play with. Finally, the day came late in the year 1972 when I gathered sufficient courage to bring my cheap Japanese-made banjo down to the weekly local musician's jam at the Unmuzzled Ox Coffee House in Ithaca, New York. As I've recounted in at least one book-intro, I was amazed to find that I could keep up pretty well on the few tunes I knew. As I went back week after week, I was also motivated to learn many of the other tunes that were locally popular. In addition to building my confidence, going down to these sessions also pointed out weaknesses that I needed to correct. My right hand was still too tight, for example, and my attack was not strong enough. My timing also needed to be more steady. Moreover, I realized that if I wanted to be heard I'd have to go out and buy a better instrument!

Three or four years passed and I had become a veteran of jam sessions — both in Ithaca and in my new home, New York City. There was still something lacking in my playing however, namely the basic assurance and drive that comes from playing in a string band. When I heard that one local group called the Fly by Night String Band had lost its banjo player and needed another, I jumped at the opportunity. Fly by Night, which featured Kevin Krajick on guitar, Bill Christopherson on fiddle, and Scott Kellogg on mandolin, played a blend of western swing, old timey, and bluegrass with a heavy vocal component. I was required not only to play fiddle tunes, but to play breaks and become proficient at backing up several styles of music. This forced me to develop the skills and techniques to play in various non-typical frailing rhythms, and to begin to seek out ways to systematically explore the upper reaches of the finger-board. I also found that my right hand technique needed further refinement to allow for greater projection. I also determined that even with all the technique in the world my second banjo (which sported a modern Whyte-Laydie tone ring on a Vega Little Wonder pot) still wasn't loud enough.

The point here is that practicing in the comfort of your living room can make you a good player, but you really need to get out there and play with people to make the leap from music student to musician. There are things to be learned both from playing at sessions and from playing in bands, and a full-fledged picker must do both at some point in his/her career .

This is not always easy to accomplish. Many of my students, for example, have families and demanding jobs and therefore have little free time available for such ventures. Even when time is not an issue, a given community may have no regularly scheduled jam sessions, and no real string-band scene.

A student of mine named Bob Solosko of Reading, Mass. had an interesting brain storm to help deal with this issue. He sent out a call for musicians over the computer bulletin board at work. His call was answered by players of several instruments such as concertina, guitar, hammer dulcimer, bass and mandolin. Bob and these other players met fairly regularly for quite a while during lunch hours and even performed at a few company functions. By the time the group ultimately disbanded, Bob's playing had improved markedly and he even had begun to arrange tunes on his own. In fact, a couple of his arrangements and co-arrangements —*Far from Home* and *Road to California* — appear in this book.

8.6 Tuning
8.7 Keeping your Banjo in Tune

(Sept. '97)
(June '95)

Tuning is a major issue for all stringed instrument players. No matter how much technique you have, your output will always sound unpolished if your strings are out of tune. On banjo — with its many tunings and a flexible head that pulls strings out of whack at the drop of a hat — the ability to get strings in tune swiftly is even more significant.

Everyone has heard performer's tuning jokes, as they struggle on stage to conquer misbehaving strings. My memory goes back to the time of "that old Chinese song, too-NING" (I even remember when I thought that was funny). Next to evolve was "Gee these were in tune when I bought them; it said so right on the package (G, B, D...)".

Some folk artists have come up with some clever epigrams to cover this embarrassing situation. I recall folksinger Michael Cooney noting on stage that his guitar always started to behave as soon as it was mentioned that there was a shortage of kindling in the house. Legendary guitarist Erik Frandsen of New York City is said to have coined a number of tuning maxims, one of which is "Find the string most out of tune, and tune all the other strings to that one."

I can't tell you how often in my teaching career I have encountered a student with perfectly good ears who claimed to be tone-deaf and incapable of tuning his/her own strings. As a longstanding teacher I think I can safely make the following statement, "Nobody who enjoys music and is capable of playing an instrument can *possibly* be tone-deaf."

In almost every case, it turned out that the student was confused about what exactly to listen for when tuning a stringed instrument. The simplest ear-tuning method, for example, involves matching a higher open string to a *stopped* (that is, fretted) lower string. You all know the procedure for G-tuning: tune string 4 to an outside source; tune open string 3 to fret 5, string 4; tune open string 2 to fret 4, string 3; tune open string 1 to fret 3, string 2; tune open string 5 to fret 5, string 1.

There are two main stumbling blocks to this method. First, if you hit the strings too hard, you begin to hear — in addition to the sound of the open strings — a whole slew of other musical sounds called *harmonics* or *overtones* (see col. 7-4). It is quite easy for a beginner (especially those with sensitive ears) to become confused and focus on overtones when tuning by this method instead of on the *fundamental* (the sound of the open-string). Note that you stand the best chance of clearly picking up the fundamental *if you strike the string fairly gently.*

The second stumbling block is that many students don't listen carefully enough. Make sure to pluck the *template* (string you want to match) first and *listen carefully to the tone.* Then pluck the string you want to tune and *listen carefully to its tone.* Finally, *compare* the tones of the two strings and decide whether the string to be tuned must go up and down. As you rotate the tuning peg, *keep plucking the string steadily* so that you can hear exactly how much the pitch of the string has changed.

There is one school of thought which holds that the best way to handle this kind of tuning is to pluck both strings in rapid succession and — like a piano tuner — listen for "beats" (sound-wave interference). The strings are in tune when these beats disappear. While this is certainly a theoretically reasonable tuning method, in my experience beginning and even intermediate players generally have a hard time with it.

As a player gains confidence, he or she is well-advised to learn a number of other, supplementary tuning methods. These can be checked one against the other, the way division and multiplication can be checked against each other.

In one very effective alternative method, harmonics are used for tuning purposes. Harmonics can be isolated by placing a fretting-hand finger on a string at certain specific points (*without pressing that string down*), then plucking the string normally with the other hand. The strongest *harmonics* are obtained by placing a finger above the fretwire that forms the upper border of the fifth, seventh and twelfth frets of any string. Because harmonics on different strings can yield equivalent tones, they can be used as tuning checks. Some examples appear in Table 7-1.

Template Harmonic	*Matching String Harmonic*
G-tuning (gDGBD)	
Fret 5, string 4	Fret 7, string 3
Fret 7, string 3	Fret 12, string 1
Fret 5, string 3	Fret 17, string 5
Fret 4, string 3 (a weak harmonic)	Fret 5, string 2
Double C tuning (gCGCD)	
Fret 7, string 4	Fret 12, String 3
Fret 5, string 3	Fret 7, string 2
Fret 7, string 3	Fret 12, string 1
Fret 5, string 3	Fret 17, string 5

Table 7-1

Another effective tuning method involves the use of *intervals*, or musical distances. Each string in a given tuning is a specified musical distance apart from its neighbor, and each of these distances has a characteristic sound that can be memorized.

The easiest musical distance to recognize is the *octave* — hearing the same note at a higher or lower level (middle C and high C on the piano, for example, are one octave apart). Most students can easily train themselves to hear an octave. If you are able to do so, this gives you the ability to check the tuning of specific pairs of strings, such as strings 1 and 4 in G-tuning — both tuned to D an octave apart — and strings 2 and 4 in double C-tuning, both of which are tuned to C an octave apart.

Musicians have developed a number of *mnemonics* (memory aids) to help students recognize other musical distances. For example, the interval called a *fifth* (also used to tune the strings of violins, violas, cellos and tenor banjos), is the same as the two first notes of the famous tune *Streets of Laredo*. Being able to recognize a fifth gives you the ability, for example to check the sound of open string 3 against open string 4 in double C-tuning, or of open string 1 against open string 3 in G-tuning.

Other common intervals in banjo tuning include:

♦ the *fourth* (used to tune string 3 to string 4 in G-tuning or mountain minor tuning). Mnemonic: the first two notes of *Here Comes the Bride*.

♦ the *major third* (used to tune string 2 to string 3 in G-tuning). Mnemonic: first two notes of *Halls of Montezuma*.

♦ the *minor third* (used to tune string 1 to string 2 in G-tuning). Mnemonic: first two notes of *Green Sleeves*.

♦ the *major second* (used to tune string 1 to string 2 in mountain minor and double C-tunings). Mnemonic: Do and Re of the major scale.

Interestingly, this tuning-by-interval method was the one employed most by traditional banjo players in the South before the old-time music revival. Instead of using mnemonics, however, musicians learned to recognize the exact sounds of the strings for each tuning.

I'll also offer two more tuning suggestions: First, make sure to tune your strings in consecutive order. Ideally, start with the lowest string, then tune the next highest to it, and so on. Above all, avoid tuning your strings to more than one template unless you know these multiple templates are in tune with each other. For example, you court disaster if you tune string 3 to string 4, and then tune string 2 to string 1. Since you haven't checked to see whether strings 1 and string 4 are in tune, you're almost certain to have an out-of-tune instrument in your hands.

Finally, you can make your tuning efforts easier by making sure to keep your banjo-head as tight as possible. The more play the head has, the more the other strings will move around when one string is tuned. You can also make sure that the neck is firmly attached to the pot, and that the tail-piece is securely fastened in place.

I'll close with a word on electronic tuners. By and large, electronic tuners are very useful inventions. They are great in the recording studio, when performing in noisy bars or when trying to create a slick impression on stage. For a student who has not yet learned to tune by ear, however, they become an addicting crutch that can atrophy the ability to distinguish slight gradations in pitch. I can say without hesitation that learning to tune by ear is an absolutely crucial stage in the development of any stringed-instrument player.

8.8 Changing Tunings on the Fly (and 5th-String Capos)
8.9 More on Rapid Retuning

(Aug. '90)
(Nov. '90)

One definite albatross for the clawhammer player is the constant tuning changes the style requires for playing in different keys or modes (see chapter 5). Old timey pickers are usually sensitive to 5-string artists and give them plenty of time to retune. Players of Irish, Scottish and contra-dance music, on the other hand, are accustomed to switching keys at will, and are often unaware that this presents a problem for banjoists. Another important situation where banjo pickers might be expected to switch keys frequently is solo-performance work, where considerations of variety encourage frequent retunings.

There are three common ways of dealing with this situation: First you can attempt to do away with retuning entirely. Second, you can alter your instrument to make retuning easier. Third, you can resort to outside aids to assist the retuning process. Let's look at each of these in turn.

There are two ways to do away with retuning in clawhammer. First, you can show up at your gig or jam session with a different banjo for each tuning (don't laugh, this is actually done by some noted artists). You could probably get away with just two banjos: one for open G tuning and one for double C tuning (or maybe three banjos if you play a lot in mountain minor), but you'd still have to deal with capoing (see below). You'd also have to get used to the idiosyncrasies of several different instruments — something I for one do not find congenial.

The second method for doing away with retuning is learning to play all keys and modes out of a single tuning, the way guitarists and many bluegrass banjo players do. This works theoretically but I think that under this system many tunes would develop impossible fingerings. I also think that you would tend to lose that open ringing resonance that makes clawhammer so special.

At any rate, all clawhammerists should at least be able to play back-up in any key from any tuning (for some hints on how to do this, see cols. 2-15 and 5.4-5). That way if you're set up say, for D major tunes and the fiddler shifts to A major without warning, you can chord along without having to retune. This is particularly important because the fiddler might just follow that A tune with another D tune, and then where would you be!

There are two primary methods for altering a banjo to make retuning easier: installing Keith pegs and/or installing a fifth string capoing device. Keith pegs — which are part of the arsenal of most self-respecting bluegrass pickers — precisely control the amount that a given peg can turn, thereby enabling you to shift a given string exactly one or two frets in pitch. Theoretically, this means that you can change the pitch of the second string from B to C and back at a touch, and that a similar touch could shift the fourth string from D to C and back. This would make shifts among standard C-, double C-, mountain minor and G-tunings child's play.

There is a down-side to Keith tuners, however. First, they add weight to your banjo neck and require wider pegholes to be drilled in the headstock. Second (the banjo being what it is), when you shift one string in this manner there's at least some tendency for the others to go out of tune. To be honest, I have owned banjos on which Keith pegs were an effective alternative for shifting among tunings, and banjos on which this was not the case. From my limited sample, I suspect that instruments with particularly dense maple necks, solid construction, and *coordinator rods* (that pair of metal rods used in modern instruments to bond neck and pot in lieu of the old fashioned — albeit more esthetically pleasing — dowel stick) stand the best chance of holding tune when you shift that Keith-peg.

Fifth string capoing devices are usually necessary when a capo is used on the long strings. Essentially, there are two kinds: rail capos and intra-fret capos. Rail capos involve a sliding device with some sort of spring mechanism capable of stopping the string at any fret within reach of the rail. The most popular intra-fret capo is the *railroad spike* — a right angle nail set in at the desired fret in such a way that the fifth string can be slipped under it, effectively raising its pitch. Interestingly, these bent nails used in banjo fretboards were in fact designed to be used for fastening model railroad tracks. The fact that they are ideal for use as banjo capoing devices is purely fortuitous!

The problem with rail capos is that they are unsightly and can get in the way of your fretting hand, although if you must get one I suppose I'd recommend the Shubb model, which is mounted flush to the neck. Railroad spikes do away with the above problems, but they create new ones. To wit: it's almost impossible to set them so that the fifth string won't go a little sharp when placed in them. And, if you really want flexibility, you'd need a spike at every fret (I usually use just a single spike set at the second fifth string fret, parallel to the seventh fret on any of the long-strings).

I ought to mention here that when tuning your instrument, it probably works a little better to place the long-string capo first, *then* tune the fifth string. This is because placing the capo may change the string tension and cause the pitch of the long strings to shift slightly. If this happens, you'd just have to retune the fifth string anyway.

Probably the best solution of all to fifth string capoing was once suggested to me by one banjo maker. This would be more or less a cross between the two capoing styles. Built into the neck at the fifth string side of each fret would be a small metal-lined cylindrical cavity. You would then have a spring mechanism (similar to the one used on a rail capo), one end of which would fit into one of these cavities, while the other end stopped the string. The only potential negatives here are that such a capoing device would probably be expensive to install, and that the little spring mechanism would be easy to misplace.

Finally, let's look at "outside aids." What I had in mind here is the now relatively commonplace electronic tuner, which allows you to follow the progress of your tuning efforts via a screen display. What's more, by attaching an electronic tuner to your banjo with an alligator-clip cord, you can even isolate the sound of your instrument to some degree when in a band or jamming situation. As usual, there are some problems here. If you're performing solo, for example, you have to take your eyes off the audience to watch the tuner's screen display, and this is never an effective tactic. Plus, it has been my experience that even with the alligator clip chord (which seems to be an avid believer in Murphy's Law and likes to disengage itself at every opportunity), it's often hard to isolate your own signal in a noisy environment.

There is yet another possibility that could be made to work in tandem with electronic tuners, which I thought of after watching bluegrass banjoist Roger Sprung playing a version of *Auld Lang Syne* using only his Keith tuners to change pitches. Roger didn't have a Keith tuner on his fifth string, however. He had merely memorized how far to turn it in order to get the pitch changes he wanted. I reasoned that this method could also be applied to old-time banjo. In other words, I could probably learn just how far to turn the pegs to get the pitch shifts I wanted. This would be a tremendous advantage in crowded settings — especially if it was coordinated with watching an electronic tuner screen display! At any rate, if you want to try this, I found that a shift on the second string from B to C took about one eighth of a turn with Planet gears, and that a shift on the fourth string from C to D took somewhat less than a quarter turn (say about one-fifth or one-sixth of a turn).

At any rate, all of the above methods have their advantages and disadvantages, and I do encourage you to try some or all of them.

8.10 How I Got Started (Excerpt from Ken Perlman Interview by Ed Britt and Jeff Davis)   (May '97)

Britt: Why the banjo and what got you started?

Ken Perlman: The guitar was actually my first fretted instrument. I took it up in my mid teens, but the first contact I had with the banjo was my first day at Cornell University in Ithaca, NY. There was a fellow named Eric Mintz sitting there and playing what I later found out was a genuine Vega Whyte Laydie. I wandered over carrying my guitar case and I said, "Hey, what key are you playing in?" And he said, "I'm a banjo player, I don't know anything about keys!"

Later on, I was exposed to a number of old-time banjo players there — Howie Bursen, Walt Koken who was to become a central figure in the Highwoods String Band, and lots of others. Towards the end of university, I got a little frustrated with the guitar and decided I'd like to try something else, bought a cheap Japanese-made banjo, and started to play. At first I was kind of playing backwards fingerpicking, because that's what I knew.

Britt: How would you define "melodic" clawhammer?

Ken Perlman: People really started using this term in the mid-70s when the Kicking Mule anthology LP *Melodic Clawhammer Banjo* was released. The idea at the time was, "Let's see if we can create a brand of clawhammer so sophisticated and flexible that we can play with authority complete *melodies* of fiddle tunes." Ultimately, my aim became to create a style of clawhammer that was essentially a full-fledged solo instrumental style. In other words, it would give the banjoist the ability to play a large range of musical genres with speed, accuracy, power, and (within the limitations of the instrument) a wide range of expression.

Britt: How did you get involved in the melodic style?

Ken Perlman: I was never involved in anything else. I picked up the banjo, and immediately what I wanted to do was play tunes. At first I learned a few tunes out of books. And when I started to go to sessions, people would turn to me periodically and say "You don't have to bother playing on this one, because it's impossible to frail." At first I would just accept that. Later though, I would go home and think, "Let's see if I can." And quite often I would be able to find a way that would work. I remember one tune that people said couldn't be played in clawhammer style was *Devil's Dream*. I tried it and actually came up with a very traditional solution — I changed the tuning! I changed the fifth string to "E" so that you could get the off-beat high notes in the second part.

Davis: Tell us about your years in New York City?

Ken Perlman: I actually had grown up in New York City, but I returned in 1975 and rented a small walk-up apartment in Greenwich Village. Even before this move, I had begun to meet a whole coterie of young local players. Among those I encountered were a lot of banjo pickers who are now associated with the "traditional" style of clawhammer, such as Bob Carlin, Ray Alden, Bruce Molsky and Paul Brown. I also met a young clawhammerist named Henry Sapoznik. It turned out that Sapoznik — and Carlin as well at the time — were both experimenting in the same area of banjo playing I was. But fairly quickly I began to realize that there were a lot of other people who didn't seem to approve of what I was doing. At first it was a very subtle thing, but it actually seemed to pick up strength as my playing improved.

Davis: What was your reaction to this perceived "opposition?"

Ken Perlman: I didn't alter my focus, but I found myself starting to also hang around Irish sessions in New York — both at the Irish Arts Center and a place called the Eagle Tavern on 14th St. and 9th Ave. There were also some wonderful older fiddle players from Ireland like Andy McGann, Johnny Cronin and Paddy Reynolds who lived in New York and came to these sessions. For the first time I found myself trying to emulate other musicians: instead of just "playing the tune," I was trying to capture on banjo the *style* that these older musicians played *on fiddle*.

Britt: Getting back to the various other banjo players you met in New York. Did you pick up anything from them?

Ken Perlman: Absolutely! I found that I was able to continue improving my own techniques of playing by watching these other pickers. Take Ray Alden for example, then the most ardent advocate of "traditional" banjo style in New York. Ray had spent tons of time in the Galax, Virginia area with Fred Cockerham and Kyle Creed learning to play like them. I really liked the tone Ray got out of the banjo. It was a lot more projecting and powerful than the tone I had at the time, which could be described as fairly "airy."

I remember watching him closely to see what he was doing different. And he was doing a thing like a lot of Southern players, where they bring the forearm straight over the strings, and kind of roll the hand over the top — so the whole arm is really driving the attack. And by watching him, I absorbed the idea of supporting my attack with the full weight of my forearm, and sure enough my tone and drive increased markedly! By now, the whole thing is very subtle, and if you watched my arm you might not see my forearm move very much. But in this way I'm influenced — not only by Alden — but through him by his mentor Kyle Creed.

CHAPTER 9. HISTORY AND OBSERVATIONS ON THE BANJO AND OLD TIME MUSIC

9.1 The Origin of the Banjo and Clawhammer   (Mar. '84)
9.2 The Origin of the Banjo and Clawhammer, Revisited   (Feb. '01)

A clawhammer player from Montreal, Quebec, named Marc Nerenberg seems to have shed some light on the question of how and where the banjo and clawhammer style originated. Back in the mid-80s, Marc and his wife Rosemary spent several weeks vacationing in a West African country called Mali. He brought along a small fretless banjo — an 8" pot with maybe a 20" scale — and as they traveled around, he would sometimes play the instrument in the central squares of some of the villages they visited.

On one such occasion a crowd gathered and he had the inspiration to ask if anyone had ever seen a similar instrument. A number of onlookers indicated that they had, but that the ones they had seen were still played only in relatively primitive communities located far in the interior of the country.

Several villages and questioning sessions later, Marc and Rosemary found themselves in the territory of an animist tribe known as the Dogon People. The Dogon live in a village set into the face of an escarpment near the southern edge of the Sahara Desert. When Marc started playing his banjo in the central square of that village, he was suddenly confronted by the local bard carrying a small instrument composed of a round, skin-covered gourd about six inches in diameter with an attached smoothed stick about ten inches long. Suspended between the gourd and the stick were two strings: one long string and one short one. Marc had found at least one of the banjo's ancestors!

After some hurried pitch adjustments, accomplished by pushing the knotted ends of each string up or down the stick, the bard began to play his instrument (known as a *kona*) along with Marc. To Marc's astonishment the bard used a down-picking style instantly identifiable as a relative of clawhammer. He played the melody on the long string with a down-picking fingernail (using his fretting hand fingers to stop different melody notes), while his thumb played a high drone on the open short string. In fact, once both musicians got over their initial shock, they were able to swap songs and tunes, and even try out each other's instruments. In fact, one well-known old-timey tune that was immediately recognizable to the bard as an African melody was *Reuben's Train*.

In the years since Marc first told me this story, it has become plain to much of the historically-minded banjo community that west Africa is more or less awash with instruments that resemble the banjo to a greater or lesser extent. There are even hieroglyphic depictions to attest that the "class" of instruments to which banjos belong — "lutes" with skin sounding-boards — were played by the ancient Egyptians.

Most of these African instruments — like the Dogon kona — have a neck made of a rounded stick or length of bamboo: their strings are fixed at the gourd end and looped around the stick in such a way that their tension can be altered to effect pitch changes. The "pots" show quite a range in terms of construction. Some use a hemispherical gourd, others an elliptical gourd, some have a carved-wood pot or a wooden frame pot. Another major variable is the manner by which neck and pot are joined. In the case of many African skin-head lutes, the neck is attached via a "spike" driven into the center of the "pot," and the bridge rises directly out of this point of attachment. In others, the neck proceeds through the entire pot (like the dowel-stick of a banjo), and a separate bridge is required to lift the strings off the pot surface.

Quite a number of west African musicians who play these instruments have appeared in the US of late. At the second Tennessee Banjo Institute festival in 1990, for example, Ba Sekou Kouyate from Mali was brought in to demonstrate his instrument, also known as the kona (or nkoni). The "pot" on his instrument was elliptical in shape, with several long strings and *two* drone strings. One drone — as in a 5-string banjo — was set above the strings, and one was set in *below* the long strings. His playing style sometimes resembled clawhammer and sometimes fingerpicking.

Similarly, a Malian named Cheick Hamala Diabate settled in the US in the '90s and is now performing extensively around the country. He plays an instrument called the Mande koni (a variant of the halam) in a style quite similar to clawhammer. His instrument itself has an elliptical rosewood "pot," spike-style construction, and four strings: three long and one short.

A recent meeting of banjo collectors near Boston featured an appearance by Daniel Jatta from the Jola tribe in Gambia. He played a stringed instrument with a hemispherical gourd "pot" and dowel-stick construction called an *akonting*. The akonting has three strings of unequal length, and is played in a style virtually identical to American clawhammer, with the longest string used for melody, and the shortest for thumb-drone; the string in between serves as an additional drone and is plucked via a technique that is unmistakably drop-thumbing. Many banjo scholars now feel that the akonting may well have been one of the prototypes for the North American banjo. Among the many points in its favor are (1) Gambia was the region from which slaves bound for North America were first drawn, (2) the style of construction is close in many details to that of early North American banjos, (3) the neck of the akonting is made of a local kind of bamboo known as bangoe (pronounced "ban-joo"), and (4) the capitol of Gambia (built on an island where this plant is found in great abundance) is known as Banjul!

According to artists' depictions and diary-accounts, North American banjos prior to the minstrel era had four strings — almost certainly in the form of three long strings and one short string (the addition of a fifth string to the banjo is often attributed to Joel Walker Sweeney: if so, he added the one now referred to as the *fourth* string).

As of this writing, it is not at all clear to banjo-scholars how the North American banjo first acquired its flat fingerboard and bona-fide peghead construction (one can surmise that these features were borrowed from European stringed instruments like the guitar, viol or violin, but there is as yet nothing to document this theory). Certainly by the 1840s when the banjo was absorbed into the European-American mainstream, construction styles borrowed from these European instruments were being applied to the banjo. For example, drum-making

techniques were borrowed for pot-construction, and European decorating techniques, such as marquetry and inlay, were applied to fingerboard decoration. Along these lines, some 8- or even 10-string banjos built around that time in England and Western Europe probably borrowed some ideas from a multi-string instrument known as the Baroque lute.

At any rate, the arrangement of *Reuben's Train* that appears here is my recollection of Marc Nerenberg's recollection of how the tune was played in the Dogon village. This arrangement — where the entire melody is played along a single string — may be representative of at least some of the original clawhammer playing brought by Africans to this country in the 1600s.

On the assumption that the two strings of the kona are tuned a perfect fifth apart (examples: gC; eA; aD), I used the banjo the tuning gCGCC. To get this *triple*-C tuning from double-C tuning (gCGCD), just tune the first string down to match the pitch of the open second string.

Reuben's Train

Banjo Arrangement: Ken Perlman

Tuning: gCGCC

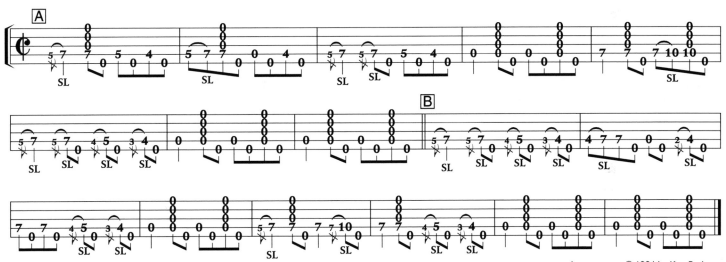

Arrangement © 1984 by Ken Perlman

9.3 Minstrel Clawhammer

(July '83)

Beginning in the mid-19th century, the banjo was a prominent feature of traveling minstrel shows. Banjo pickers of that era played clawhammer style (then called *stroke style*) exclusively. Instead of using a fingernail or bare finger on the downstroke, however, some minstrel-style players wore a pointed wire rig known as a *thimble* on the index or middle finger to aid in sound production. They may also have worn a similar device on the thumb. Banjos of the period were fretless and had gut strings. They also had much longer necks and were tuned substantially lower than present day instruments. Standard tunings for banjos started at roughly dGDF♯A (five frets or a *fourth* lower than present day standard C tuning [gCGBD]), then moved up to eAEG♯B (three frets or a *minor third* lower than present day standard C tuning).

Because the style was so popular, numerous instruction books and tune collections were published at the time. Many of the tunes presented in these collections were jigs, reels and hornpipes, and the arrangements often called for techniques that we now think of as melodic clawhammer techniques. The strange part is that the present day melodic style was developed by players who were not even aware that the minstrel style existed, and who were exposed only to the "traditional" style of playing. It seems that the human mind, when faced with the problem of playing similar types of melodies on the same instrument will come up with similar solutions and technical modifications even in completely different eras.

Eli Kaufman of Amherst, New York, who is president of the American Banjo Fraternity and an avid collector of banjo memorabilia, was kind enough to provide me with photocopies of a few tunes from an 1858 volume entitled *Phil Rice's Banjo Instructor*. The tune I chose to tab out is Rice's arrangement of *Mrs. McCloud's Reel* (you may know it as *Hop High Ladies*).

For comparison's sake, check out my tablature version of the tune in *Basic Clawhammer Banjo*.

Rice's arrangement was written out in standard notation for the tuning eAEG♯B. All notes to be played by the middle or index finger were marked with an arabic "1" subscript, while all notes to be played with the thumb were marked with an "x" subscript.

The first step in making the transcription was transposing the music from the key of E up a minor third to the key of G. I was fascinated by the result. As I tabbed out the tune, I felt a kinship with this man who played banjo so long ago. I knew exactly what he was trying to do and why he made the choices he did.

This particular arrangement is not completely melodic in its approach; it often substitutes "banjo-isms" for certain fiddle phrases. The arrangement does employ many melodic techniques, however. The arpeggio, for example, appears frequently (col. 2.9), the open fifth string and alternate string pull-offs are often used for melody (cols. 2.1 and 1.8 respectively), M and T "reversal" is not uncommon (col. 2.12), and so on. One maneuver that may be unique to Rice's era is a T-P-T triplet starting on the fifth string (Parts A and B, measures 2, 4, 6 and 7). I think they are performed as follows:

♦ At the last preceding M note, bring T into contact with the fifth string
♦ Pluck the fifth string with T, and bring a left-hand finger into contact with the first string at the same time. If the first string notation calls for a fretted note, have a finger at that fret and one at a higher fret.
♦ Pull off the open first string, (or pull off from the higher to the lower first-string fret). At the same time, bring T into contact with the second string.
♦ Pluck the second string with T.

Mrs. McCloud's Reel (Minstrel Version)

Banjo Arrangement: Phil Rice   Tuning: eAEG♯B (or gCGBD)

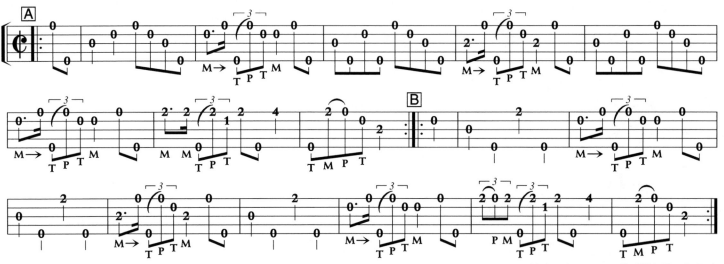

Modern Arrangement © 1983 by Ken Perlman

9.4 Briggs' Banjo Instructor   (Feb. '88)

I recently came across a copy of Thomas F. Briggs' *Briggs Banjo Instructor*, a clawhammer tutor published by the Oliver Ditson Company of Boston in 1856.[1] Although the work is primarily a loosely graded banjo-tune collection with a minimum of actual teaching, It does give us some idea of what banjo playing was like in Briggs' day.

Briggs recommends a system of playing substantially similar to the modern style. He calls for using the first fingernail (he uses the symbol "f") and the thumb (symbol: x.) to pluck the banjo, and he goes on to describe basic hand position as follows:

"[T]he thumb should be extended and rest on the 5th string. The fingers should not be separated, but held closely together, and move simultaneously with the first finger; the first finger should be held a little farther out from the hand than the other fingers. The fingers should be held stiff; except at the third joint. The wrist should be held limber."

[1] *Briggs' Banjo Instructor* was reprinted in 1997 by Centerstream Music Co., with all banjo settings translated from standard notation to tablature by Joe Weidlich.

Basic picking technique is also described in familiar terms:

"In playing, the thumb and first finger only of the right hand are used; the 5th string is touched by the thumb only; this string is always played open, the other strings are touched by the thumb and the first finger… The first finger should strike the strings with the backs of the nail…"

As Briggs continues his description of the style, one important difference with modern technique emerges. He states that when using the thumb, "the first fingernail should rest against the first string (or on the head or on the string immediately below the one that has just been 'touched'); when using the first finger the thumb should rest on the fifth string…"

If this directive is to be taken literally (and quite often musical directives are not meant to be taken at face value), it's hard to imagine how players of that period were able to achieve much in the way of rapid tempos.

Briggs also describes the several basic maneuvers that form the heart of the style. I translated to tab five short exercises from his books that illustrate them. These appear in Example 9-1:

♦ Example 9-1a shows what I call the single-string brush.
♦ Example 9-1b shows double thumbing.
♦ Example 9-1c illustrates double thumbing with a change of note in the middle.
♦ Examples 9-1d and 9-1e show maneuvers not much used today: a two-string *arpeggio* followed by a T-M-T triplet (his notation is "x-f-x"). (I've Illustrated these maneuvers in two ways: the top staff is in Briggs' notation, while the bottom staff shows what I think he means).

Tuning: dGDF♯A

159

Briggs also describes three kinds of "slurs" used by banjoists of the period. Two of these are identical to our hammer-ons and pull-offs. The third kind of slur involves dragging the picking finger from string to string with a roll-like motion. This last slur seems to be another name for the arpeggio technique (col. 2.9). In his pieces, Briggs combines all three kinds of slurs in very interesting and (from the modern point of view) unusual ways to obtain rhythms and melodic figures.

If this book is any indication, left hand fingering does not seem to have been very adventurous in the 1850s. At any rate, Briggs clearly states that the fifth string was never stopped and that strings two through four were stopped only in first position. A "second position" was recognized only for the first string in which the first finger played the equivalent of fret 5 (D above middle C, given a tuning of dGDF#A), the second finger played the equivalent of fret 7 (E), the third finger played the equivalent of fret 9 (F#) and the fourth finger played the equivalent of fret 10 (G).

I've translated two of Briggs' tunes into tablature: *Turkey in the Straw* (Briggs uses the old title *Old Zip Coon*) and *Fisher's Hornpipe* (he calls it *Darkey's Fisher's Hornpipe*). If you're familiar with the full-fledged versions of these tunes (see my books *Clawhammer Style Banjo* and *Basic Clawhammer Banjo*, respectively), you'll quickly note that Briggs altered them all significantly so that they'd fit comfortably in clawhammer style. It's not clear, however, if these are the arrangements Briggs played himself, or if they were toned down student versions.

Turkey in the Straw (Minstrel Version)

Banjo Arrangement: Thomas F. Briggs

Tuning: dGDF#A (or gCGBD)

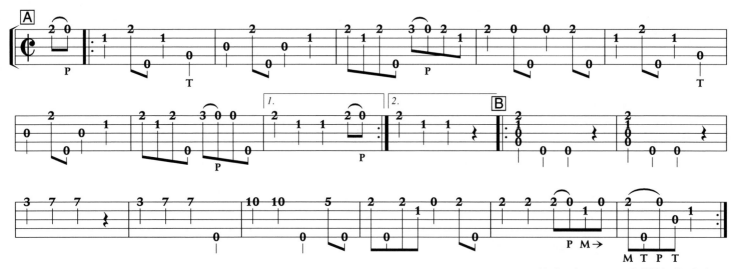

Modern Arrangement © 1988 by Ken Perlman

Fisher's Hornpipe (Minstrel Version)

Banjo Arrangement: Thomas F. Briggs

Tuning: dGDF#A (or gCGBD)

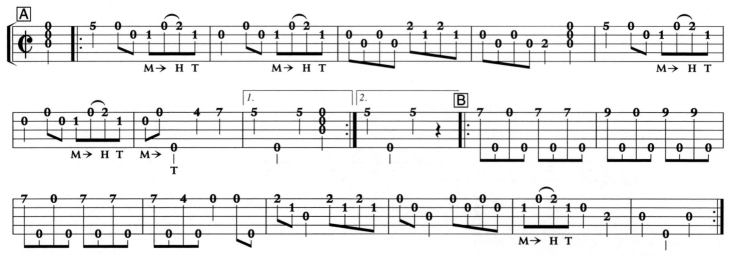

Modern Arrangement © 1988 by Ken Perlman

To get the full flavor of these tunes, tune down to 1850s tuning (dGDF♯A). To obtain this tuning from modern G tuning (gDGBD):

♦ Tune string 4 down an octave below string 3 (two G's below middle C on the piano)
♦ Tune string 3 to the new pitch of fret 7, string 4 (D below middle C)

♦ Tune string 2 to the new pitch of fret 4, string 3 (F♯ below middle C)
♦ Tune string 1 to the new pitch of fret 3, String 2 (A below middle C)
♦ Tune string 5 to the new pitch of fret 5, String 1 (D above middle C).

9.5 The Minstrel-Melodic Connection

(Dec. '98)

Back in the early days of this column, and several years before the current rebirth of interest in minstrel style got underway, I did a couple of articles on the subject accompanied by a few 1850s banjo settings.

Of most interest for me at the time was the many techniques that appeared in minstrel arrangements that I had thought were unique to melodic clawhammer — like the use of off-string pull-offs for melody, extensive use of drop-thumbing on the "inner" strings (that is, strings 2, 3 and 4), plus the use of lots of fretted hammer-ons and pull-offs, triplets, and ornaments. Even more remarkable from my point of view were the numerous situations that called for a technique they called a right hand slur and which I call an *arpeggio* (column 2.9). This technique — an elaboration of the Galax lick — was something I thought I had actually invented!

Then there was the content of the material. These early minstrels had devoted much of their talents to playing jigs, reels, hornpipes and other tunes of that ilk. Plus, they clearly were attempting to get in a very healthy percentage of the notes. Again, both of these are also common traits of modern melodic playing.

At the time, I thought it might be an interesting exercise to resurrect more of these old minstrel tunes. I never got around to it myself, but I've been gratified to see a number of others get involved in such re-creations, such as Bob Winans, Bob Flesher, Clarke Beuhling, George Wunderlich and Bob Carlin.

It was with some of these thoughts in mind that I arrived not long ago on the doorstep of Clarke Beuhling's home in Fayetteville, Arkansas. I was on tour in the area and had a couple of days to kill and Clarke had graciously offered me a place to stay. Naturally we spent much of our time together playing tunes.

Considering that Clarke's repertoire comes almost entirely from 19th century banjo manuals, and mine comes primarily from late 20th century fiddle players, one might think we would have had little repertoire in common. In point of fact we knew dozens of tunes in common — most of them Irish and Scottish fiddle tunes that had been set for banjo during the minstrel era

(many of these banjo arrangements were published at the time under other names, almost all of which began with the word "Darkey").

Even when it came to style of performance, Clarke's minstrel approach and my melodic one were not really too far apart — especially if one takes into consideration that he had never heard some of these tunes played by a bona-fide fiddler. In terms of the minstrel banjo settings themselves, if you discount the seemingly obligatory banjo-clichés that were occasionally thrown in for effect, by and large these are arrangements that a modern melodic player would be happy to own up to.

If one is looking for an ultimate ancestor-in-spirit for the modern melodic approach to clawhammer, it is the minstrel tradition that probably serves this role. By this I mean that the principles which gave rise to the minstrel style of arranging are quite similar to those that gave rise to the melodic, and that the musical aims of minstrel practitioners seem to have been quite similar to those of modern melodic players.

Having said this, I should also point out the areas in which melodic clawhammer and the minstrel style differ. First of all, modern melodic players have had the benefit of exposure to the great drive of Galax clawhammer — a style that, of course, didn't exist back in the minstrel era. This allows modern melodic players to approach fiddle-music with greater depth and power than was once possible.

Another factor here is the influence on melodic clawhammer of melodic bluegrass players such as Bill Keith and Tony Trischka. The old minstrel players, for example, did not use much in the way of Keith-like melodic fingering forms or fifth-string fretting — options that are certainly open nowadays (see cols. 2.13-17). Of course, one reason minstrel players neglected these techniques was that they played on fretless instruments with a non-standardized 5th-string scale length. On the other hand, an accomplished fretless player could very well have used these techniques on the more sophisticated instruments built in the years following the Civil War (I offer by way of "proof" that Beuhling was able to accomplish all kinds of up-the-neck work on some of his fretless instruments).

I recently had the chance to visit the much-touted *Ring the Banjar!* exhibit, held at the Massachusetts Institute of Technology in Cambridge, Massachusetts. From the exhibit itself, its accompanying booklet and some subsequent research, I was able to piece together much of the history of banjo design and manufacture through the 1920s.

♦ The early minstrels did not play much above the "fifth fret" region of the fingerboard (they played fretless instruments, but you know what I mean). Banjo necks of that period were thin and playable below that point but then widened abruptly to unplayable proportions.

♦ Many minstrel-era banjo fingerboards were deeply scalloped where the neck and pot met. Apparently, the practice of stationing the plucking hand over the upper fingerboard (instead of over the head) was popular even in the 1850s. I had always assumed that this stylistic variation originated in the Galax area of North Carolina.

♦ The pots of the first banjos were made from dried calabash gourds. When wooden-hoop pots became popular, many of the craftsmen who felt themselves equipped to build banjos were drum-makers (see cols. 7.8 and 9.1). At least one small flat drum with an attached banjo neck was on display, and it was plain to see that pot-construction still owes much to drum-building technology.

♦ In the pre-frets era, banjo decoration usually consisted of a unified design that covered the entire headstock and fingerboard surface. The most handsome such designs were created via *marquetry* (inlays of contrasting woods). As fretted banjos became more and more popular through the 1860s and beyond, it was simply more practical to use discrete decorations that could also double as fret markers. What's more, mother-of-pearl and abalone made much handsomer fret markers than did contrasting woods. One popular fretless-era fingerboard decoration that has survived into modern times is the *tree of life* design.

♦ The 19th-century name for the fifth string was *chanterelle* (French for "little singer"). I think we should re-adopt this term!

The genealogy of the major Boston banjo makers is fascinating and makes good reading. In the beginning (1880 or so), there was *Fairbanks & Cole* — a partnership that produced a line of instruments comparable to that of S.S. Stewart of Philadelphia. In 1890, William Cole and Albert Fairbanks parted company. Cole continued to make Stewart-style banjos, such as the Cole's Eclipse model. Fairbanks, on the other hand, experimented with both rim and tone-ring design and, late in 1890, introduced his Fairbanks Electric model. The Electric featured a laminated wood rim and the first modern complex tone ring: a scalloped metal "truss" topped by a brass rod. Fairbanks also dabbled in bicycle manufacture and is credited with the invention of the wooden bicycle rim. He withdrew from the *Fairbanks Co.* in 1896, and was replaced as technical director by David Day.

Day soon modified the Electric model by devising a bracket band with attached "shoes" that eliminated the need for drilling through the rim. This new model, which featured a blonde finish, was called the Fairbanks Whyte Laydie. Day continued as technical head after the Vega Co. took over Fairbanks in 1904. He is sometimes also credited for designing the Tubaphone tone ring, a square-in-cross-section bell-brass tube perforated by regularly spaced small holes. Documents filed with the U.S. patent office, however, attest that the ring was invented by one N.J. Nelson. At any rate, the first "Vega-Fairbanks Tu-Ba-Phone" appeared in 1909.

From 1905-12, Vega built a series of banjos for Fred Bacon of Hartford, Connecticut, called the Bacon Professional. From 1912 to about 1920, some Bacon banjos were built by the Wm. Lange Co. of New York City, which also manufactured both the Orpheum and Paramount lines of banjos. In 1922 David Day left Vega to join the Bacon Banjo Co., which had since re-located to Groton, Connecticut. This company later produced the "B&D" (presumably short for "Bacon & Day") line of instruments. The best known banjo model bearing the B&D imprint was the Silver Belle.

Also of interest: there were literally hundreds of banjo-related patents before 1933, but there have been less than a dozen since. There is certainly plenty of room for improvement in banjo design: so let's get cracking, all you banjo builders!

9.7 A European Model for the Banjo? (Excerpt from Readers' Mailbag)   (Feb. '96)

Joe Weidlich of Washington, DC wrote in with some historical notes concerning parallels between the playing style used for frailing banjo, and that employed for a five-stringed instrument known as the *baroque guitar*:

"The baroque guitar — an instrument with five *courses* (sets of doubled strings) tuned ADGBE — was popular in the 17th

century. One common technique associated with the instrument is similar to one frequently used on banjo. The fifth *course* of the baroque guitar was tuned in octaves so that the high A could be used as a melody note, particularly in elaborate scale passages where you could play a cluster of notes by combining open strings, up-the-neck fretted notes and the high fifth string. This technique — which bares an uncanny resemblance to what 20th century banjoists call 'Keith-picking' — was then known as *campanellas* (literally, 'ringing of the bells') and was associated particularly with the playing of the Italian guitarist Ludovico

Ronalli, and the French guitarist Robert de Visée, who was attached to the court of Louis XIV."

The Banjo and Old-Time Music in Australia
9.8 Adventures in Aussie Land
9.9 The Banjo Down-Under, Revisited
9.10 Another Visit to Oz

(Mar. '92)
(Jan. '96)
(Mar. '98)

During my three Australian tours, I learned quite a few interesting facts concerning local banjo history. It seems that the Australian Gold Rush of the 1850s got underway just as our '49 rush in California was winding down. Quite a number of our 49ers who had not struck it rich headed for Australia to try to improve their luck, and (you guessed it) some of them brought their banjos along.

In the second half of the 19th century, there was a major trade route going between San Francisco and Sydney, and numerous American minstrel bands made Australia a stop on their touring itineraries. Some of these bands even chose to settle "down under" on a permanent basis. This much groundwork having been laid, Australia proved to be fertile ground for the establishment of banjo orchestras in the late 19th century, along the lines of those formed in the United States at the time. As a result, there are plenty of original American made vintage 5-string banjos in Australia, such as Vega and Fairbanks Tubaphones and Whyte Laydies, S.S. Stewarts, Bacons and the like.

In the 1920s and 1930s, Australia proved to be a ready market for recordings of old-time American country music. Quite a number of Australian bands formed at the time with a repertoire derived from these recordings, some of them made up entirely of Aborigine musicians. I met one octogenarian named "Tex" (he haled from the town of Texas, New South Wales) who had been performing old-time American country songs for over half a century. Given this background, it's not surprising that the folk, bluegrass and old-timey revivals of the 1950s through the 70s took firm root here.

There has also been a strong indigenous country music scene in Australia since the 1930s. Australian country music is an offshoot of the Nashville sound (and it tends to follow The

musical trends coming out of Nashville), but it has its own record companies and pantheon of stars. The spiritual heart of Australian country music is the city of Tamworth, New South Wales, which features a wax museum devoted to better known Aussie artists, not to mention a 25-foot high gilt statue of a semi-acoustic f-hole single-cutaway guitar.

Tamworth is not really a second Nashville (the record companies are located elsewhere), but it has made itself the Mecca for what amounts to an annual country-music pilgrimage. For ten days each January thousands of Aussie country-music fans don their cowboy hats and boots, and descend en masse on this town, where they mill about the streets, fill the bars, and congregate briefly to listen to a myriad of country-music street singers.

While in Canberra I had the chance to visit the National Library, where scholars are doing quite a bit to help preserve and disseminate recordings of traditional Australian music. According to archivist Kevin Bradley, Australia had a far different musical experience than did North America. First of all, the concentrations of Irish and Scottish immigrants that allowed Celtic music to thrive in the New World rarely developed in Australia. Second, by the mid-19th century when Australia was settled, the jigs and reels that had previously dominated the ballrooms of England had been superseded by music from Central Europe — waltzes, mazurkas, polkas, and schottisches. Consequently, these Central European tunes were the ones that were typically played at Australian rural dances — a trend that was naturally amplified later in the century by an influx of a large number of German and other central European immigrants. What's more, in most Australian rural communities, the dance-accompaniment instrument of choice was the accordion: not the fiddle.[2]

The Banjo and Old-Time Music in Britain
9.11 Clawhammer and the Current UK Folk Scene
9.12 Clawhammer Today in the UK and North-West Europe
9.13 The Banjo in Britain: an Update

(Aug. '87)
(Aug. '95)
(Aug. '00)

first thing that strikes you about Britain is how much live music there is, relative to the United States. Just about every hamlet — no matter how small — seems to have at least one pub where musicians gather for a weekly session. And just about

every sizable town has at least one folk club. Consequently, there are just more folk gigs per capita in the U.K. than in the U.S. And you don't need to travel nearly as far between gigs when you're on tour.

---

[2] The point could be raised here: "What about the 49ers: didn't some of them play fiddle?" I'll bring this up the next time I visit Canberra!

Most folk clubs are run by a group of dedicated *residents*, who are usually excellent performers in their own right. A few residents get up to do short opening spots during the course of each concert. The main act, who is called the *guest*, does two sets per concert.

There are strong old time and bluegrass scenes in Britain, but both are still closely tied to musical developments in the States — not only through the distribution of CDs and visits to the US by British musicians — but also by a small but steady stream of American concert artists and American bands living or touring in Britain. American banjoists Peggy Seeger, Sara Grey and Tom Paley lived in the UK for years, for example. Among the American banjoists of note whose recent concert appearances and workshops have been highly influential are Bob Carlin, Tony Ellis, Debby McClatchy and Dwight Diller.

Of course, such influences are nothing new. The banjo was firmly ensconced in Britain as far back as the minstrel show days, and both classic banjo and banjo orchestras were almost as much a passion here in the late 19th and early 20th centuries as they were during the same period in America. Excellent banjos have been manufactured here as well over the years, and I am constantly running into players who proudly show off their vintage Clifford Essex, Windsor or Jedson instruments — many of which are in the same league in terms of sound and playability as those produced by our famous vintage manufacturers.

9.14 Origins of the 5-String Banjo Renaissance and "Folk-Song" Revival (Excerpts from Ken's Interview with Pete Seeger)

Interest in playing the 5-string banjo had declined dramatically in much of the Western world with the onset of the jazz age c. 1915: for the most part anyone drawn to the banjo-sound took up jazz-friendly 4-string *plectrum* or *tenor* banjos (the plectrum has the same scale-length as the 5-string and is tuned to the long-string portion of standard C-tuning, or CGBD; the tenor has a shorter scale length and is tuned CGDA like a cello). It was Pete Seeger's performances and recordings with the Almanac Singers and the Weavers in the 1940s and 50s that both rekindled interest in the 5-string banjo, and helped launch the American folk-song revival. In the 50s and 60s, his example made the banjo a respectable alternative instrument during the guitar-dominated folk-song "boom." He more or less invented and popularized the long-neck banjo as a means of lowering the modern banjo's range to make it more effective for song accompaniment. He is also the guy whose instruction manual, *How to Play the 5-string Banjo* (originally penned in 1948 and still in print) introduced two generations of players to the instrument. Following are a few excerpts from an interview I did with Pete on January 16, 2000.[3]

KP: How did you get started playing the 5-string banjo?

PS: I was about 16 when I heard a 5-stringer for the first time down in Asheville, North Carolina and it just non-plussed me. How did Samantha Baumgartner get all those wonderful notes out of it? And she seemed to be having so much fun leaning back in her rocking chair. And then Bascom Lunsford visited my father's house when we were in Washington DC, and in a few brief minutes I got a nice introduction to what I still call the Lunsford style, which I now play more than most anything else. It involves plucking up on the 3rd string and then the 1st string next and then you add the 5th string. And then you add the pulling off and hammering on.

But it wasn't until the spring of 1940 when I hitch-hiked west and south — mainly in the south — that I really learned to play. What I did was, every time I found some one who played a banjo I'd say, "Can you play me a tune?" and I'd watch him closely. By the end of the summer I realized there were several different styles of picking — double thumbing, frailing (some called it "beating"), and there was up-picking (which I call "the basic strum" in my book), and there was Lunsford-style which was up-up.[4] By the end of '40, I was about 200% better on the banjo than I had been eight months earlier...

But after I'd been through Kentucky and Tennessee and Alabama, Georgia and North Florida, I had learned basically what I passed on to people eight years later when I wrote my banjo book.

KP: How did you come to write your banjo book?

PS: My father[5] said, "Why don't you try writing something about how to play the banjo?" Because the old books written in the 19th century like Converse's and Briggs' really didn't show the folk styles... I worked on it when I was in the army, and I typed out the mimeograph stencils in hotel rooms while I was touring with Henry Wallace in the presidential campaign of '48. I had somebody take a few pictures of me playing the various techniques: that picture in my book of me playing a roll, for example, was taken with me still in my G.I. fatigues.

Around January 1948, I finished the job. I had 52 pages then, and a nice left-wing outfit called the Cooperative Mimeograph Shop on Union Square in Manhattan mimeoed 100 copies. I collated and stapled them, and it took me three or four years before I sold the hundred at $1.59 a copy. Then I went back to Cooperative Mimeo, and they ran off 500 more copies... Finally in 1962, the current edition came out through the Music Sales Company.

---

[3] The entire interview was published in the Sept. and Oct., 2000 issues of *Banjo Newsletter*.
[4] That is, a bumm-titty rhythm composed entirely of up-strokes.
[5] Musicologist Charles Seeger

KP: It seems that you started with basic elements you had learned from a variety of people in 1940, but by the late 40s you had developed that into a highly sophisticated and quite personal style. How did this develop?

PS: Well, I was playing all different kinds of music — Caribbean music, for example, which had a certain kind of syncopation. And I was curious about any kind of music I heard. In 1949, a young Indonesian was trying to raise money to go back home now that the Dutch had been kicked out of his country. We had a fund raising party for him and I'll never forget the dance he did, where he held a saucer with a small candle stuck to it and these two candles were the only light in the room. Then he sang a song, and clinked rings on his fingers on the two saucers. Then he turned the saucers in great circles under his arms and up in the air, and the candles never went out. At the end of the song he brought the candles together to snuff them out! He said this was a harvest dance in his part of Indonesia. The song he taught us was "Suli Ram" which I later taught to the Weavers, and it's still one of my favorite songs...

So I tried playing these strange songs with the banjo and found I could get away with it and I've been doing it ever since...

KP: What can you tell us about the beginnings of the folk revival?

PS: In 1929 when the crash came, it seemed to my father that it was going to take some kind of very disciplined method of government to feed all the people. He got together with some other musicians — Aaron Copeland was one of them — and they started what they called the Composer's Collective. They were going to use all their knowledge to invent a new style of music for the proletariat to sing while they were marching to the barricades. Well, after four or five years they had to face up to it — their atonal music and their Germanic stamping rhythms: unfortunately the working people of the country proved pretty much uninterested in them.

Well around that time a woman named Aunt Molly Jackson out of Kentucky sang at a rally held in New York City for striking coal miners. My father said, "Maybe we should learn from her," so he brings Aunt Molly around to the composers' collective. But they were quite baffled by her. They said, "Charlie, this is interesting but this music represents the past and we're supposed to be creating the music of the future." Then my father took Molly back to her apartment and he said, "I'm sorry they didn't understand you, but I know some young people who are going to want to learn your songs." And I was one of them. And when I was about 17, I went and knocked on her door...

KP: Can you describe early folk-song revival scene in New York City?

PS: There was Leadbelly, there was Burl Ives, there was Aunt Molly Jackson, there was Alan Lomax and a few friends... The folk revival literally started in Alan's living-room...

But it was mainly the left wing movement that got the folk "revival" going. And it was in 1941 that the Almanac Singers — Lee Hayes, Mil Lampell and myself — burst on the scene. The trained musicians said, "Oh that was nice, but after all they are just amateurs." But some other lefties like Mike Gold said, "This is the kind of music they should have given us back ten years ago instead of those hifalutin things the Composers' Collective was trying to give us." And Mike just wrote column after column about this great group, the Almanac Singers... When there was a big rally in New York's Madison Square Garden for the Transport Workers Union, they said, "Get those Almanac Singers." And we sang them a song about the *Train that Never Returned*... And we had them all stamping their feet and joining in on Woody Guthrie's song, *Union Maid*...

But it was the Almanac Singers who set off a great enthusiasm on the Left, and that Transport Workers' Union rally in New York was probably when the folk song revival began to spread beyond that initial group of people.

9.15 Tom Paley and the Clawhammer Revival

(Nov '84)

Most of you are well-acquainted with the roles of musicians like Pete Seeger and Earl Scruggs in re-popularizing the 5-string banjo and teaching us how to play it. Scruggs, of course, more or less invented bluegrass picking, while Seeger developed his own unique fingerpicking style.

Scruggs and Seeger were essentially instrumental *innovators*: they both blended together elements of several folk banjo styles to form entirely new ways of playing the banjo. They were not strictly speaking what you might call banjo *revivalists*. In other words, painstakingly working out the licks of the great pickers of yore was neither their forte not their aim.

The first true 5-string banjo revivalists came along in the mid-to-late 1940s. For the most part, these were young men and women so inspired by the music of Scruggs and Seeger that they

began to seek out recordings of other 5-string pickers. Most of the recordings they found were old 78's issued in the 1920s and 1930s, which featured an assortment of two-finger, three-finger, and clawhammer pickers playing a hodge-podge of regional styles. Without the benefit of lessons, instruction books, or even much visual exposure to the players they sought to emulate, the first revivalists attempted to recreate these old styles note-for-note by a process of musical dead-reckoning. That these first revival pickers laid the foundation for the modern clawhammer movement goes without saying

Tom Paley, a founding member of the New Lost City Ramblers, was one of the first 5-string banjo revivalists. I met him for the first time at the September 1984 Eisteddfodd Folk Festival in North Dartmouth, Massachusetts, where we were both scheduled performers. We got to talking about the old days, and he mentioned that he started playing banjo in the 1940s. He had seen Pete Seeger clawhammer and fingerpick the 5-string on a number of occasions, but he taught himself to play by working out note-for-note the banjo music on a Library of Congress collection that included recordings by Wade Ward, Herbert Smoke, Pete Steele, Thaddeus Willingham and Justice Begley. He also attempted to reproduce the music he heard on recordings by Clarence ("Tom") Ashley and Uncle Dave Macon. When he first started airing out his revivalist style in the late 40s, he remembers being criticized by some folk enthusiasts for sounding too much like the traditional pickers, and not enough like Seeger.

I asked Tom about the origin of the Ramblers. He noted that he first met John Cohen in New York when they were both active in the Greenwich Village folk scene. Later on, both found themselves at Yale University in New Haven, Connecticut — Tom as a graduate student and John as an undergraduate. One weekend, Peggy Seeger (then still in college and an accomplished instrumentalist in her own right) visited New Haven with her brother Mike and introduced him to Tom and John.

A couple of years later, Tom was living near Washington, D.C. John Cohen was down for a visit one weekend when they got a phone call from a local folk-music D.J. named John Dildine. Dildine noted that Mike Seeger was in town and wondered if they were interested in doing his radio show as a trio. Paley, Cohen and Seeger rehearsed a bunch of folk standards (which were still relatively fresh at the time) like *Old Joe Clark*, *Cluck Old Hen* and *Flop Eared Mule*, and did the show. The response was so overwhelming that they started performing together regularly.

Just before their first big New York concert, they met with promoter Moe Asch, founder of Folkways records. Asch was dismayed the trio had no name except "Paley, Cohen and Seeger," and insisted that a new, more catchy name be adopted: a few hours of tossing ideas back and forth produced the name "The New Lost City Ramblers."

For more on the clawhammer revival, see col. 9.28.

I asked Tom to contribute a tune to this column and he chose *Wolves Howling*, which he learned from a County Records reissue of a recording by the Stripling Brothers of Alabama. As he was playing the tune, folksinger and uillean piper Patrick Sky happened by and observed that the tune was more or less a stripped-down version of the Irish reel *The Silver Spear*. Note that the piece is in open C tuning (explained in col. 4.19).

Wolves Howling

Banjo Arrangement: Tom Paley

Tuning: gCGCE (capo–2)

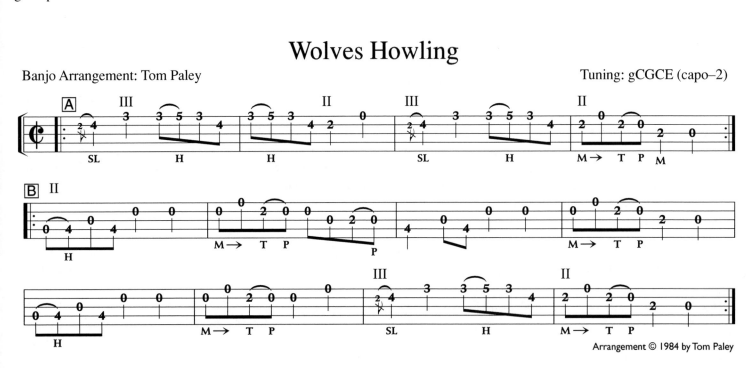

Arrangement © 1984 by Tom Paley

9.16 The Rebirth of Tablature

(Mar. '96)

Tablature is a system of music writing that is instrument specific. Notes are indicated as a series of activities. In other words — what does the player have to do in order to obtain the note in question.

Standard music notation gives us pure musical information via a system of dots on a staff. You are told that a series of specific pitches are called for; it is up to you to find those pitches on an instrument.

On some instruments — such as keyboards and winds — there is a direct association between pitch and standard notation. If you see the notation for middle C on a staff, for example, there is one (and only one) place to find that pitch on the piano. Similarly, the notation for high D on a staff calls for one (and only one) fingering combination on a flute. For instruments like these, there is no real advantage in using a tablature system.

Example 9-2

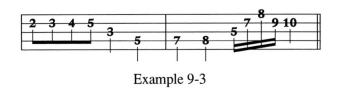

Example 9-3

Using "tab" does offer distinct benefits for players of instruments where there is no one-to-one correspondence between a notated pitch and the activity required to produce that pitch. For these instruments, a given pitch notation can indicate any one of several activities, depending on the context.

As probably comes as no surprise, players of fretted instruments in particular stand to benefit from a tablature system. Not only can the same pitch appear in different locations on several different strings, but the mental process involved in pitch location can involve three separate steps (identifying the note on the staff, learning where the various notes appear on the fingerboard, then associating staff notations with specific fingerboard locations). To make matters worse, a fretboard has a schematic aspect that intimidates novices (there's no nice pattern of black and white keys, for example, that indicates where to find the note C).

Writing "tab" is not exactly a new idea. Fretted-instrument pieces have been written in some form of tablature since at least the Renaissance. In fact, pieces in tablature for lute, viol, guitar, and other instruments were written almost exclusively in tab until the late eighteenth century.

In the seventeenth century, some of the first collectors of Scottish music were lutenists who set folk tunes for their instruments. In some cases, their surviving tablatures were the only means by which these tunes were preserved for posterity.

Some of these early tablature systems were remarkably like those used today. Most were written on a staff of lines, with each line signifying a string or *course* on the instrument (a "course" is a multiple-string set treated as a unit by the player, such as the doubled strings on a mandolin or 12-string guitar). In the Italian system, frets were indicated by numbers; in the French system, frets were indicated by letters (a = open string, b = 1st fret, c = 2nd fret, etc.).

In most of these early systems, rhythm notation was shown by placing a stem or entire note shape above the staff. Example 9-2 shows how this system operates, using numbers and modern note-shapes for the readers's convenience.

Music instruction became more and more formalized in the eighteenth and 19th centuries, and the use of tablature was largely abandoned. After 1800, Spanish guitar pieces, etudes and exercises were preserved via standard notation. Even minstrel-era banjo tutors employed standard notation exclusively.

Modern experimentation with fretted-instrument tablature dates from the publication of Pete Seeger's book, *How to Play the 5-String Banjo*, in 1948.[6] Seeger's main innovation in writing tablature was moving rhythm notation *into* the staff, as illustrated in Example 9-3.

In the decades that followed, tablature gradually found its way into teaching materials for most fretted instruments. By the 1970s, tablature books became quite common. For some instruments (notably banjo), standard notation seems to have been entirely supplanted.

Why did tablature suddenly reappear at the dawn of the post-industrial age? I think for the answer to that question we have to look at the nature of the folk revival, which was then just getting underway. Many of the idealists who joined the revival were rebelling against a world where politics, industry and science had led Europe and North America into two major wars within thirty years, and had together created weapons so destructive that man faced annihilation. There was a strong urge to get back to simpler things — relics of a pre-industrial age — like ballads, sailor's songs, old-time country music, fiddle tunes. There was also a drive to experience the world in a more elemental, emotional manner, which led to a fascination with country blues.

Translating folk music to tablature at that time, then, served a variety of needs. First (and most obviously), it made the music more immediately accessible (the presumption was that "tab" allowed the material to transcend barriers of education and economic class). Second, it allowed players to feel that they were experiencing the music more immediately — that they didn't require standard notation as a go-between. Third, since classical music and note reading has long been associated with the social elite, it permitted the player to believe that he or she had rejected the values of that elite.

---

[6] When Pete introduces his system in the book, he acknowledges his debt to the fretted-instrument tab systems of the past.

Perhaps the most noteworthy thing about most folk-festival workshops is that they are not really workshops at all. Strictly speaking, a workshop is a group class or group lesson presented by an expert (or group of experts) in the field. A true banjo workshop, then, would be a clinic on playing techniques, or a forum where different approaches to playing the instrument could be compared and contrasted in detail.

I have no doubt that festival banjo workshops started out as true workshops. The earliest folk festivals in the late 1920s and 30s featured a high percentage of what you might call "folk-originals" — musicians who learned their art in something approaching a traditional setting, or who appeared on old 78s or Library of Congress field recordings. Since frailing, two-finger picking and other banjo playing styles were in danger of becoming lost arts, these early festival banjo workshops served as forums where a new generation of players could learn the tools of their trade.

By the mid-1970s, however, most folk-originals were gone from the scene, and the torch, so to speak, had been passed to the first generation of revivalist pickers. By the mid-eighties, many workshop participants were two or three playing-generations removed from the "originals" generation.

As the nature of workshop artists changed, so did the function of the festival banjo workshop. In the early days of festivals, a fast-moving, round-robin approach proved a valuable teaching method because most old-timers were much better musicians than they were explainers, and one demonstration of an art in danger of dying out was worth more than the proverbial thousand words. Nowadays, however, we have retained this format even though basic banjo techniques are well-known and most workshop artists are well-educated and well-spoken.

As a result, the present-day festival banjo workshop has evolved into a musical "Whitman's Sampler." From the artist's point of view, the focus has shifted from teaching to creating a lasting impression on the audience, from passing on elements of a musical tradition to competing for attention with the other workshop artists.

Bearing all this in mind, festival banjo workshops can still serve a number of important functions if run properly. New talent can be introduced, different playing styles can be compared and contrasted, and new developments in banjo techniques, technology or accessories can be touched on. Most importantly, by creating the impression of a living, growing playing tradition, workshops can offer new inspiration to those who already play, and even motivate non-players to take up the instrument.

9.18 Military Bands and their Influence on Old Time Music: (Sept. '86)

During a recent Midwest tour, I stopped off for a few days in Chicago to visit family and got dragged along to Evanston, Illinois' July 4th celebration. Before the fireworks display, about fifty musicians in period costume with period brass instruments performed the arrangements of a Civil War-era Wisconsin regimental band.

I found the band's repertoire quite intriguing. First of all, they played several military tunes called *quicksteps*, designed to encourage rapid troupe movement. These certainly had to be the origin of such fiddle-tunes as *Steamboat Quickstep, Avalon Quickstep* and *Texas Quickstep*.[7]

Secondly, quite a bit of the band's repertoire consisted of arranged fiddle-tunes. These were played with both syncopa-tion and with counter-melodies from support instruments. They were also played quite a bit faster than dance tempo.

It's a reasonable assumption that military and other brass bands had a major role in spreading tunes that were eventually absorbed in fiddling repertoires throughout the South and other portions of North America. It is also likely that some changes in the way that fiddle tunes were performed in the rural South can be traced to Civil War era marching-band arrangements. Anyone who served in such bands — or merely listened to them perform — would have been exposed to syncopation, accidentals, swing-eighths, counter-melodies, rapid tempos, and so on. Surely it is not too much of a stretch to presume that after the war, some of this new perspective found its way home with the returning soldiery.

---

[7] Military quicksteps are often in 6/8-time: many tunes called "quickstep" in the old-time repertoire may very well have been "converted" from 6/8 to reel-time: see col. 3-14.

9.19 More on Military Bands

In response to my first column on military bands, BNL columnist Clarke Beuhling sent along a copy of the forward by George P. Carroll from a reissue of *The Drummer's and Fifer's Guide* by George Barrett Bruce and Dan D. Emmett, originally published in 1865.

Dan Emmet wrote the fifers' portion of the book, but he is better known as one of the great minstrel-style banjoists. He is perhaps best known as the composer of the famous songs *Dixie, Boatman* and *Old Dan Tucker*. Emmet joined the US Army as a fifer and drummer in the 1820s at the age of 17; he later wrote the first U.S. Army drummers' manual. He studied drumming with John J. "Juba" Clark, who was known for his syncopated approach to military drum rhythms (the term "juba" — which traces to an African hand-clapping game — was often applied to the style of dance associated with minstrel shows: in fact, many banjo tunes of the period feature the word "Juba" in the title). George B. Bruce, who taught for many years at the Military School for Practice on Governor's Island in New York City harbor, wrote the drummers' portion of the 1865 guide.

According to Carroll's forward, the training of the military musician was quite rigorous. In the ante-bellum period (1820-60), boys were recruited between the ages of 12 and 16, and quartered at the old South Battery in Manhattan, near the present location of the Brooklyn Bridge. They lived in crowded, uncomfortable conditions, they were fed sparingly and worked hard. A typical morning schedule involved early reveille, one hour of physical exercise, a meager breakfast, two hours of schooling and one hour of music instruction. A hearty lunch was typically followed by two more hours of music instruction and two hours of military drill. Evenings were occupied with *Tattoo* and *Taps* duty. For all this these boys were paid the princely sum of $7 per month.

9.20 A Short History of Square and Contra Dancing

Since so much of the music we 5-string banjoists play evolved along with the kind of dancing we now refer to as "squares" and "contras," it makes sense for us to understand the general course of their development.

The traceable story starts about 1650. London-based John Playford, having collected and adapted a large number of *figure dances* from among those being taught at the time by rural dancing masters, compiled a book of tunes and dancing directions called *The English Dancing Master*. It was so successful it was carried over into several editions, and eventually the idea was continued in several additional volumes. These figure dances — so-called because each was composed of different combinations of a relatively few easily walked through routines or "figures" — were conducted out of three basic formations. In some the dancers formed a circle, in others a square, but most were done *longways* (that is, in two facing lines like modern contra dances).

In the decades that followed, longways *country dancing* (as this dance style became known) became the dominant social dance for all levels of society in England and — to a somewhat lesser extent — in Scotland. The French were also taken with the style, and by the early eighteenth century their version of longways dancing (known as *contre danse*) was a major factor in that country, and it was even danced at the royal court.

By mid-century, the French developed a variation of the longways dance, in which all maneuvers were carried out with four couples lined up in the form of a square. This became known as the *contre danse française* (French country dance), or *cotillon* (cotillion), while the longways style came to be referred to as *contre danse anglaise* (English country dance).

Around the same time, a new kind of music was evolving to take advantage of the possibilities of the violin, which had only just become the dominant dance instrument of the era. This kind of music — the generally two-part, 32-bar jigs and reels we now refer to as "fiddle tunes" — was created for the most part to accompany both country dancing and another dance-genre that is now usually referred to as the Scotch Reel. (See col. 3.1).

In the aftermath of the American Revolution, things English were not so popular in America, while things French became all the rage. A number of French dancing masters saw a good opportunity and traveled throughout the new nation, teaching their cotillions wherever they went. These square-formation dances eventually became dominant, although longways dancing remained strong in New England. One longways dance that continued in currency throughout much of the new nation was *Sir Roger de Coverly*, now generally known as *The Virginia Reel*.

Around the beginning of the 19th century, the French developed another square-formation dance known as the *quadrille*. Essentially, each quadrille was a medley, or "suite" of cotillions. In other words, to make a single quadrille, several cotillions — each with different steps and music — were danced in succession with pauses in between. Each of these component cotillions became known as a *figure* of the quadrille, and most quadrilles were made up of five figures (note that the term "figure" has two different meanings in regards to this kind of dancing: [1] a square or contra routine or "step," and [2] a complete component of the quadrille).

Quadrilles were introduced to Britain just after the Napoleonic Wars, and spread soon afterwards to North America.

Eventually, several quadrille variants became particularly popular, such as the Lancers, the Saratoga Lancers and the Caledonians.

The music played for quadrilles in 19th century urban and upper class ballrooms was different from that played for eighteenth century country dancing. Instead of violin-centered jigs and reels, quadrille music reflected for the most part the tastes of "refined" classes of society, and was often drawn from marches, operas, operettas, and popular songs of the day. Accompaniment was usually provided by a band or small orchestra. In *Hillgrove's Call Book* (published 1863), for example, the ideal ballroom ensemble is described as consisting of first and second violins, viola, bass, flute, clarinet, first and second cornets and a trombone.

Throughout rural North America in the 19th century, local people took these cotillions and quadrilles and created new versions of them that suited their own tastes and predilections. The pace of dancing increased and demeanor became less restrained. Steps were altered or recombined in ways that seemed convenient or pleasing. The centrifugal waltz-grip swing was invented and replaced the more sedate two handed turn. Callers — who in many cases extemporized combinations of steps — replaced the old dancing masters. The fiddle remained the dominant instrument, and the music best suited to it — that music we now call fiddle tunes — was retained, elaborated and adapted to local tastes.

These localized variants of the old cotillions and quadrilles eventually became known simply as *square dances*, while the longways dances of New England — as a legacy from the old French term "contre danse" — were often referred to as *contra* dances.

The surviving calls for both square and contra dancing also reveal the French influence. A few examples: *dosey doh* (French: dos sur dos, or back to back), *allemande* left/right (French: á la main gauche/droit, or left/right hand to…), *promenade* (French for "walk"), *sashay* (from the French "chassez:" meaning "chase," "gallop" or "skip"), and *haye* (from haie, an old French dance in which dancers wound about each other).

Much of the old rural square and longways dancing that evolved in 19th century North America is now gone, victims of the decline in rural community life that characterized so much of the 20th century. Most of what we see danced nowadays is the product of two separate revivals originating in the 1930s, each of which radically changed the steps, atmosphere and musical accompaniment styles of the dancing. These two revivals are the New England contra dance movement (sparked by Ralph Page) and the Western square dance movement (set in motion by Lloyd Shaw).

Two important revivals of country dancing also took place in Britain. About 1900, Cecil Sharp and the Country Dance Society he helped found set the English country dance movement in motion. In the late 1920s, the Royal Scottish Country Dance Society revived country dancing in Scotland.

9.21 Dances in the Tennessee Mountains (Excerpt from "The Festival of American Fiddle Tunes") (Aug. '99)

While on the faculty at The Festival of American Fiddle Tunes in Port Townsend, Washington I got to room in the same wing as Bobby Fulcher (organizer of the old Tennessee Banjo Institute festivals), guitarist Mike De Fosche and 99-year old Tennessee fiddler Bob Douglas. This was a truly wonderful experience, because I got to hear Bob practicing quite a bit with Bobby and Mike: it was like hearing a genuine performance off an old 78, without any of the scratches. (Naturally, everyone who heard him said, "I hope I can play like that when I'm 99," but I guess the main problem here is that first you have to get to be 99!) During a brief interview session, Bob told me about the old square dances they used to have in the east-Tennessee mountains, and I'd like to share part of that information here. One intriguing item: the dance he mentions had three distinct parts with stops in between, a trait that is characteristic only of the quadrille — a style of square-dancing not generally associated with the southern mountains.

"The dances were in somebody's house, country-peoples' houses: some of 'em would have a pretty good sized room you know, 'specially to dance in. Somebody'd come along before the dance and say, 'We want you down at our house tomorrow night.' Me and Dad and the banjo player — he played clawhammer banjo just like Bobby [Fulcher], we just walked, we didn't ride or nothin'. Dad [Tom Douglas] he carried his fiddle in an old flour sack. We'd walk in and eat supper before we played anything, then we'd start playin' about sundown: lots of times we'd be playin' when the sun come up the next mornin'. There was always one in the crowd that was a caller.

"What they'd do, so many couples would line up on the floor, say six or eight couples and when they'd go to dance they'd pay 'on the corner.' Each couple would pay us 10¢ and they would dance a set, which would take about 15 minutes. Now to make it a set, they had to dance three rounds, three times. They had to dance three times to call it a set. [Question: They would dance and stop?] Yeah, and dance again. But here's where the catch was: they didn't pay us but one time. They'd pay us the first time. When they'd dance a full set they'd line up again, we'd start all over again, and they'd pay us again. We finally went up to 25¢ on a set and we done pretty good at it at that. We didn't have to spend no money for our board or sleep or nothin'. They'd almost fight one another to get us to stay all night with them."

Although waltzing spread rapidly throughout much of Europe and urban North America in the first half of the 19th century, it wasn't nearly as readily adopted in rural North America. After all, the waltz was one of the first modern "couple dances." As such, it called for a much closer proximity between male and female partners than was thought proper by many religious and social groups of that era. In fact, it is pretty well documented that it was the rise of the waltz and related couple dances in the 19th century that prompted many religious denominations to drop their long-standing vehement opposition to square and contra dancing (just as it was the rise of jazz and its accompanying dance forms in the 1920s that got churches and social conservatives interested in *reviving* square and contra dancing: see col. 9-24).

In Cape Breton, Prince Edward Island and other mostly rural areas of Atlantic Canada, for example, waltzing didn't become widespread until the 1930s and 40s. When the dance did indeed catch on, not surprisingly there were only a few waltz tunes in circulation, making it necessary for fiddlers to search out suitable tunes in waltz-time (that is, 3/4 time). What's more, they also had to develop a suitable waltz-playing style.

In terms of playing style, fiddlers pretty much adapted what they were already familiar with to the new genre. Since waltzes had a high proportion of relatively long notes, fiddlers employed the kind of longer bow strokes they were already using to play set tunes (cols. 3.3-4). Similarly, they instinctively brought to waltz-playing an approach to ornamentation and double-string usage that was similar to the one they already used for playing jigs and reels.

One major source for waltz repertoire was folk- and popular-song melodies in 3/4 time. Just as any cut-time or 4/4 time song can be transformed into a *set tune*, any song in 3/4 time (or slowed-down 6/8 time) can be pressed into service as a waltz. Some examples of songs I heard converted to waltzes on Prince

Niel Gow's Lament for His Second Wife

Banjo Arrangement: Ken Perlman

Tuning: gCGCD (capo–2)

Arrangement © 1989 by Ken Perlman

Edward Island are the old Scottish song *The Four Marys*, several late 19th century American pop songs such as *My Wild Irish Rose*, *Sidewalks of New York* and *My Old Homestead*, and such relatively modern songs as *Mockingbird Hill* and *Music-Box Dancer*.

Fiddlers also reached into their repertoires for old Scottish or Irish airs and *laments* in 3/4 or 6/8 time that made good waltzing melodies.

Laments are melodies written for sad occasions, such as the demise of a loved one or patron (this is not always the case: one of the most famous laments is entitled *Farewell to Whiskey!*). In the latter half of the 18th Century, laments written by such famous Scottish fiddlers as Niel Gow and William Marshall were much influenced by the art music of the day, resulting in compositions that resemble pieces from the Baroque or early classical periods.

Celtic airs and laments are generally played with much feeling and high levels of ornamentation. They are also played with a considerable amount of *rubato* (that is, the musician is not held to a steady pulse). When such tunes are transformed into waltzes, they are played in steady time but at least some of their original feeling and ornamentation comes along for the ride. The result can be quite striking and beautiful.

I was reminded of this not long ago when I heard Cape Breton fiddler Joe Cormier play for a Saturday night dance at the French-American Club in Waltham, Massachusetts near Boston. When the call went up for a waltz, he played an exquisite, highly ornamented conversion of an 18th century composition entitled *Niel Gow's Lament For His Second Wife*. A banjo arrangement inspired by Cormier's approach to this tune accompanies this column.

It is very likely that the process just described for Atlantic Canada also accompanied the development of waltzes and waltz playing in the Southern US a couple of generations earlier. In other words, when the newly-popular waltz needed accompaniment, fiddlers reached into their repertoires of Scottish and Irish dance tunes, songs and airs for suitable tunes, bringing to the task both the overall feel and style of ornamentation with which they were already familiar.

Observe that in order for *Gow's Lament* to fit on banjo, the tune had to be taken up an octave (see col. 2.19).

9.24 Old Time Music Contests (Mar. '00)

Instrument-competitions have had a major role in the development of old-time music in the 20th century. In order to more fully understand the music we play, it makes sense to take a look at how these contests originated and developed.

Much has been made in the literature of a fiddle contest held as part of a St. Andrews Day celebration in the Williamsburg, Virginia area in 1736, which offered a "fine Cremona fiddle" as first prize. Given the time-frame, however, it can be inferred that the music played at this event would almost certainly have borne but small resemblance what we now think of as fiddling. For one thing, the kind of music we now call "reels" (the parent-genre of Southern breakdowns) was just coming into its own in the Highlands of Scotland, and was then virtually unknown outside its home area. More important, the date precedes by about a decade the emergence of Niel Gow, the Scottish musician who is generally credited with developing the powerful rhythmically-articulated sawstroke technique that ultimately served as the foundation for country fiddling.

Throughout the 19th century, *fiddlers' conventions* were frequently held in the towns and villages of the United States, often on courthouse lawns in conjunction with the arrival of the local circuit court. Although the term "fiddlers' convention" is associated with contests nowadays, it is not at all clear that competition was a major aspect of these 19th century gatherings. Instead, these conventions seem for the most part to have been just what the name implies: occasions for conviviality, swapping tunes and telling stories. Concerts featuring fiddling were often held in association with these events, with proceeds going to support local schools or other public causes.

Competitions involving only fiddling begin to come into play in certain parts of the US beginning about the last third of the 19th century (banjos and other fretted instruments didn't really come into the old-time contest picture until much later). There are records of fiddle contests taking place in Atlanta, Georgia as early as the 1870s. In the 1880s and 90s, fiddle contests were held along-side city-wide holiday festivities in Knoxville, Tennessee. A thriving fiddle-contest scene grew up in west Texas near Amarillo around the turn of the 20th century. In 1907, an eight-day contest — eventually won by future Grand Ol' Opry star Uncle Jimmy Thompson — was held in Dallas. In 1913, an annual contest was established in Atlanta and continued there for over twenty years.

Some of these early contest scenes were breeding grounds for many of the first successful commercial old-time music entertainers. I have already mentioned Uncle Jimmy Thompson. Eck Robertson — the first southern fiddler to record on a major label — was a product of the West Texas contest scene. Fiddlin' John Carson — probably the first southern fiddler to play on radio, and the first country-music artist to produce a commercially successful recording — came out of the Atlanta contest scene. Other products of Atlanta contests include such well known artists as Gid Tanner, Clayton McMichen and Lowe Stokes, all three of whom played with the famous Skillet Lickers Band.

It is interesting to note that in most cases, contests were established in particular areas only after local community fiddle-dance scenes had begun to decline. This interpretation is often supported by published comments of organizers and observers. For example, one William Van Jacoway, who organized a 1920s-era contest in De Kalb County, Alabama hoped by way of this event "to perpetuate the memory and the music of the old time fiddle, to revere the past, [and] to show the present generation… that there was sweeter and more inspiring music emanating from the fiddle and the bow than will ever be found in the present day jazz…"[8]

The true heyday of these contests in terms of media interest came in the mid-1920s as a result of famed industrialist Henry Ford's campaign to revive fiddling and square dancing throughout the United States. Ford's campaign — which had its roots in an avowed aim to rid American music and dance of its foreign and Afro-American influences — got underway in 1923 when he began holding old-time dances at an inn he had purchased in Sudbury, Massachusetts. In 1925, he sponsored a contest in Detroit at which 80-year old Jasper "Jep" Bisbee of Michigan was crowned "King of Old-time Fiddlers." Not long afterwards, a fiddler of similar vintage named Mellie Dunham of Norway, Maine received national publicity when Ford invited him to spend a few days as his personal guest in Dearborn, Michigan (there was talk at the time of setting up a grudge-match with North vs. South overtones between Uncle Jimmy Thompson and Dunham, but it never came off).

By 1926 media interest in fiddling was at an all time high, and literally hundreds of contests were held that year all over North America. In January '26, for example, the three-day "All New England Contest" was held in Providence, Rhode Island, involving dozens of contestants and thousands of spectators. In April, the four-day "World Champion Old-Time Fiddlers' Contest" was held in Lewiston, Maine. The biggest contest of all was national in scope: some 1,865 fiddlers competed in local and regional playoffs organized through Ford dealerships. In a "playoff" held in Detroit, Uncle Bunt Stephens of Lewisburg, Tennessee was declared national champion.

Although general interest in old-time music competitions paled after 1927 and plummeted at the onset of the Great Depression, contests at the local and regional levels continued to be held in many areas through the 1930s. In the mid-30s, a promoter named Larry Sunbrock created a touring commercialized version of the fiddle contest in which well known players

such as Fiddlin' Arthur Smith and Clayton McMichen would face-off with lesser lights. As in modern professional wrestling, the outcomes of these matches were often scripted. Few old-time contests of any kind were held through the 1940s, although the now famous Union Grove Fiddlers' Convention (which has run continuously since its founding in 1924) was a notable exception.

Most of the larger old time fiddling contests around nowadays have grown up with the fiddle association movement, which started in the early 1950s. About 1950, The Canadian Open Old-time Fiddlers' Contest was founded in Shelburne, Ontario. In 1953, a small annual fiddle contest was established at Weiser, Idaho by amateur folklorist Blaine Stubblefield. In 1962 the event was taken over by the newly formed Idaho Old-time Fiddlers' Association, and renamed the National Old-Time Fiddlers' Contest (interestingly, the 1973 Senior Division prize was won by none other than Eck Robertson!). Before long, comparable groups had formed in Missouri (1962), Montana ('63), Oregon ('64), Nebraska ('64) and Vermont ('65). By the mid-seventies, fiddle associations had also formed in Washington, California, Kansas, Illinois, Tennessee, Indiana, Texas, Wyoming and British Columbia.

For most of these organizations, sponsoring contests ultimately became the most important activity. Essentially, organizers simply felt that offering members the opportunity to compete was the best way to maintain their interest in playing.

How have contests affected the practice of old-time music? For one thing, as contests replace playing-for-dances as a major focus, there is a strong tendency for musicians to de-emphasize strong dance rhythms in favor of the kind of smooth, showy virtuosity that impresses judges. This was certainly one of the factors that led to the rise in the mid- to late-1920s of the "longbow" style (many notes off a single stroke) which now dominates bluegrass, swing and contest fiddling nationwide. Another common theme — also noted by those who have studied the effects of Scottish and Irish traditional-music competitions — is that contests tend to quickly push up the general level of expertise, but they also tend to create homogenization among players. In other words, because those eager to succeed soon adopt the general approach of previous contest winners, both individual idiosyncrasies and variation among regional styles tend to be suppressed.

9.25 It's Traditional! (Or Is It?)   **(May '00)**
9.26 Some Thoughts on Fiddle Tunes   **(Feb. '92)**
9.27 The Prince Edward Island-Old Time Southern Connection   **(Nov. '92)**

We old time music "revivalists" sometimes need to ask ourselves if we've adopted a particular practice because it actually was an integral part of a tradition, or merely because it has recently become fashionable among our friends or other contemporary role models.

Asking questions like this does not carry a subtext condemning all changes in an original musical tradition. Traditional music cultures have always changed from generation to generation as different influences and interests passed through

8 Quoted in the De Kalb [Alabama] Republican, Aug. 14, 1924.

a given region. What I am getting at is that every effort should be made to understand what a tradition really was before assuming that we know it thoroughly.

By way of illustrating the issues involved, I'd like to cite a few practices and notions that are quite widespread within the old-timey revival movement. Although these practices and notions are generally believed to be carry-overs from long-standing traditions, the truth of the matter is that they themselves are either relatively new, or represent the adoption of isolated practices.

First myth: Old time music (defined as vibrant fiddling and square-dancing communities) was confined to the southern Appalachians.

The reality: Old time music was widespread throughout the eastern two-thirds of North America well into the 20th century. We are now aware mostly of the southern traditions because the attention of early record companies and music collectors was focused southward.

Second myth: It is completely *un*traditional to accompany southern music with a piano or other keyboard instrument.

The reality: Keyboard accompaniment was actually quite common in the south, whenever it was available. The record companies and scholars who recorded the music in the 1920s favored banjo and guitar accompaniment despite the fact that the latter instrument at least was then quite new to the genre (along these lines: Bob Clayton of the Washington DC area pointed out to me that Charlie Poole and the North Carolina Ramblers routinely performed with piano accompaniment but were never allowed to use it on a recording).

Third myth: Clawhammer banjo approximating the contemporary Galax (or Round Peak) style was the dominant form of banjo playing in the South prior to the rise of Scruggs-picking.

The reality: Very little Southern banjo playing in the period 1900-1945 could be described as pure frailing or pure three-finger picking. Just about every hybrid one could imagine was practiced somewhere. It was the post New Lost City Ramblers folk-revival that focused on frailing as the dominant old time style, and it was the 1970s before the Galax style was adopted by the revival as the dominant frailing variant (see col. 9.28). It is also important to remember here that the highly rhythmic Galax style as practiced by Tommy Jarrell, Fred Cockerham and others evolved in the post World War II era and was quite different from the style of frailing practiced in that region by the previous generations of pickers.

Fourth myth: Jigs (6/8 time fiddle tunes) are not traditional to the southern repertoire.

The reality: The oldest southern players alive today remember their parents' generation playing jigs, and they themselves knew some examples of the genre when they were young. This in itself should not be surprising, since the late 19th century is only a few decades removed from the major waves of Scottish and Irish immigration that provided much of this country's early fiddling stock. Jigs were also an integral part of the accompaniment for quadrille and cotillion dancing, but as such forms of square dancing declined in the latter years of the 19th century the need for jigs decreased. I also suspect that the record companies and scholars who first recorded the music steered away from jigs as being not consistent with their image of the southern "mountaineer." Jig melodies linger on in the southern repertoire converted to reel or "hoedown" form. Two examples that come directly to mind: *Green Willis* (derived from the Scottish jig *New Rigged Ship*) and *North Carolina Breakdown* (derived from *The Cowboy Jig*).

Fifth Myth: So-called "crooked tunes" (those with odd or uneven numbers of beats or measures) were widespread regionally.

The reality: Square and country dancing in the old days was pretty well dependent on having music with a relatively dependable structure. While some latitude in the number of measures and beats could slip by without doing substantial harm to an evenings dance-party, the kind of extreme time-variations perpetuated by some contemporary old-time players would have probably made the average square dancer fall on their face. These time variations were for the most part the individual eccentricities of players who — following the decline of square dancing in their communities — had been playing in relative isolation, in some cases for decades.

On Prince Edward Island where I had the first-hand opportunity to study a living North American traditional fiddling community, it does sometimes happen that particular fiddlers develop the habit of deleting beats from or adding beats to particular tunes. Since these stray beats do not generally interfere with the ability of dancers to perform their steps, this habit is generally regarded as a harmless eccentricity. However, it should be stressed that fiddlers who are highly "eccentric" in this manner are not generally well regarded by their peers, and that tune versions with added or deleted beats and measures are rarely emulated by other fiddlers.

Sixth Myth: Just about every tune that I don't know the origin of is generations old.

The reality: Many tunes considered traditional today by the old time revival scene are quite new, and in some cases the composers are contemporary old-time revivalists themselves. One such case is *Ashokan Farewell*, a wonderful air written in the 1980s by fiddler Jay Unger and named for the Ashokan (ash-OH-ken) Music Camps that he runs. The tune was used as theme music for an American public-television documentary on the Civil War, and Cape Breton fiddling star Natalie MacMaster subsequently recorded it. It has since spread like proverbial wild-fire through North America, Britain and Australia and by now probably half the world's traditional Celtic and old time musicians are convinced the tune is traditional. In fact, a few years' ago a musician at a session in Queensland Australia asked me if I knew an ancient Celtic air she pronounced "ASH-o-kan's Farewell."

The major source for the style we call clawhammer in the early stages of the "urban" folk revival was a banjoist from the town of Allen in Floyd County, Kentucky named Rufus Crisp. Pete Seeger in fact credits Crisp with teaching him to "frail," but apparently it was Stu Jamieson who was Crisp's major disciple and the main revivalist exponent of the downpicking style through the 1940s. Jamieson was extremely active in the 40s and 50s in both New York City and California, and taught Rufus' style to quite a number of students, including Woody Wachtel (who also studied directly with Crisp) and Al Hjerpe. In turn, Wachtel (in New York) and Hjerpe (in California) were extremely active teachers of "down picking": Hjerpe taught Ry Cooder to play clawhammer, and Wachtel taught Hank Schwartz, who later recorded on the seminal *Old Time Banjo Project* album.

Interestingly, Jamieson — who did a considerable amount of collecting and field recording in Appalachia in the late 1930s through the mid 40s — claims that neither *frailing* nor *clawhammer* were then the common names for our downpicking style. The term "frailing," is apparently an urban-based misunderstanding of "flailing," which is itself an analogy to the motion employed to thresh grain. The term "clawhammer" was indeed sometimes applied to down-picking, but it was also used in parts of the South to describe certain forms of 3-finger picking (Jamieson's maternal grandfather, Wm. Wallace Simpson of White Co., Tennessee played banjo and referred to his own 3-finger style as "clawhammer"). Jamieson notes that Crisp himself referred to the style as "flogging," and that other players called it "rapping." Well-known folklorist Alan Jabbour notes that among upper South banjoists and fiddlers in the 60s he heard the term "knocking" most often, but that "thumping" and "flailing" were also current.

As an indication of how confused the nomenclature was at one time, in 1965 a Chicagoan named John Carbo published a guide — to 3-finger picking — called "How to Play 5-String Bluegrass Banjo, Clawhammer Style." It was the late 60s when "clawhammer" permanently entered the revival lexicon in association with downpicking. Two books which may have had a hand in this were John Burke's "Old-Time Fiddle Tunes for Banjo" and Art Rosenbaum's "Old-Time Mountain Banjo."

Tom Paley claims that he learned to frail as an extension of the Pete Seeger style. In other words, the Seeger basic strum was an up-pick movement followed by a brush-thumb. Paley notes that he was merely instructed to substitute a down stroke for an up-pick, and that he later taught his own students to proceed similarly. It seems likely that quite a number of other players from that era learned in exactly this manner.

Paley also notes that the music of the New Lost City Ramblers did not particularly emphasize "frailing": he himself and fellow band member John Cohen both used the style on only a few numbers. If any banjo style could be said to particularly

feature in the Ramblers' recordings according to Paley, it would be 3-finger picking à la Charlie Poole.

Once the art of down-picking was launched in the revival, a number of other models were available on Library of Congress and other field and commercial recordings. Paley singles out Clarence "Tom" Ashley as being particularly influential: Ashley was presented in concert in New York City about 1960 and also appeared at a Newport Folk Festival around the same time. Similarly, Frank Hamilton mentions Hobart Smith, and several sources bring up Wade Ward.

It should be emphasized here that collectors of banjo music in the 1930s and 40s had found a wealth of banjo styles. In fact, what might be termed "pure" clawhammer was only one of a constellation of playing styles circulating among Southern rural banjoists. What had happened was this: in the years following the American Civil War, a three-finger based method known as classic banjo had virtually superseded stroke style in the United States, and various rural players had begun to partially incorporate or borrow wholesale various elements of this new style. When collectors and scholars began to look at rural banjo playing in earnest then, they found — not only clawhammer — but two-finger picking, three-finger picking, thumb-lead, finger-lead, up-pick clawhammer (the Seeger basic strum), not to mention dozens of variants and hybrids of the above.

This variety was very well represented in the early stages of the revival. In fact many pickers who learned during the 40s, 50s and early 60s prided themselves on mastering a variety of styles and substyles. When I interviewed Art Rosenbaum, for example, his take on the matter was that focusing on just one banjo-picking style was in fact short-sighted or even "wrong headed" (see his book, "Old-Time Mountain Banjo" for a sampling of some of the styles he learned).

Frank Hamilton notes that in the mid-to late 50s, frailing was seen in much of the revival primarily as a song-accompaniment style. He notes that when he helped found the Old Town School of Folk Music in Chicago in 1957, the two banjo teachers — Fleming Brown and the aforementioned John Carbo — both taught frailing.

The period in the revival when clawhammer began to eclipse all other old time styles was roughly the mid-1960s. One factor involved here is that by this time the balance of power among styles in the South was changing, under pressure from a general fascination with the then relatively new "Scruggs-picking" style. Alan Jabbour makes the point that at the fiddlers' contests he went to during that period in Virginia and North Carolina, you would see lots of Scruggs-pickers and a fair amount of down-pickers. What you no longer saw so much was the old time fingerpickers, because most of them had either made the transition to bluegrass, or — presumably — been intimidated into silence by the high levels of sound-volume and speed that the new style permitted.

And it was to these very contests in the mid 60s, of which Galax and Union Grove were only the most famous, that scores of young urban, college-educated pickers began to flock in search of musical inspiration. What they saw at that time, was mostly clawhammer associated with old-time music, and three finger picking associated with bluegrass music.

By the late 60s, this new generation of revival banjo pickers had focused on the styles of a few banjoists from the Round Peak region, which — not entirely coincidentally — was right in the heart of the area where all these fiddlers' conventions were taking place. One of the first new-generation players who modeled his style on the Round-Peak banjoists was Tommy Thompson, who was then playing with the Hollow Rock String Band, and who later was banjoist for the Red Clay Ramblers.

Banjo player and builder Bob Flesher was on the scene as the process was unfolding:

"When I went to the Galax Old Time Fiddlers' Convention in 1969, I had a small tape recorder and I recorded every banjo player that moved. Kyle Creed was the only person playing anything remotely resembling the Round Peak style. Other contemporary banjo players from the Northeast who camped out on Tommy Jarrell's front porch added Fred Cockerham's 'chuck' to Kyle Creed's style to 'invent' [what we now call] the Round Peak style.

"I was selling banjo parts for Liberty Banjo Co. at a festival in West Virginia one time, and Kyle Creed was taking a nap under my table. When he awoke he heard someone playing the new 'Round Peak' style. He said, 'Everywhere I go I hear myself playing.' I think that quote from Kyle says it all. There are those that claim the style goes back many years and they name all the fellows in the past who played it, but I believe that is just an effort to give their style legitimacy."

In the early 70s, quite a number of revivalist banjo pickers made pilgrimages to Galax/Round Peak and learned the banjo styles of Kyle Creed and Fred Cockerham. One of the most influential such "pilgrims" was Ray Alden of New York City, who was later to produce a number of seminal banjo recordings involving Round Peak and Round-Peak influenced musicians. As this Creed/Cockerham style spread and was adopted by newcomers to the banjo-revival, a myth spread with it, namely that this very style had once been widespread throughout much of the South, and that it was in fact the only truly "traditional" way to play old-time banjo. By 1977, as Bob Carlin once reported in a letter to BNL, musicians at a gathering of prominent old time revivalists in Lexington, Virginia were sufficiently secure in this perspective to reject the then just released "Melodic Clawhammer" recording as "not having any relevance to the banjo."

There's one more piece of the puzzle that needs to be sorted out more fully, namely just why the revival focused so heavily on Creed and Cockerham. One factor certainly was that Creed for one was an extremely visible presence at the '60s fiddlers' conventions, and that he was particularly open to sharing his musical expertise with the newcomers. In effect, he became the "un-" or "anti-Scruggs" for those who were drawn to old-time music instead of bluegrass. Tom Paley puts it this way:

"I think the readiness of [the Round Peak players] to teach outsiders about their music was the main thing. And the music does have a drive and verve that's very attractive. It also has a sound of authenticity that was just what a lot of the city converts were looking for. By that, I mean that, though it can be pretty intricate, it doesn't sound over-polished like Bluegrass and contest-style fiddling can."

Ken with fiddler Archie Stewart and guitarist Chester MacSwain near Montague, Prince Edward Island, July '91
(Photo courtesy Earthwatch)

Minstrel-Era string band (Image courtesy Jim Bollman collection)

Rural musicians' gathering, c.1920s
(Photo courtesy Jim Bollman collection)

CHAPTER 10: MORE GREAT TUNES!!

Far From Home

Banjo Arrangement: Bob Solosko
Kind of Tune: Reel

Tuning: gDGBD
Origin: Scotland

Arrangement © 1996 by Bob Solosko

Country Waltz

I learned this one from fiddler Alvin Bernard of Long River, Prince Edward Island.

Setting: Ken Perlman
Kind of Tune: Waltz

Tuning: gCGCD (capo–2)
Origin: Southern US?

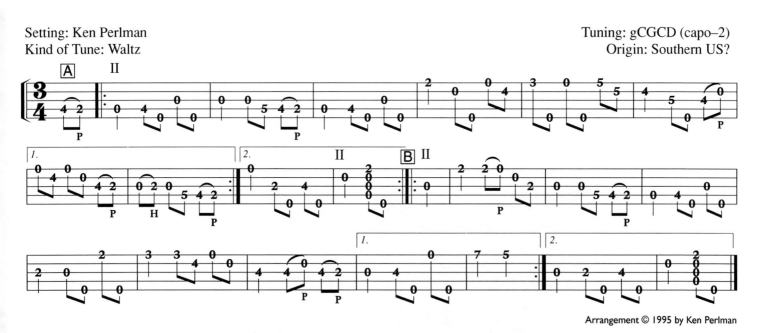

Arrangement © 1995 by Ken Perlman

Over the Briny Ocean

As played on my recording, *Island Boy;* learned from fiddler Stephen Toole of Bonshaw, Prince Edward Island. Techniques to review: dotted quarter notes, fretting the 5th string.

Banjo Arrangement: Ken Perlman
Kind of Tune: Set tune

Tuning: gDGBD
Origin: Atlantic Canada

Arrangement © 1993 by Ken Perlman

Plaza Polka

Learned from fiddler Danny MacLean of Eldon, Prince Edward Island. Techniques to review: dotted quarter notes, off-string P's.

Banjo Arrangement: Ken Perlman
Kind of Tune: Set tune

Tuning: gCGCD (capo–2)
Origin: Canada

Arrangement © 1994 by Ken Perlman

The Dashing White Sergeant

A popular song associated with the Jacobite Uprising of 1745, when Scottish clans supported Bonnie Prince Charlie's claim to the British throne. Techniques to review: playing up the neck.

Banjo Arrangement: Rob Mairs
Kind of Tune: Scotch measure (set tune)

Tuning: gDGBD
Origin: Scotland

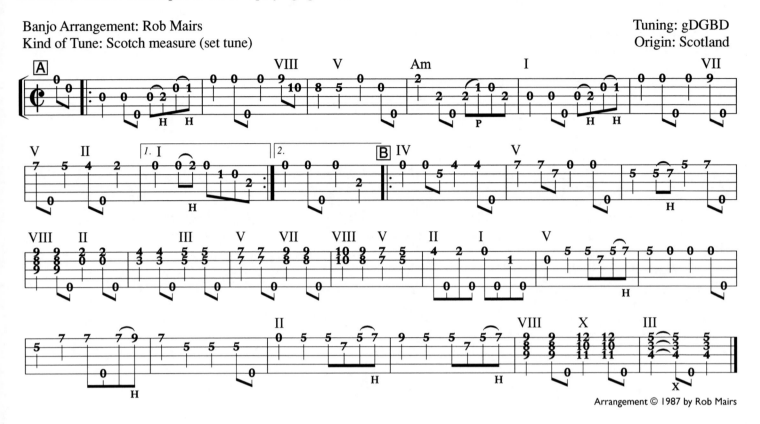

Arrangement © 1987 by Rob Mairs

Honeymoon Polka

Learned from fiddler Sterling Baker of Montague, Prince Edward Island. Techniques to review: dotted quarter notes , off-string P's, arpeggios, off-beat H's and P's.

Banjo Arrangement: Ken Perlman
Kind of Tune: Set tune

Tuning: gDGBD (capo–2)
Origin: North America

Arrangement © 1999 by Ken Perlman

The Black Mill

As recorded on my CD, *Devil in the Kitchen*. Technique to review: fretting the 5th string.

Banjo Arrangement: Ken Perlman
Kind of Tune: Reel

Tuning: gDGCD (capo–2)
Origin: Scotland

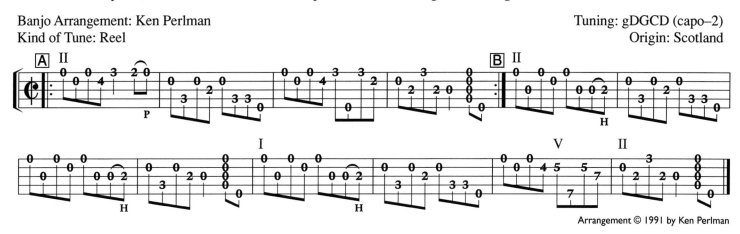

Arrangement © 1991 by Ken Perlman

Dinah

Techniques to review: skip strokes, arpeggios, rolls.

Banjo Arrangement: Ken Perlman
Kind of Tune: "Hoedown"

Tuning: gDGBD (capo–2)
Origin: Southern US

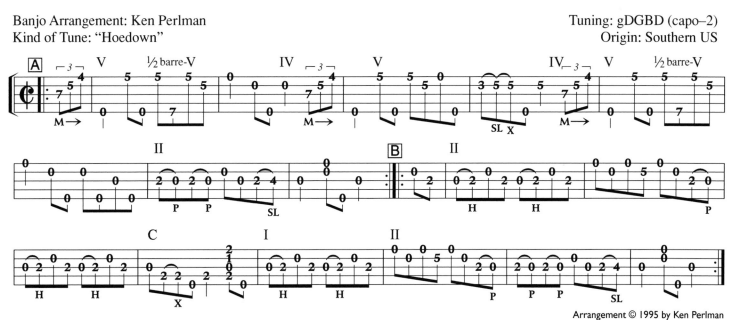

Arrangement © 1995 by Ken Perlman

Whalen's Breakdown

Learned from Sid Baglole of Freetown, Prince Edward Island; popularized by well-known radio fiddler Don Messer. Techniques to review: off-string P's, skip strokes, fretting the 5th string.

Banjo Arrangement: Ken Perlman
Kind of Tune: Set tune

Tuning: gCGCD
Origin: Canada

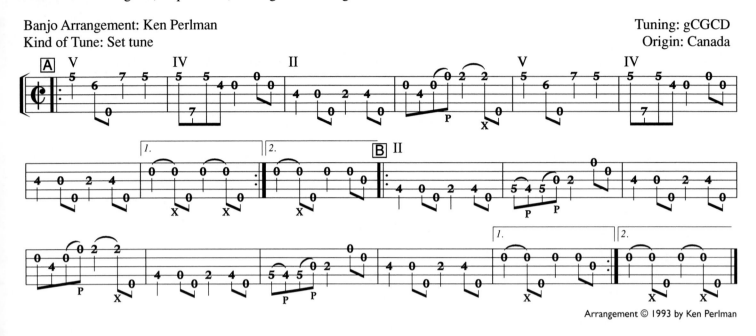

Arrangement © 1993 by Ken Perlman

Westphalia Waltz

Learned from fiddler Attwood O'Connor of Milltown Cross, Prince Edward Island. Techniques to review: dotted quarter notes, off-string P's, "Keith-picking."

Banjo Arrangement: Ken Perlman
Kind of Tune: Waltz

Tuning: gDGBD
Origin: Central Europe

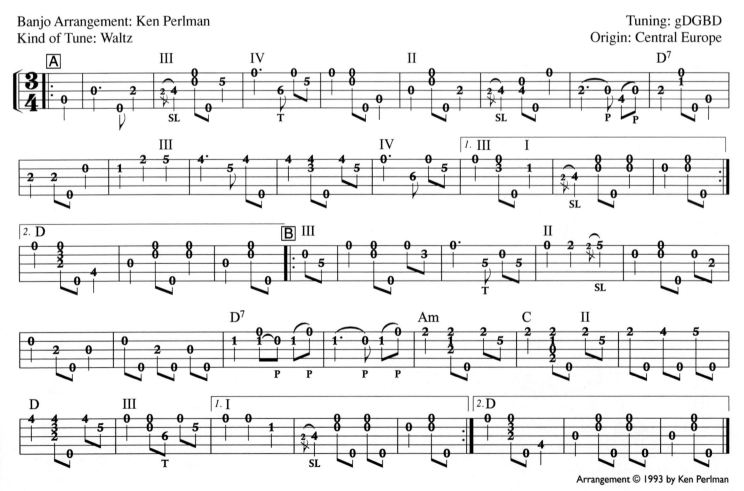

Arrangement © 1993 by Ken Perlman

Pipe Major Christie of Wick

Learned from fiddler Gus Longaphie of Souris, Prince Edward Island. Techniques to review: off-string P's .

Banjo Arrangement: Ken Perlman
Kind of Tune: March Converted to Reel

Tuning: gDGCD (capo–2)
Origin: Scotland

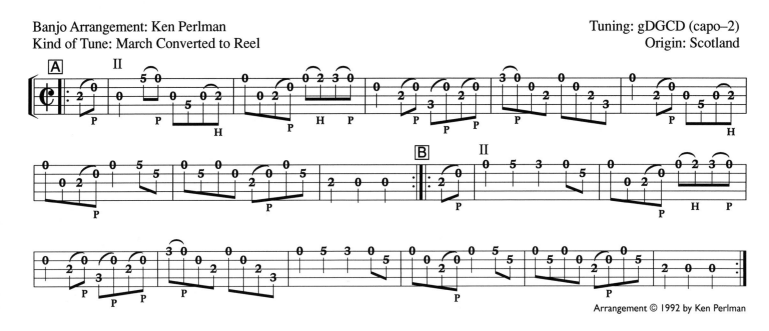

Arrangement © 1992 by Ken Perlman

The Sailor's Wife

Techniques to review: off-string P's, melodic fingering forms.

Banjo Arrangement: Ken Perlman
Kind of Tune: Jig

Tuning: gDGBD
Origin: Scotland

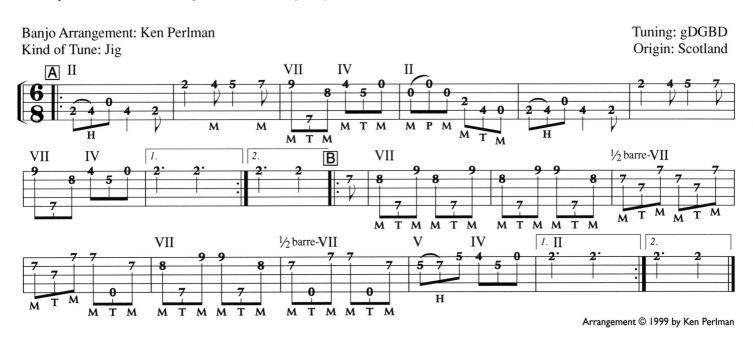

Arrangement © 1999 by Ken Perlman

Indian Nation

Techniques to review: dotted quarter notes, syncopation and skip strokes, arpeggios.

Banjo Arrangement: Ken Perlman
Kind of Tune: "Hoedown"

Tuning: gDGBD
Origin: US

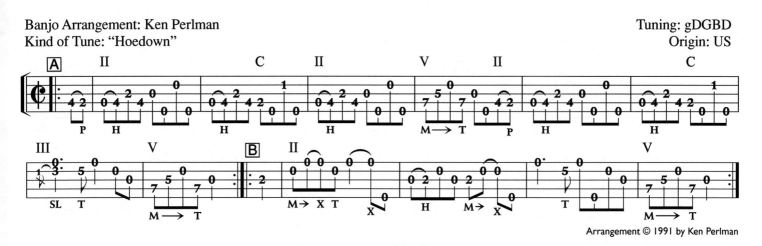

Arrangement © 1991 by Ken Perlman

Island Boy

As played on my recording *Island Boy*. Learned from Ervan Sonier of Summerside, Prince Edward Island. Converted from the jig, *Larry O'Gaff* and also known as *Larry O'Gaff Reel*. Techniques to review: off-string P's, dotted quarter notes, arpeggios, ragtime, syncopation Acadian style, up-strokes.

Banjo Arrangement: Ken Perlman
Kind of Tune: Reel converted from Irish Jig, *Larry O'Gaff*

Tuning: gCGCD (capo–2)
Origin: Prince Edward Island

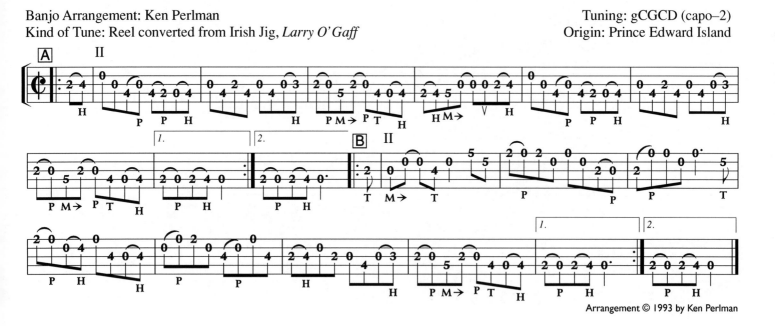

Arrangement © 1993 by Ken Perlman

The Twin Sisters

This version comes from fiddler Andrew Jones of Pleasant View, Prince Edward Island. Techniques to review: off-string P's, arpeggios, cross-overs.

Banjo Arrangement: Ken Perlman
Kind of Tune: Reel

Tuning: gDGCD (capo–2)
Origin: Prince Edward Island variant of *Pigeon on the Gate* (Irish)

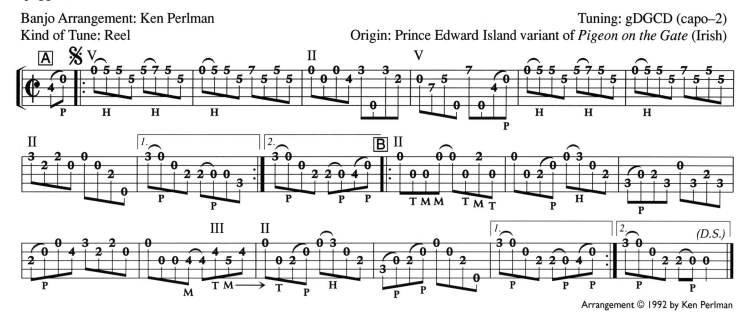

Arrangement © 1992 by Ken Perlman

George V's Army

This three-part version, learned from fiddler Sterling Baker of Montague, Prince Edward Island is condensed from the original Scottish version, which has four parts. Techniques to review: off-string P's, skip strokes, dotted quarter notes, multiple H's and P's, arpeggios, grace notes.

Banjo Arrangement: Ken Perlman
Kind of Tune: Pipe-march

Tuning: gDGBD (capo–2)
Origin: Scotland

Arrangement © 1993 by Ken Perlman

The Flowers of Edinburgh

This is more or less the arrangement I played on the anthology recording, *Melodic Clawhammer Banjo*. Techniques to review: off-string P's, melodic fingering forms, triplets, Keith-picking.

Banjo Arrangement: Ken Perlman
Kind of Tune: Reel

Tuning: gDGBD
Origin: Scotland

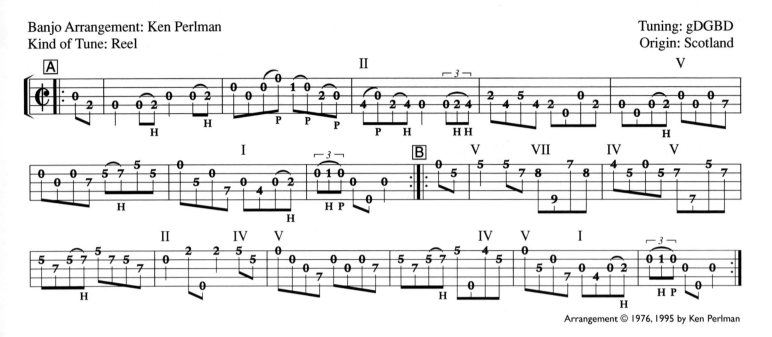

Arrangement © 1976, 1995 by Ken Perlman

Sheehan's Reel

As played on my CD, *Devil in the Kitchen*. This version is from fiddler George MacPhee of Monticello, Prince Edward Island. Techniques to review: off-string P's, arpeggios, melodic fingering forms.

Banjo Arrangement: Ken Perlman
Kind of Tune: Reel

Tuning: gDGBD
Origin: Ireland

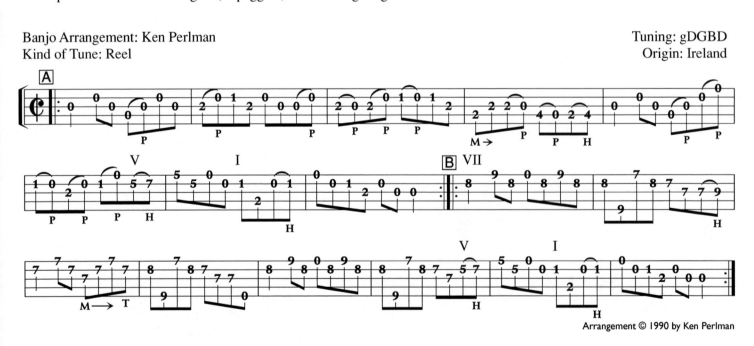

Arrangement © 1990 by Ken Perlman

Sally Gardens

Learned from fiddlers Carl and Jackie Webster of Cardigan, Prince Edward Island. Techniques to review: off-string P's, triplets, multiple H's and P's, arpeggios, fretting the 5th string, melodic fingering forms.

Banjo Arrangement: Ken Perlman
Kind of Tune: Reel

Tuning: gDGBD
Origin: Ireland

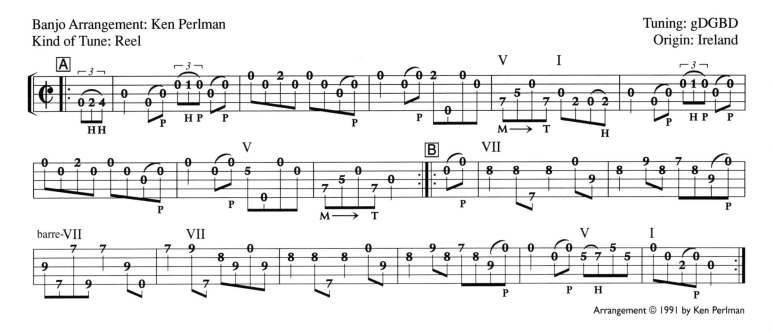

Arrangement © 1991 by Ken Perlman

Upper Denton Hornpipe

As played on my CD, *Island Boy;* this version is from fiddler Peter Chaisson, Jr. of Bear River, Prince Edward Island. Techniques to review: off-string P's, triplets, multiple H's and P's, arpeggios, fretting the 5th string, grace notes.

Banjo Arrangement: Ken Perlman
Kind of Tune: Reel "converted" from Hornpipe

Tuning: gCGCD (capo–2)
Origin: Scotland

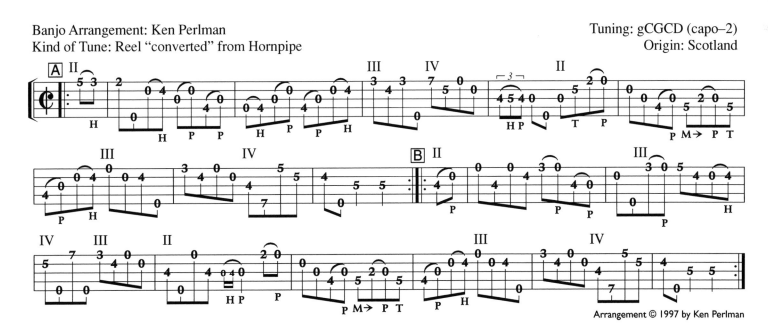

Arrangement © 1997 by Ken Perlman

The Black Hoe

Techniques to review: triplets, melodic fingering forms.

Banjo Arrangement: Ken Perlman
Kind of Tune: Jig

Tuning: gDGBD
Origin: Ireland

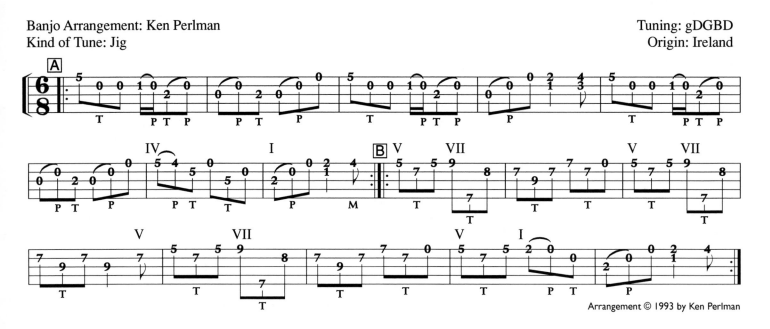

Arrangement © 1993 by Ken Perlman

Green Meadow Reel

As played on my CD, *Island Boy;* learned from fiddler Eddy Arsenault of St. Chrysostom, Prince Edward Island. Also known as *Over the Moor to Maggie, The Willow Tree* and (in the southern US) *Waynesboro.* Techniques to review: off-string P's, melodic fingering forms, ragtime licks, arpeggios.

Banjo Arrangement: Ken Perlman
Kind of Tune: Reel

Tuning: gDGBD
Origin: Ireland

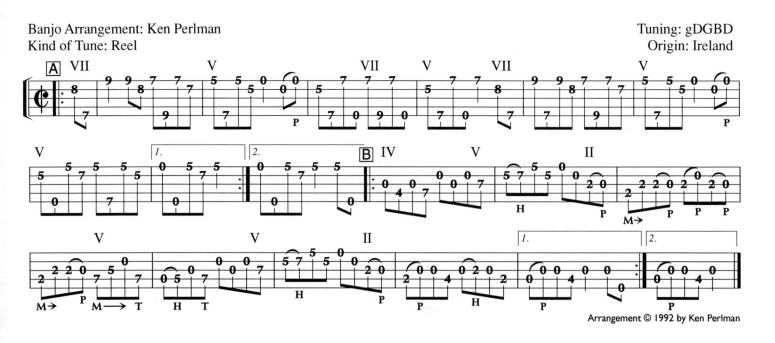

Arrangement © 1992 by Ken Perlman

Phiddlin' Phil

As played on my CD, *Island Boy;* this version learned from fiddler George MacPhee of Monticello, Prince Edward Island. A relative of such Southern old-time tunes as *Dubuque* and *Possum Up a Gum Stump*. Techniques to review: off-string P's, melodic fingering forms, ragtime licks.

Banjo Arrangement: Ken Perlman
Kind of Tune: Reel

Tuning: gCGCD (capo–2)
Origin: 19th Century US

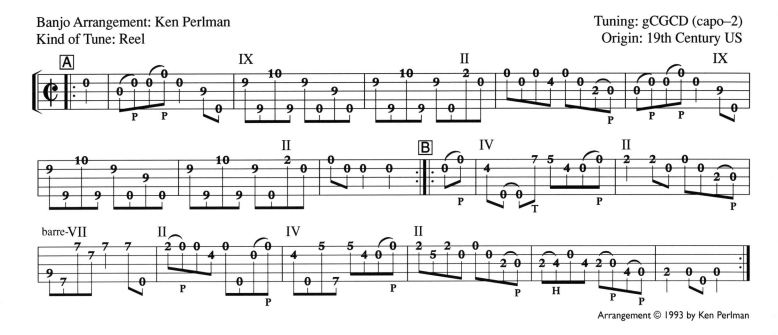

Arrangement © 1993 by Ken Perlman

Heather on the Hill

As played on my CD, *Devil in the Kitchen*. This version learned from fiddler George MacPhee of Monticello, Prince Edward Island. Techniques to review: off-string P's, melodic fingering forms.

Banjo Arrangement: Ken Perlman
Kind of Tune: Reel

Tuning: gDGBD
Origin: Cape Breton

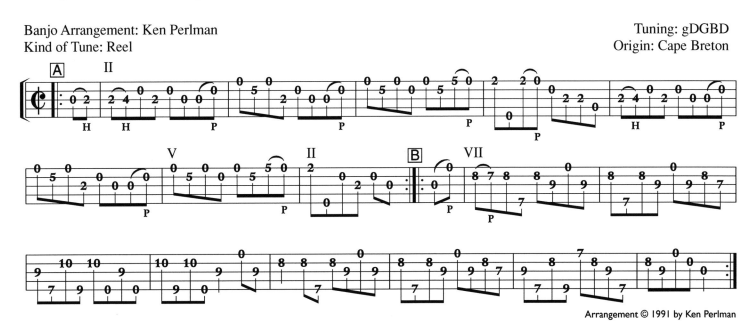

Arrangement © 1991 by Ken Perlman

Road to California

Techniques to review: skip strokes, off-string P's, melodic fingering forms.

Banjo Arrangement: Bob Solosko & Ken Perlman
Kind of Tune: Reel

Tuning: gCGCD (capo–2)
Origin: US

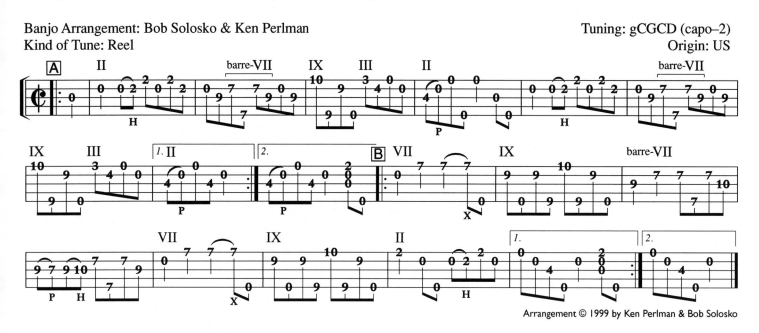

Arrangement © 1999 by Ken Perlman & Bob Solosko

Nine Points of Roguery

As recorded on my *Clawhammer Banjo & Fingerstyle Guitar Solos* recording. Modeled on a version by Northern Irish fiddler Tommy Peoples. Techniques to review: triplets, grace notes, sixteenth notes, arpeggios, off-string pull-offs.

Banjo Arrangement: Ken Perlman
Kind of Tune: Reel

Tuning: gCGCD (capo–2)
Origin: Ireland

Arrangement © 1983, 1989 by Ken Perlman

190

Dill Pickle Rag

Techniques to review: ragtime licks, arpeggios, melodic fingering forms.

Banjo Arrangement: Joe McGuire
Kind of Tune: Fiddle Rag

Tuning: gDGBD
Origin: US

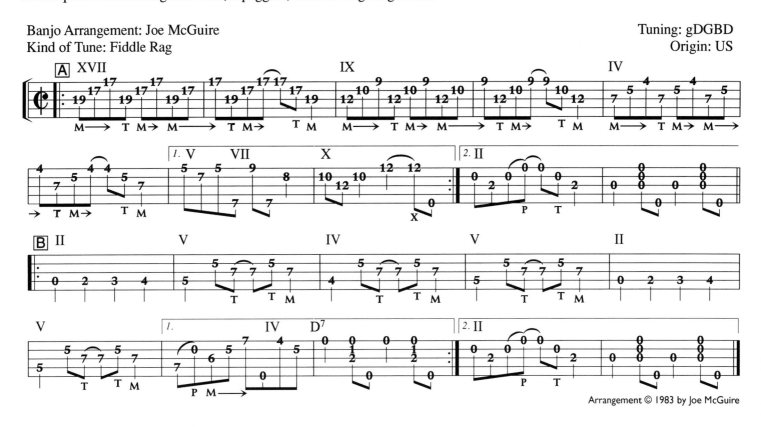

Arrangement © 1983 by Joe McGuire

Ken with fiddler George MacPhee of Monticello, Prince Edward Island, Aug. '91
(Photo by Mike Hird)

Beaumont Rag

As played on my first recording, *Clawhammer Banjo and Fingerstyle Guitar Solos*. Techniques to review: ragtime licks, arpeggios, melodic fingering forms.

Banjo Arrangement: Ken Perlman
Kind of Tune: Fiddle Rag

Tuning: gCGCD
Origin: Texas

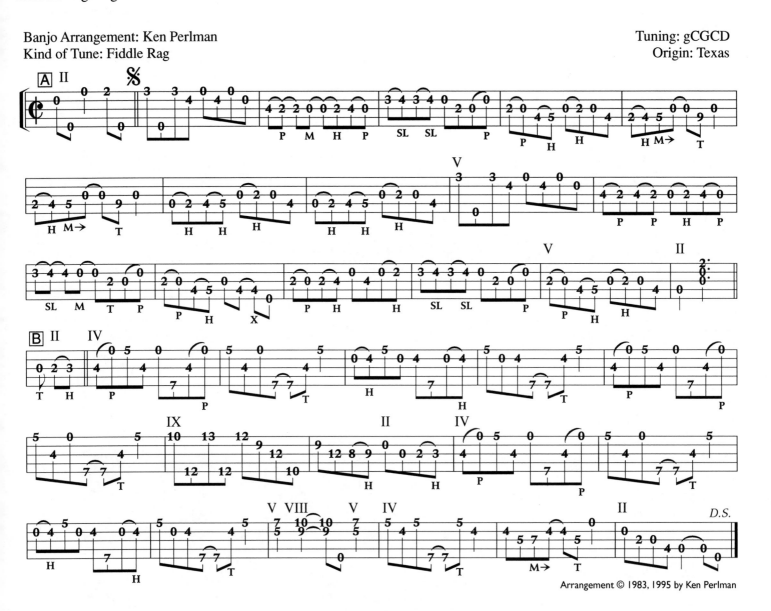

Arrangement © 1983, 1995 by Ken Perlman

BIBLIOGRAPHY

Alburger, Mary Anne. *Scottish Fiddlers and Their Music*. London: Victor Gallaway, 1983.

Arsenault, Georges. *The Island Acadians*. Trans. Sally Ross. Charlottetown: Ragweed Press, 1989.

Benford, Mac. *Kentucky Favorites*. Trumansburg, NY: private printing, 2000.

Breathnach, Breandán, *Folk Music and Dances of Ireland*. Cork: Mercier Press, 1971.

[Briggs, Thomas F.], *Briggs Banjo Instructor,* Joseph Weidlich, Ed. Anaheim Hills, California: Centerstream, 1997.

Bronner, Simon J. *Old-Time Music Makers of New York State*. Syracuse University Press, 1987.

Burke, John. *John Burke's Book of Old Time Fiddle Tunes for Banjo*. New York: Amsco, 1968.

Carolan, Nicholas. *A Harvest Saved: Francis O'Neill and Irish Music in Chicago*. Cork: Ossian Publications, 1997.

Cauthen, Joyce. *With Fiddle and Well Rosined Bow: Old-Time Fiddling in Alabama*.
    Tuscaloosa: University of Alabama Press, 1989.

Christeson, R. P. *The Old-Time Fiddler's Repertory*. Columbia, Mo.: University of Missouri Press, 1973.

Cohen, John and Mike Seeger, eds. *The New Lost City Ramblers Song Book*. New York: Oak Publications.

Collinson, Francis. *The Traditional and National Music of Scotland*. Knoxville: Vanderbilt University Press, 1966

Cooke, Peter. *The Fiddle Tradition of the Shetland Isles*. Cambridge University Press, 1986.

Damon, S. Foster. *The History of Square Dancing*. Barre, Mass.: Barre Gazette, 1957. Rpt. from Proceedings of the American
    Antiquarian Society.

Downer, Alan S., Ed. *The Memoir of John Durang, American Actor 1785-1816*. Historical Soc. of York Co. [Pennsylvania], 1966.

Dunlay, Kate and David Greenberg. *Traditional Celtic Violin Music of Cape Breton*. Toronto: DunGreen Music, 1996.

Emmerson, George. *Rantin' Pipe and Tremblin' String*. 1972. 2nd ed. London, Ontario: Galt House, 1988.

—. *A Social History of Scottish Dance*. Montreal: McGill-Queens University Press, 1972.

Epstein, Dena J. *Sinful Tunes And Spirituals: Black Folk Music to the Civil War*. U. of Illinois Press, 1997.

Fiske, Roger. *Scotland in Music*. New York: Cambridge University Press, 1983.

Flett, J.F. and T.M. Flett. *Traditional Dancing in Scotland*. London: Routledge and Kegan Paul, 1966.

Gura, Phillip F. and James F. Bollman. *America's Instrument: The Banjo in the Nineteenth Century*. Chapel Hill: The Univ. of North
    Carolina Press, 1999.

Hillgrove, Thomas. *Hillgrove's Call-Book and Dancing Master*. New York: Dick & FitzGerald, 1863.

Johnson, David. *Music and Society in Lowland Scotland in the Eighteenth Century*. London: Oxford University Press, 1972.

—. *Scottish Fiddle Music in the Eighteenth Century: A Music Collection and Historical Study*. Edinburgh:
    John Donald Publishers, 1984.

Kerr's Collection of Merry Melodies for the Violin. 4 vols. Glasgow: James S. Kerr, n.d. Rpt. of *Kerr's Collection of Reels &
    Strathspeys [. . .]*. Glasgow, 1870.

Linn, Karen. *That Half-Barbaric Twang: The Banjo in American Popular Culture*. Urbana: University of Illinois Press, 1994.

Mac Aoidh, Caoimhín, *Between the Jigs and the Reels: The Donegal Fiddling Tradition*. Nure, Co. Leitrim: Drumlin Publications,
    1994.

MacDonald, Keith Norman. *The Skye Collection*. 1887. Ed. Paul Cranford. London, Ontario: Scott's Highland Services, 1979.

MacGillivray, Allister. *The Cape Breton Fiddler*. 1981. Marion Bridge, NS: Sea Cape Music, 1997.

Malone, Bill C. *Country Music U.S.A.* Austin: University of Texas Press, 1985. American Folklore Society, 1968.

Milnes, Gerald. *Play of a Fiddle: Traditional Music, Dance, and Folklore in West Virginia*. Univ. Press of Kentucky, 1999.

Nathan, Hans. *Dan Emmett and the Rise of Negro Minstrelsy*. Norman: University of Oklahoma Press, 1962.

O hallmhurain, Gearold. *A Pocket History of Traditional Irish Music*. Dublin: The O'Brien Press, 1998.

Oliver, Paul. *Savannah Syncopators: African Retentions in the Blues*. New York: Stein and Day, 1970.

One Thousand Fiddle Tunes. Chicago: M.M. Cole Publishing Co., 1967. Rpt. of Ryan, Wm. Bradbury.
    Ryan's Mammoth Collection of More than 1050 Reels [. . .].

O'Neill, Capt. Francis. *O'Neill's Music of Ireland*. Chicago, 1903. Bronx, NY: Private Printing, 1973.

Perlman, Ken. *The Fiddle Music of Prince Edward Island: Celtic and Acadian Tunes in Living Tradition*.
    Pacific, MO: Mel Bay, Inc., 1996.

—. *Basic Clawhammer Banjo*. Pacific, MO: Mel Bay, Inc., 1996; Formerly *New England and Irish Fiddle Tunes for
    Clawhammer Banjo*, 1979.

—. *Clawhammer Style Banjo.*, 1983. Fullerton, California: Centerstream Music, 1989.

—. *Melodic Clawhammer Banjo*. New York: Oak Publications, 1979.

Roche Collection of Traditional Irish Music, The . 1912. Cork: Ossian Publications, 1982

Rosenberg, Neil, ed. *Transforming Tradition: Folk Music Revivals Examined*. Urbana and Chicago: Univ. of Illinois Press, 1993.

Seeger, Pete. *How to Play the 5-String Banjo*, 1948. 3rd ed. Beacon NY: Private Printing, n.d.

—. *The Incomplete Folksinger*. New York: Simon & Schuster, 1972.

Shapiro, Henry D. *Appalachia on Our Mind: The Southern Mountains and Mountaineers in the American Consciousness.* Chapel Hill: U. Of North Carolina Press, 1978.

Sharp, Cecil. *The English Folk Song: Some Conclusions.* London: Simpkin & Co., 1907.

—. *English Folk Songs from the Southern Appalachians.* 1917. Ed. Maud Karpeles. vol. 1. London: Oxford University Press, 1932, 1952.

Shaw, Lloyd. *Cowboy Dances.* 1939. Caldwell, Idaho: Caxton Printers, 1952.

Stewart-Robinson, James. *The Athole Collection* . 1884. Edinburgh: Oliver & Boyd, 1961.

Voyer, Simonne. *La danse traditionnelle dans l' est du Canada.* Québec: Les Presses de L'Université Laval, 1986.

Webb, Robert Lloyd. *Ring the Banjar!: The Banjo in America...* Cambridge, Mass.: The MIT Museum, 1984.

Wiggins, Gene. *Fiddlin' Georgia Crazy: Fiddlin' John Carson, His Real World and the World of His Songs.* U. Of Illinois Press, 1987.

Wolfe, Charles. *The Devil's Box: Masters of Southern Fiddling.* Nashville: The Country Music Foundation Press & Vanderbilt University Press, 1997.

—. *Kentucky Country.* Lexington: U. Press of Kentucky, 1982.

—. *Tennessee Strings: The Story of Country Music in Tennessee.* Knoxville: U. Of Tennessee Press, 1977.

The family that plays together... From the Ithaca, NY area c.1890s
(Photo courtesy Jim Bollman collection)

194

DISCOGRAPHY OF CLAWHAMMER AND OTHER OLD-TIME BANJO STYLES[1]

Roots Anthologies:
Alan Lomax Collection of American Folk Music: Voices from the American South. Rounder 1701.
—. *Ballads & Breakdowns.* Rounder 1702.
—. *Ozark Frontier-Ballads & Old-timey Music from Arkansas.* Rounder 1707.
Altamont: Black String Band Music. Rounder 02238.
Black Appalachia. Rounder 11823.
Hammons Family, The. 2 Vols. Rounder 1504-5.
Harry Smith Anthology of American Folk Music. 3 vols. Folkways 40090.
Kentucky Old Time Banjo. Rounder 0394.
Kentucky, Mountain Music of. 2 vols. Smithsonian Folkways 40077.
Mountain Banjo Songs and Tunes. County 515.
North Carolina Banjo Collection. Rounder 0439-40.

Roots Soloists, Living and Gone By:
Ashley, Clarence. *Old Time Music at Clarence Ashley's.* 2 vols. Folkways FA 2355, 2359.
Best, Carroll. *The Carroll Best Band.* Ivy Creek 250.
Blizzard, Ralph. *Southern Ramble.* Rounder 0352.
Boggs, Dock. 2 vols. Rounder FA 2351, 2392.
Crisp, Rufus. Folkways FA2342.
Davenport, Clyde. *Puncheon Camps.* Appalachian Center 002C.
George, Frank. *Traditional Music for Banjo, Fiddle, and Bagpipes.* County 2703.
Holcomb, Roscoe. *The High Lonesome Sound.* Folkways FA2368.
Kazee, Buell. Folkways FA 3810.
Keys, Will. *Banjo Original.* County 2720.
Lunsford, Bascom Lamar. *Ballads, Banjo Tunes […] of Western North Carolina.* Folkways 40082.
Macon, Uncle Dave . RBF RF 51.
—. *Laugh Your Blues Away.* Rounder 1028.
Poole, Charlie and the North Carolina Ramblers. 2 vols. County 3501, 3508.
Profitt, Frank. Folk Legacy FSA 1.
Sexton, Morgan. *Shady Grove: Traditional Appalachian Banjo Player.* June Appal JA0066.
Smith, Hobart. Folk Legacy FSA 17.
Steele, Pete. *Banjo Tunes and Songs.* Folkways 3828.
Ward, Wade. *Uncle Wade: The Playing of Wade Ward.* Folkways FA 2380.
—. *The Music of Wade Ward and Roscoe Holcomb.* Folkways FA 2363.
—. *Fields & Wade Ward.* Biograph RC-6002.

Galax Soloists and Anthologies:
Clawhammer Banjo. County 701.
Clawhammer Banjo, Vol. 3. County 757.
Cockerham, Fred and Kyle Creed. *The Camp Creek Boys.* County 709.
Cockerham, Fred, Tommy Jarrell and Oscar Jenkins. *Back Home in the Blue Ridge.* County 723.
—. *Stay All Night.* County 741.
Creed, Kyle et. al. *Liberty.* Heritage HRC028.
Jarrell, Tommy. *Come and Go With Me: Tommy Jarrell's Banjo Album.* County 748.
—, Fred Cockerham et. al. *Tommy & Fred.* County 2702.
—, Kyle Creed et. al. *June Apple.* Heritage HRC 38.
More Clawhammer Banjo Songs and Tunes. County 717.
Round the Heart of Old Galax. 2 Vols. County 534-5.

---

[1] Some privately released recordings have no label name or record number.

Minstrel Re-Creations:
Ayers, Joe. *Old Dan Tucker: Melodies of Dan Emmett & the Virginia Minstrels*. Tuckahoe C1989.
Buehling, Clarke. *Out of His Gourd: Gourd Banjo Instrumentals*.
Early Minstrel Show, The. New World 338.
Flesher, Bob. *Dr. Horsehair: Minstrel Banjo*.
Minstrel Banjo Style. Rounder 0321.
Skirtlifters, The. *Wait for the Wagon*.

Contemporary Players:
American Fogies, The. 2 Vols. Rounder 0379/0389.
Benford, Mac. *Backwoods Banjo*. Rounder 0115.
—. *Willow*. Rounder 0371.
Brown, Fleming. Folk Legacy FSI 1.
Bursen, Howie. *Banjo Manikin*. Folk Legacy CD-130.
—. *Building Boom*. Flying Fish 441.
—. *Cider in the Kitchen*. Folk Legacy FSI 74.
Carlin, Bob. *Fiddle Tunes for Clawhammer Banjo*. Rounder 0132.
—. *Banging and Sawing*. Rounder 0197.
Cooney, Michael. *Still Cooney After All these Years*. Front Hall 016.
Darling, Eric. *Instrumental Music & Songs of The Southern Appalachians*. Bescol 329.
Diller, Dwight, *Just Banjo*.
—. *New Plowed Ground*. Yew Pine IX-4.
—. *Harvest*. Yew Pine IX3.
Fennigs' All Stars. *The Hammer Dulcimer*. Front Hall 302.
Fink, Cathy. *Banjo Haiku*. Comm 202.
—. *Doggone My Time*. Sugar Hill 3783.
Folk Banjo Styles. Elektra EKL 7217.
Freight Hoppers, The. *Where'd You Come From, Where'd You Go?* Rounder 0403.
Fuzzy Mountain String Band, The. Rounder 0010.
Gellert, Dan. *Forked Deer*. Marimac 9000 C.
Holt, David. *Grandfather's Greatest Hits*. High Windy 1251.
Holy Modal Rounders. *Anthology*. Fantasy 24711.
Highwoods String Band, The. *Dance All Night*. Rounder 0045.
—. *Fire on the Mountain*. Rounder 0023.
Hollow Rock String Band, The. *Traditional Dance Tunes*. County 2715
Johnson, Mark, *Clawgrass*.
—, and Clawgrass. *Bridging the Gap*. Pinecastle 1069.
Jones, Grandpa. *16 Greatest Hits*. Hollywood 224.
Kimmel, Dick. *Fishin' Creek Blues*. Copper Creek 0173.
Koken, Walt. *Banjonique*. Rounder 0337.
—. *Hei-wa Hoedown*. Rounder 0367.
Leftwich, Brad & Dan Gellert. *Moment in Time*. Marimac 9038C.
—, & Linda Higginbotham. *Say Old Man*. County 2714.
Levenson, Dan. *Barenaked Banjos*. Buzzard 2002.
—. *Light of the Moon*. Buzzard 2001.
Levy, Bertram. *That Old Gut Feeling*. Flying Fish 27271.
Mabus, Joel. *Flatpick & Clawhammer*. Fossil 793.
Martin, Reed. *Old-Time Banjo*.
McClatchy, Debby. *Light Years Away*. Marimac 4010.
Melodic Clawhammer Banjo. Kicking Mule KM 209.
Miles, Michael. *American Bach*. RTOR 822.
—. *Counterpoint*. RTOR-821.
Molsky, Bruce & Big Hoedown. Rounder 0421.
Mullenex, Ron. *Taking Yesterday Along*. Bluestone 001.
Naiman, Arnie & Chris Coole. *5 Strings Attached with No Backing*. Merriweather 01.
New Lost City Ramblers, The. Vols. 1-5. Folkways FA 2395-2399.
—. *String Band Instrumentals*. Folkways FA 2492.

Old Time Banjo in America, The. Kicking Mule KM 204.

Old-Time Banjo Project, The. Elektra S7-276.

Perlman, Ken. *Northern Banjo.* Copper Creek 0191.

—. *Clawhammer Banjo & Fingerstyle Guitar Solos.* Folkways 31098.

—. *Devil in the Kitchen.* Marimac 6502.

—. *Island Boy.* Wizmak 579-27.

—. *Live in the U.K.* Halshaw.

Powell, Dirk. *If I Go Ten Thousand Miles.* Rounder 0384.

—, Tim O'Brien & John Herrmann. Howdyskies.

Red Clay Ramblers, The. *Stolen Love.* Flying Fish 009.

Rosenbaum, Art. *The Art of the Mountain Banjo.* Kicking Mule KM 203.

—. *Art Rosenbaum and Al Murphy.* Meadowlands MS2.

Roustabout. Yodelahee 27CD.

Schatz, Mark. *Brand New Old Tyme Way.* Rounder 0342.

Seeger, Mike. *Old Time Country Music.* Folkways FA 2325.

—. *Southern Banjo Styles.* Folkways 40107.

—, and Paul Brown. *Way Down in North Carolina.* Rounder 0383.

Seeger, Pete. *The Essential Pete Seeger.* VSD 97-8.

—, and Frank Hamilton. *Nonesuch and other Folk Tunes.* Folkways FA 2439.

Southern Clawhammer Banjo. Kicking Mule KM 213.

Stecher, Jody & Brislin, Kate. *A Song That Will Linger.* Rounder 0274.

Tenenbaum, Molly. *And the Hillsides Are All Covered with Cakes.* Cathair C94.

Volo Bogtrotters, The. *Old Time String Band With Vocal Accompaniment.* Marimac 9067.

Wade, Stephen. *Dancin' in the Parlor.* County 2721.

Watson, Doc. *Memories.* United Artists LA423-H2 0798.

Still life with banjo and cigar... c.1880s (Photo courtesy Jim Bollman collection)

SUBJECT INDEX

Ken simulates thumbing a ride with banjo near English pub, July '88.
Sign reads, "No Travellers or Pickers." (Photo by John Collins).